iko Takahashi

The spotlight on Rumiko Takahashi's career began in 1978 when she won an honorable mention in Shogakukan's annual New Comic Artist Contest for *Those Selfish Aliens*. Later that same year, her boy-meets-alien comedy series, *Urusei Yatsura*, was serialized in *Weekly Shonen Sunday*. This phenomenally successful manga series was adapted into anime format and spawned a TV series and half a dozen theatrical-release movies, all incredibly popular in their own right. Takahashi followed up the success of her debut series with one blockbuster hit after another—*Maison Ikkoku* ran from 1980 to 1987, *Ranma ½* from 1987 to 1996, and *Inuyasha* from 1996 to 2008. Other notable works include *Mermaid Saga*, *Rumic Theater*, and *One-Pound Gospel*.

Takahashi won the prestigious Shogakukan Manga Award twice in her career, once for *Urusei Yatsura* in 1981 and the second time for *Inuyasha* in 2002. A majority of the Takahashi canon has been adapted into other media such as anime, live-action TV series, and film. Takahashi's manga, as well as the other formats her work has been adapted into, have continued to delight generations of fans around the world. Distinguished by her wonderfully endearing characters, Takahashi's work adeptly incorporates a wide variety of elements such as comedy, romance, fantasy, and martial arts. While her series are difficult to pin down into one simple genre, the signature style she has created has come to be known as the "Rumic World." Rumiko Takahashi is an artist who truly represents the very best from the world of manga.

RIN-NE
VOLUME 15
Shonen Sunday Edition

STORY AND ART BY
RUMIKO TAKAHASHI

KYOKAI NO RINNE Vol. 15
by Rumiko TAKAHASHI
© 2009 Rumiko TAKAHASHI
All rights reserved.
Original Japanese edition published by SHOGAKUKAN.
English translation rights in the United States of America,
Canada, the United Kingdom and Ireland arranged with
SHOGAKUKAN.

Translation/Christine Dashiell
Touch-up Art & Lettering/Evan Waldinger
Design/Yukiko Whitley
Editor/Mike Montesa

Printed in the U.S.A.

Published by VIZ Media, LLC
P.O. Box 77010
San Francisco, CA 94107

10 9 8 7 6 5 4 3 2 1
First printing, July 2014

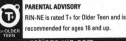

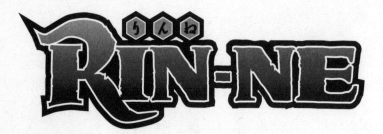

Story and Art by
Rumiko Takahashi

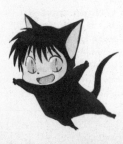

RIN-NE

りんね

Characters

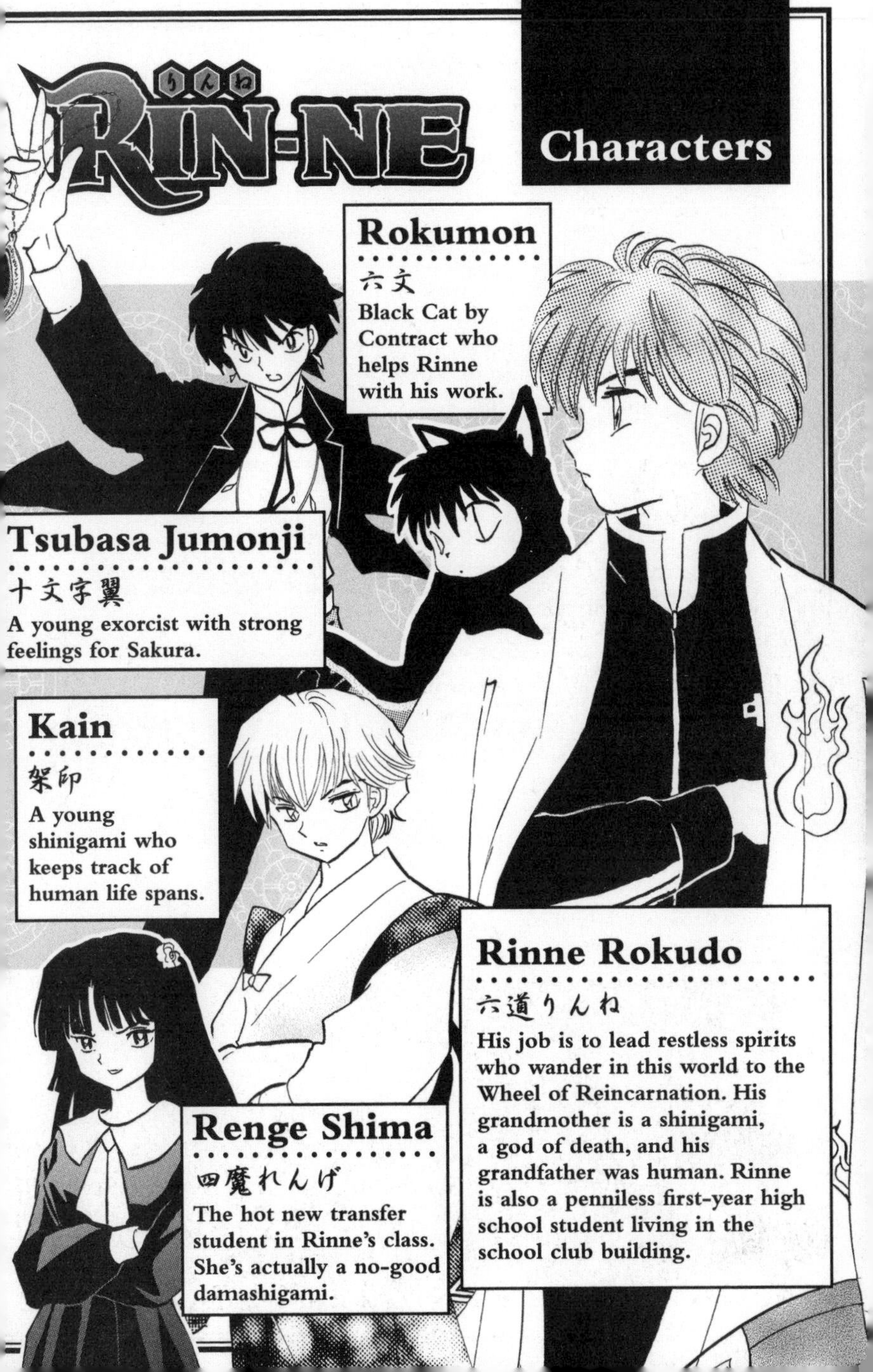

Rokumon

六文

Black Cat by Contract who helps Rinne with his work.

Tsubasa Jumonji

十文字翼

A young exorcist with strong feelings for Sakura.

Kain

架印

A young shinigami who keeps track of human life spans.

Rinne Rokudo

六道りんね

His job is to lead restless spirits who wander in this world to the Wheel of Reincarnation. His grandmother is a shinigami, a god of death, and his grandfather was human. Rinne is also a penniless first-year high school student living in the school club building.

Renge Shima

四魔れんげ

The hot new transfer student in Rinne's class. She's actually a no-good damashigami.

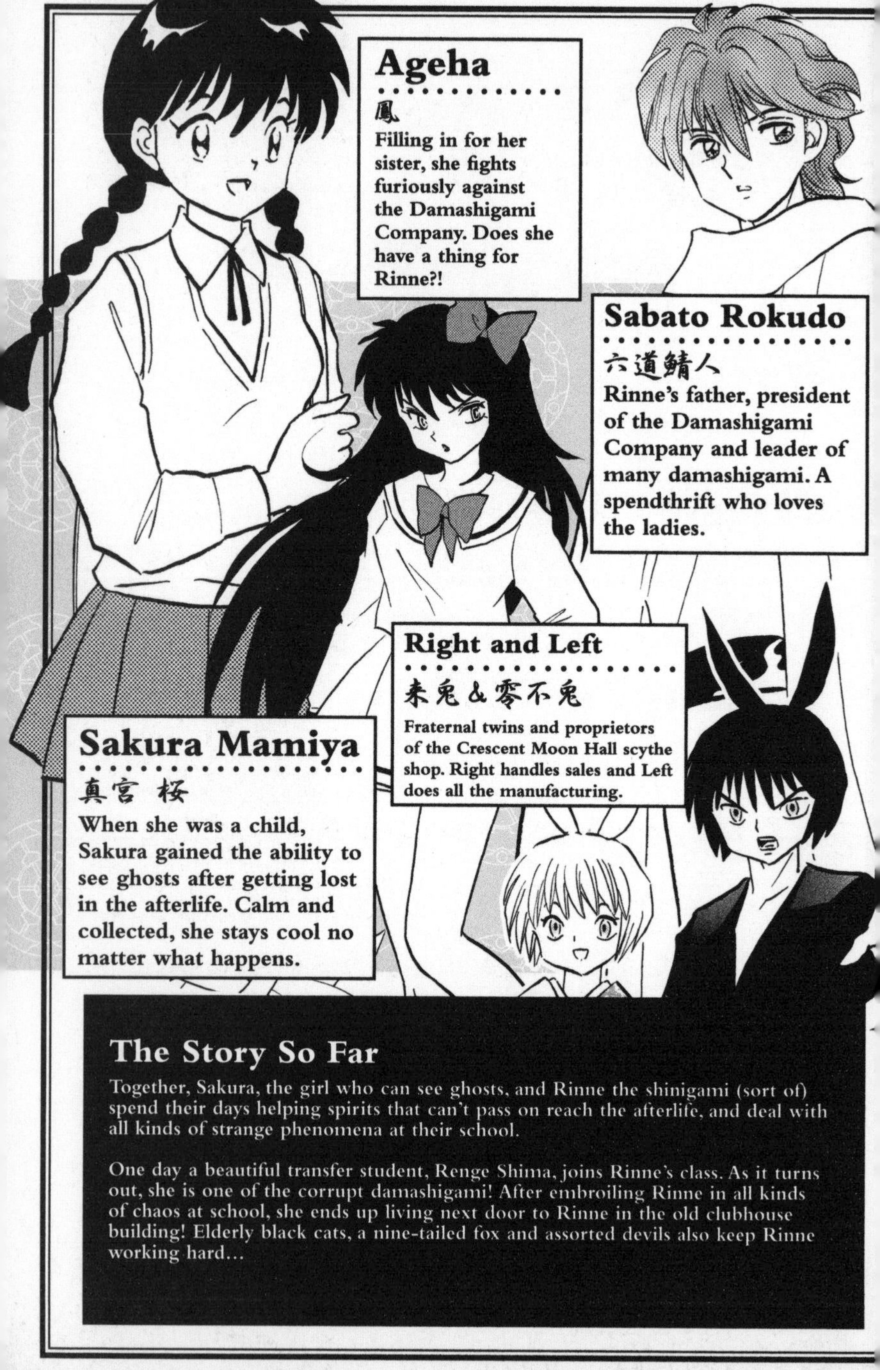

Ageha

鳳

Filling in for her sister, she fights furiously against the Damashigami Company. Does she have a thing for Rinne?!

Sabato Rokudo

六道鯖人

Rinne's father, president of the Damashigami Company and leader of many damashigami. A spendthrift who loves the ladies.

Right and Left

来兎&零不兎

Fraternal twins and proprietors of the Crescent Moon Hall scythe shop. Right handles sales and Left does all the manufacturing.

Sakura Mamiya

真宮 桜

When she was a child, Sakura gained the ability to see ghosts after getting lost in the afterlife. Calm and collected, she stays cool no matter what happens.

The Story So Far

Together, Sakura, the girl who can see ghosts, and Rinne the shinigami (sort of) spend their days helping spirits that can't pass on reach the afterlife, and deal with all kinds of strange phenomena at their school.

One day a beautiful transfer student, Renge Shima, joins Rinne's class. As it turns out, she is one of the corrupt damashigami! After embroiling Rinne in all kinds of chaos at school, she ends up living next door to Rinne in the old clubhouse building! Elderly black cats, a nine-tailed fox and assorted devils also keep Rinne working hard...

RIN-NE

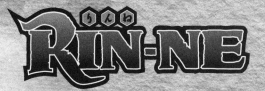

Contents

CHAPTER 139: THE LUCKY PHONE CHARM

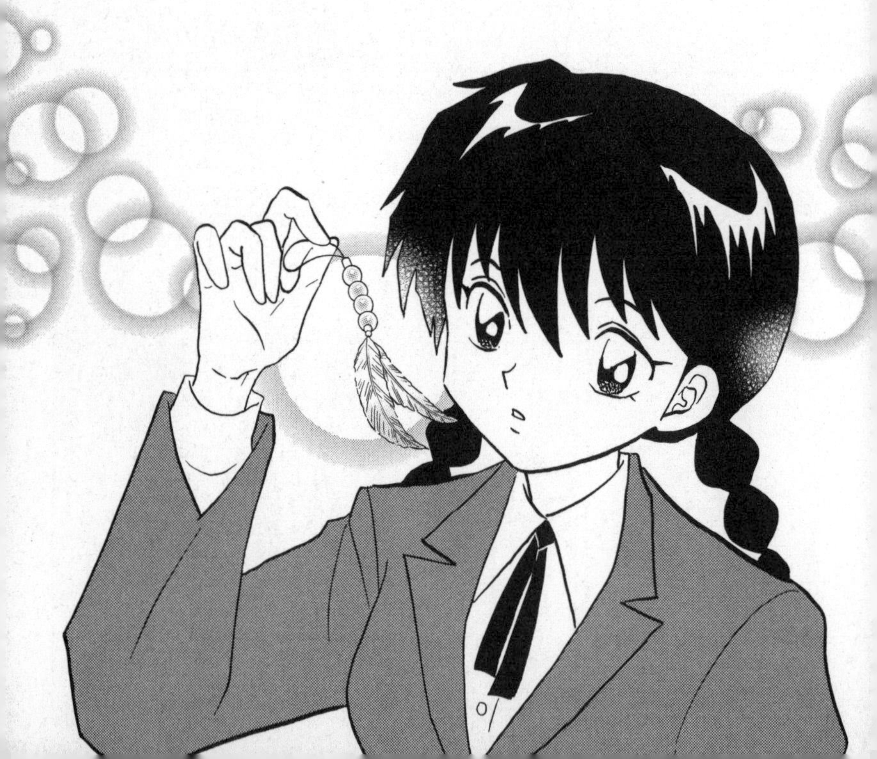

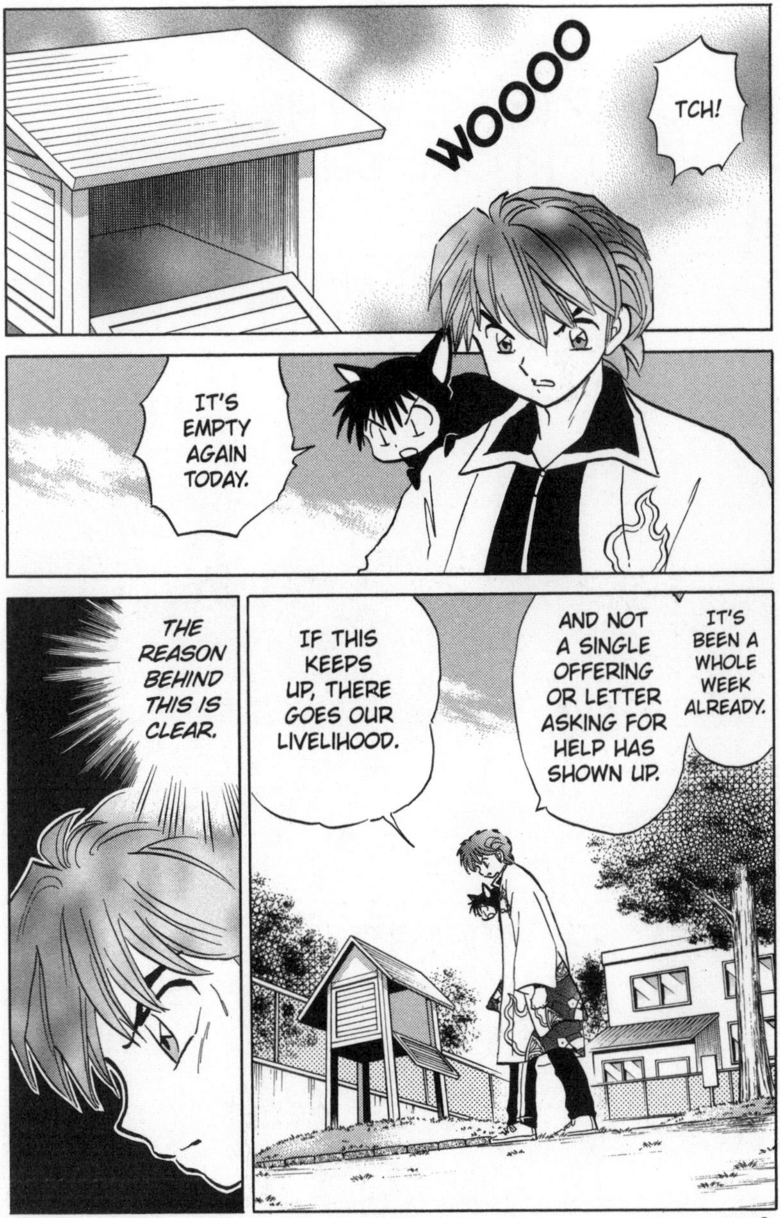
TCH!
WOOOO
IT'S EMPTY AGAIN TODAY.
IT'S BEEN A WHOLE WEEK ALREADY.
AND NOT A SINGLE OFFERING OR LETTER ASKING FOR HELP HAS SHOWN UP.
IF THIS KEEPS UP, THERE GOES OUR LIVELIHOOD.
THE REASON BEHIND THIS IS CLEAR.

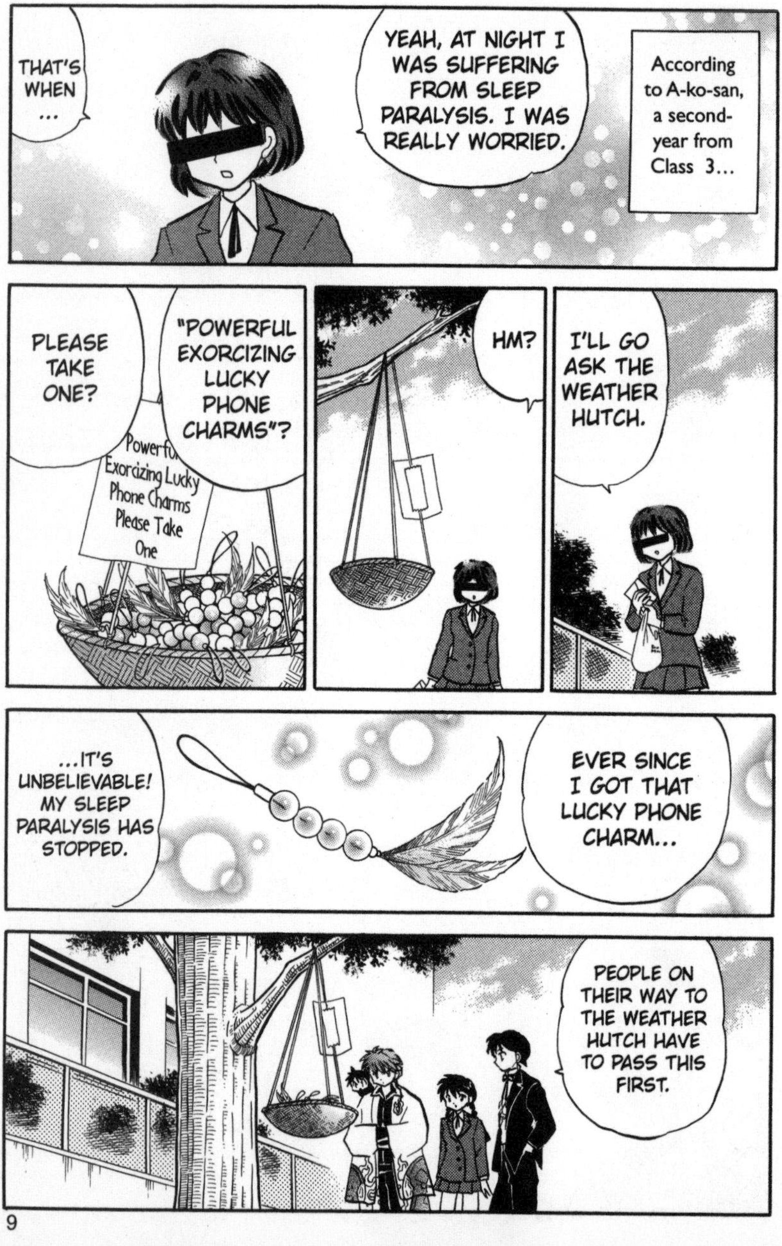
According to A-ko-san, a second-year from Class 3…
YEAH, AT NIGHT I WAS SUFFERING FROM SLEEP PARALYSIS. I WAS REALLY WORRIED.
THAT'S WHEN …
I'LL GO ASK THE WEATHER HUTCH.
HM?
"POWERFUL EXORCIZING LUCKY PHONE CHARMS"?
PLEASE TAKE ONE?
Powerfu Exorcizing Lucky Phone Charms Please Take One
EVER SINCE I GOT THAT LUCKY PHONE CHARM…
…IT'S UNBELIEVABLE! MY SLEEP PARALYSIS HAS STOPPED.
PEOPLE ON THEIR WAY TO THE WEATHER HUTCH HAVE TO PASS THIS FIRST.

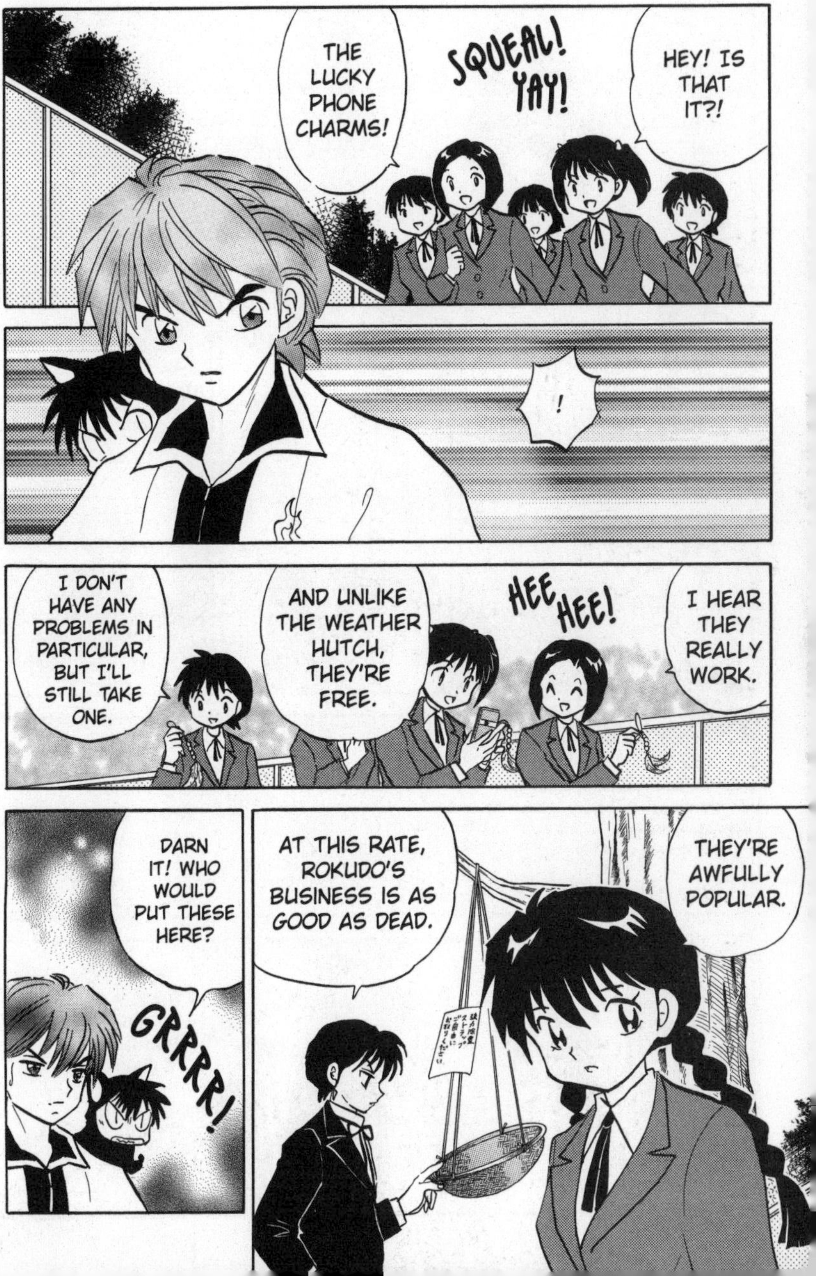
HEY! IS THAT IT?!
SQUEAL! YAY!
THE LUCKY PHONE CHARMS!
!
I HEAR THEY REALLY WORK.
HEE HEE!
AND UNLIKE THE WEATHER HUTCH, THEY'RE FREE.
I DON'T HAVE ANY PROBLEMS IN PARTICULAR, BUT I'LL STILL TAKE ONE.
THEY'RE AWFULLY POPULAR.
AT THIS RATE, ROKUDO'S BUSINESS IS AS GOOD AS DEAD.
DARN IT! WHO WOULD PUT THESE HERE?
GRRRR!

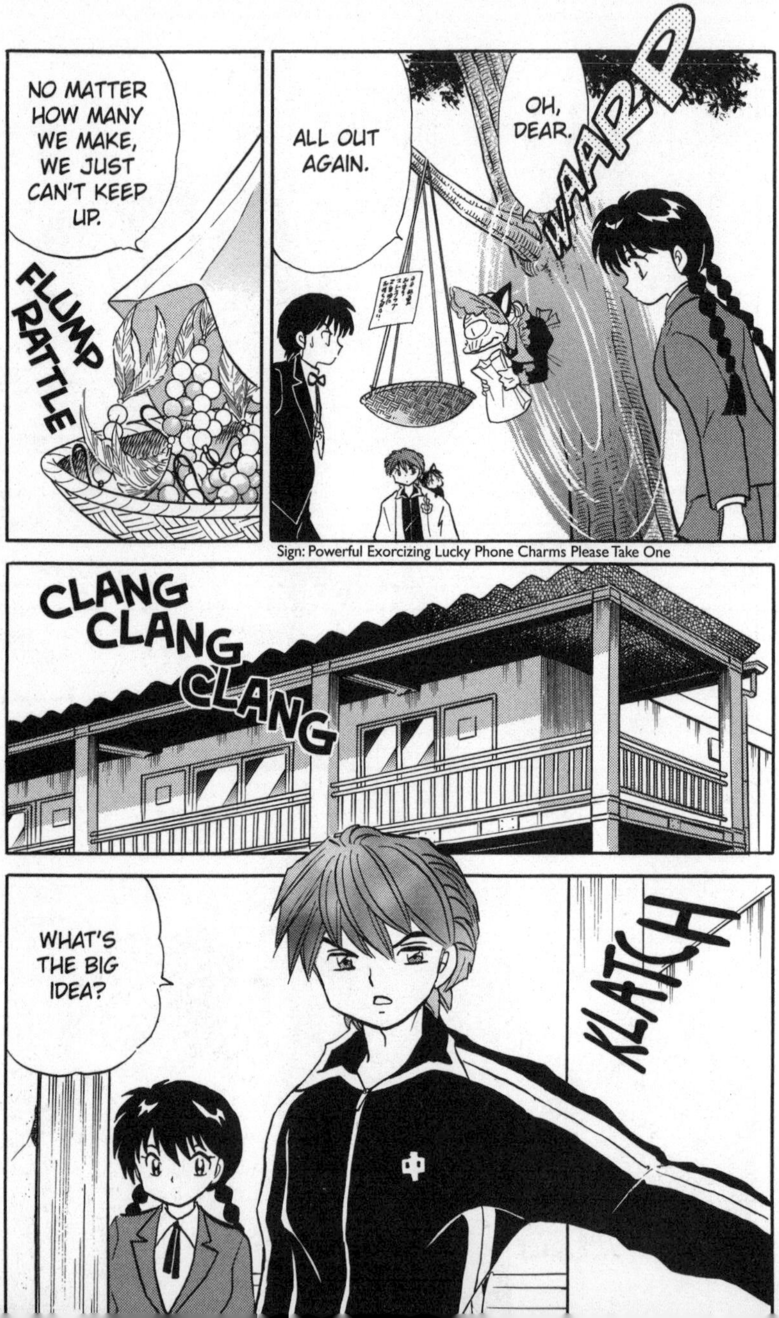
WAAAP
OH, DEAR.
ALL OUT AGAIN.
NO MATTER HOW MANY WE MAKE, WE JUST CAN'T KEEP UP.
FLUMP RATTLE
CLANG CLANG CLANG
KLATCH
WHAT'S THE BIG IDEA?
Sign: Powerful Exorcizing Lucky Phone Charms Please Take One

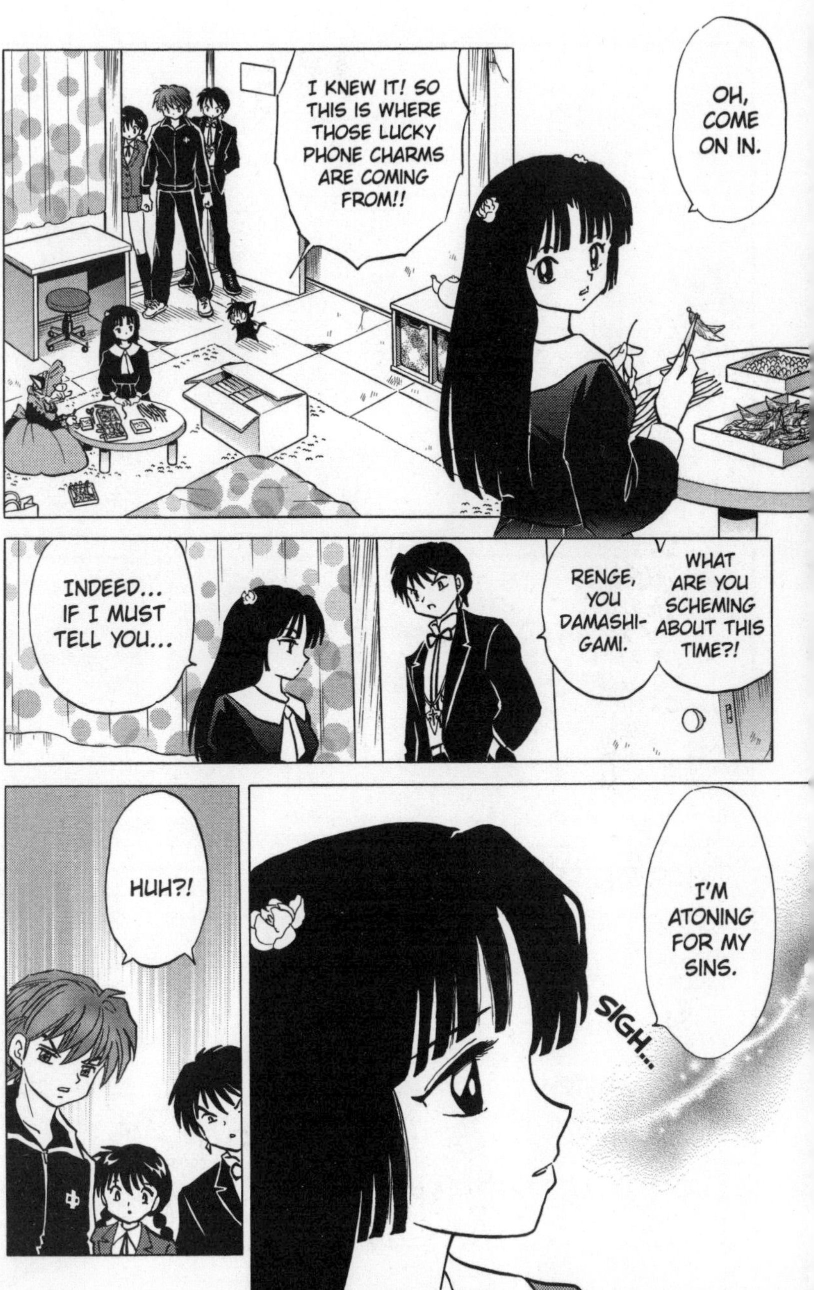
OH, COME ON IN.
I KNEW IT! SO THIS IS WHERE THOSE LUCKY PHONE CHARMS ARE COMING FROM!!
WHAT ARE YOU SCHEMING ABOUT THIS TIME?!
RENGE, YOU DAMASHI-GAMI.
INDEED... IF I MUST TELL YOU...
I'M ATONING FOR MY SINS.
SIGH...
HUH?!

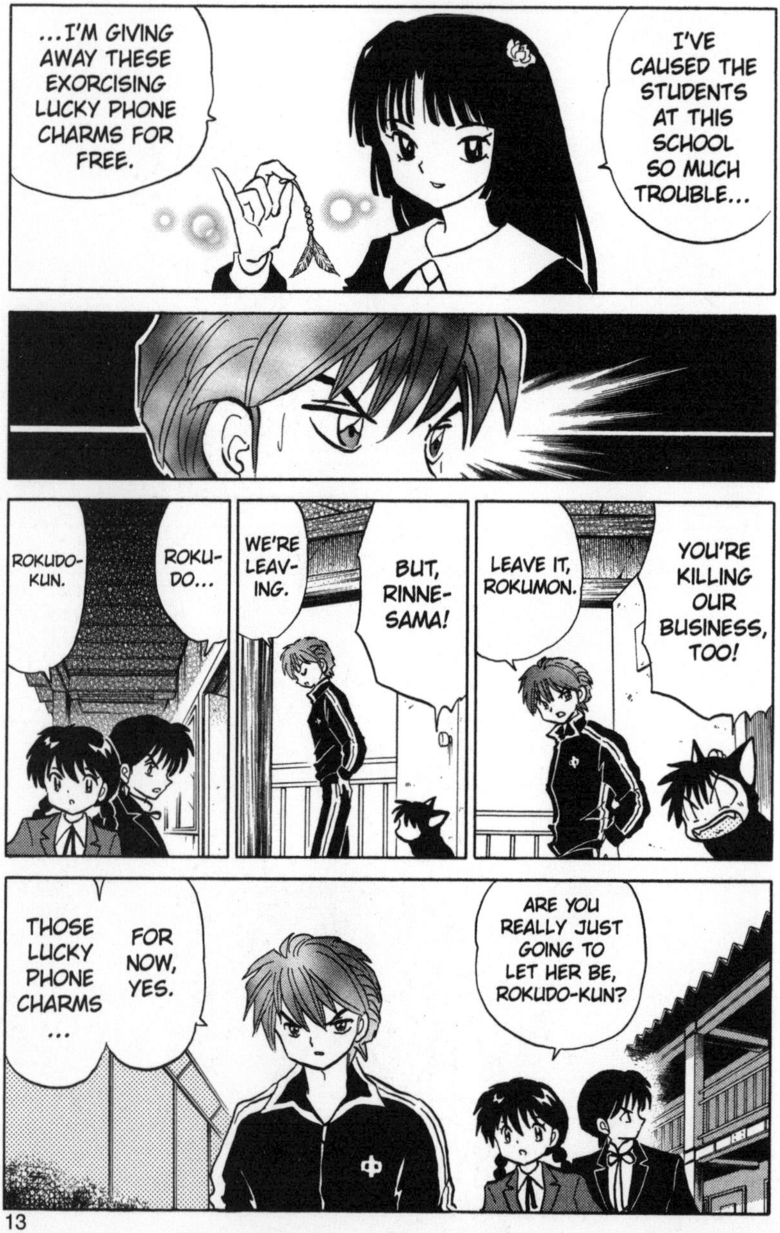
I'VE CAUSED THE STUDENTS AT THIS SCHOOL SO MUCH TROUBLE...
...I'M GIVING AWAY THESE EXORCISING LUCKY PHONE CHARMS FOR FREE.
YOU'RE KILLING OUR BUSINESS, TOO!
LEAVE IT, ROKUMON.
BUT, RINNE-SAMA!
WE'RE LEAV-ING.
ROKU-DO...
ROKUDO-KUN.
ARE YOU REALLY JUST GOING TO LET HER BE, ROKUDO-KUN?
FOR NOW, YES.
THOSE LUCKY PHONE CHARMS ...

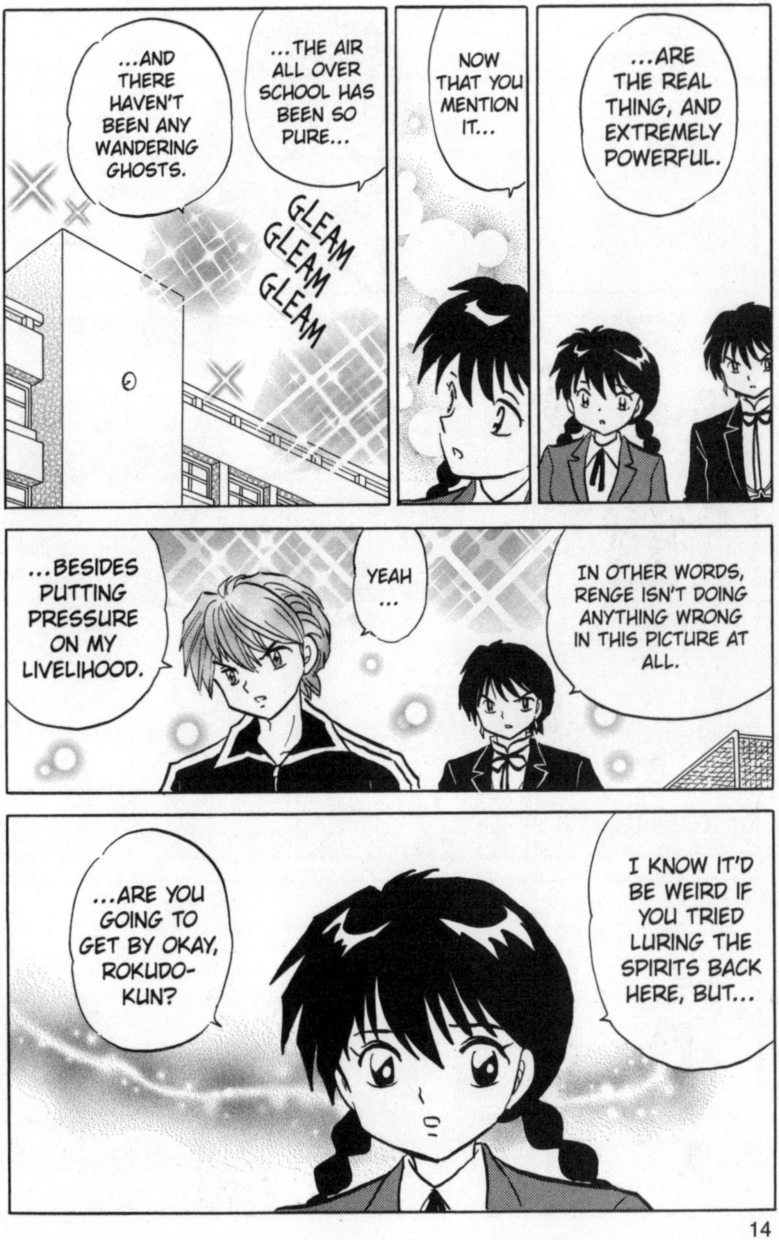
...ARE THE REAL THING, AND EXTREMELY POWERFUL.
NOW THAT YOU MENTION IT...
...THE AIR ALL OVER SCHOOL HAS BEEN SO PURE...
...AND THERE HAVEN'T BEEN ANY WANDERING GHOSTS.
GLEAM GLEAM GLEAM
IN OTHER WORDS, RENGE ISN'T DOING ANYTHING WRONG IN THIS PICTURE AT ALL.
YEAH ...
...BESIDES PUTTING PRESSURE ON MY LIVELIHOOD.
I KNOW IT'D BE WEIRD IF YOU TRIED LURING THE SPIRITS BACK HERE, BUT...
...ARE YOU GOING TO GET BY OKAY, ROKUDO-KUN?

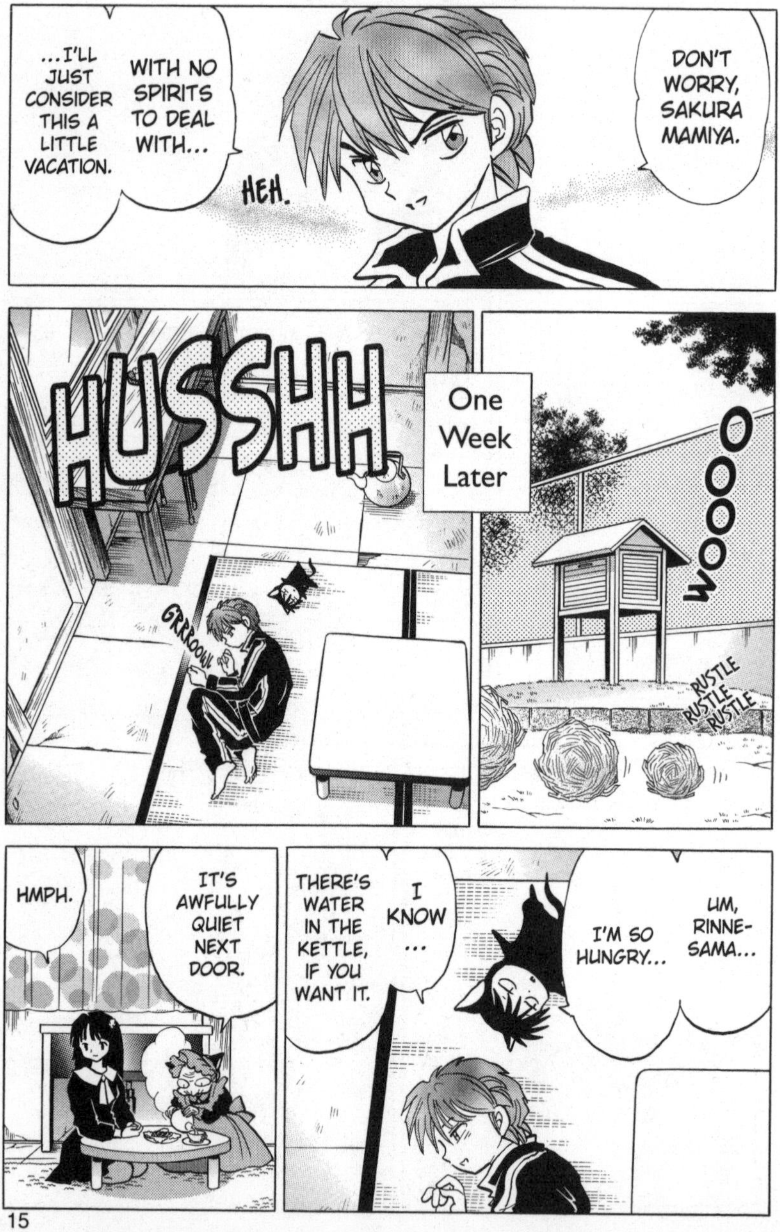
DON'T WORRY, SAKURA MAMIYA.
HEH.
WITH NO SPIRITS TO DEAL WITH...
...I'LL JUST CONSIDER THIS A LITTLE VACATION.
One Week Later
WOOOO
RUSTLE RUSTLE RUSTLE
HUSSHH
GRRROOWL
UM, RINNE-SAMA...
I'M SO HUNGRY...
I KNOW...
THERE'S WATER IN THE KETTLE, IF YOU WANT IT.
IT'S AWFULLY QUIET NEXT DOOR.
HMPH.

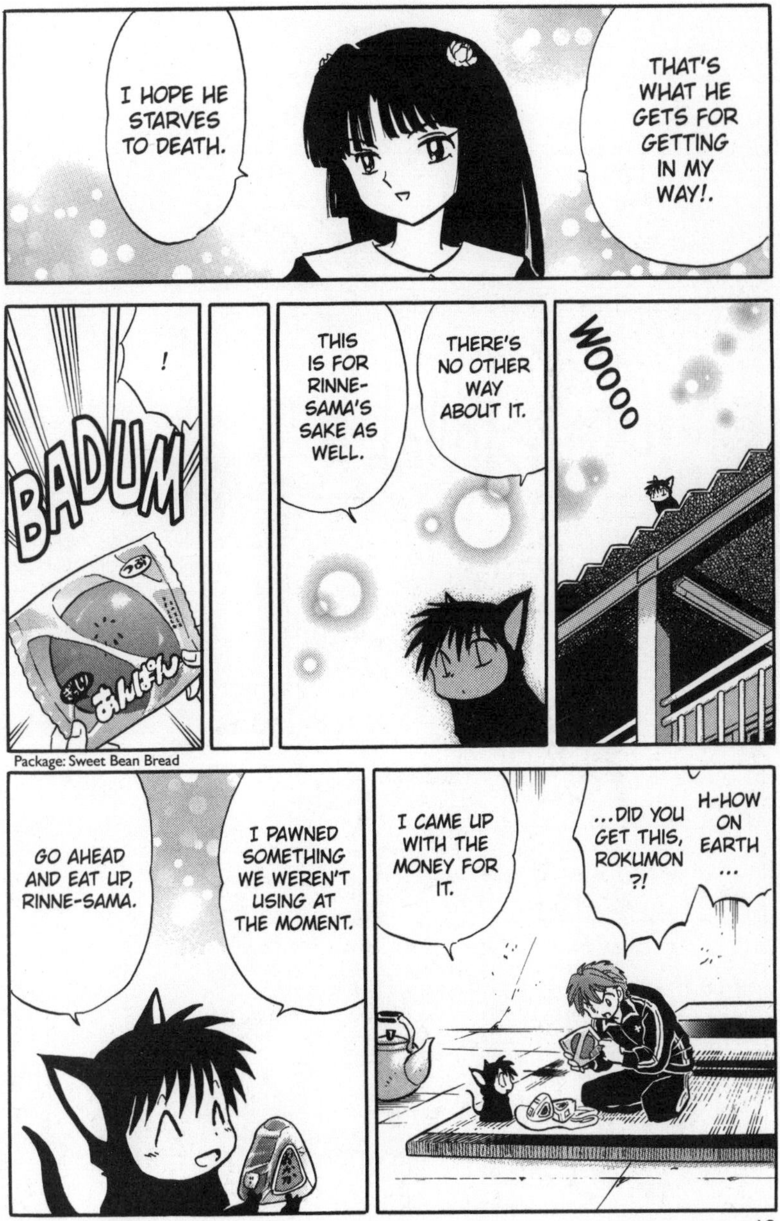
THAT'S WHAT HE GETS FOR GETTING IN MY WAY!.
I HOPE HE STARVES TO DEATH.
WOOOO
THERE'S NO OTHER WAY ABOUT IT.
THIS IS FOR RINNE-SAMA'S SAKE AS WELL.
!
BADUM
H-HOW ON EARTH ...
...DID YOU GET THIS, ROKUMON ?!
I CAME UP WITH THE MONEY FOR IT.
I PAWNED SOMETHING WE WEREN'T USING AT THE MOMENT.
GO AHEAD AND EAT UP, RINNE-SAMA.
Package: Sweet Bean Bread

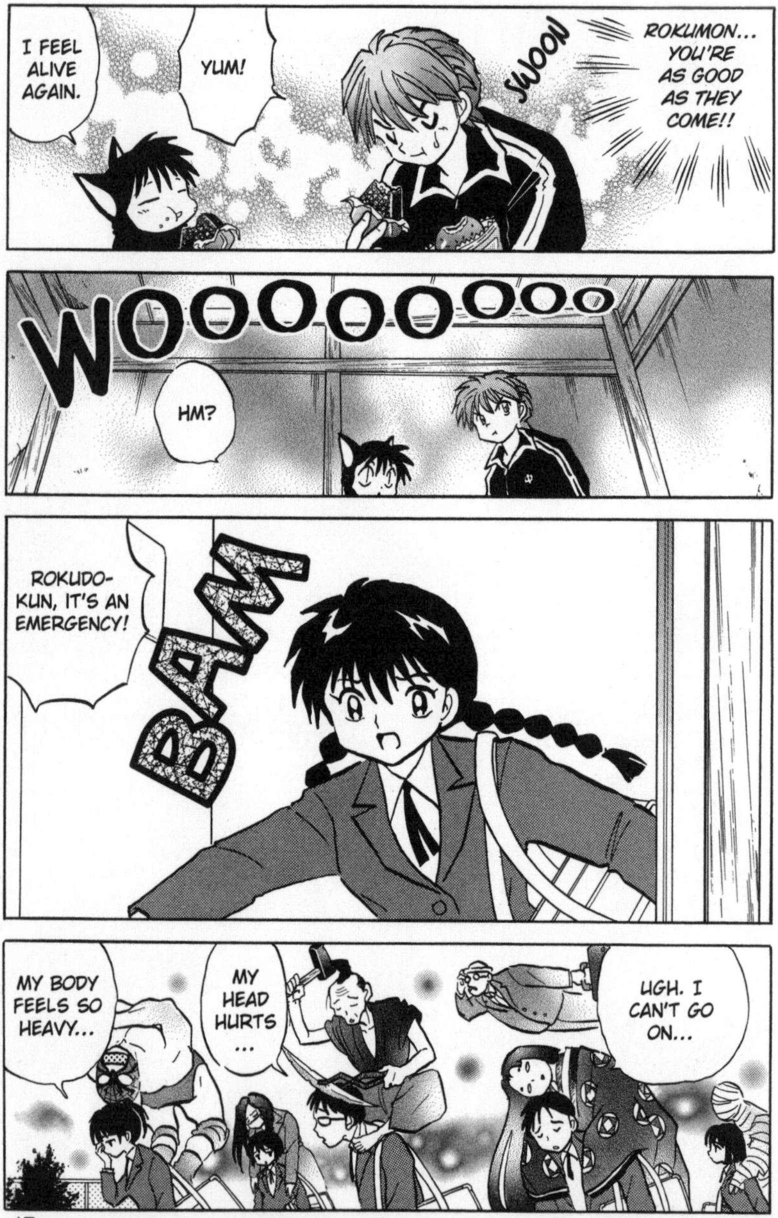
ROKUMON... YOU'RE AS GOOD AS THEY COME!!
SWOON
YUM!
I FEEL ALIVE AGAIN.
WOOOOOOOOO
HM?
BAM
ROKUDO-KUN, IT'S AN EMERGENCY!
UGH. I CAN'T GO ON...
MY HEAD HURTS...
MY BODY FEELS SO HEAVY...

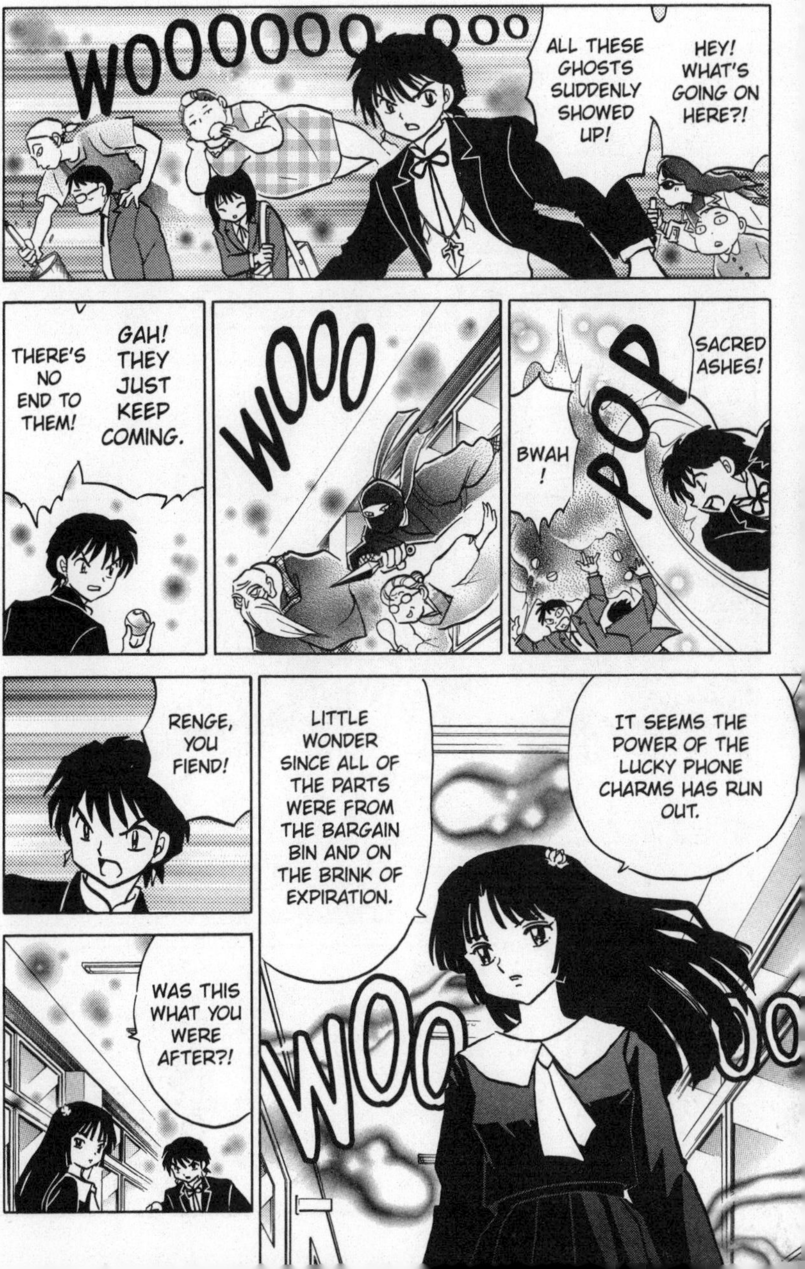
HEY! WHAT'S GOING ON HERE?!
ALL THESE GHOSTS SUDDENLY SHOWED UP!
WOOOOOO OOO
SACRED ASHES!
POP
BWAH!
WOOO
GAH! THEY JUST KEEP COMING.
THERE'S NO END TO THEM!
IT SEEMS THE POWER OF THE LUCKY PHONE CHARMS HAS RUN OUT.
LITTLE WONDER SINCE ALL OF THE PARTS WERE FROM THE BARGAIN BIN AND ON THE BRINK OF EXPIRATION.
WOOOOO
RENGE, YOU FIEND!
WAS THIS WHAT YOU WERE AFTER?!

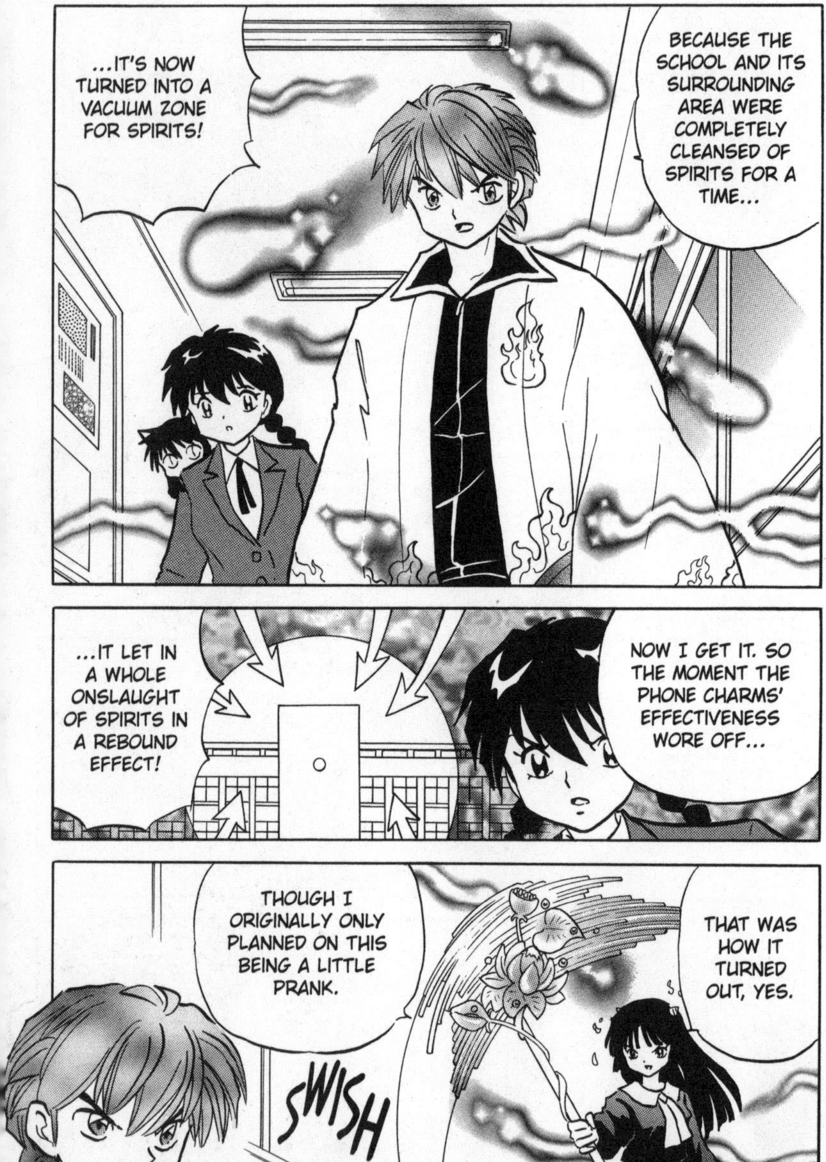
BECAUSE THE SCHOOL AND ITS SURROUNDING AREA WERE COMPLETELY CLEANSED OF SPIRITS FOR A TIME...
...IT'S NOW TURNED INTO A VACUUM ZONE FOR SPIRITS!
NOW I GET IT. SO THE MOMENT THE PHONE CHARMS' EFFECTIVENESS WORE OFF...
...IT LET IN A WHOLE ONSLAUGHT OF SPIRITS IN A REBOUND EFFECT!
THAT WAS HOW IT TURNED OUT, YES.
THOUGH I ORIGINALLY ONLY PLANNED ON THIS BEING A LITTLE PRANK.
SWISH

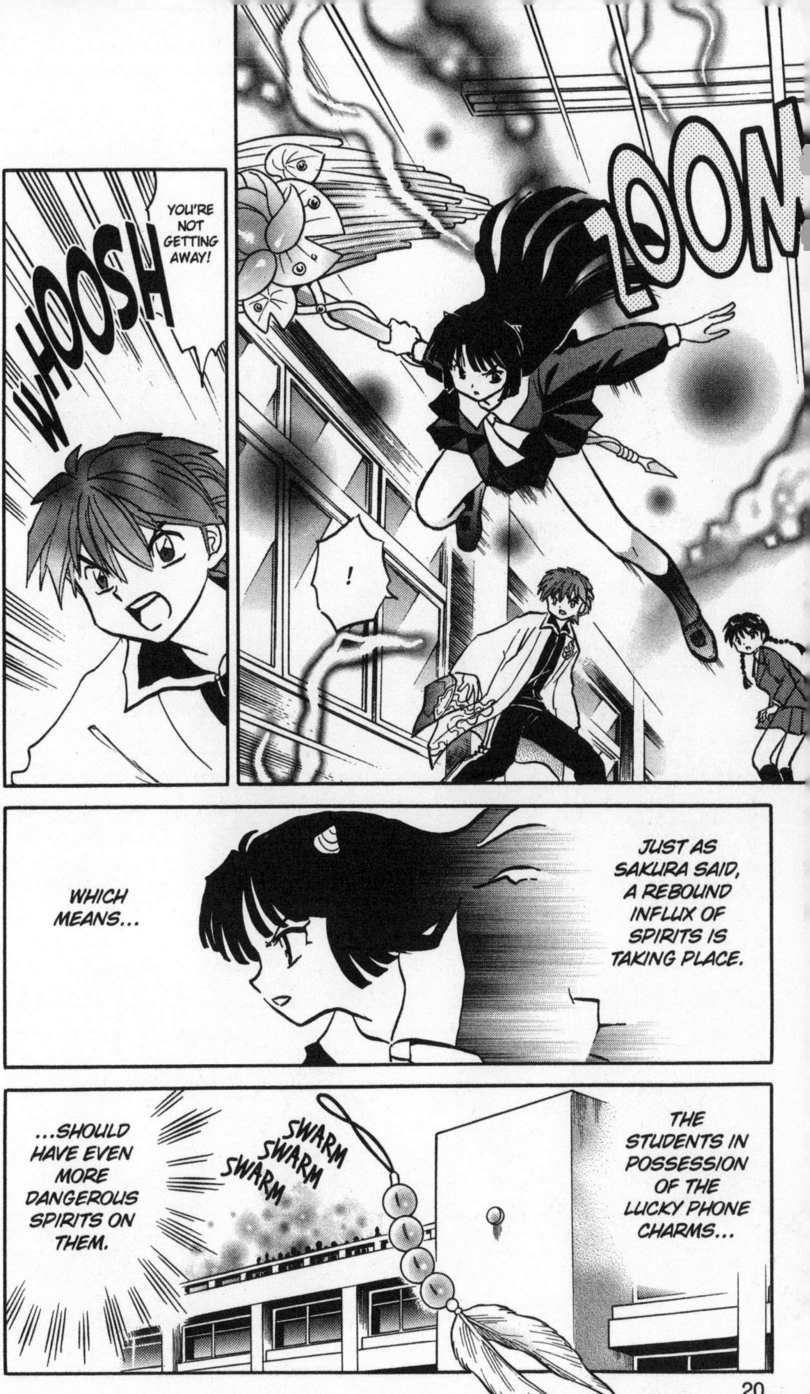
ZOOM
!
WHOOSH
YOU'RE NOT GETTING AWAY!
JUST AS SAKURA SAID, A REBOUND INFLUX OF SPIRITS IS TAKING PLACE.
WHICH MEANS...
THE STUDENTS IN POSSESSION OF THE LUCKY PHONE CHARMS...
SWARM SWARM SWARM
...SHOULD HAVE EVEN MORE DANGEROUS SPIRITS ON THEM.

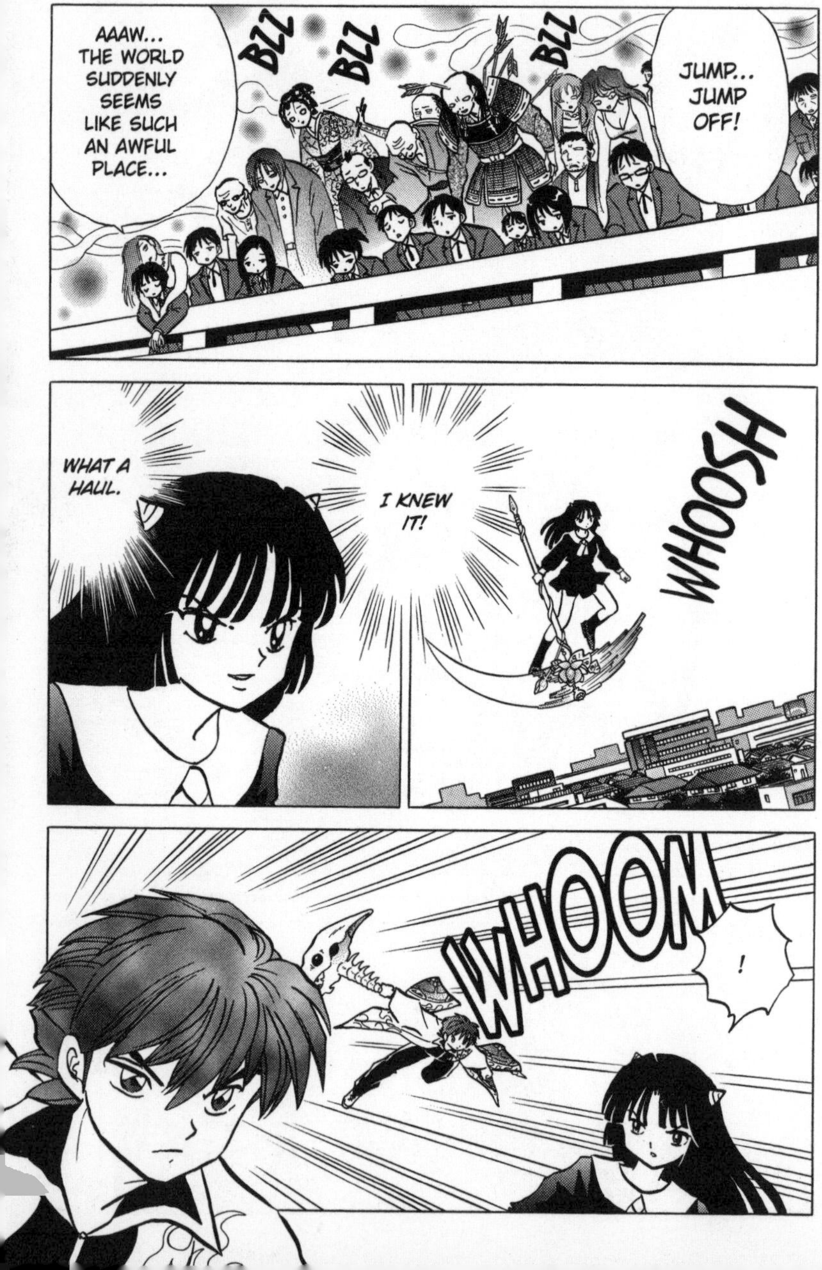
JUMP... JUMP OFF!
BZZ
BZZ
BZZ
AAAW... THE WORLD SUDDENLY SEEMS LIKE SUCH AN AWFUL PLACE...
WHOOSH
I KNEW IT!
WHAT A HAUL.
!
WHOOM

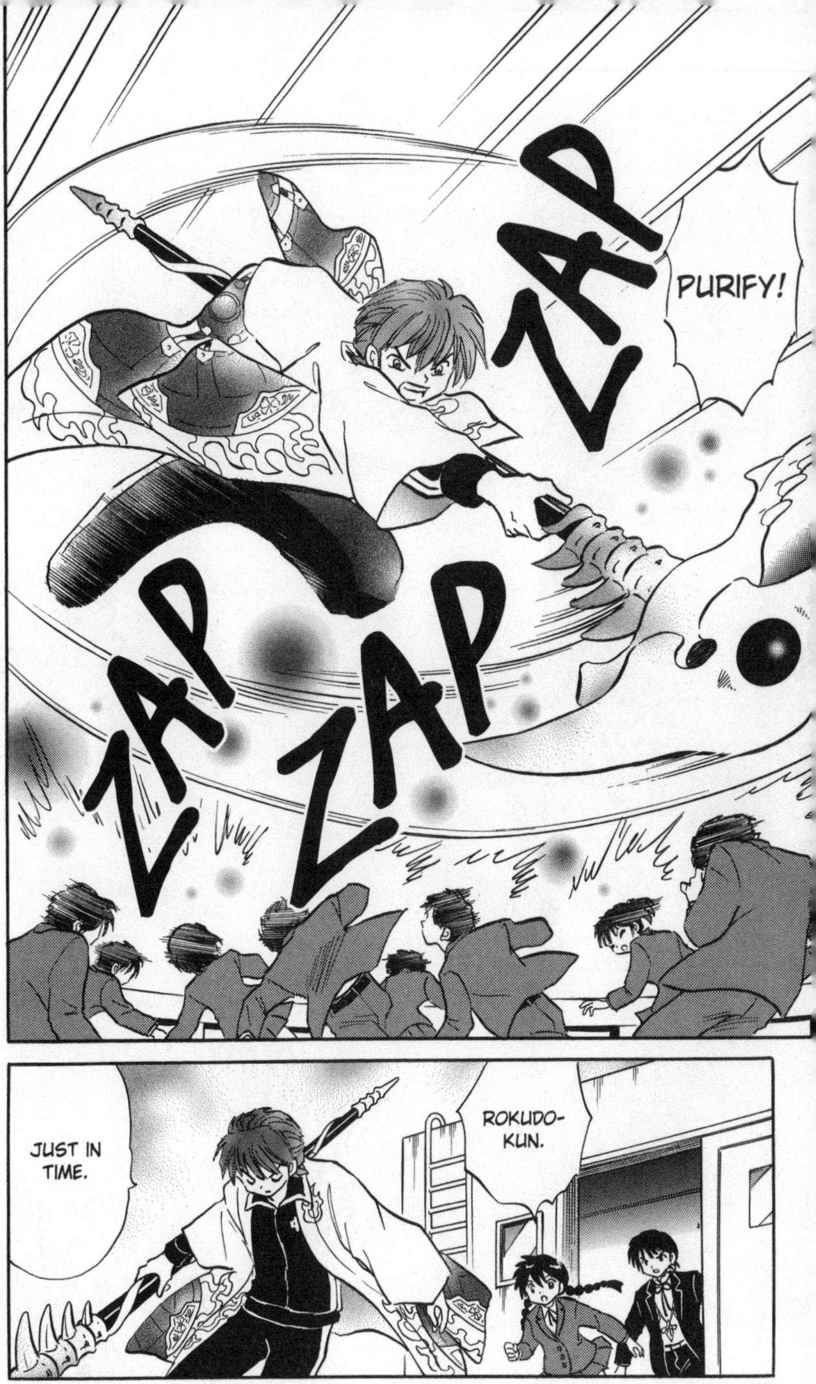
PURIFY!
ZAP
ZAP
ZAP
ROKUDO-KUN.
JUST IN TIME.

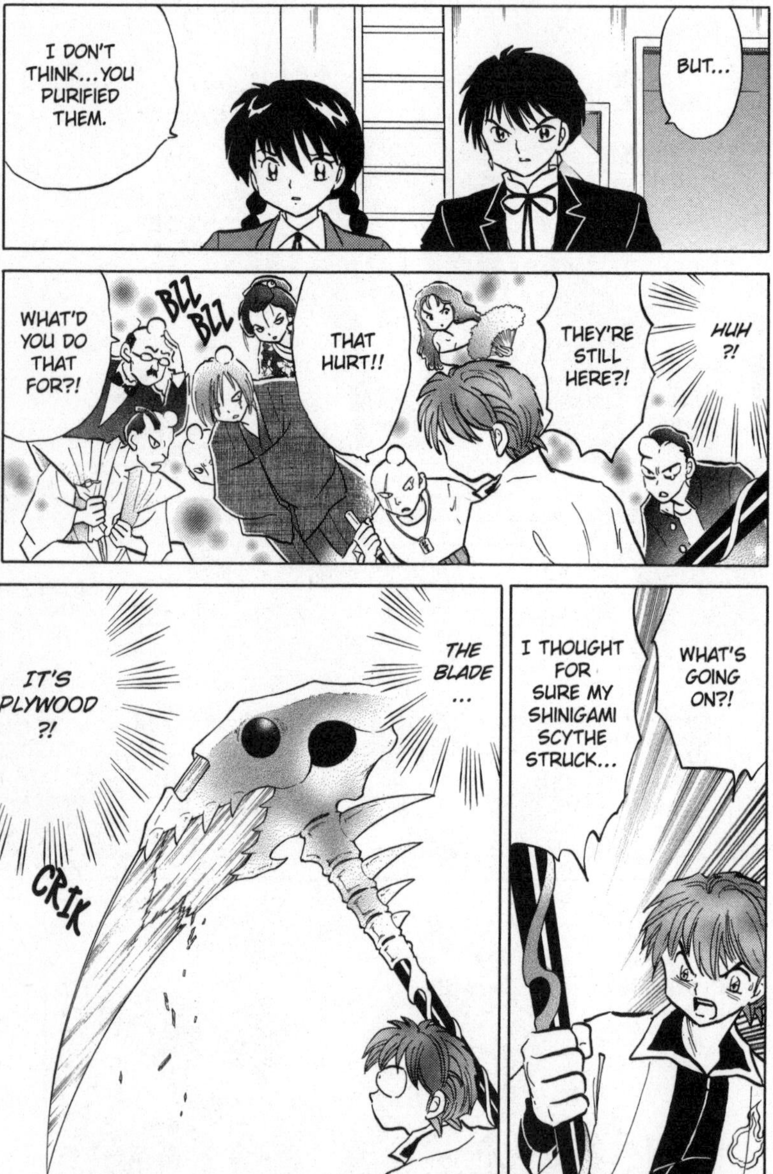
BUT...
I DON'T THINK...YOU PURIFIED THEM.
HUH?!
THEY'RE STILL HERE?!
THAT HURT!!
BZZ BZZ
WHAT'D YOU DO THAT FOR?!
WHAT'S GOING ON?!
I THOUGHT FOR SURE MY SHINIGAMI SCYTHE STRUCK...
THE BLADE...
IT'S PLYWOOD?!
CRIK

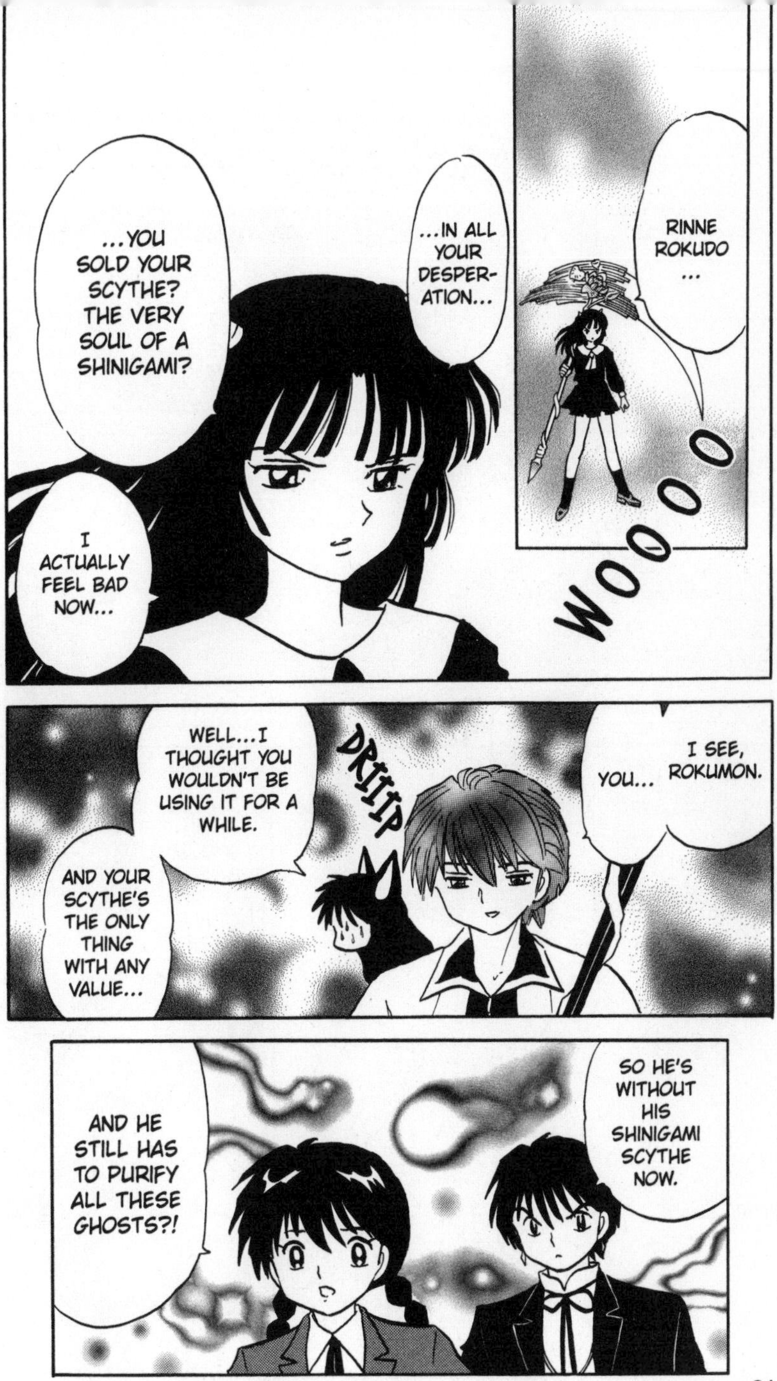
RINNE ROKUDO ...
WOOOOOO
...IN ALL YOUR DESPERATION...
...YOU SOLD YOUR SCYTHE? THE VERY SOUL OF A SHINIGAMI?
I ACTUALLY FEEL BAD NOW...
I SEE, ROKUMON.
YOU...
WELL...I THOUGHT YOU WOULDN'T BE USING IT FOR A WHILE.
DRIIIP
AND YOUR SCYTHE'S THE ONLY THING WITH ANY VALUE...
SO HE'S WITHOUT HIS SHINIGAMI SCYTHE NOW.
AND HE STILL HAS TO PURIFY ALL THESE GHOSTS?!

CHAPTER 140:
EVIL SPIRIT SURGE

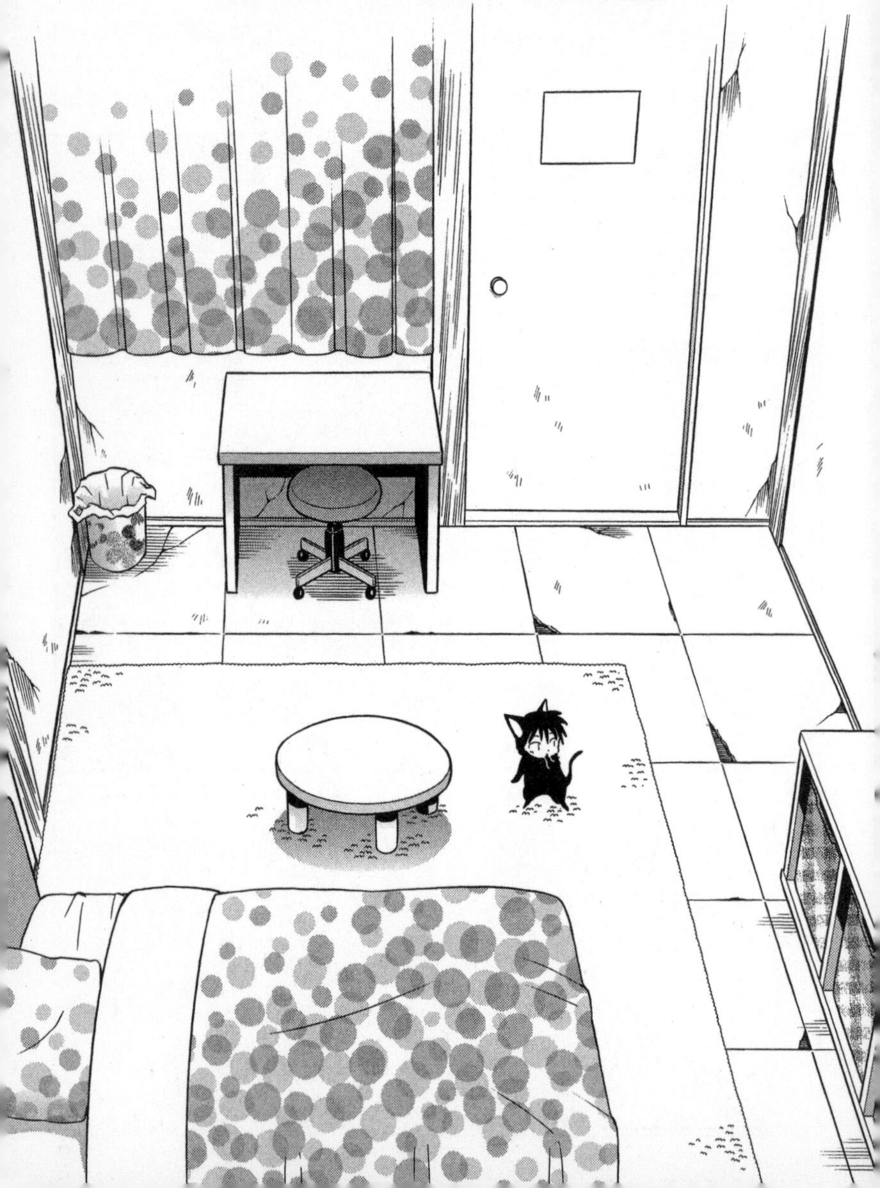

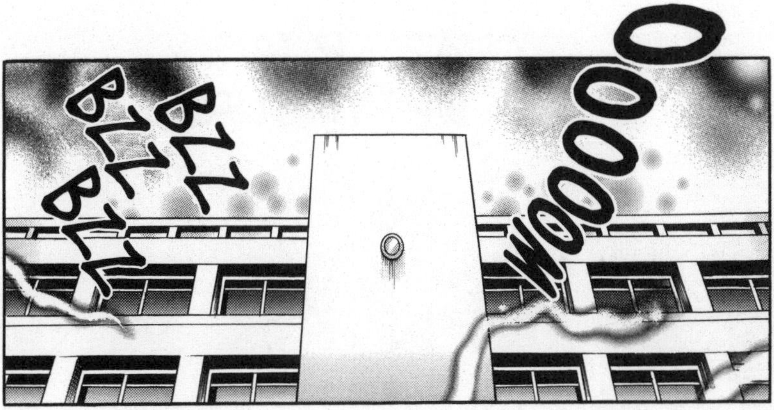
WOOOOO
BZZ
BZZ
BZZ

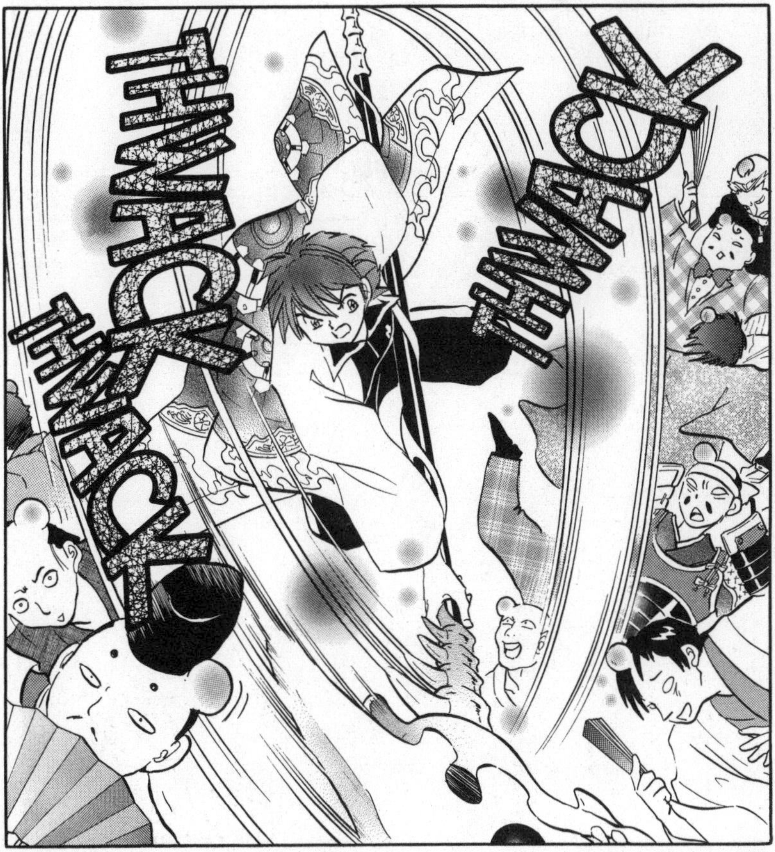
THWACK
THWACK
THWACK

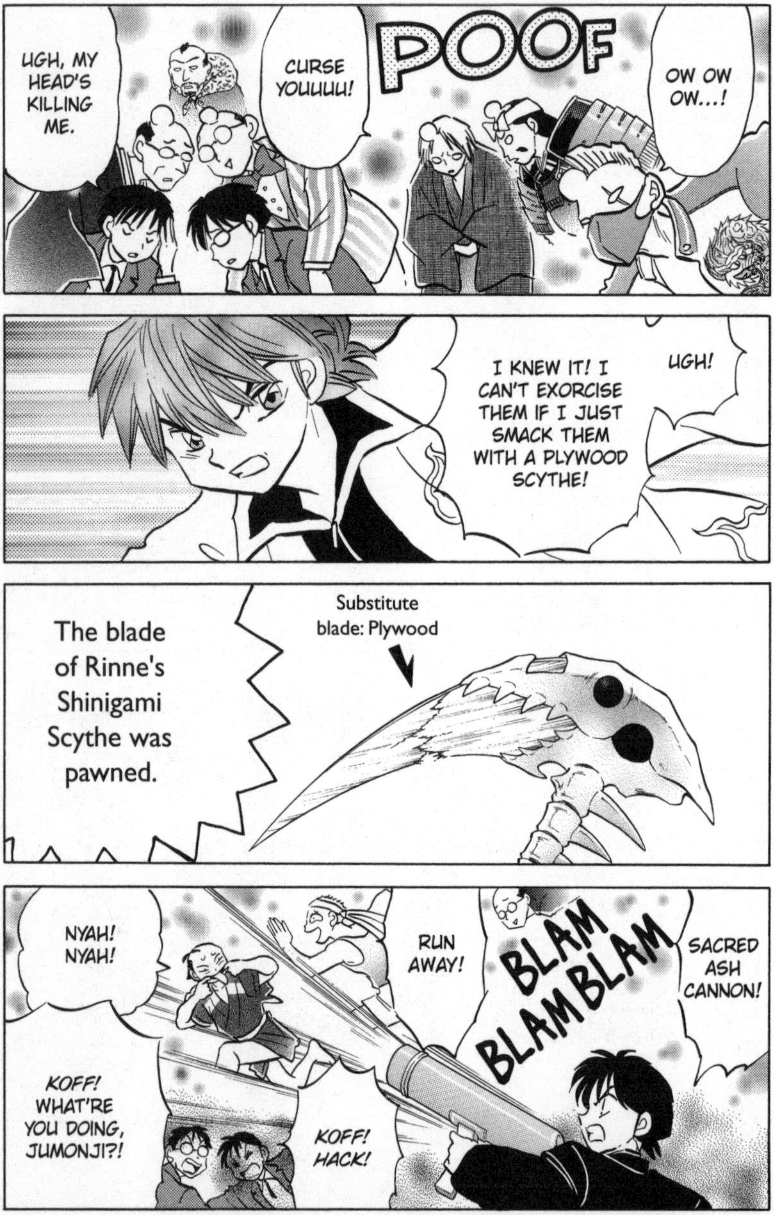
OW OW OW...!
POOF
CURSE YOUUUU!
UGH, MY HEAD'S KILLING ME.
UGH!
I KNEW IT! I CAN'T EXORCISE THEM IF I JUST SMACK THEM WITH A PLYWOOD SCYTHE!
Substitute blade: Plywood
The blade of Rinne's Shinigami Scythe was pawned.
SACRED ASH CANNON!
BLAM BLAM BLAM
RUN AWAY!
NYAH! NYAH!
KOFF! HACK!
KOFF! WHAT'RE YOU DOING, JUMONJI?!

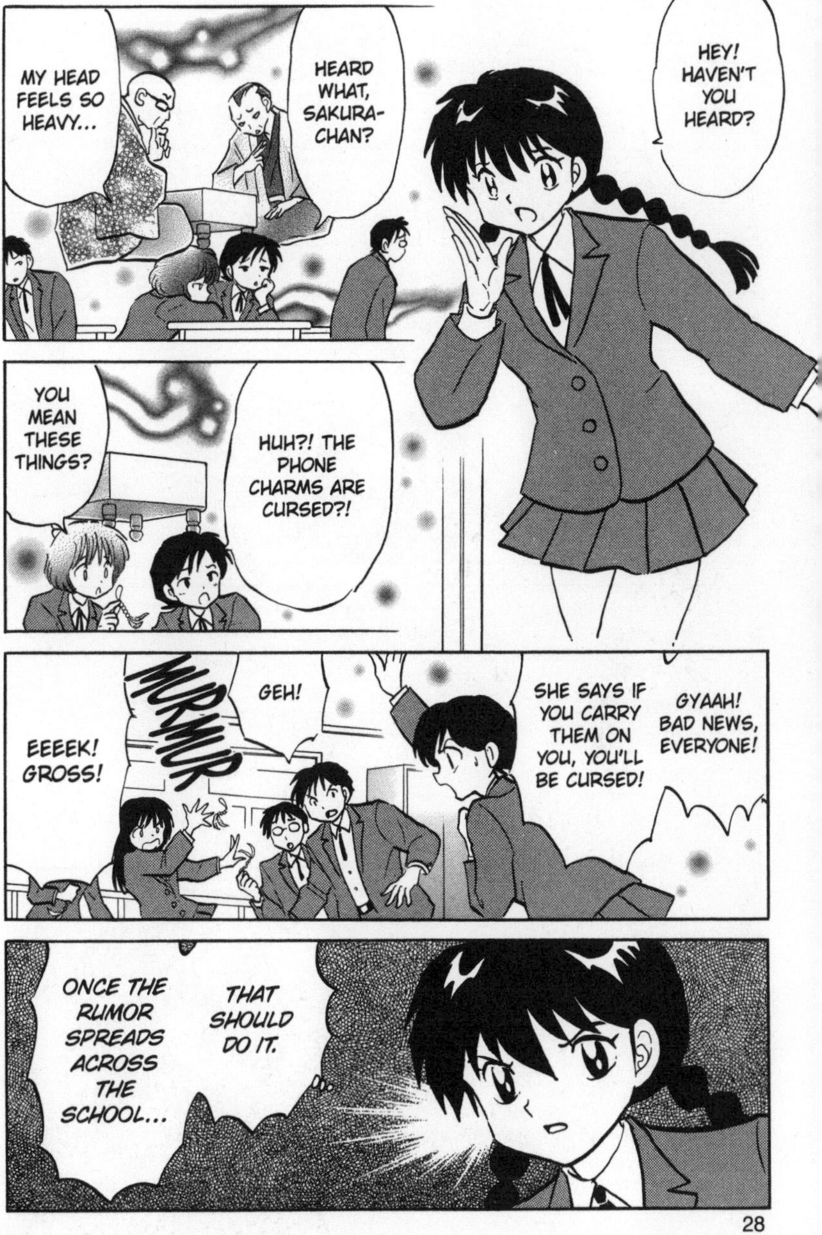

HEY! HAVEN'T YOU HEARD?
HEARD WHAT, SAKURA-CHAN?
MY HEAD FEELS SO HEAVY...
HUH?! THE PHONE CHARMS ARE CURSED?!
YOU MEAN THESE THINGS?
GYAAH! BAD NEWS, EVERYONE!
SHE SAYS IF YOU CARRY THEM ON YOU, YOU'LL BE CURSED!
GEH!
MURMUR
EEEEK! GROSS!
THAT SHOULD DO IT.
ONCE THE RUMOR SPREADS ACROSS THE SCHOOL...

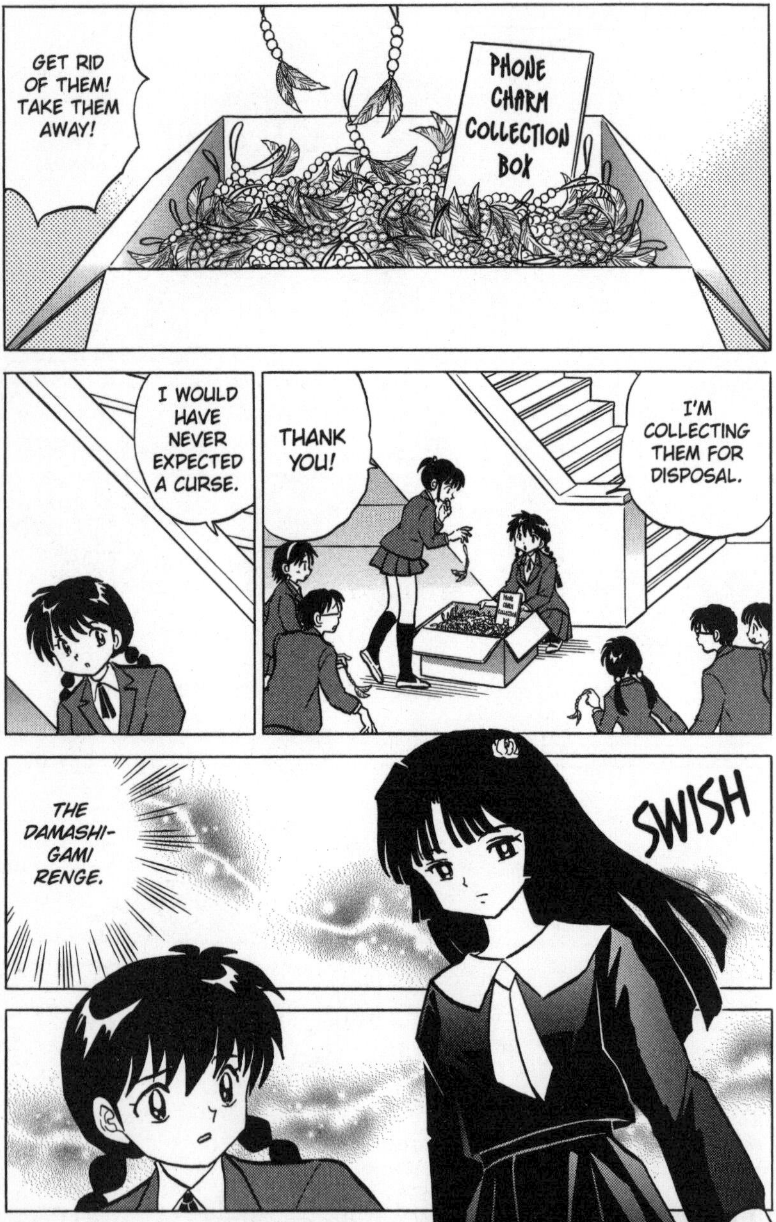
PHONE CHARM COLLECTION BOX
GET RID OF THEM! TAKE THEM AWAY!
I'M COLLECTING THEM FOR DISPOSAL.
THANK YOU!
I WOULD HAVE NEVER EXPECTED A CURSE.
SWISH
THE DAMASHI-GAMI RENGE.

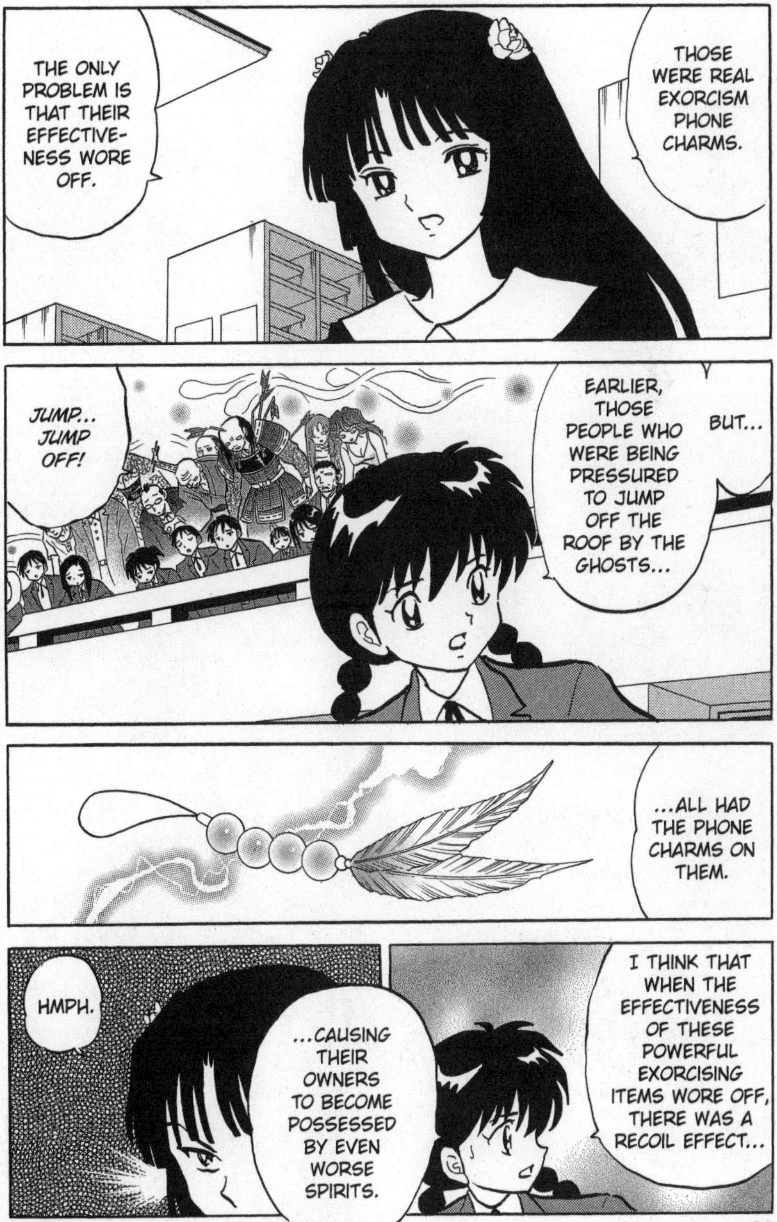
THOSE WERE REAL EXORCISM PHONE CHARMS.
THE ONLY PROBLEM IS THAT THEIR EFFECTIVENESS WORE OFF.
BUT...
EARLIER, THOSE PEOPLE WHO WERE BEING PRESSURED TO JUMP OFF THE ROOF BY THE GHOSTS...
JUMP... JUMP OFF!
...ALL HAD THE PHONE CHARMS ON THEM.
I THINK THAT WHEN THE EFFECTIVENESS OF THESE POWERFUL EXORCISING ITEMS WORE OFF, THERE WAS A RECOIL EFFECT...
...CAUSING THEIR OWNERS TO BECOME POSSESSED BY EVEN WORSE SPIRITS.
HMPH.

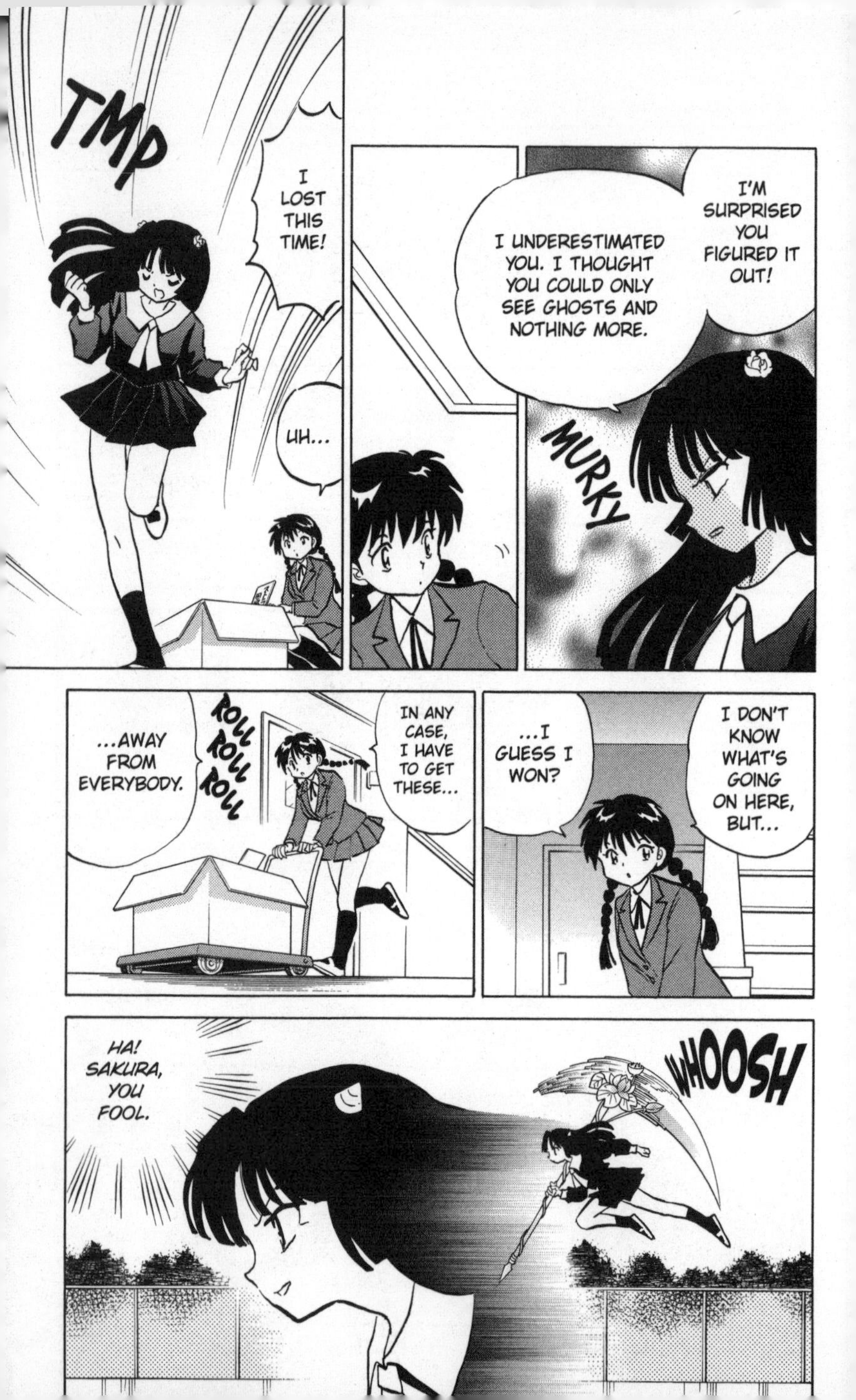
I'M SURPRISED YOU FIGURED IT OUT!
I UNDERESTIMATED YOU. I THOUGHT YOU COULD ONLY SEE GHOSTS AND NOTHING MORE.
MURKY
I LOST THIS TIME!
TMP
UH...
I DON'T KNOW WHAT'S GOING ON HERE, BUT...
...I GUESS I WON?
IN ANY CASE, I HAVE TO GET THESE...
ROLL ROLL ROLL
...AWAY FROM EVERYBODY.
WHOOSH
HA! SAKURA, YOU FOOL.

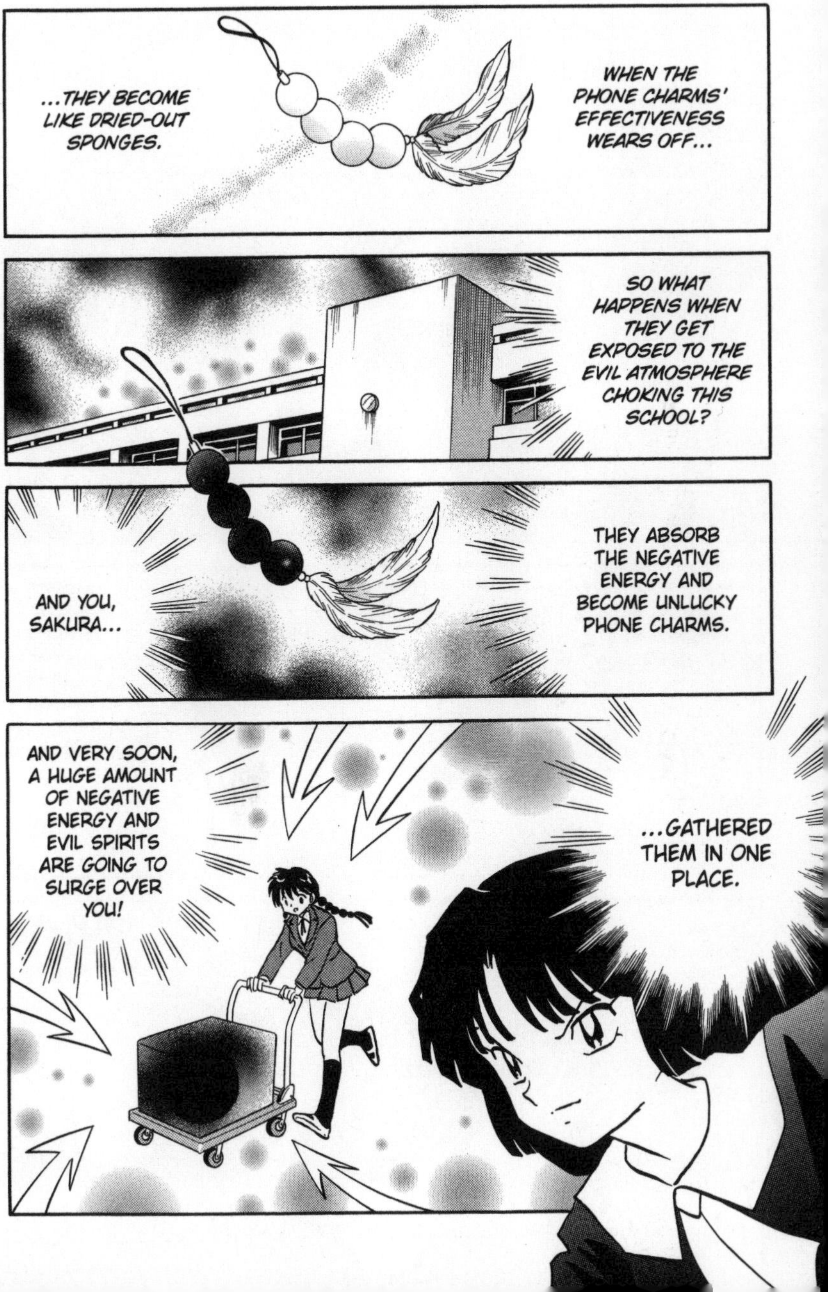
WHEN THE PHONE CHARMS' EFFECTIVENESS WEARS OFF...
...THEY BECOME LIKE DRIED-OUT SPONGES.
SO WHAT HAPPENS WHEN THEY GET EXPOSED TO THE EVIL ATMOSPHERE CHOKING THIS SCHOOL?
THEY ABSORB THE NEGATIVE ENERGY AND BECOME UNLUCKY PHONE CHARMS.
AND YOU, SAKURA...
...GATHERED THEM IN ONE PLACE.
AND VERY SOON, A HUGE AMOUNT OF NEGATIVE ENERGY AND EVIL SPIRITS ARE GOING TO SURGE OVER YOU!

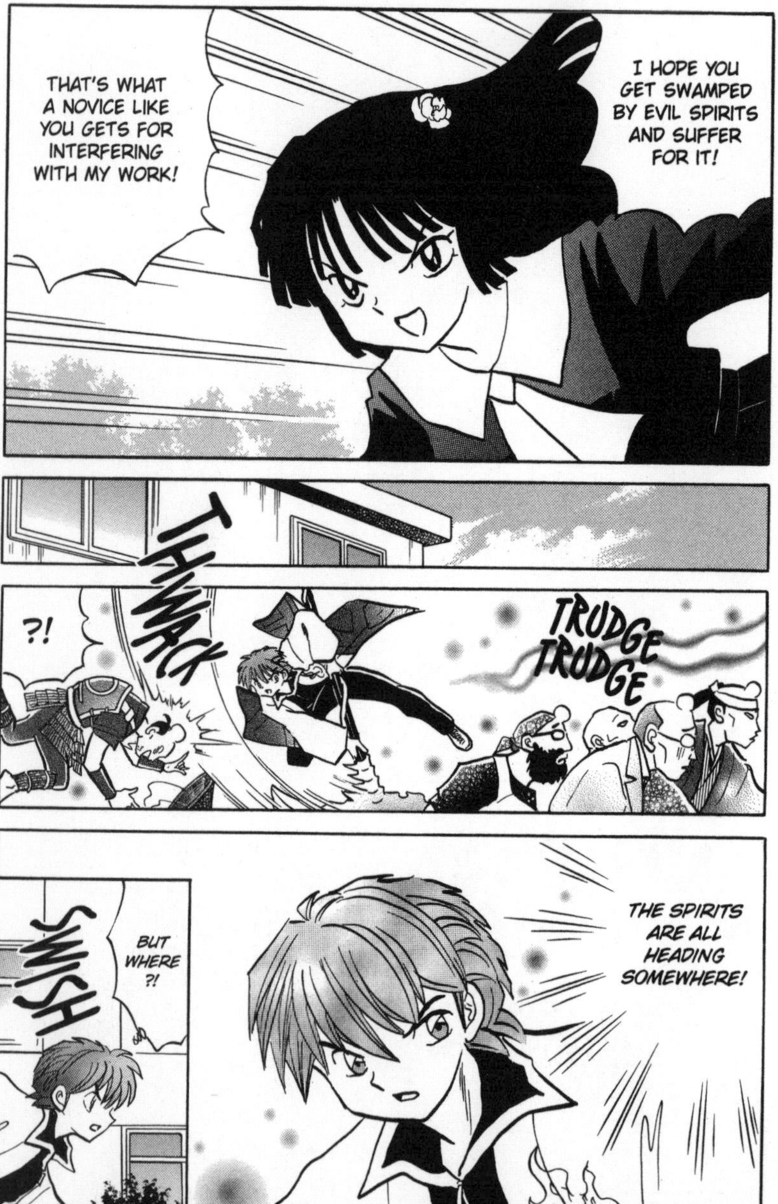
I HOPE YOU GET SWAMPED BY EVIL SPIRITS AND SUFFER FOR IT!
THAT'S WHAT A NOVICE LIKE YOU GETS FOR INTERFERING WITH MY WORK!
THWACK
TRUDGE TRUDGE
?!
THE SPIRITS ARE ALL HEADING SOMEWHERE!
SWISH
BUT WHERE?!

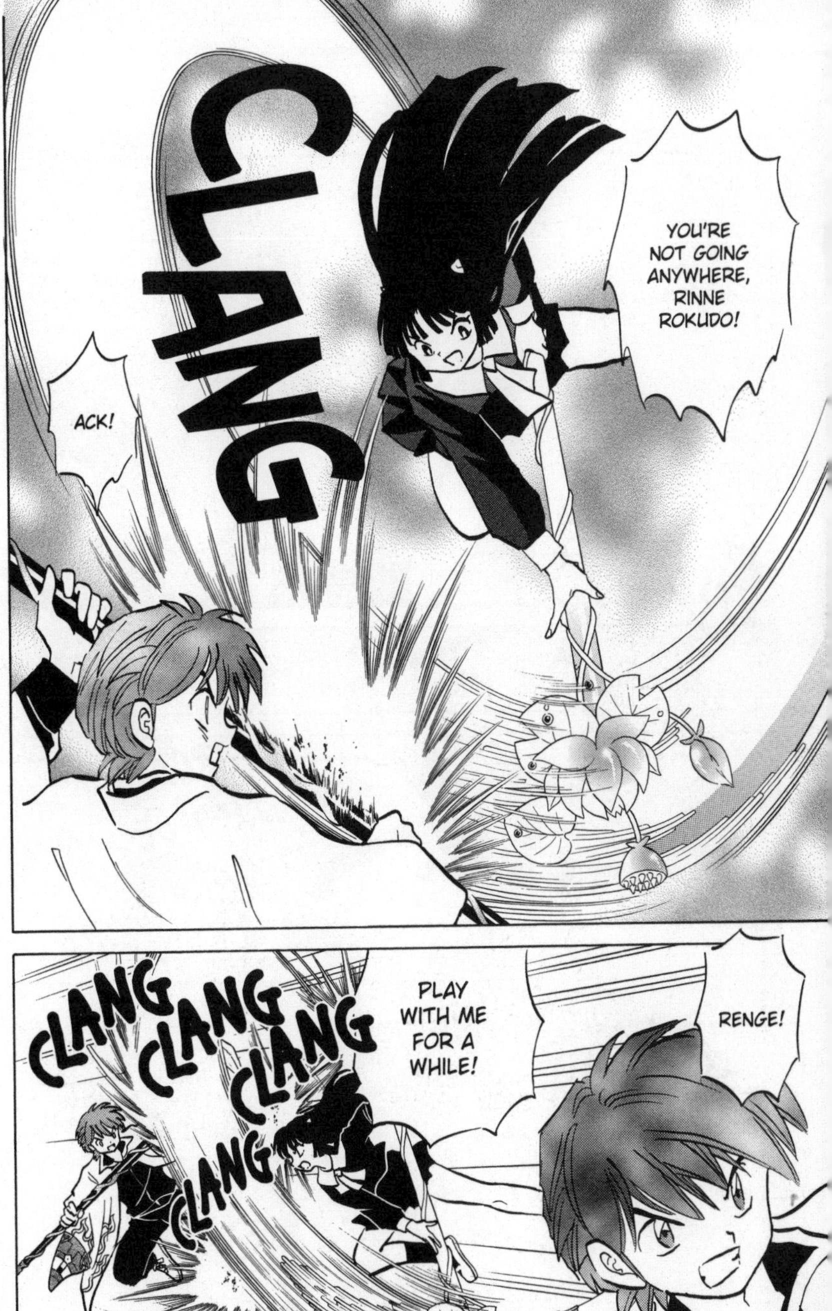
YOU'RE NOT GOING ANYWHERE, RINNE ROKUDO!
CLANG
ACK!
RENGE!
PLAY WITH ME FOR A WHILE!
CLANG CLANG CLANG CLANG

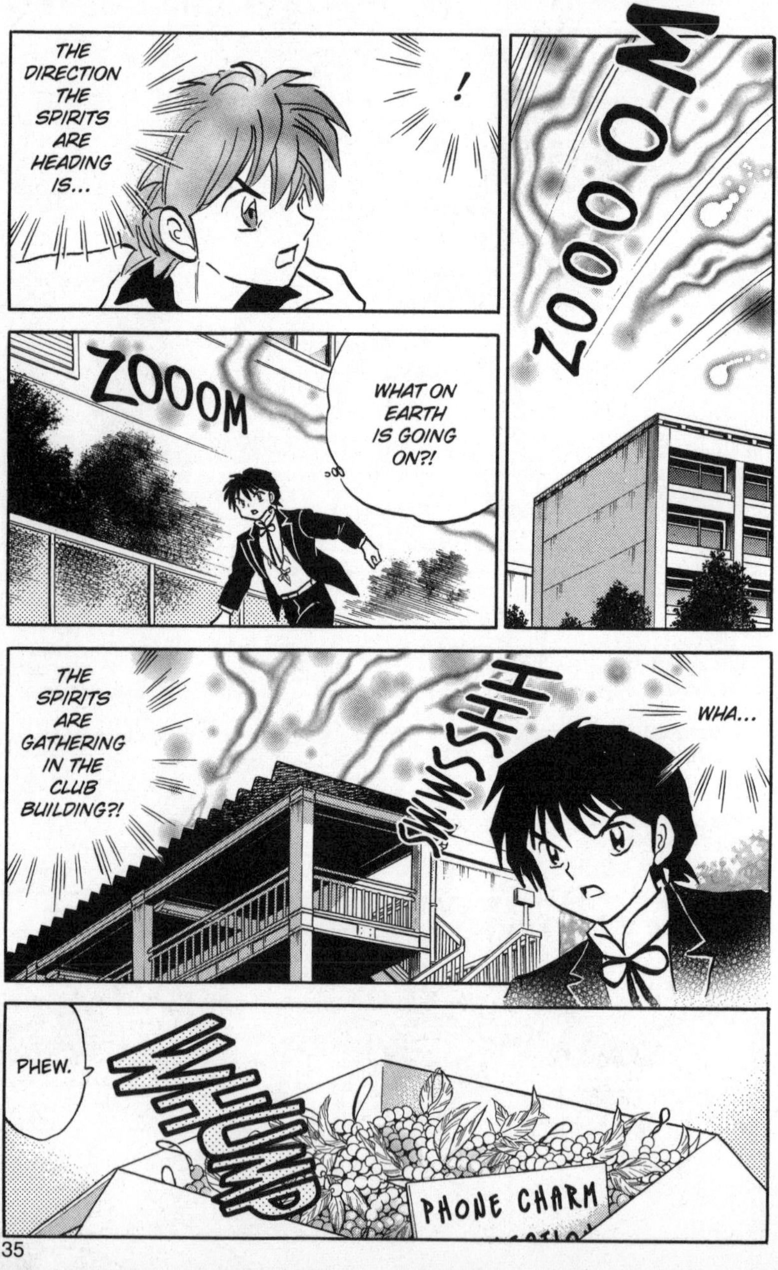
ZOOOOM
!
THE DIRECTION THE SPIRITS ARE HEADING IS...
WHAT ON EARTH IS GOING ON?!
ZOOOM
WHA...
SWSHH
THE SPIRITS ARE GATHERING IN THE CLUB BUILDING?!
PHEW.
WHUMP
PHONE CHARM

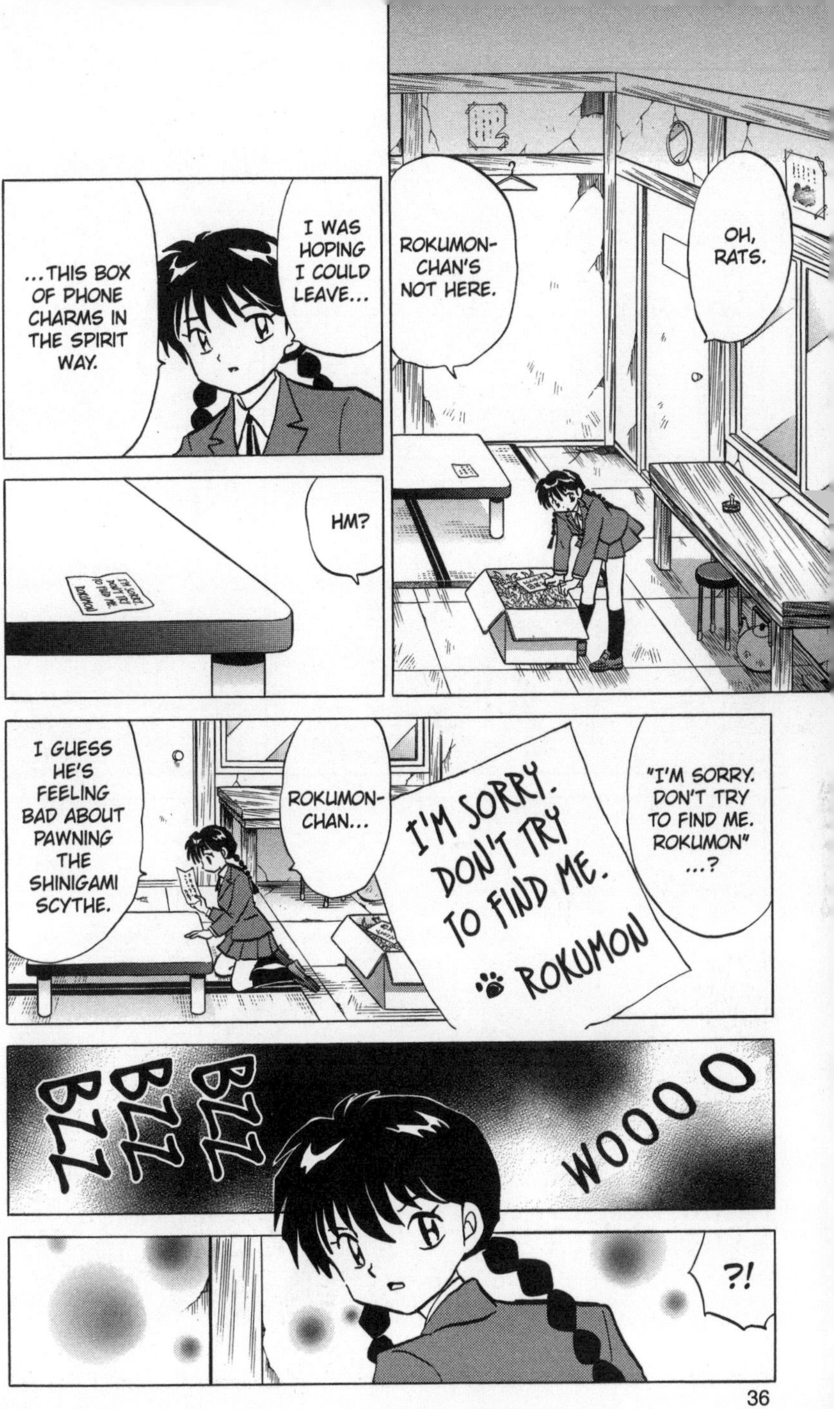
OH, RATS.
ROKUMON-CHAN'S NOT HERE.
I WAS HOPING I COULD LEAVE...
...THIS BOX OF PHONE CHARMS IN THE SPIRIT WAY.
HM?
"I'M SORRY. DON'T TRY TO FIND ME. ROKUMON" ...?
I'M SORRY. DON'T TRY TO FIND ME.
ROKUMON
ROKUMON-CHAN...
I GUESS HE'S FEELING BAD ABOUT PAWNING THE SHINIGAMI SCYTHE.
WOOOO
BZZ BZZ BZZ
?!

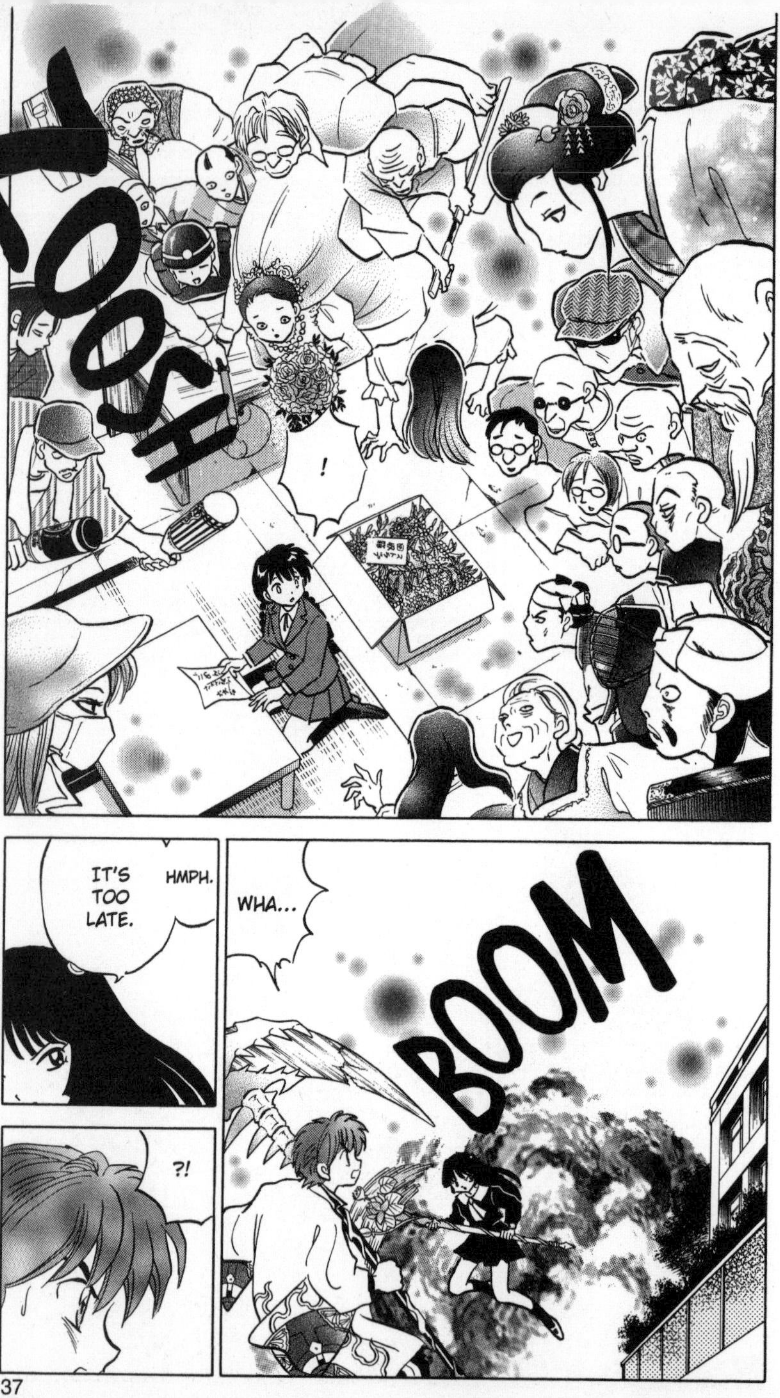
WOOSH
!
WHA...
BOOM
HMPH.
IT'S TOO LATE.
?!

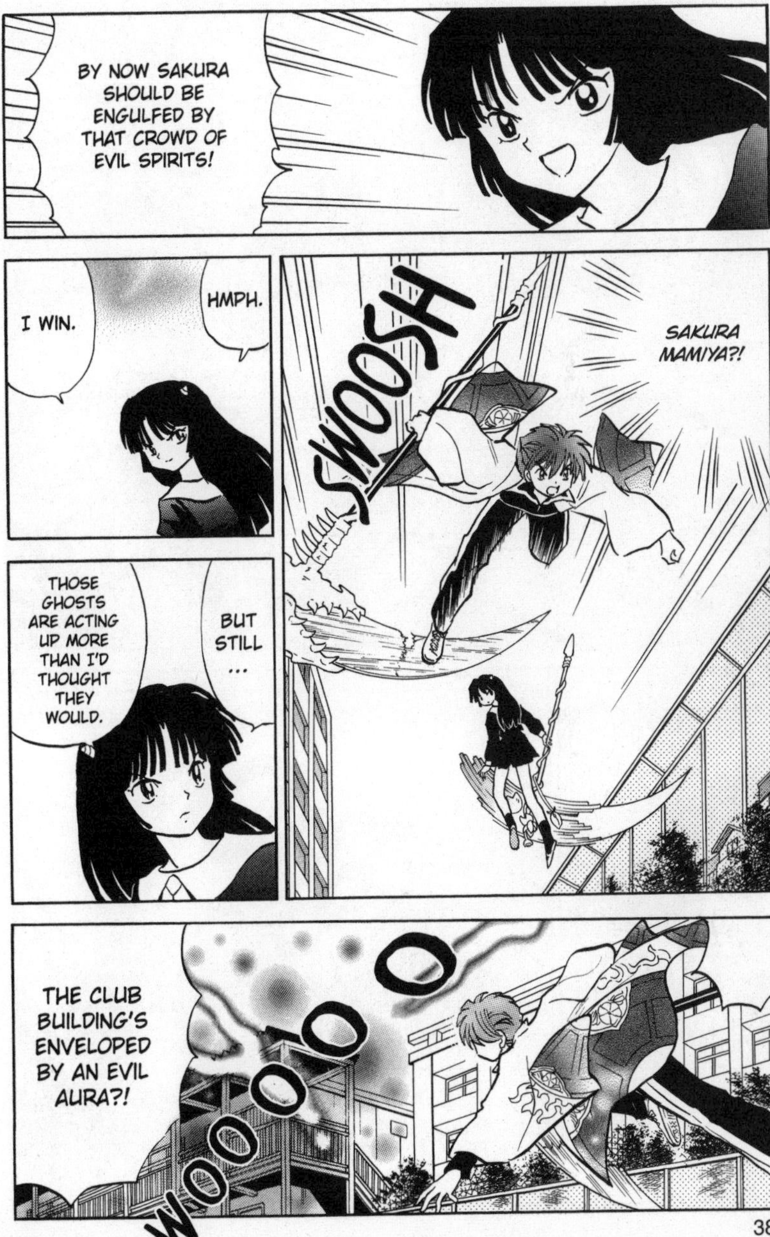
BY NOW SAKURA SHOULD BE ENGULFED BY THAT CROWD OF EVIL SPIRITS!
SWOOSH
SAKURA MAMIYA?!
HMPH.
I WIN.
BUT STILL ...
THOSE GHOSTS ARE ACTING UP MORE THAN I'D THOUGHT THEY WOULD.
WOOOOOO
THE CLUB BUILDING'S ENVELOPED BY AN EVIL AURA?!

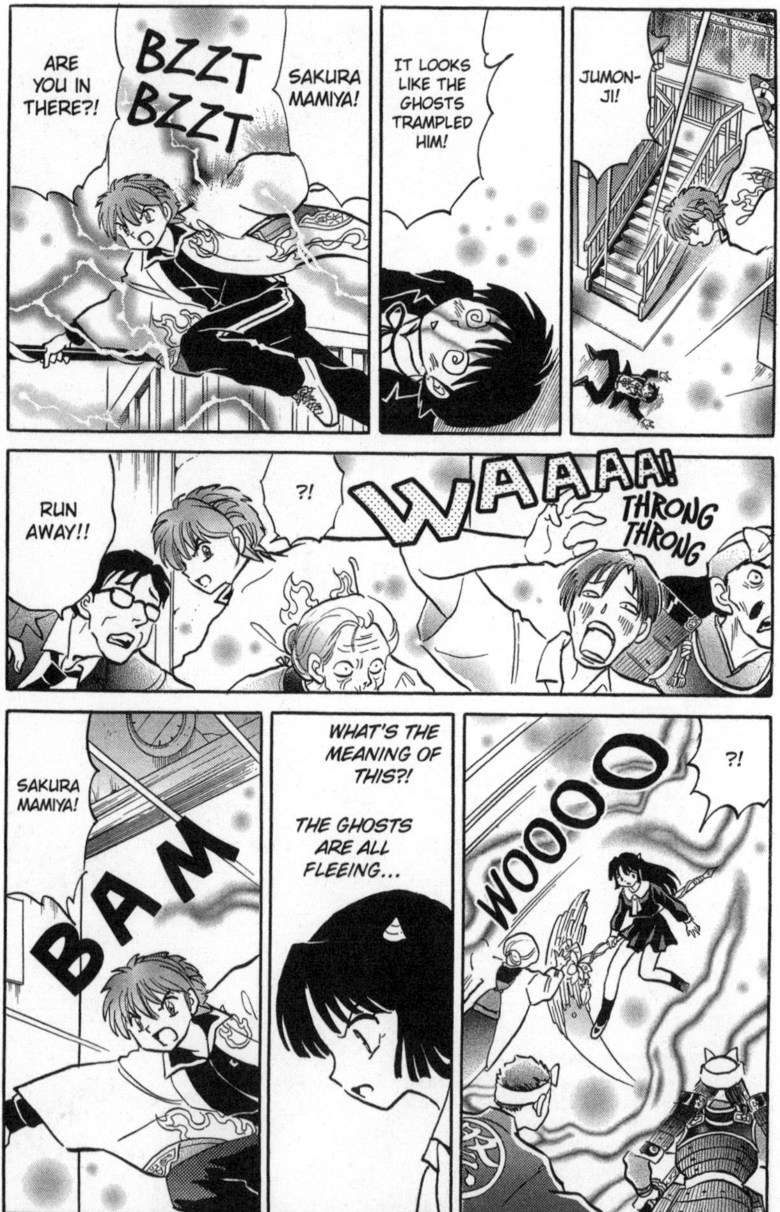
JUMON-JI!
IT LOOKS LIKE THE GHOSTS TRAMPLED HIM!
SAKURA MAMIYA!
BZZT BZZT
ARE YOU IN THERE?!
THRONG THRONG
WAAAAA!
?!
RUN AWAY!!
?!
WOOOO
WHAT'S THE MEANING OF THIS?!
THE GHOSTS ARE ALL FLEEING...
SAKURA MAMIYA!
BAM

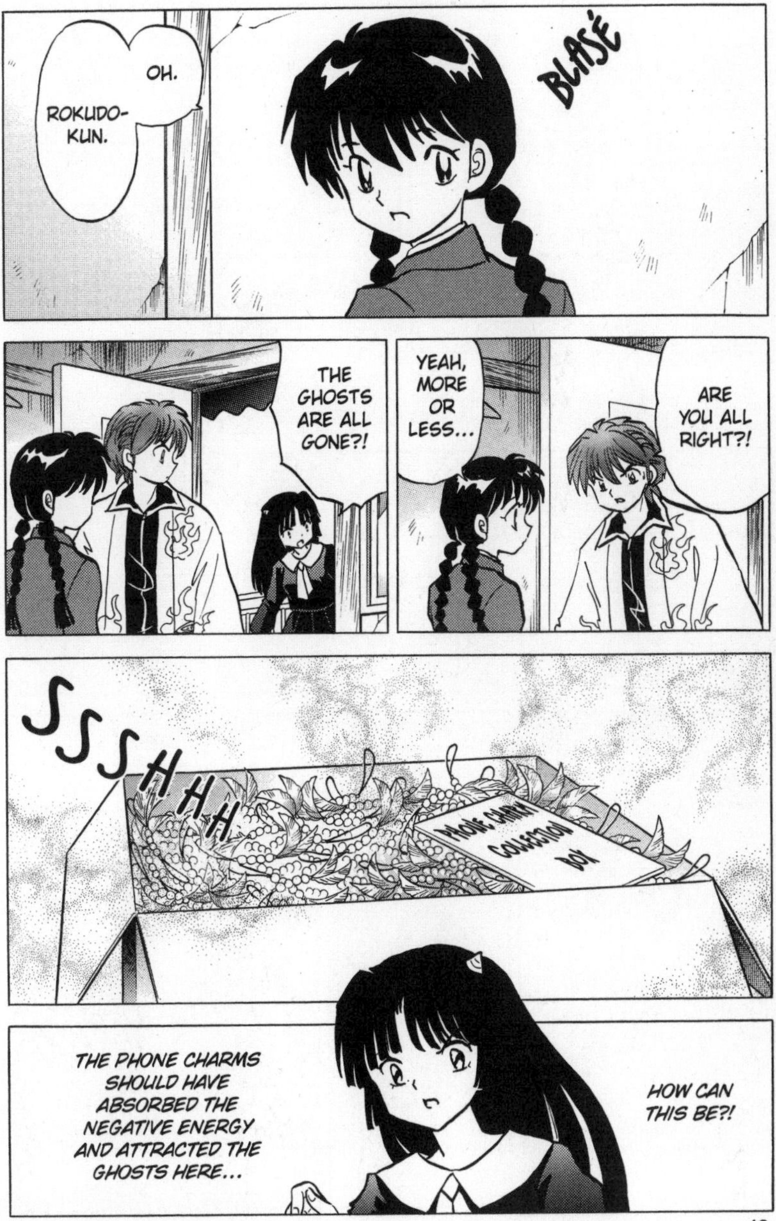
OH.
ROKUDO-KUN.
BLASÉ
ARE YOU ALL RIGHT?!
YEAH, MORE OR LESS...
THE GHOSTS ARE ALL GONE?!
SSSHHH
PHONE CHARM COLLECTION BOX
THE PHONE CHARMS SHOULD HAVE ABSORBED THE NEGATIVE ENERGY AND ATTRACTED THE GHOSTS HERE...
HOW CAN THIS BE?!

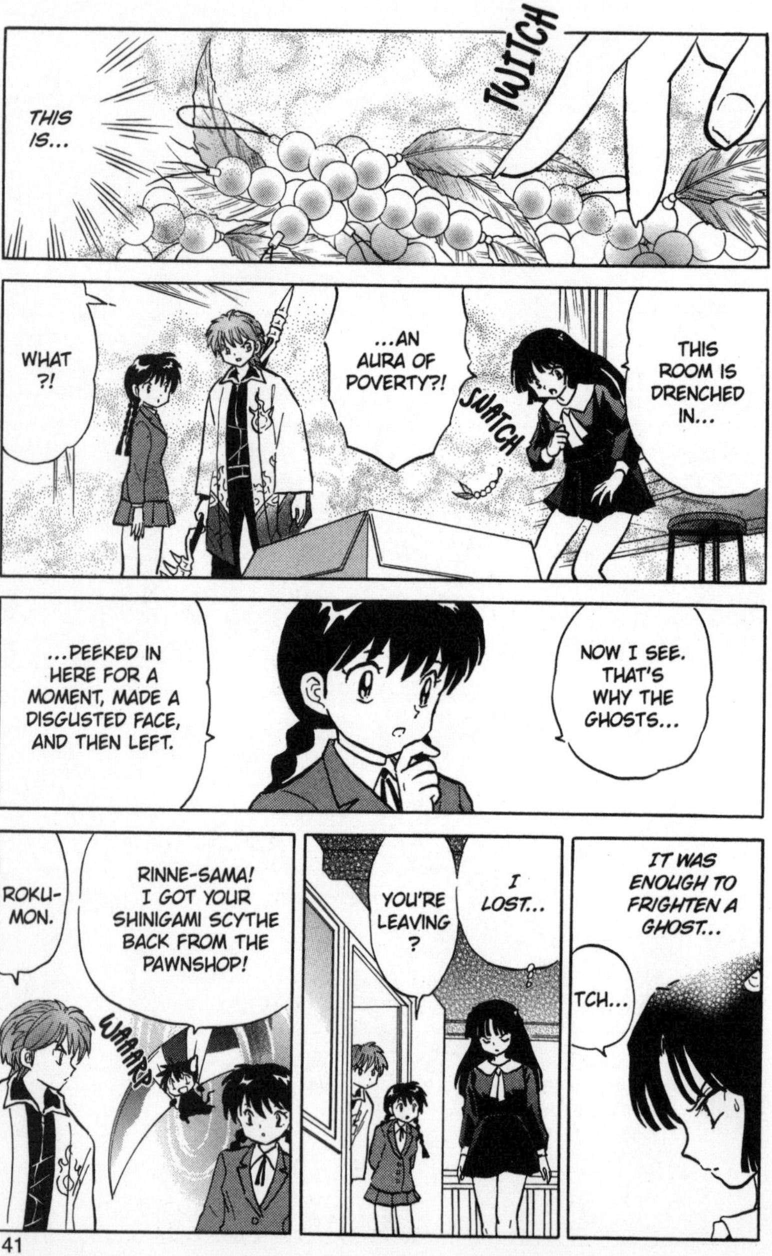
TWITCH
THIS IS...
THIS ROOM IS DRENCHED IN...
SWATCH
...AN AURA OF POVERTY?!
WHAT ?!
NOW I SEE. THAT'S WHY THE GHOSTS...
...PEEKED IN HERE FOR A MOMENT, MADE A DISGUSTED FACE, AND THEN LEFT.
IT WAS ENOUGH TO FRIGHTEN A GHOST...
TCH...
I LOST...
YOU'RE LEAVING ?
RINNE-SAMA! I GOT YOUR SHINIGAMI SCYTHE BACK FROM THE PAWNSHOP!
ROKU-MON.
WAAARP

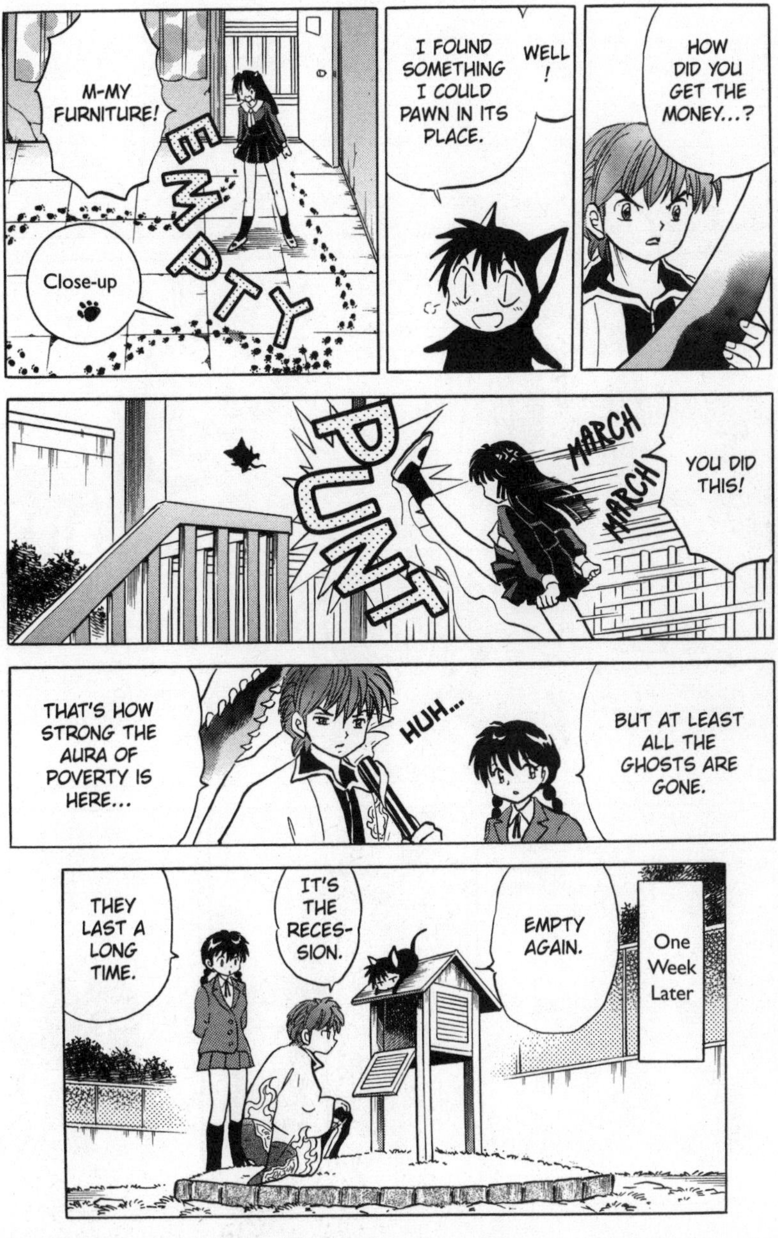
HOW DID YOU GET THE MONEY...?
WELL!
I FOUND SOMETHING I COULD PAWN IN ITS PLACE.
M-MY FURNITURE!
EMPTY
Close-up
YOU DID THIS!
MARCH
MARCH
PUNT
BUT AT LEAST ALL THE GHOSTS ARE GONE.
HUH...
THAT'S HOW STRONG THE AURA OF POVERTY IS HERE...
One Week Later
EMPTY AGAIN.
IT'S THE RECES-SION.
THEY LAST A LONG TIME.

CHAPTER 141: PRINCESS WHISPERS

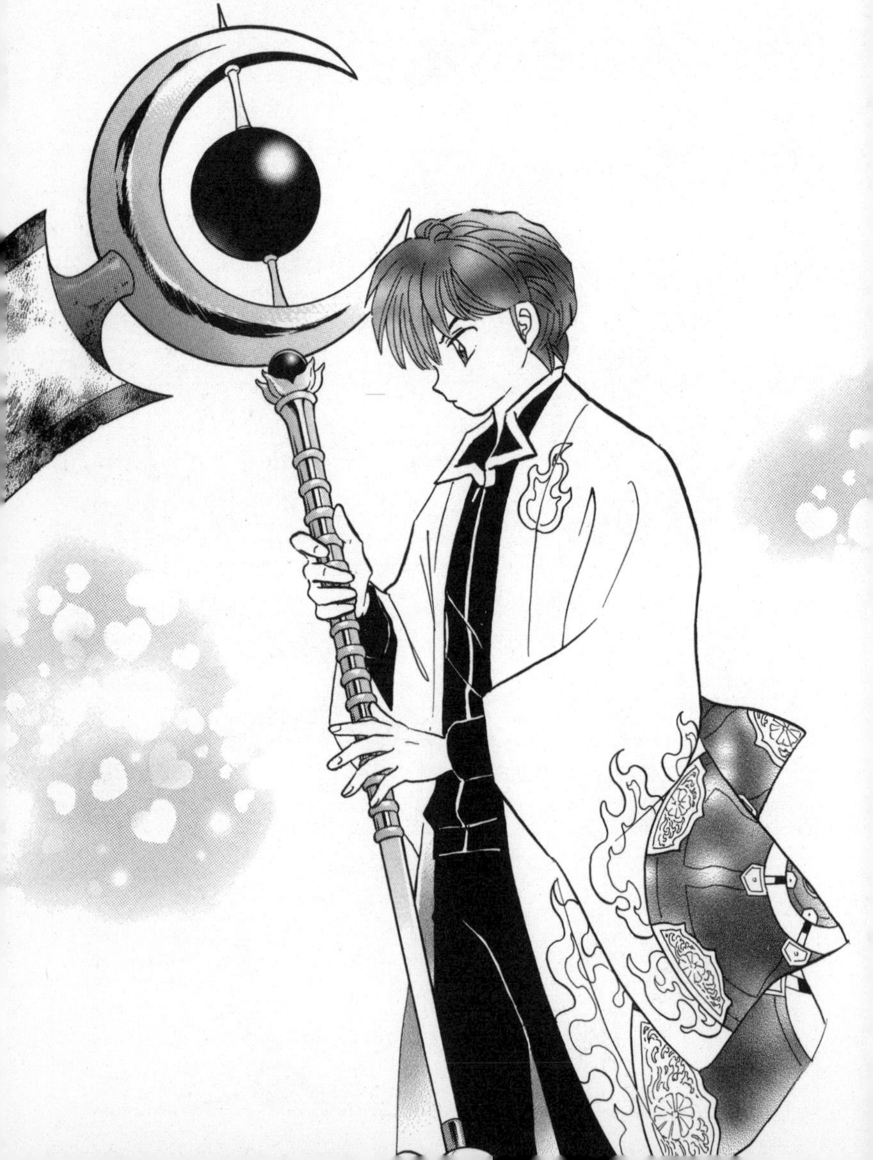

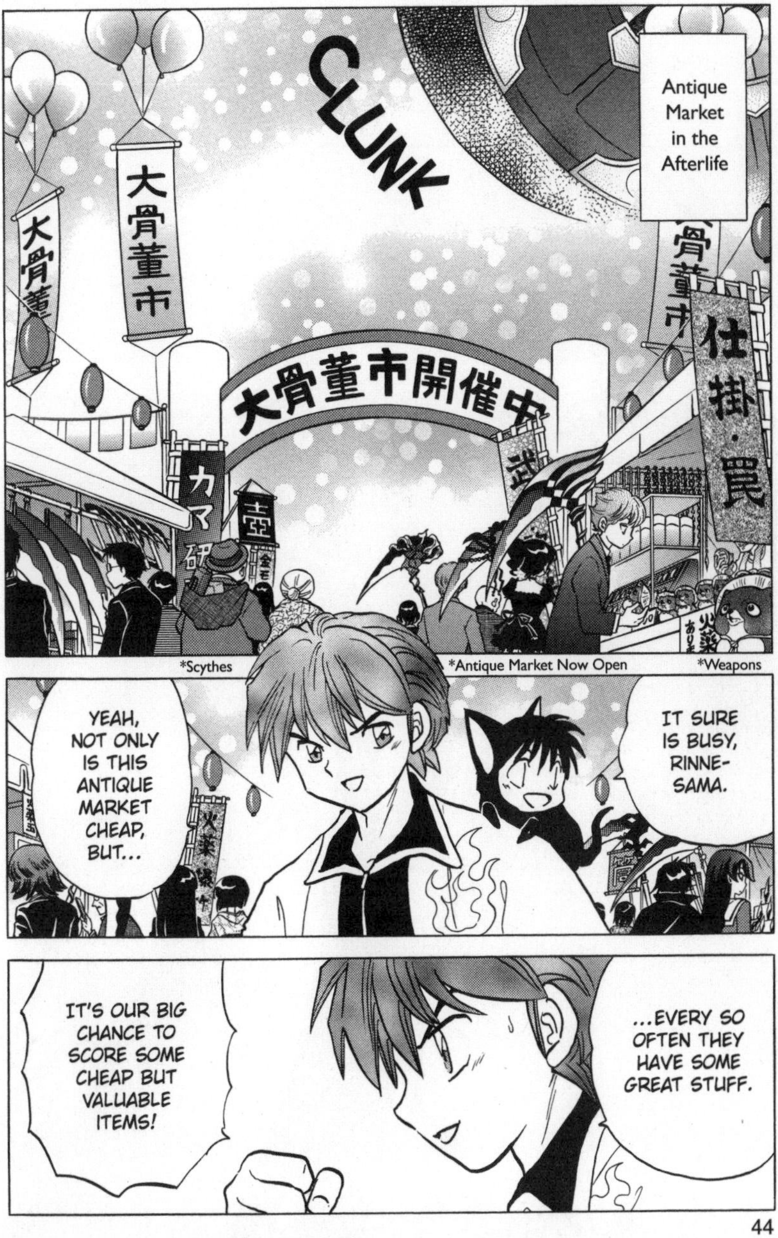
Antique Market in the Afterlife
CLUNK
大骨董市
大骨董市開催中
仕掛・罠
武
壺
カマ
*Weapons
*Antique Market Now Open
*Scythes
IT SURE IS BUSY, RINNE-SAMA.
YEAH, NOT ONLY IS THIS ANTIQUE MARKET CHEAP, BUT...
...EVERY SO OFTEN THEY HAVE SOME GREAT STUFF.
IT'S OUR BIG CHANCE TO SCORE SOME CHEAP BUT VALUABLE ITEMS!

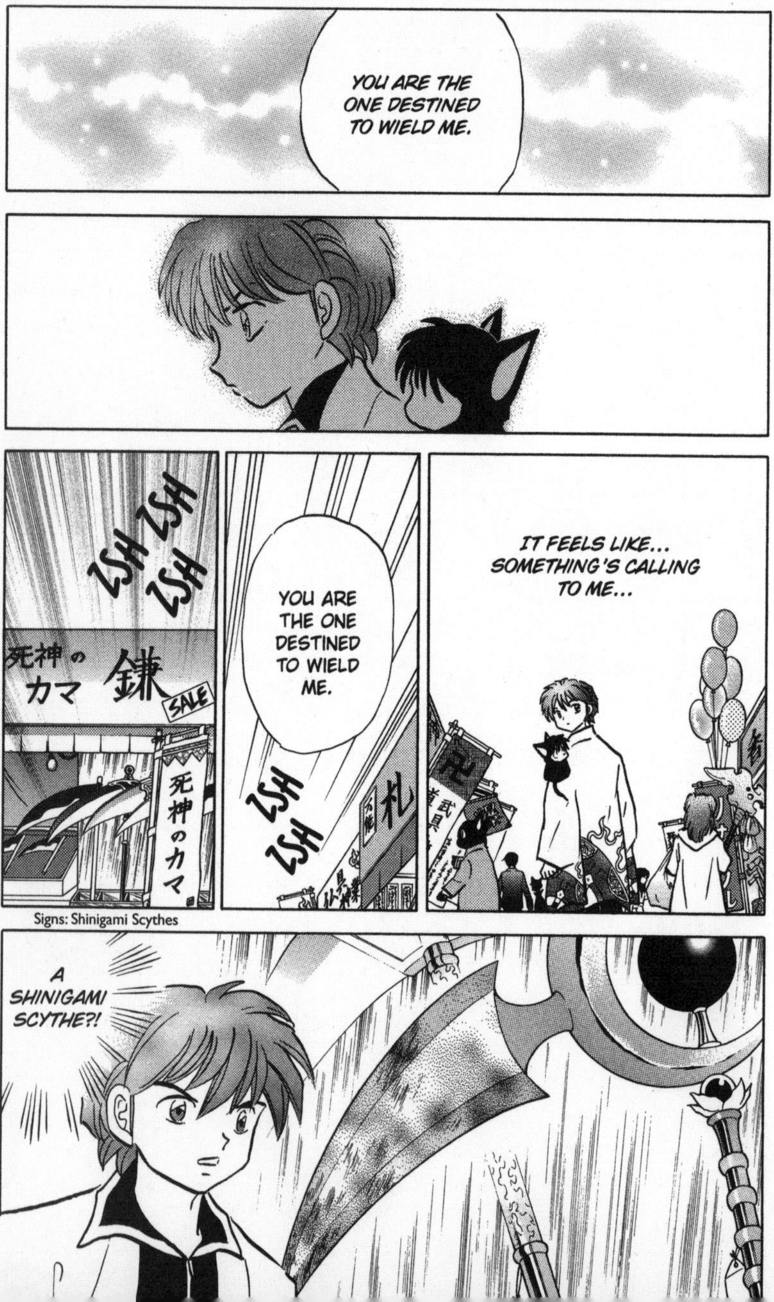
YOU ARE THE ONE DESTINED TO WIELD ME.
IT FEELS LIKE... SOMETHING'S CALLING TO ME...
YOU ARE THE ONE DESTINED TO WIELD ME.
ZSH ZSH
ZSH ZSH ZSH
死神のカマ
鎌
SALE
死神のカマ
A SHINIGAMI SCYTHE?!
Signs: Shinigami Scythes

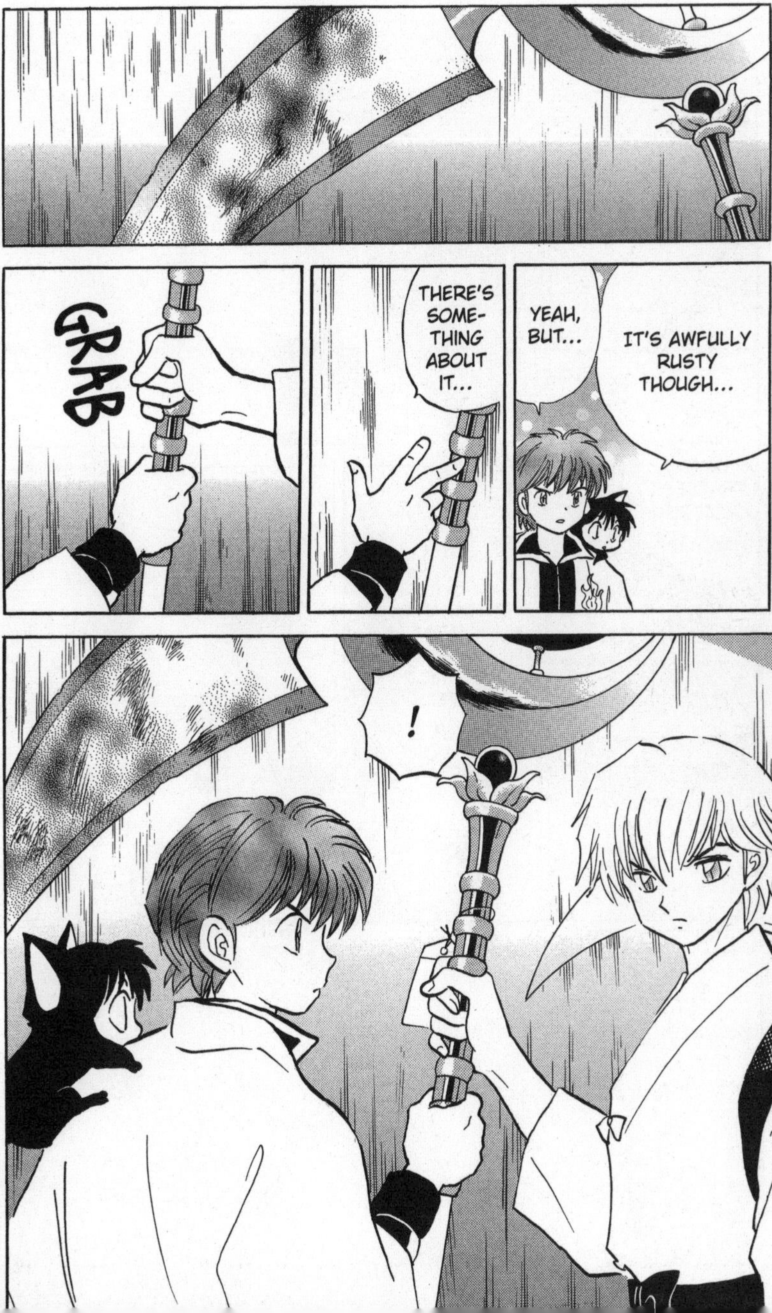
IT'S AWFULLY RUSTY THOUGH...
YEAH, BUT...
THERE'S SOME- THING ABOUT IT...
GRAB
!

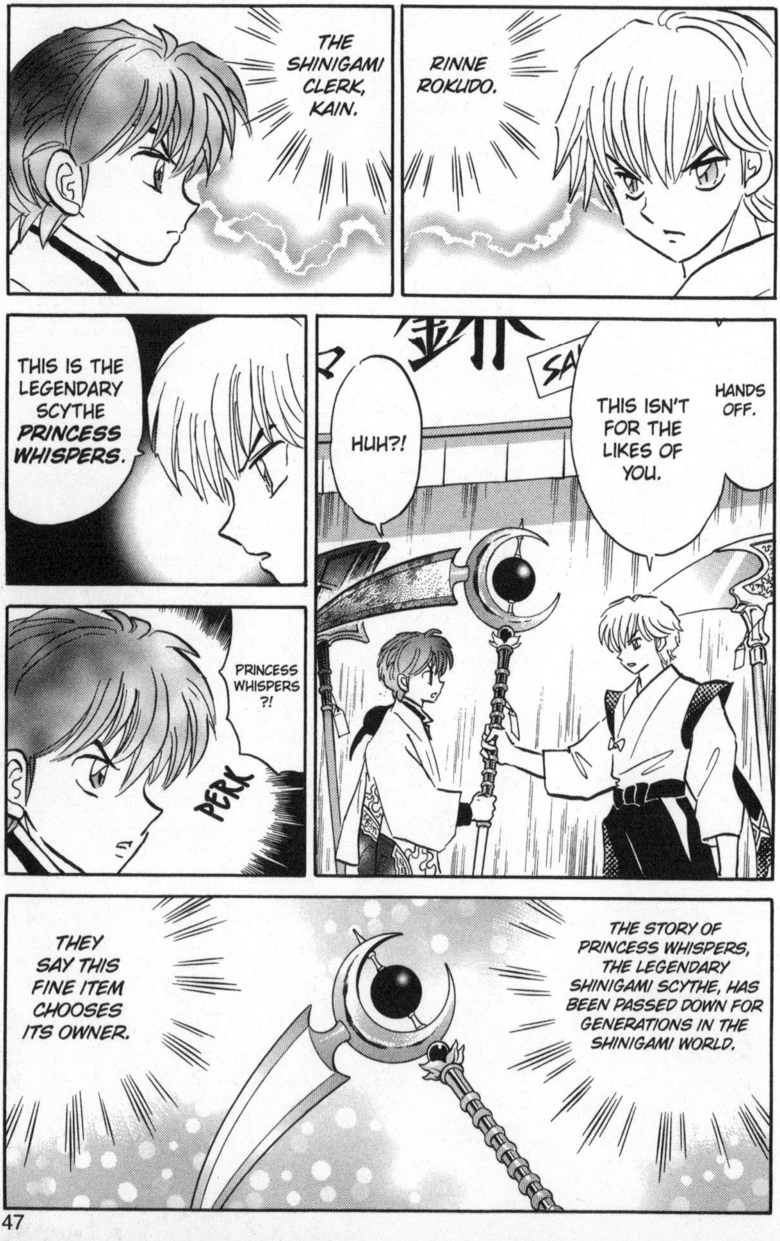
RINNE ROKUDO.
THE SHINIGAMI CLERK, KAIN.
HANDS OFF.
THIS ISN'T FOR THE LIKES OF YOU.
HUH?!
THIS IS THE LEGENDARY SCYTHE *PRINCESS WHISPERS*.
PRINCESS WHISPERS ?!
PERK
THE STORY OF PRINCESS WHISPERS, THE LEGENDARY SHINIGAMI SCYTHE, HAS BEEN PASSED DOWN FOR GENERATIONS IN THE SHINIGAMI WORLD.
THEY SAY THIS FINE ITEM CHOOSES ITS OWNER.

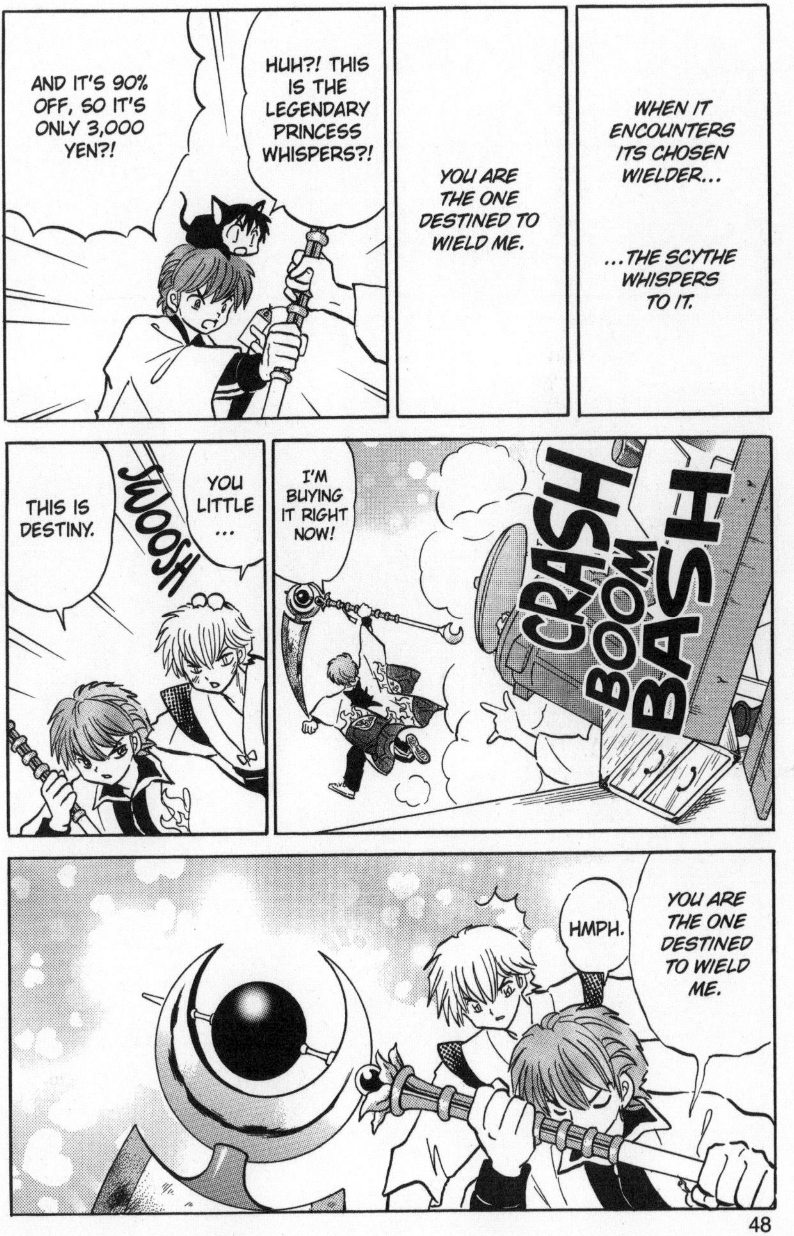
WHEN IT ENCOUNTERS ITS CHOSEN WIELDER...
...THE SCYTHE WHISPERS TO IT.
YOU ARE THE ONE DESTINED TO WIELD ME.
HUH?! THIS IS THE LEGENDARY PRINCESS WHISPERS?!
AND IT'S 90% OFF, SO IT'S ONLY 3,000 YEN?!
CRASH BOOM BASH
I'M BUYING IT RIGHT NOW!
YOU LITTLE ...
SWOOSH
THIS IS DESTINY.
YOU ARE THE ONE DESTINED TO WIELD ME.
HMPH.

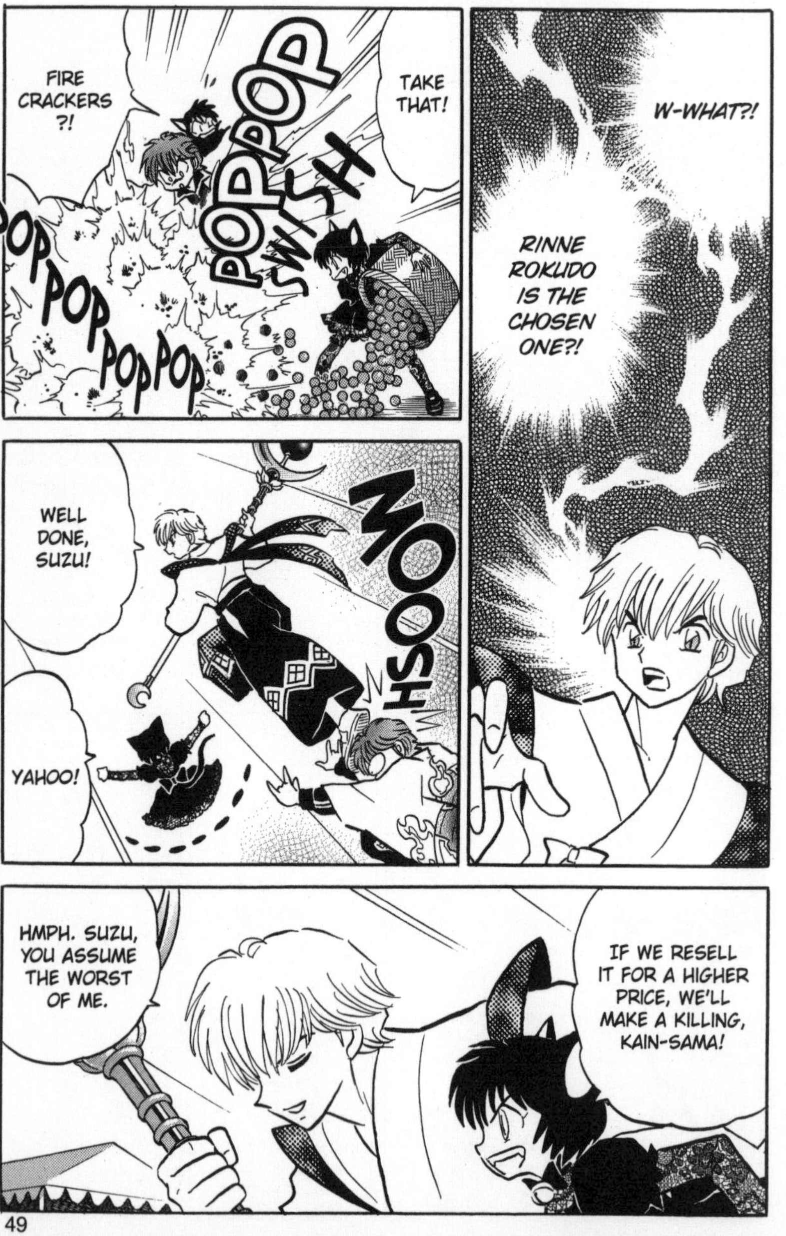
W-WHAT?!
RINNE ROKUDO IS THE CHOSEN ONE?!
TAKE THAT!
POPPOP
SWISH
FIRE CRACKERS ?!
POP POP POP POP
WHOOSH
WELL DONE, SUZU!
YAHOO!
IF WE RESELL IT FOR A HIGHER PRICE, WE'LL MAKE A KILLING, KAIN-SAMA!
HMPH. SUZU, YOU ASSUME THE WORST OF ME.

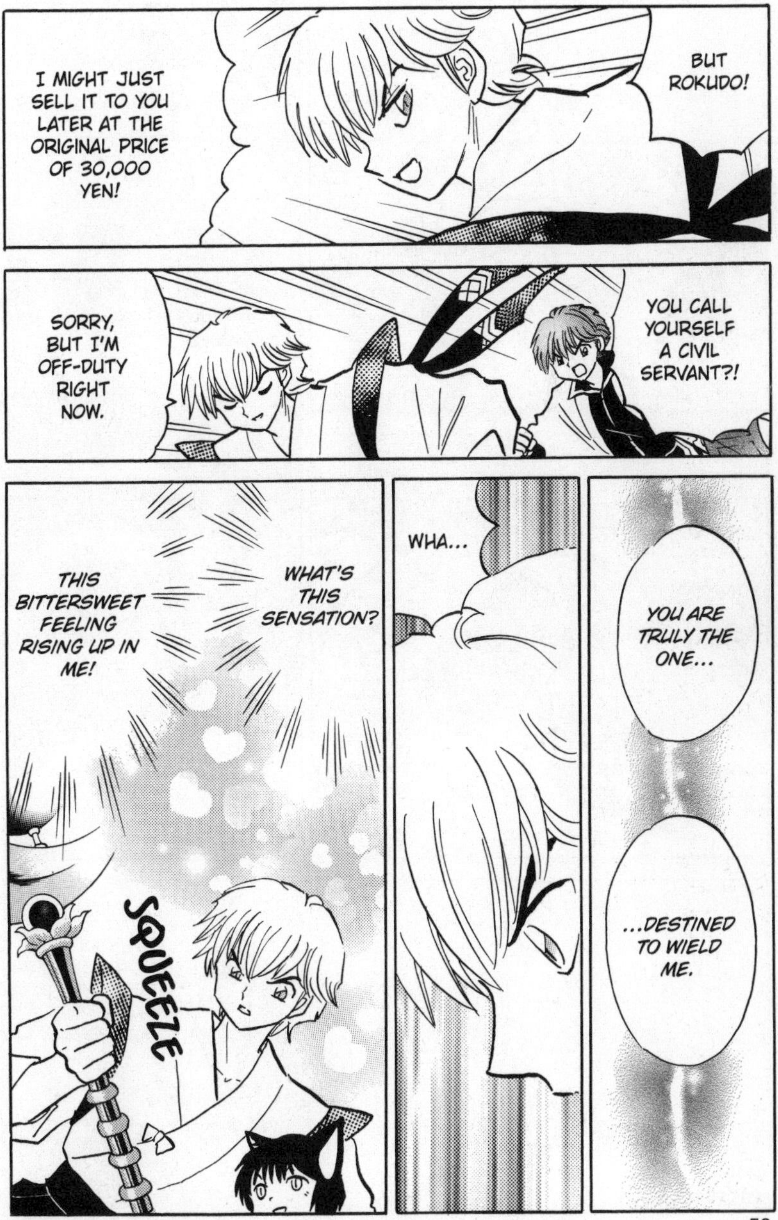
BUT ROKUDO!
I MIGHT JUST SELL IT TO YOU LATER AT THE ORIGINAL PRICE OF 30,000 YEN!
YOU CALL YOURSELF A CIVIL SERVANT?!
SORRY, BUT I'M OFF-DUTY RIGHT NOW.
YOU ARE TRULY THE ONE...
...DESTINED TO WIELD ME.
WHA...
WHAT'S THIS SENSATION?
THIS BITTERSWEET FEELING RISING UP IN ME!
SQUEEZE

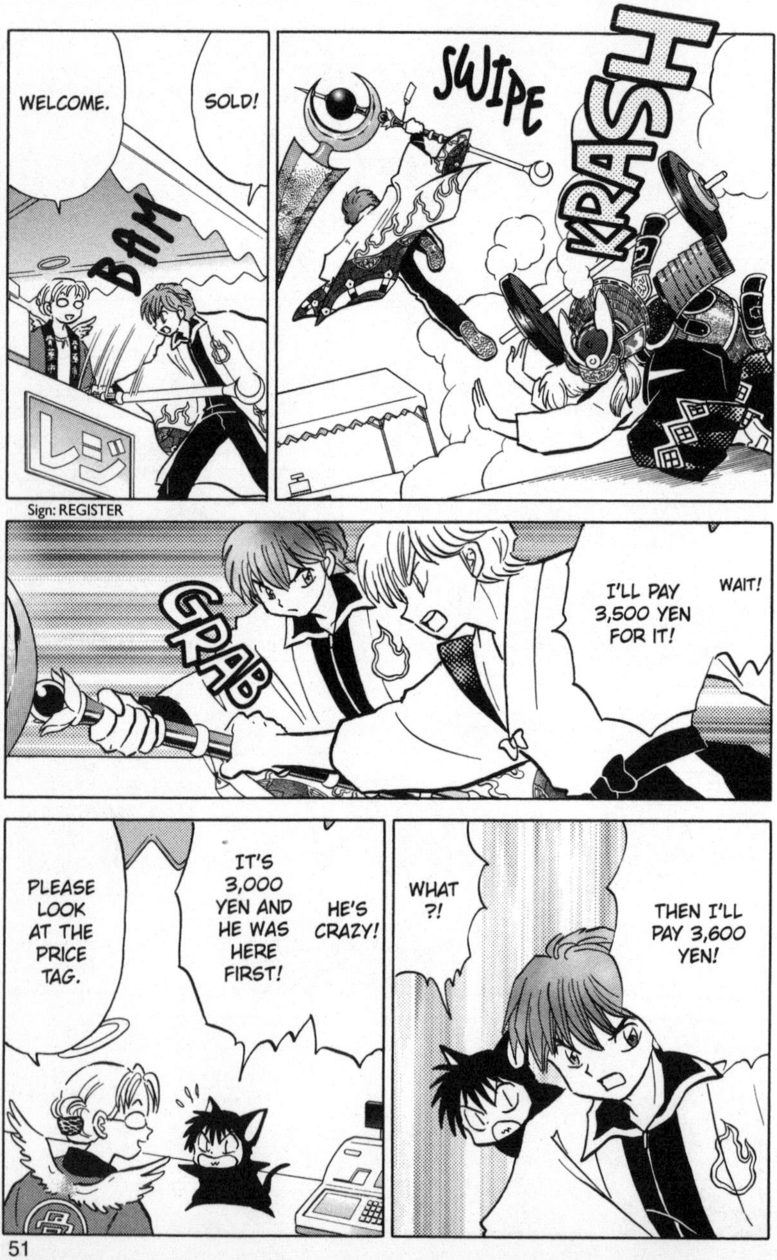
KRASH
SWIPE
SOLD!
WELCOME.
BAM
WAIT!
I'LL PAY 3,500 YEN FOR IT!
GRAB
THEN I'LL PAY 3,600 YEN!
WHAT ?!
HE'S CRAZY!
IT'S 3,000 YEN AND HE WAS HERE FIRST!
PLEASE LOOK AT THE PRICE TAG.
Sign: REGISTER

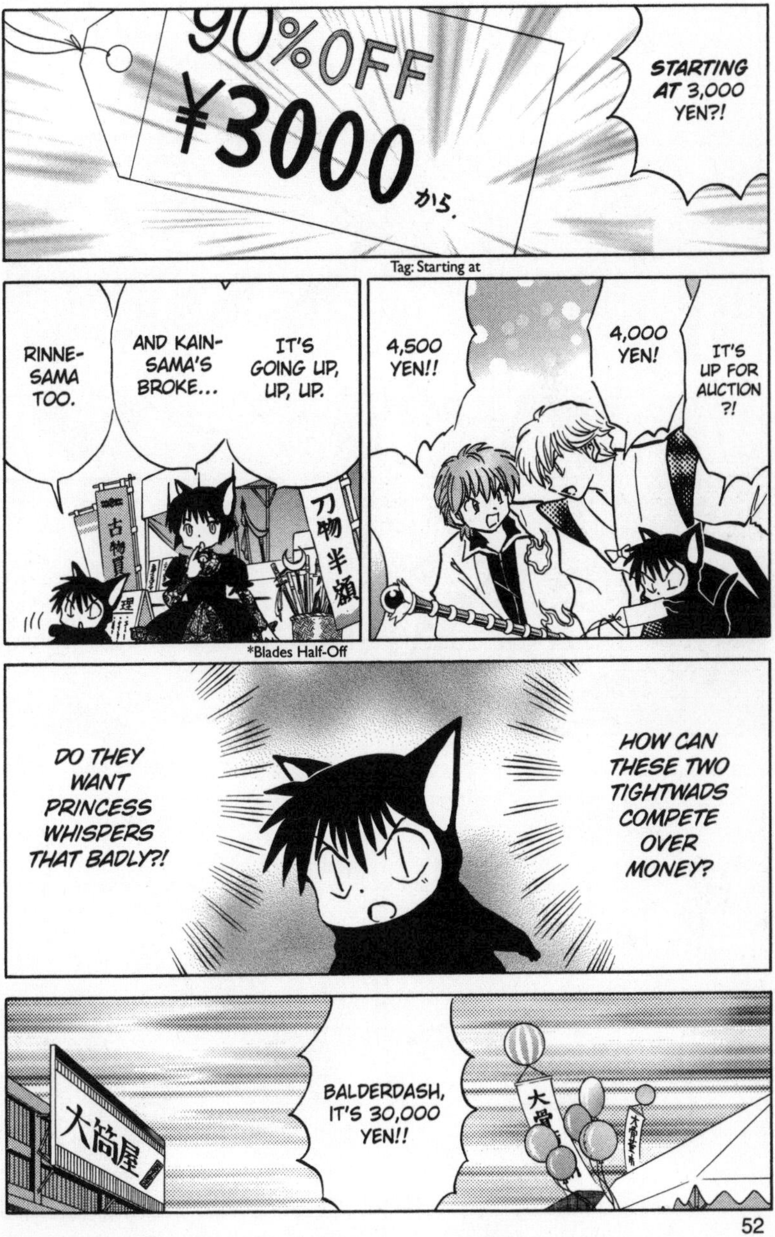
STARTING AT 3,000 YEN?!
90%OFF
¥3000
から.
IT'S UP FOR AUCTION?!
4,000 YEN!
4,500 YEN!!
刀物半額
IT'S GOING UP, UP, UP.
AND KAIN-SAMA'S BROKE...
RINNE-SAMA TOO.
古物買
HOW CAN THESE TWO TIGHTWADS COMPETE OVER MONEY?
DO THEY WANT PRINCESS WHISPERS THAT BADLY?!
BALDERDASH, IT'S 30,000 YEN!!
大筒屋
Tag: Starting at

*Blades Half-Off

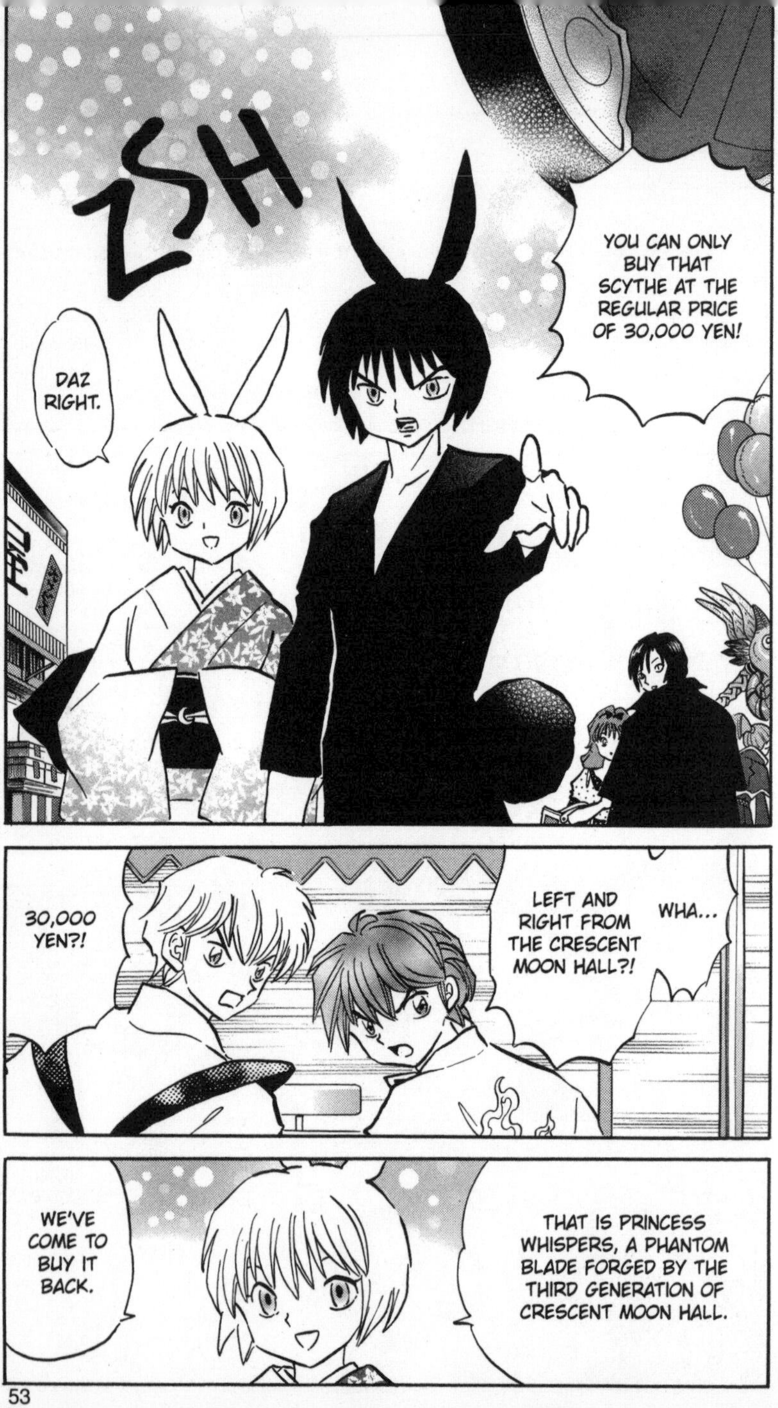
ZSH
YOU CAN ONLY BUY THAT SCYTHE AT THE REGULAR PRICE OF 30,000 YEN!
DAZ RIGHT.
WHA...
LEFT AND RIGHT FROM THE CRESCENT MOON HALL?!
30,000 YEN?!
THAT IS PRINCESS WHISPERS, A PHANTOM BLADE FORGED BY THE THIRD GENERATION OF CRESCENT MOON HALL.
WE'VE COME TO BUY IT BACK.

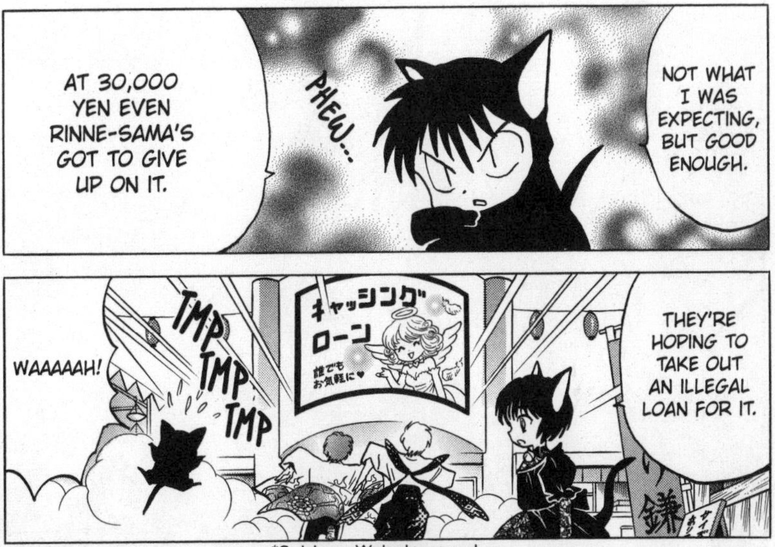
NOT WHAT I WAS EXPECTING, BUT GOOD ENOUGH.
PHEW...
AT 30,000 YEN EVEN RINNE-SAMA'S GOT TO GIVE UP ON IT.
THEY'RE HOPING TO TAKE OUT AN ILLEGAL LOAN FOR IT.
キャッシング
ローン
誰でもお気軽に♥
TMP TMP TMP
WAAAAAH!
*Cash Loans We lend to anyone!

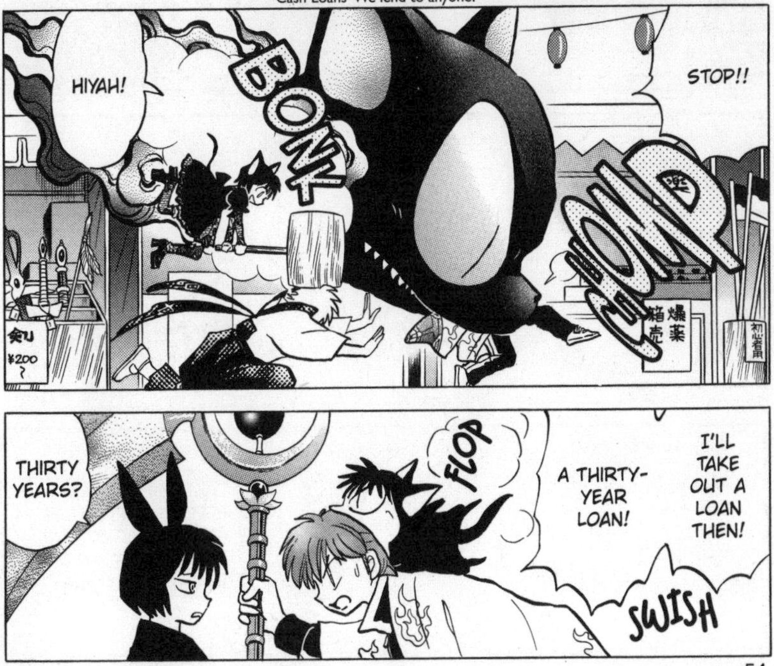
STOP!!
CHOMP
BONK
HIYAH!
爆薬
箱売
¥200
I'LL TAKE OUT A LOAN THEN!
A THIRTY-YEAR LOAN!
FLOP
THIRTY YEARS?
SWISH

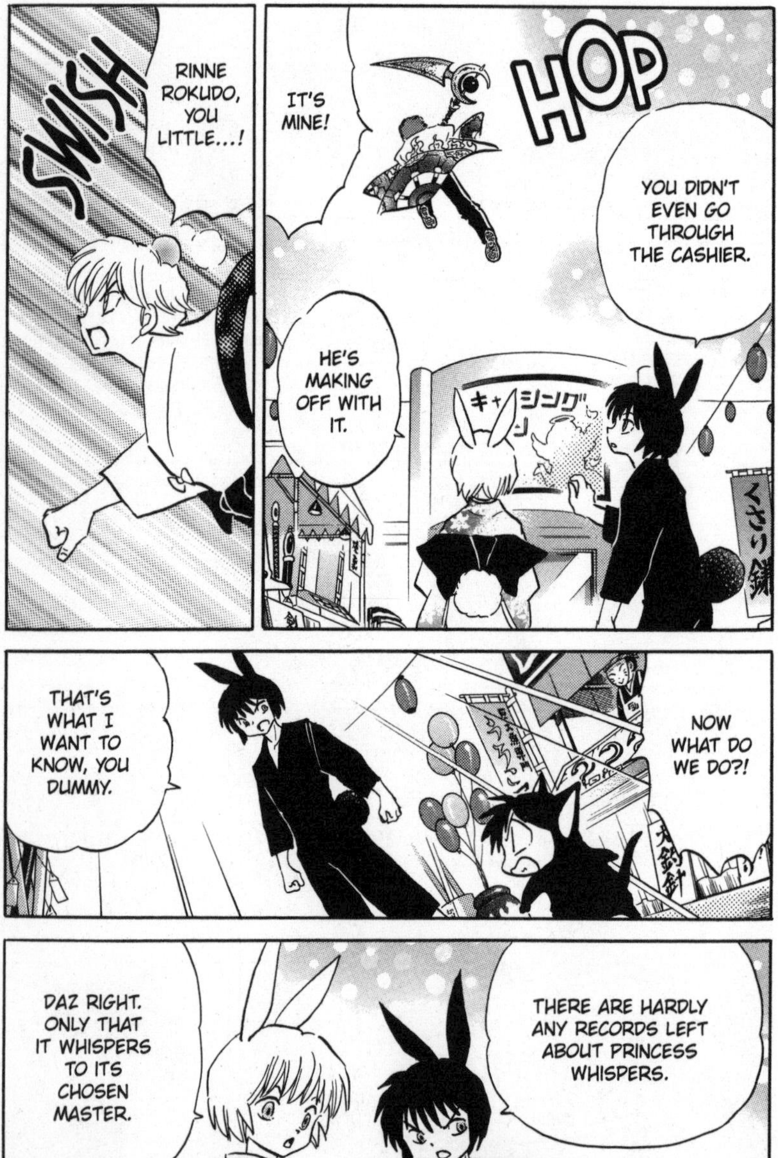
HOP
IT'S MINE!
YOU DIDN'T EVEN GO THROUGH THE CASHIER.
HE'S MAKING OFF WITH IT.
SWISH
RINNE ROKUDO, YOU LITTLE...!
NOW WHAT DO WE DO?!
THAT'S WHAT I WANT TO KNOW, YOU DUMMY.
THERE ARE HARDLY ANY RECORDS LEFT ABOUT PRINCESS WHISPERS.
DAZ RIGHT. ONLY THAT IT WHISPERS TO ITS CHOSEN MASTER.

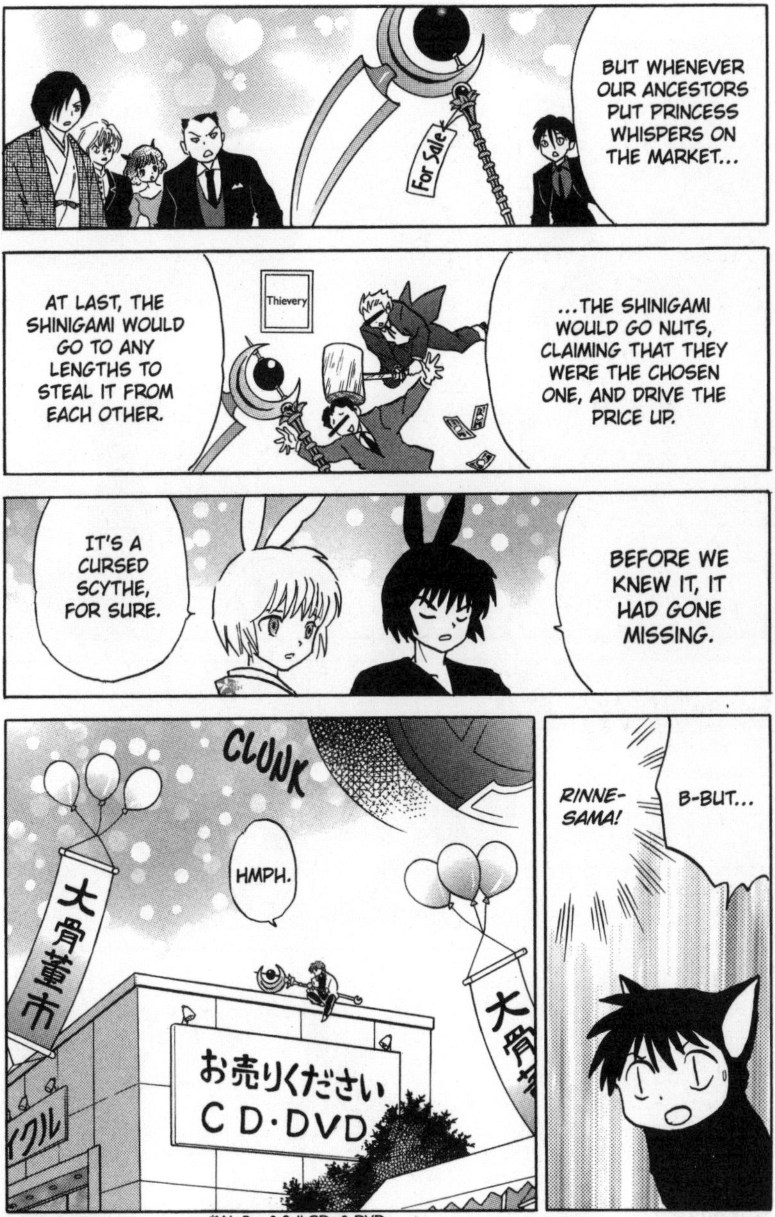
BUT WHENEVER OUR ANCESTORS PUT PRINCESS WHISPERS ON THE MARKET...
For Sale
...THE SHINIGAMI WOULD GO NUTS, CLAIMING THAT THEY WERE THE CHOSEN ONE, AND DRIVE THE PRICE UP.
Thievery
AT LAST, THE SHINIGAMI WOULD GO TO ANY LENGTHS TO STEAL IT FROM EACH OTHER.
BEFORE WE KNEW IT, IT HAD GONE MISSING.
IT'S A CURSED SCYTHE, FOR SURE.
B-BUT...
RINNE-SAMA!
CLUNK
HMPH.
大骨董市
お売りください
CD・DVD

*Antique Market

*We Buy & Sell CDs & DVDs

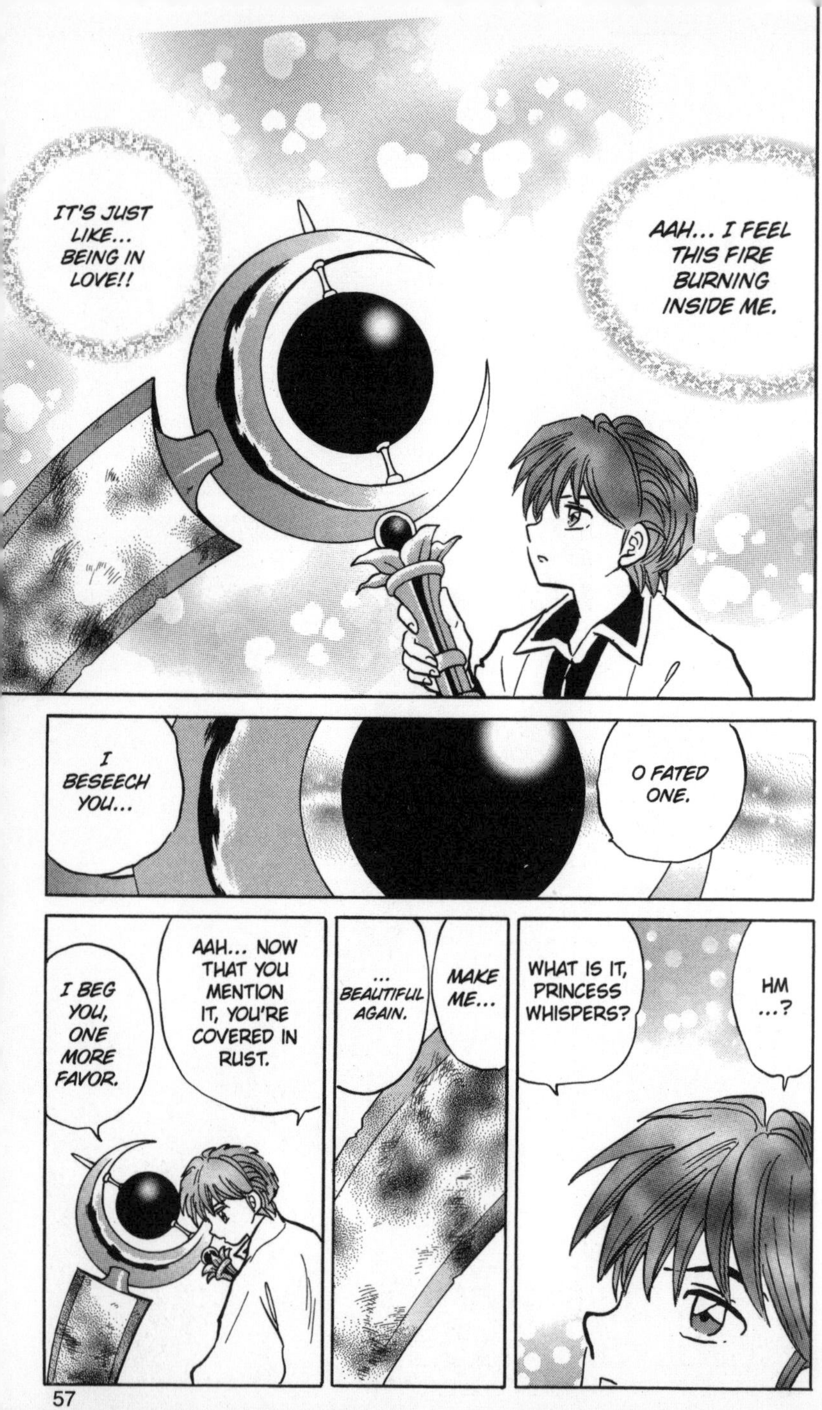
AAH... I FEEL THIS FIRE BURNING INSIDE ME.
IT'S JUST LIKE... BEING IN LOVE!!
O FATED ONE.
I BESEECH YOU...
HM ...?
WHAT IS IT, PRINCESS WHISPERS?
MAKE ME...
... BEAUTIFUL AGAIN.
AAH... NOW THAT YOU MENTION IT, YOU'RE COVERED IN RUST.
I BEG YOU, ONE MORE FAVOR.

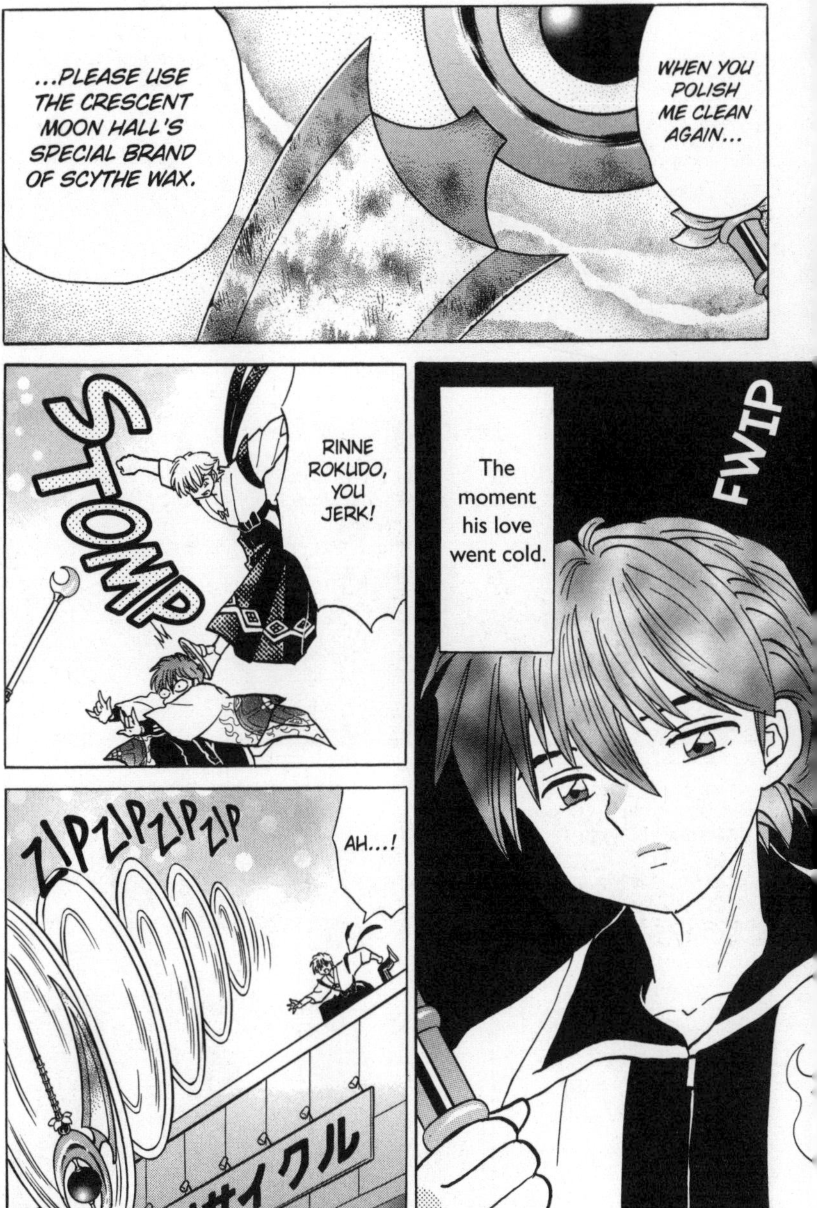
WHEN YOU POLISH ME CLEAN AGAIN...
...PLEASE USE THE CRESCENT MOON HALL'S SPECIAL BRAND OF SCYTHE WAX.
FWIP
The moment his love went cold.
RINNE ROKUDO, YOU JERK!
STOMP
AH...!
ZIPZIPZIPZIP
サイクル

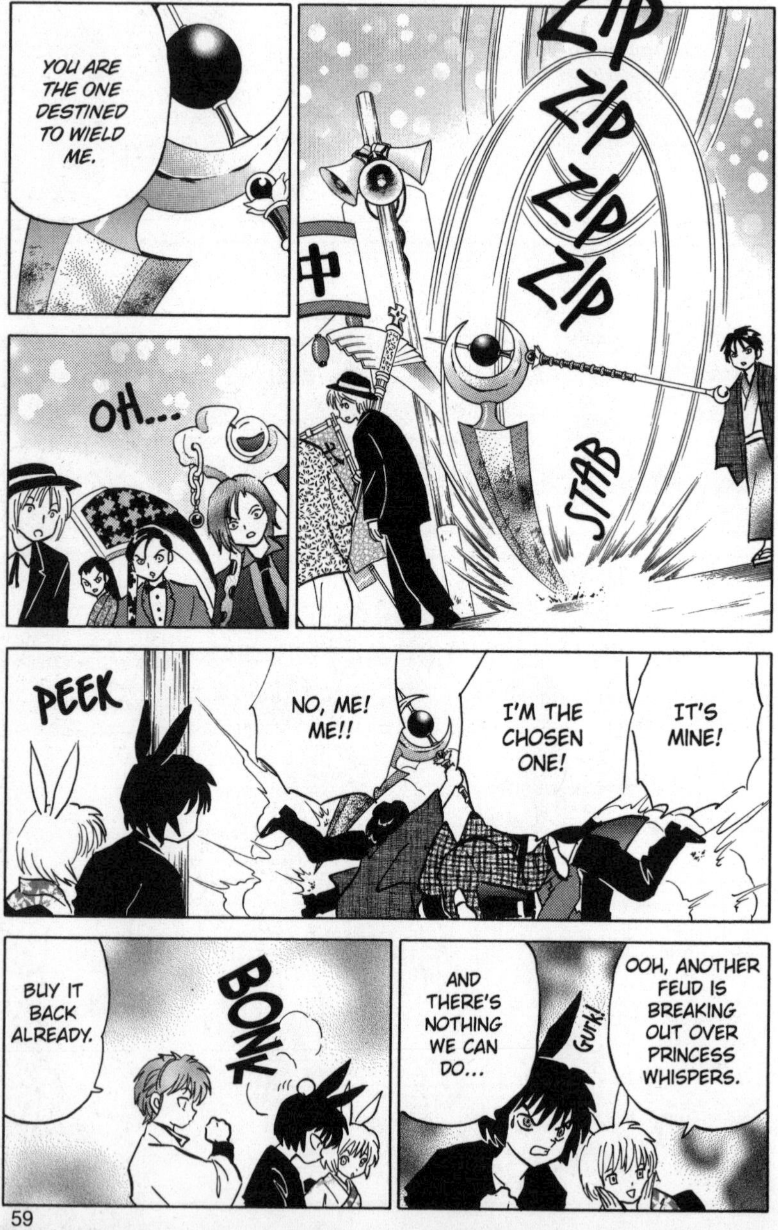
ZIP
ZIP
ZIP
ZIP
STAB
YOU ARE THE ONE DESTINED TO WIELD ME.
OH...
IT'S MINE!
I'M THE CHOSEN ONE!
NO, ME! ME!!
PEEK
OOH, ANOTHER FEUD IS BREAKING OUT OVER PRINCESS WHISPERS.
Gurk!
AND THERE'S NOTHING WE CAN DO...
BONK
BUY IT BACK ALREADY.

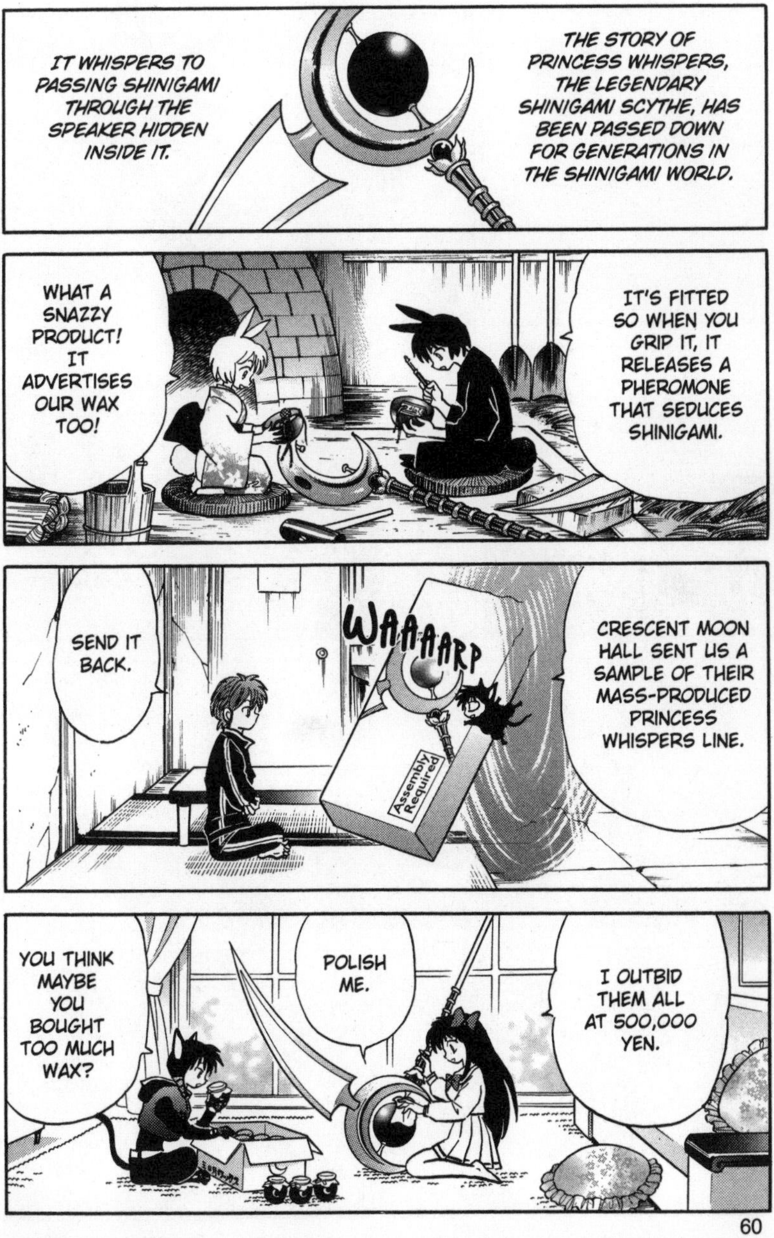
THE STORY OF PRINCESS WHISPERS, THE LEGENDARY SHINIGAMI SCYTHE, HAS BEEN PASSED DOWN FOR GENERATIONS IN THE SHINIGAMI WORLD.
IT WHISPERS TO PASSING SHINIGAMI THROUGH THE SPEAKER HIDDEN INSIDE IT.
IT'S FITTED SO WHEN YOU GRIP IT, IT RELEASES A PHEROMONE THAT SEDUCES SHINIGAMI.
WHAT A SNAZZY PRODUCT! IT ADVERTISES OUR WAX TOO!
CRESCENT MOON HALL SENT US A SAMPLE OF THEIR MASS-PRODUCED PRINCESS WHISPERS LINE.
WAAAARP
Assembly Required
SEND IT BACK.
I OUTBID THEM ALL AT 500,000 YEN.
POLISH ME.
YOU THINK MAYBE YOU BOUGHT TOO MUCH WAX?

CHAPTER 142: THE BREAK-UP SET

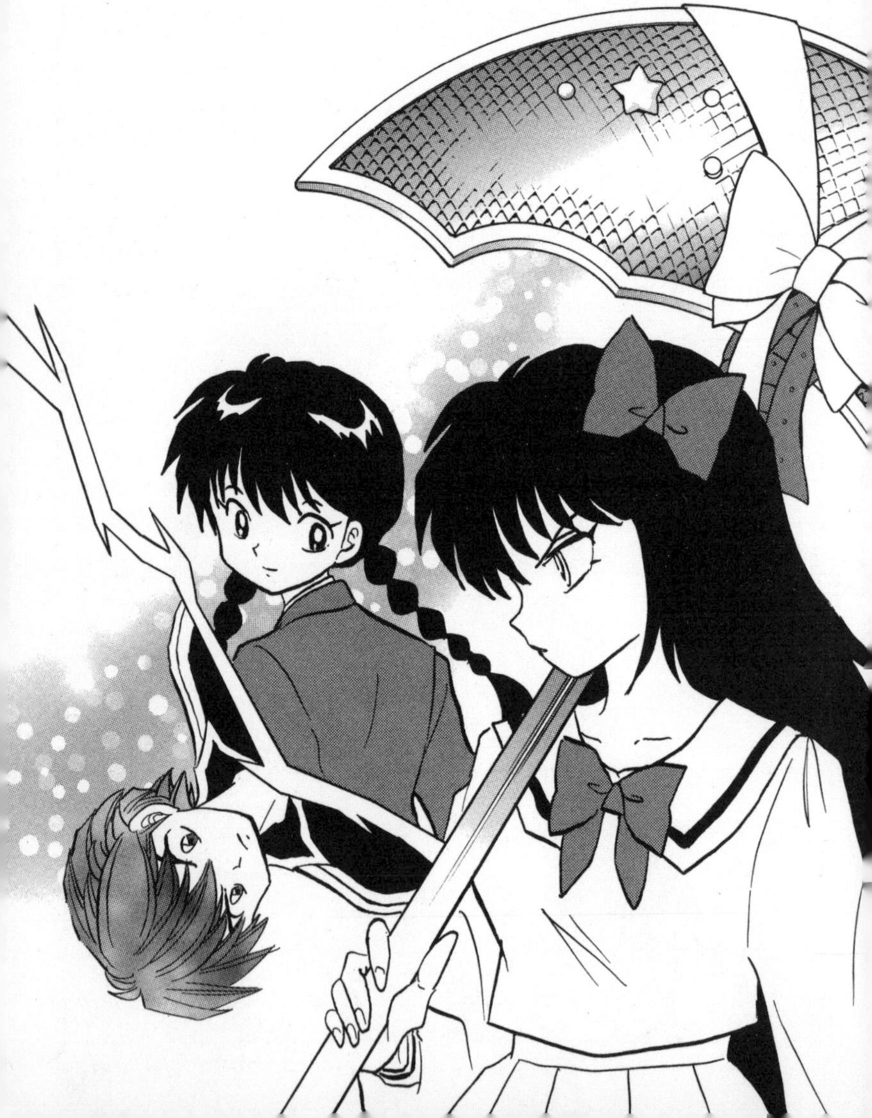

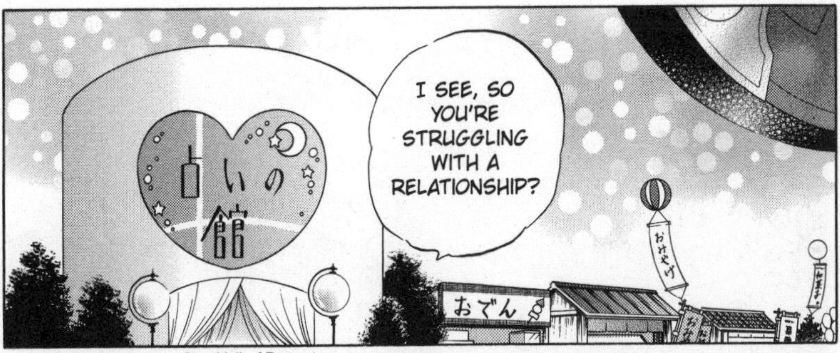
I SEE, SO YOU'RE STRUGGLING WITH A RELATIONSHIP?
占いの館
おでん
Sign: Hall of Divination

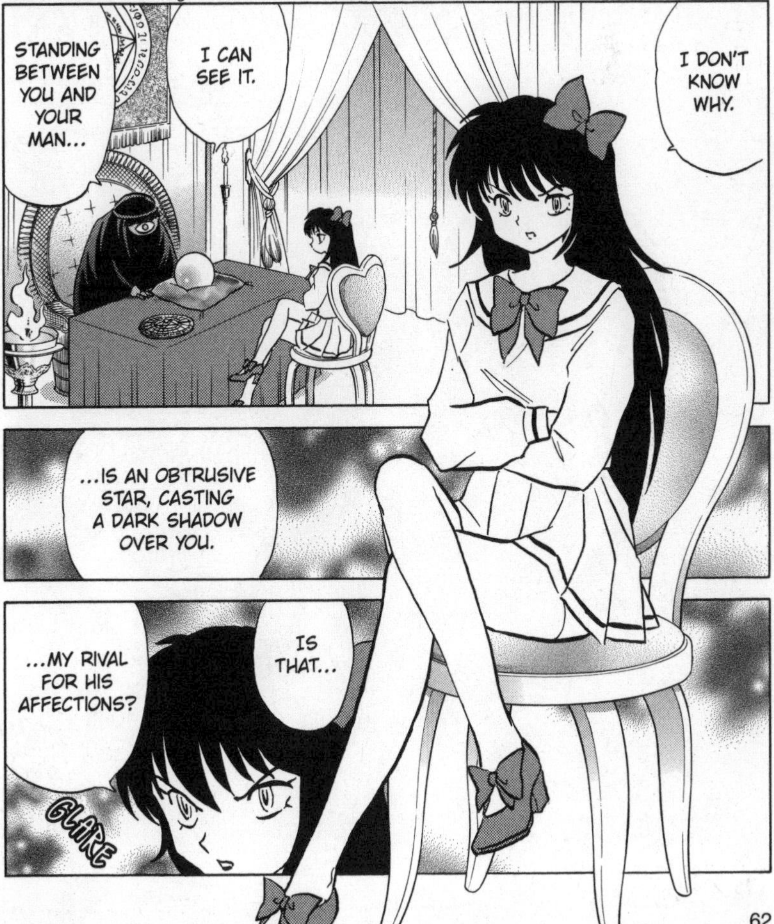
I DON'T KNOW WHY.
I CAN SEE IT.
STANDING BETWEEN YOU AND YOUR MAN...
...IS AN OBTRUSIVE STAR, CASTING A DARK SHADOW OVER YOU.
IS THAT...
...MY RIVAL FOR HIS AFFECTIONS?
GLARE

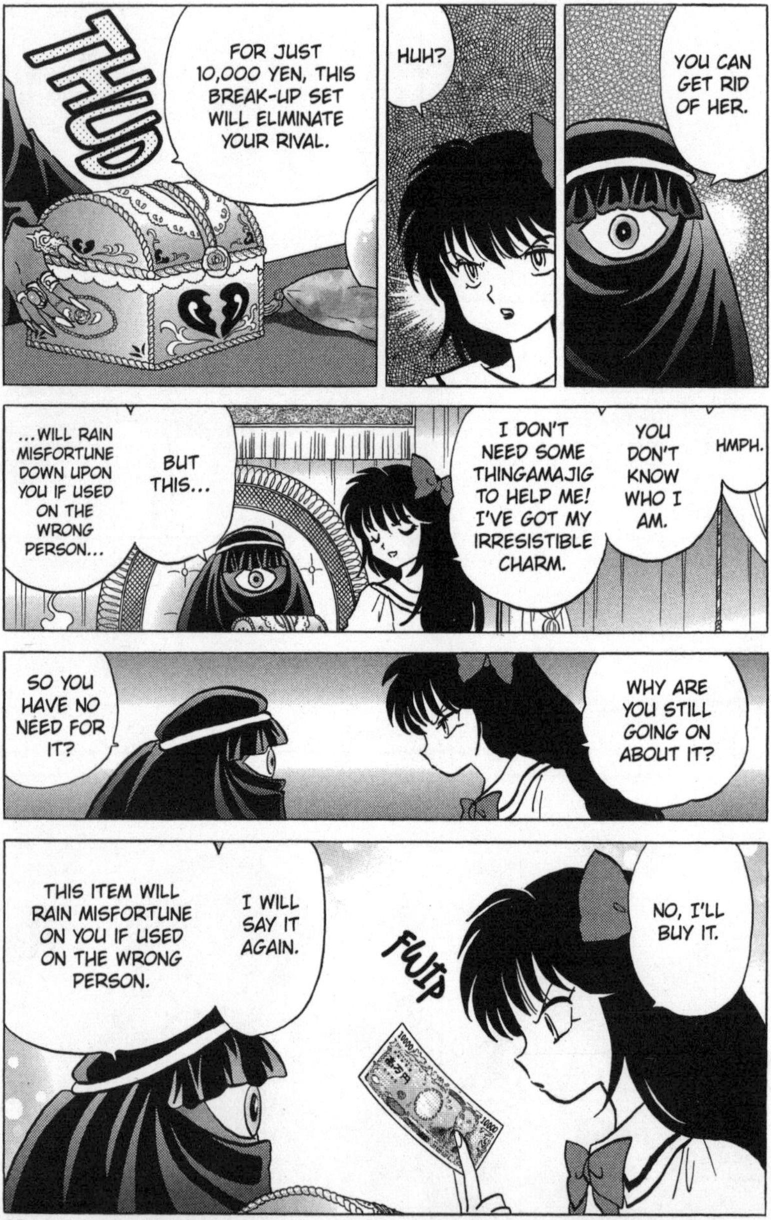
YOU CAN GET RID OF HER.
HUH?
FOR JUST 10,000 YEN, THIS BREAK-UP SET WILL ELIMINATE YOUR RIVAL.
THUD
HMPH.
YOU DON'T KNOW WHO I AM.
I DON'T NEED SOME THINGAMAJIG TO HELP ME! I'VE GOT MY IRRESISTIBLE CHARM.
BUT THIS...
...WILL RAIN MISFORTUNE DOWN UPON YOU IF USED ON THE WRONG PERSON...
WHY ARE YOU STILL GOING ON ABOUT IT?
SO YOU HAVE NO NEED FOR IT?
NO, I'LL BUY IT.
FWIP
I WILL SAY IT AGAIN.
THIS ITEM WILL RAIN MISFORTUNE ON YOU IF USED ON THE WRONG PERSON.

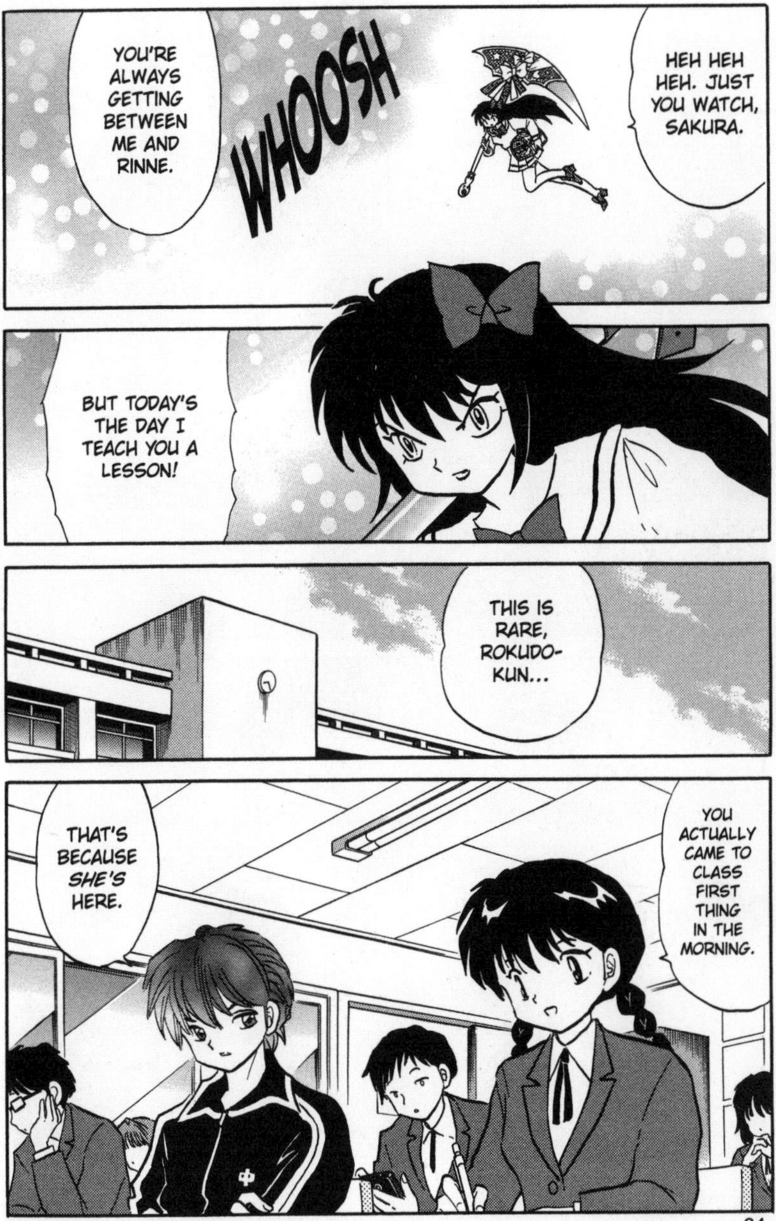
HEH HEH HEH. JUST YOU WATCH, SAKURA.
WHOOSH
YOU'RE ALWAYS GETTING BETWEEN ME AND RINNE.
BUT TODAY'S THE DAY I TEACH YOU A LESSON!
THIS IS RARE, ROKUDO-KUN...
YOU ACTUALLY CAME TO CLASS FIRST THING IN THE MORNING.
THAT'S BECAUSE *SHE'S* HERE.

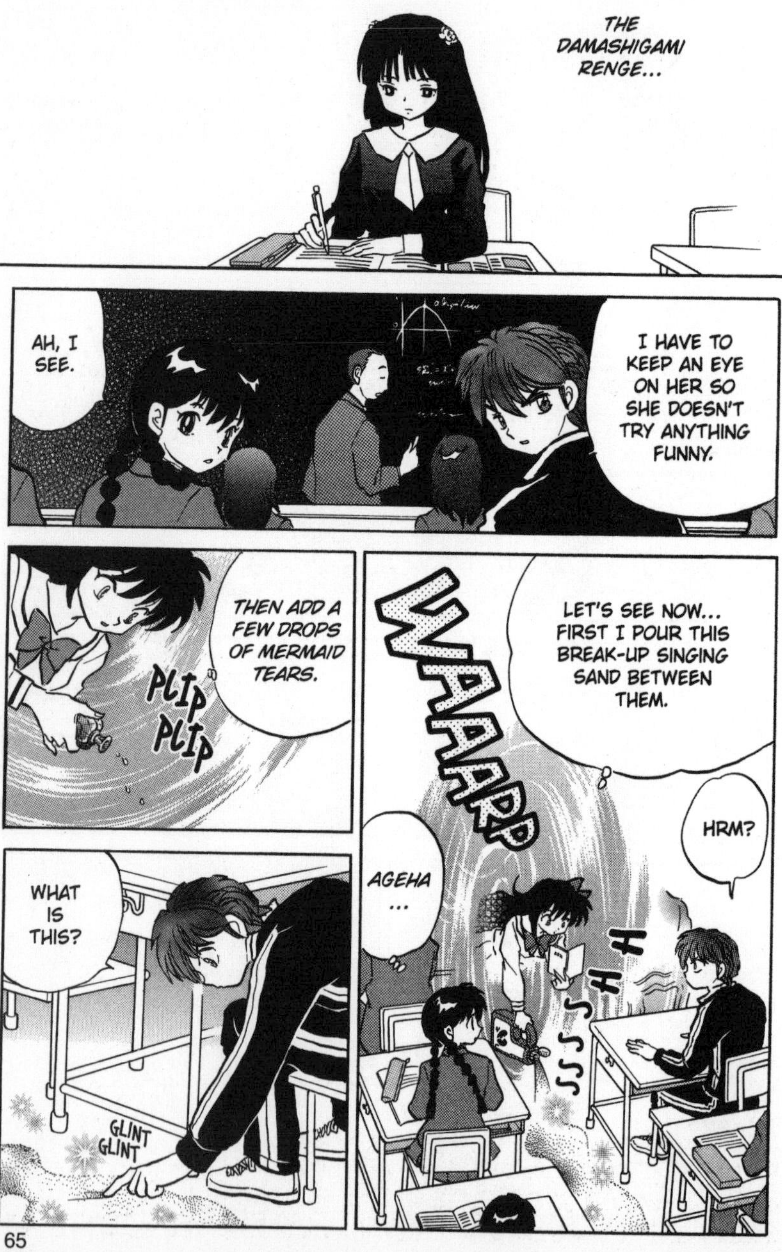
THE DAMASHIGAMI RENGE...
I HAVE TO KEEP AN EYE ON HER SO SHE DOESN'T TRY ANYTHING FUNNY.
AH, I SEE.
LET'S SEE NOW... FIRST I POUR THIS BREAK-UP SINGING SAND BETWEEN THEM.
WAAARP
HRM?
AGEHA...
H H
SSSS
THEN ADD A FEW DROPS OF MERMAID TEARS.
PLIP PLIP
WHAT IS THIS?
GLINT GLINT

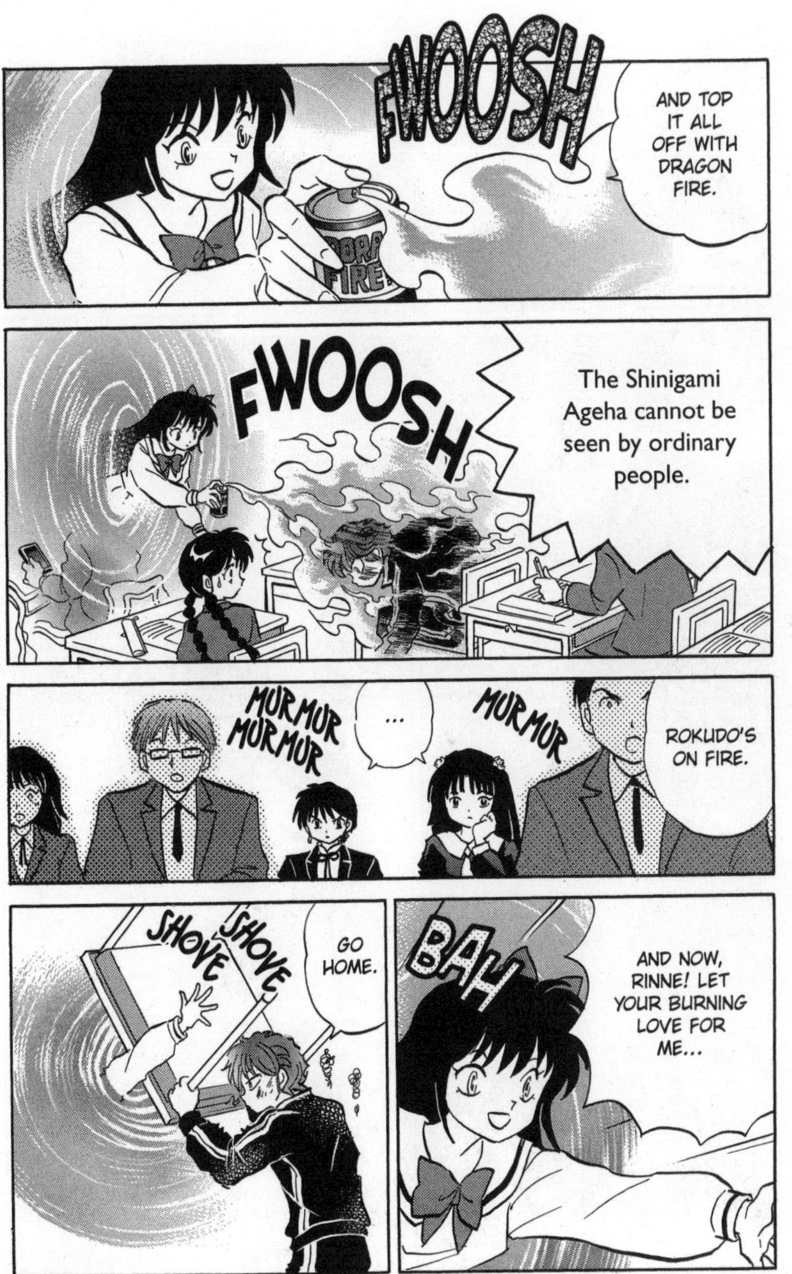
FWOOSH
AND TOP IT ALL OFF WITH DRAGON FIRE.
The Shinigami Ageha cannot be seen by ordinary people.
FWOOSH
ROKUDO'S ON FIRE.
MURMUR
...
MURMUR MURMUR
BAH
AND NOW, RINNE! LET YOUR BURNING LOVE FOR ME...
GO HOME.
SHOVE
SHOVE

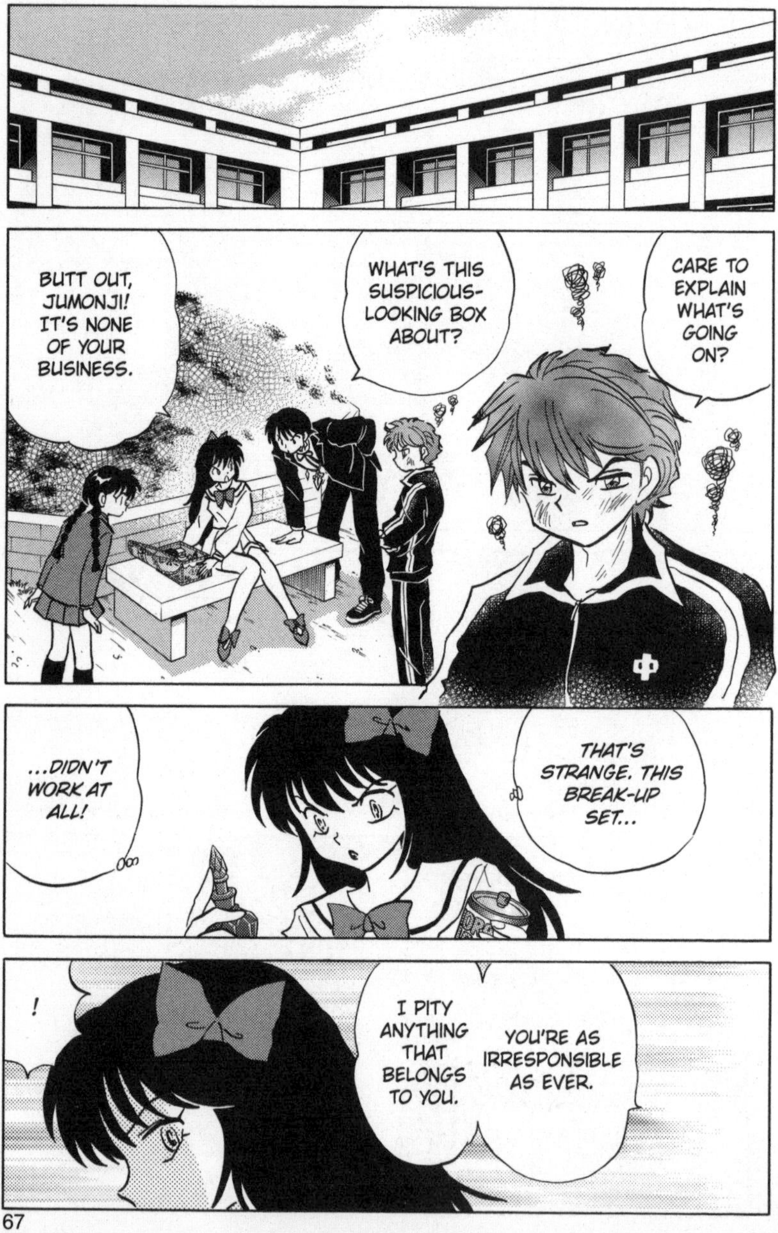
CARE TO EXPLAIN WHAT'S GOING ON?
WHAT'S THIS SUSPICIOUS-LOOKING BOX ABOUT?
BUTT OUT, JUMONJI! IT'S NONE OF YOUR BUSINESS.
THAT'S STRANGE. THIS BREAK-UP SET...
...DIDN'T WORK AT ALL!
YOU'RE AS IRRESPONSIBLE AS EVER.
I PITY ANYTHING THAT BELONGS TO YOU.
!

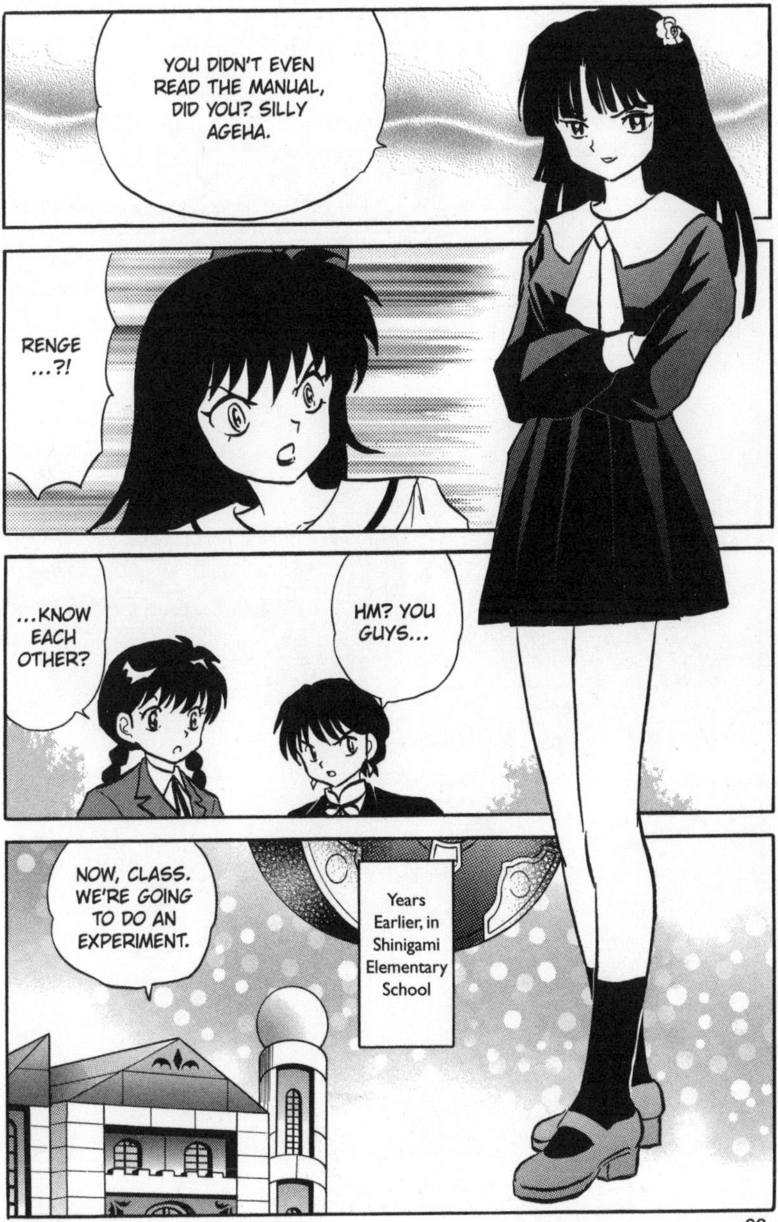
YOU DIDN'T EVEN READ THE MANUAL, DID YOU? SILLY AGEHA.
RENGE ...?!
HM? YOU GUYS...
...KNOW EACH OTHER?
Years Earlier, in Shinigami Elementary School
NOW, CLASS. WE'RE GOING TO DO AN EXPERIMENT.

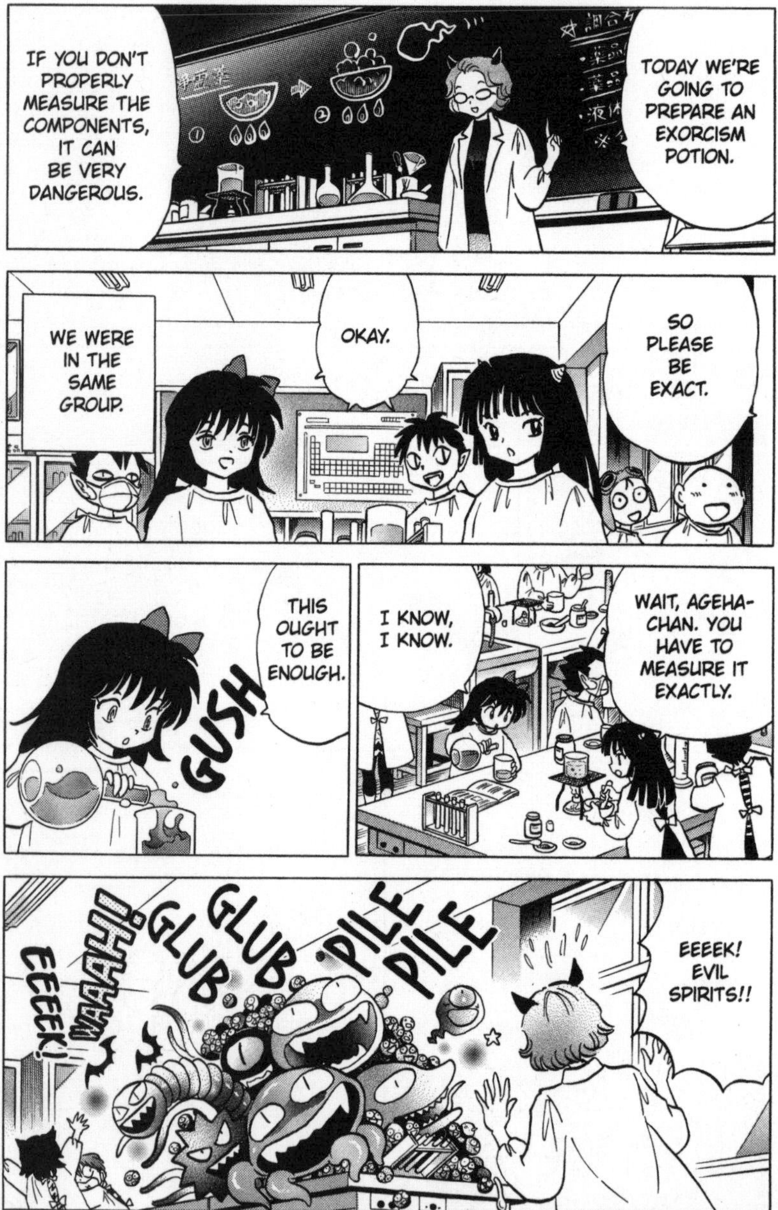
TODAY WE'RE GOING TO PREPARE AN EXORCISM POTION.
IF YOU DON'T PROPERLY MEASURE THE COMPONENTS, IT CAN BE VERY DANGEROUS.
SO PLEASE BE EXACT.
OKAY.
WE WERE IN THE SAME GROUP.
WAIT, AGEHA-CHAN. YOU HAVE TO MEASURE IT EXACTLY.
I KNOW, I KNOW.
THIS OUGHT TO BE ENOUGH.
GUSH
EEEEK! EVIL SPIRITS!!
PILE PILE
GLUB GLUB
WAAAH!
EEEEK!

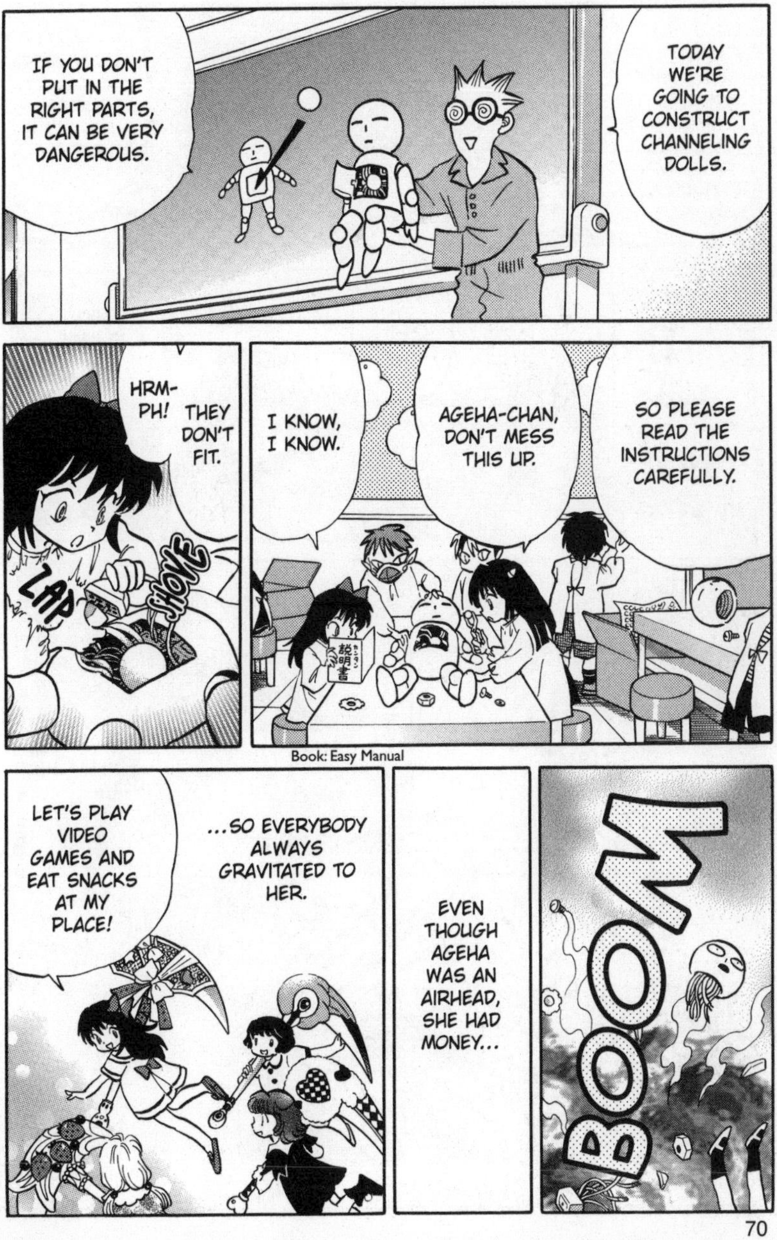
TODAY WE'RE GOING TO CONSTRUCT CHANNELING DOLLS.
IF YOU DON'T PUT IN THE RIGHT PARTS, IT CAN BE VERY DANGEROUS.
SO PLEASE READ THE INSTRUCTIONS CAREFULLY.
AGEHA-CHAN, DON'T MESS THIS UP.
I KNOW, I KNOW.
カンタン説明書
HRM-PH!
THEY DON'T FIT.
SHOVE
ZAP
BOOM
EVEN THOUGH AGEHA WAS AN AIRHEAD, SHE HAD MONEY...
...SO EVERYBODY ALWAYS GRAVITATED TO HER.
LET'S PLAY VIDEO GAMES AND EAT SNACKS AT MY PLACE!
Book: Easy Manual

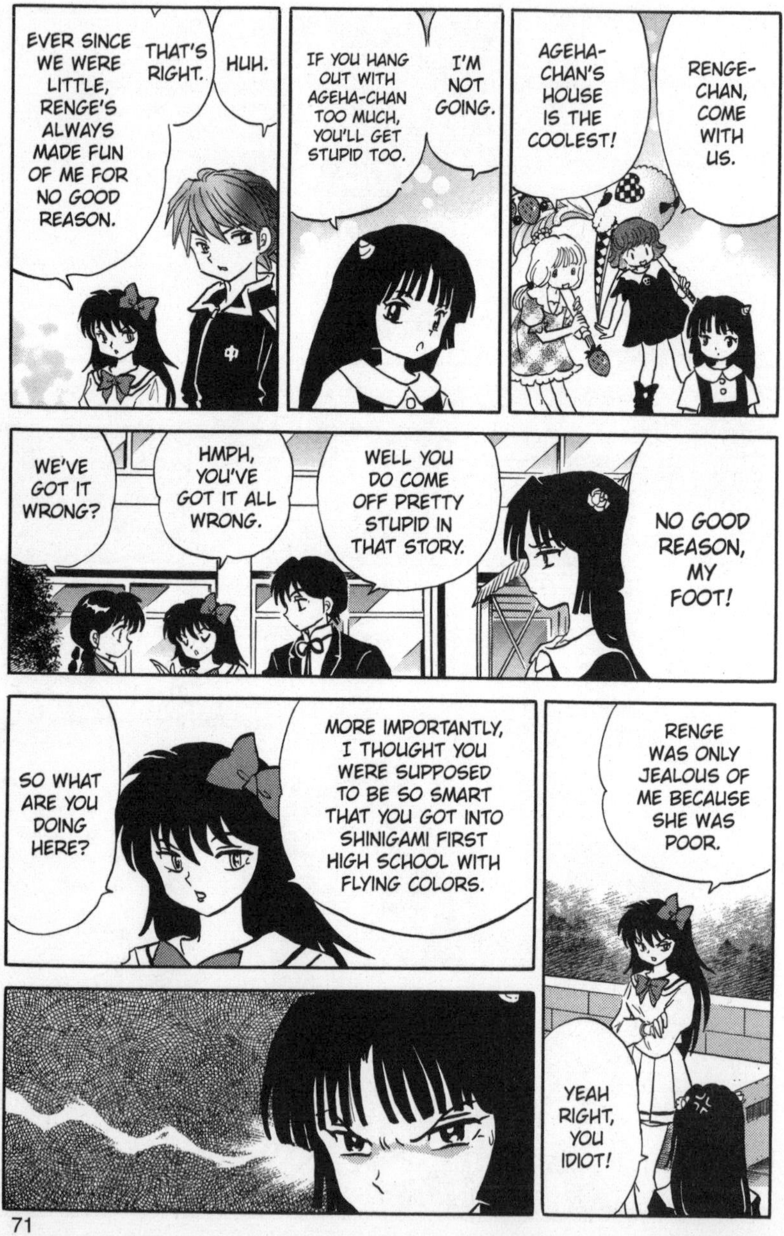
RENGE-CHAN, COME WITH US.
AGEHA-CHAN'S HOUSE IS THE COOLEST!
I'M NOT GOING.
IF YOU HANG OUT WITH AGEHA-CHAN TOO MUCH, YOU'LL GET STUPID TOO.
HUH.
THAT'S RIGHT.
EVER SINCE WE WERE LITTLE, RENGE'S ALWAYS MADE FUN OF ME FOR NO GOOD REASON.
NO GOOD REASON, MY FOOT!
WELL YOU DO COME OFF PRETTY STUPID IN THAT STORY.
HMPH, YOU'VE GOT IT ALL WRONG.
WE'VE GOT IT WRONG?
RENGE WAS ONLY JEALOUS OF ME BECAUSE SHE WAS POOR.
YEAH RIGHT, YOU IDIOT!
MORE IMPORTANTLY, I THOUGHT YOU WERE SUPPOSED TO BE SO SMART THAT YOU GOT INTO SHINIGAMI FIRST HIGH SCHOOL WITH FLYING COLORS.
SO WHAT ARE YOU DOING HERE?

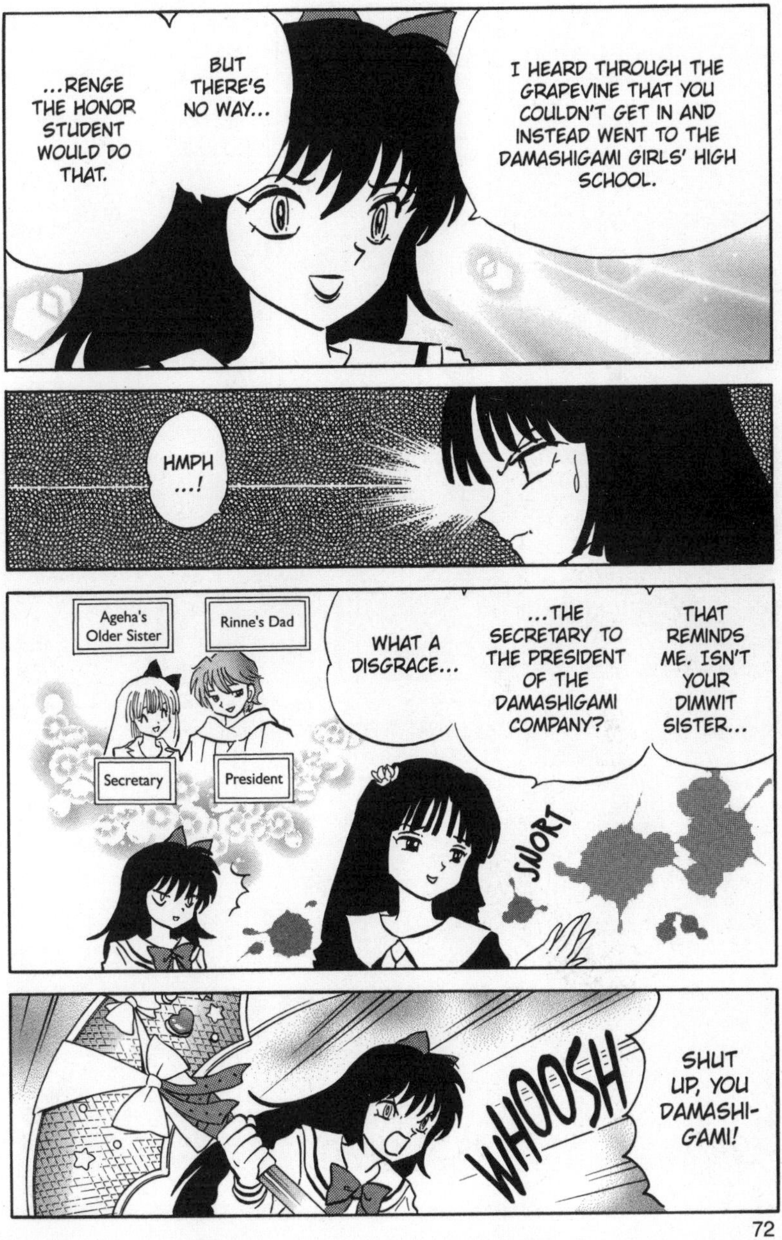
I HEARD THROUGH THE GRAPEVINE THAT YOU COULDN'T GET IN AND INSTEAD WENT TO THE DAMASHIGAMI GIRLS' HIGH SCHOOL.
BUT THERE'S NO WAY...
...RENGE THE HONOR STUDENT WOULD DO THAT.
HMPH ...!
THAT REMINDS ME. ISN'T YOUR DIMWIT SISTER...
...THE SECRETARY TO THE PRESIDENT OF THE DAMASHIGAMI COMPANY?
WHAT A DISGRACE...
Rinne's Dad
Ageha's Older Sister
President
Secretary
SNORT
SHUT UP, YOU DAMASHI-GAMI!
WHOOSH

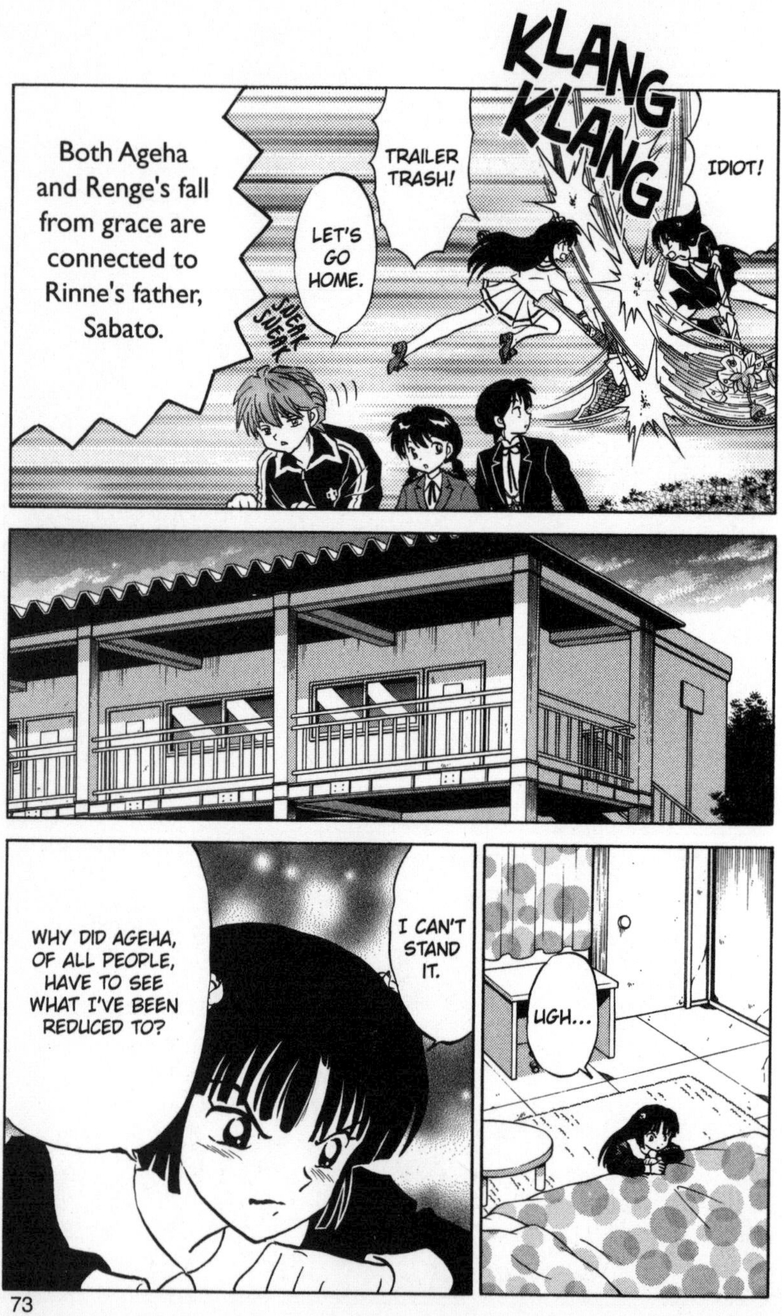
KLANG KLANG
IDIOT!
TRAILER TRASH!
LET'S GO HOME.
SWEAK SWEAK
Both Ageha and Renge's fall from grace are connected to Rinne's father, Sabato.
UGH...
I CAN'T STAND IT.
WHY DID AGEHA, OF ALL PEOPLE, HAVE TO SEE WHAT I'VE BEEN REDUCED TO?

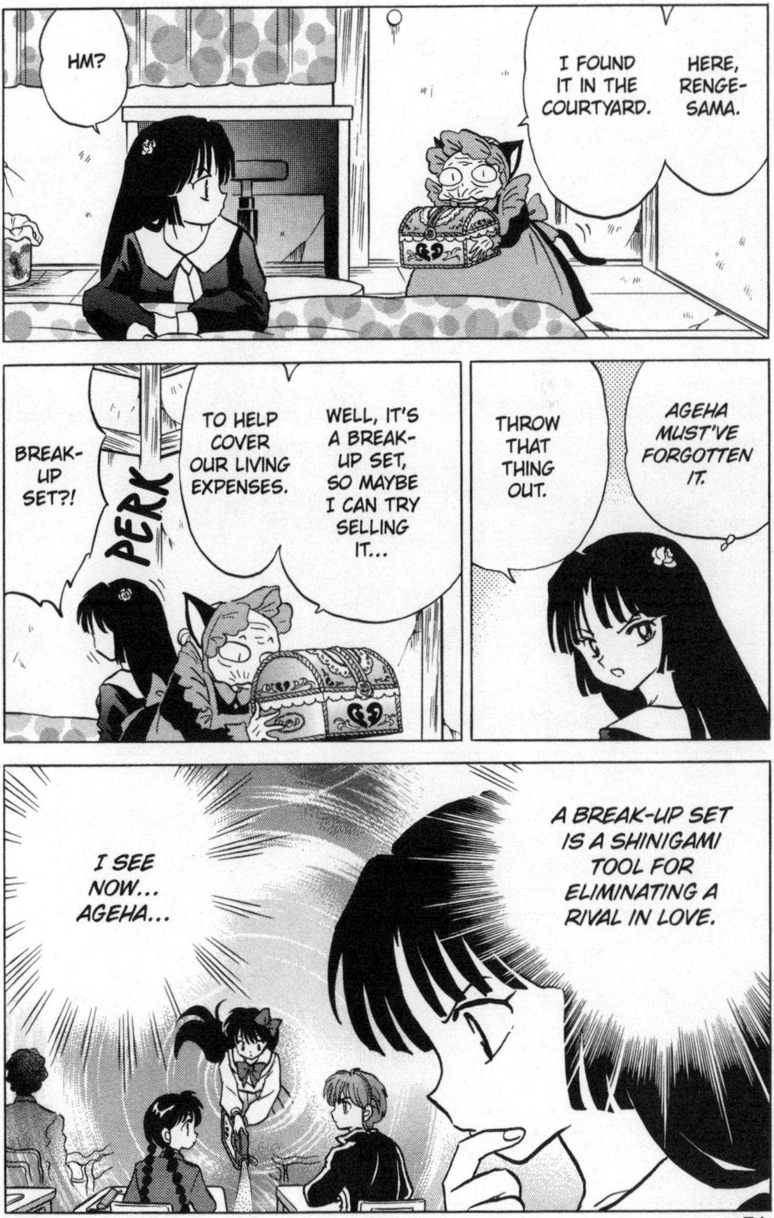
HERE, RENGE-SAMA.
I FOUND IT IN THE COURTYARD.
HM?
AGEHA MUST'VE FORGOTTEN IT.
THROW THAT THING OUT.
WELL, IT'S A BREAK-UP SET, SO MAYBE I CAN TRY SELLING IT...
TO HELP COVER OUR LIVING EXPENSES.
PERK
BREAK-UP SET?!
A BREAK-UP SET IS A SHINIGAMI TOOL FOR ELIMINATING A RIVAL IN LOVE.
I SEE NOW... AGEHA...

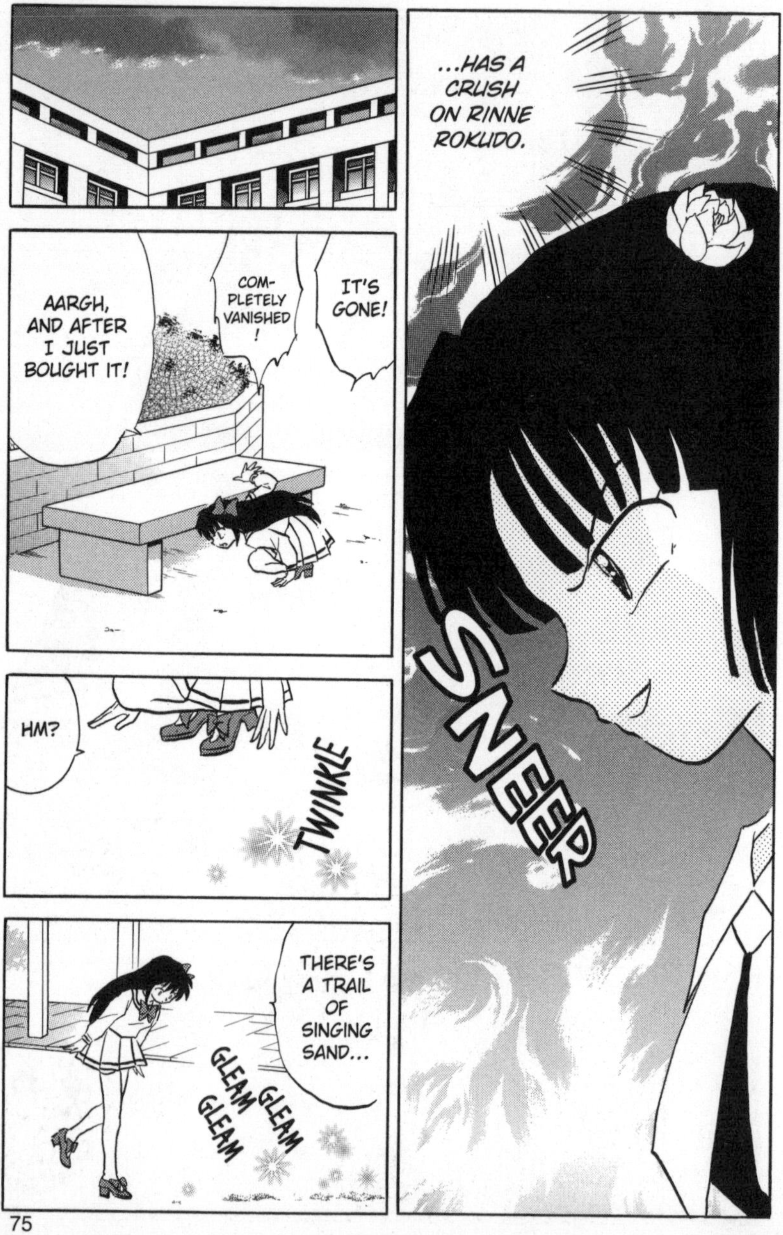

...HAS A CRUSH ON RINNE ROKUDO.
SNEER
IT'S GONE!
COM-PLETELY VANISHED!
AARGH, AND AFTER I JUST BOUGHT IT!
HM?
TWINKLE
THERE'S A TRAIL OF SINGING SAND...
GLEAM GLEAM
GLEAM

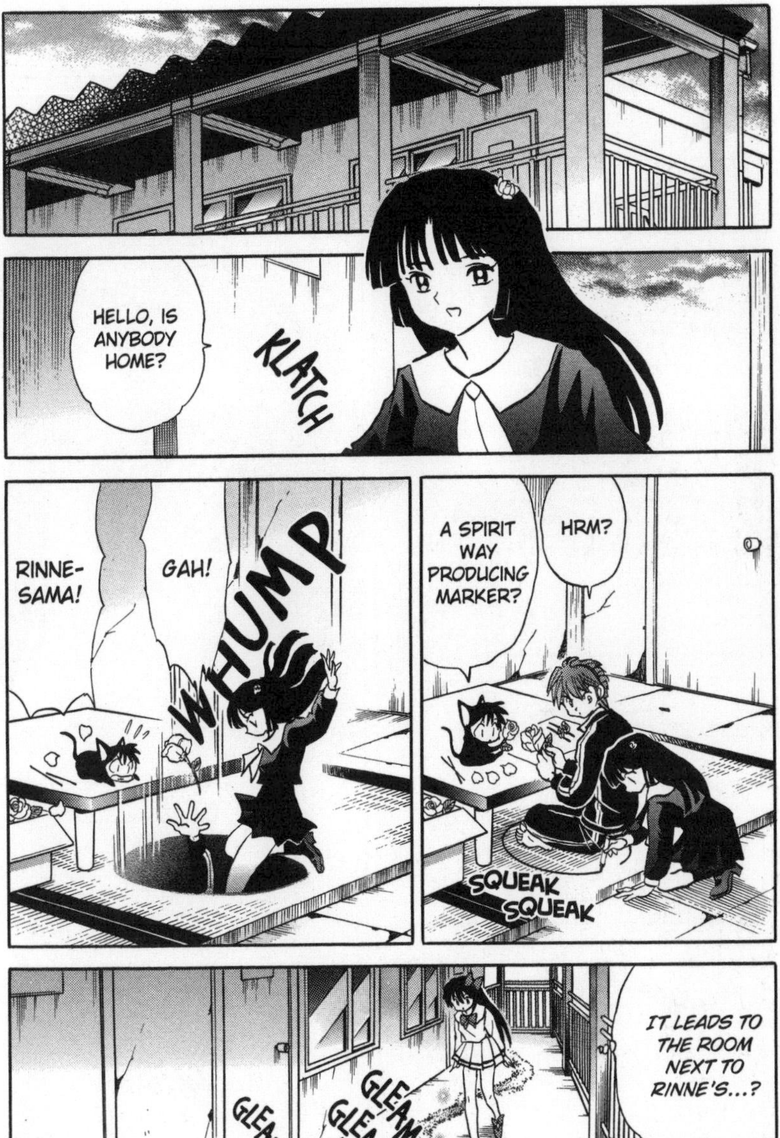
HELLO, IS ANYBODY HOME?
KLATCH
HRM?
A SPIRIT WAY PRODUCING MARKER?
SQUEAK SQUEAK
GAH!
RINNE-SAMA!
WHUMP
IT LEADS TO THE ROOM NEXT TO RINNE'S...?
GLEAM GLEAM
GLEAM

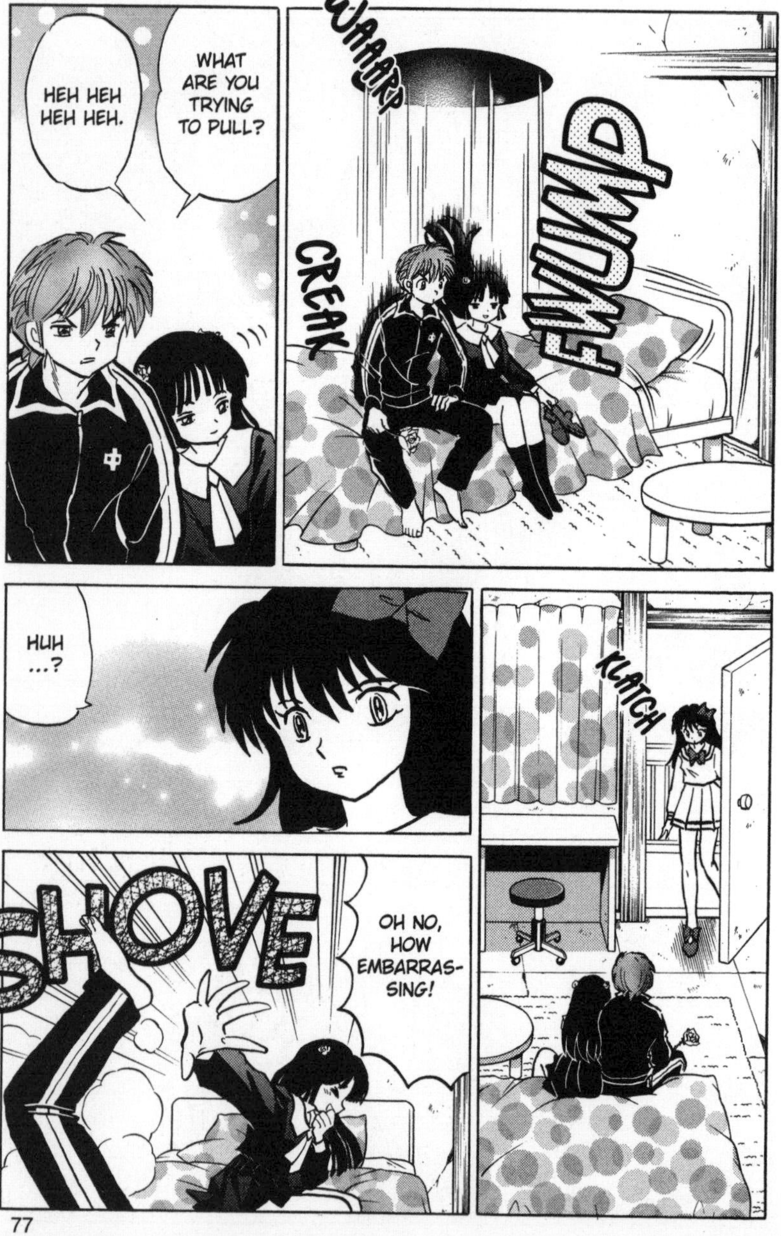
WAAARP
FWUMP
CREAK
WHAT ARE YOU TRYING TO PULL?
HEH HEH HEH HEH.
KLATCH
HUH ...?
OH NO, HOW EMBARRAS-SING!
SHOVE

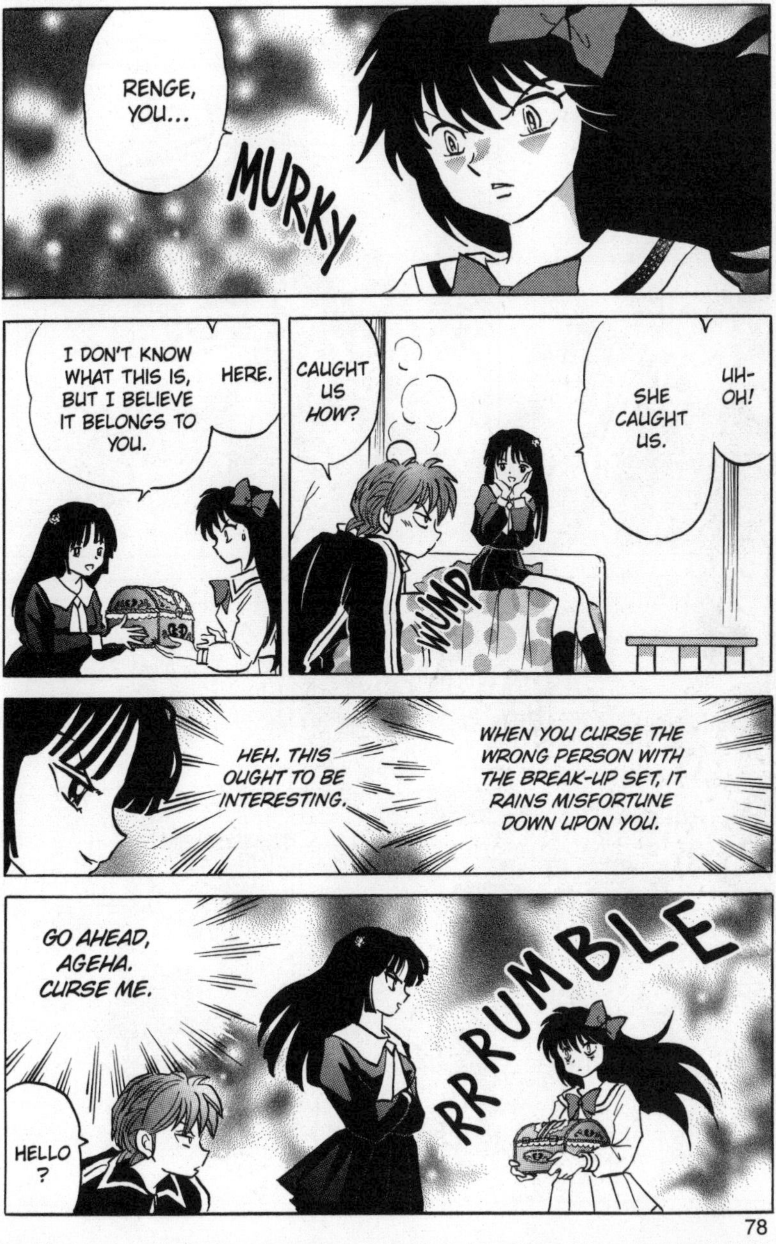
RENGE, YOU...
MURKY
UH-OH!
SHE CAUGHT US.
CAUGHT US HOW?
WUMP
HERE.
I DON'T KNOW WHAT THIS IS, BUT I BELIEVE IT BELONGS TO YOU.
WHEN YOU CURSE THE WRONG PERSON WITH THE BREAK-UP SET, IT RAINS MISFORTUNE DOWN UPON YOU.
HEH. THIS OUGHT TO BE INTERESTING.
RRUMBLE
GO AHEAD, AGEHA. CURSE ME.
HELLO?

CHAPTER 143: THE FAKE COUPLE

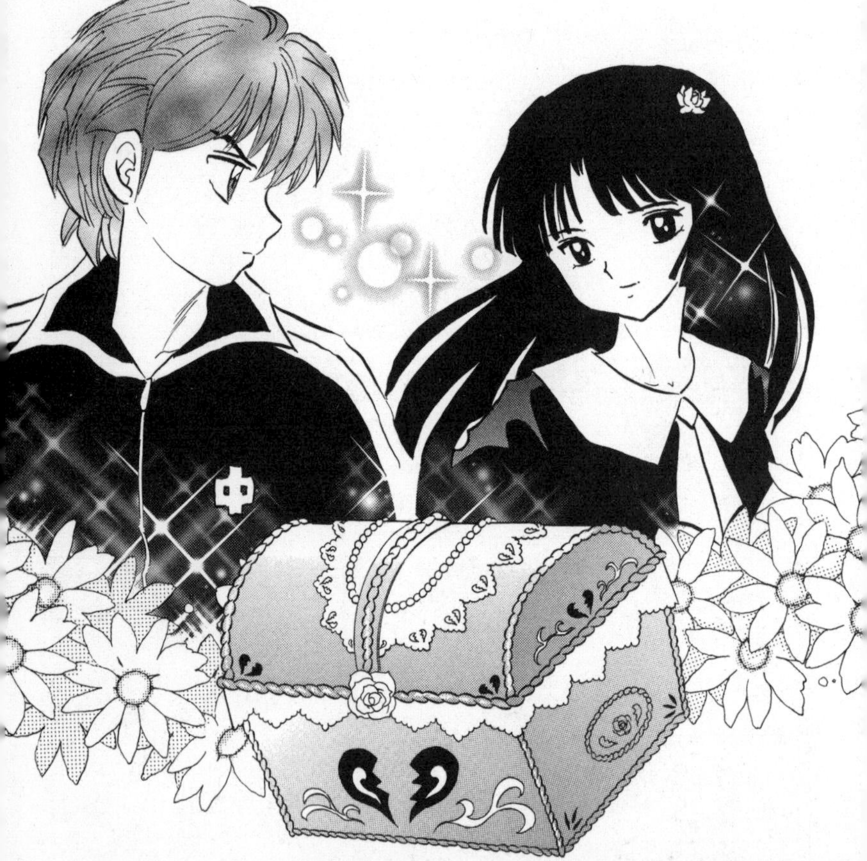

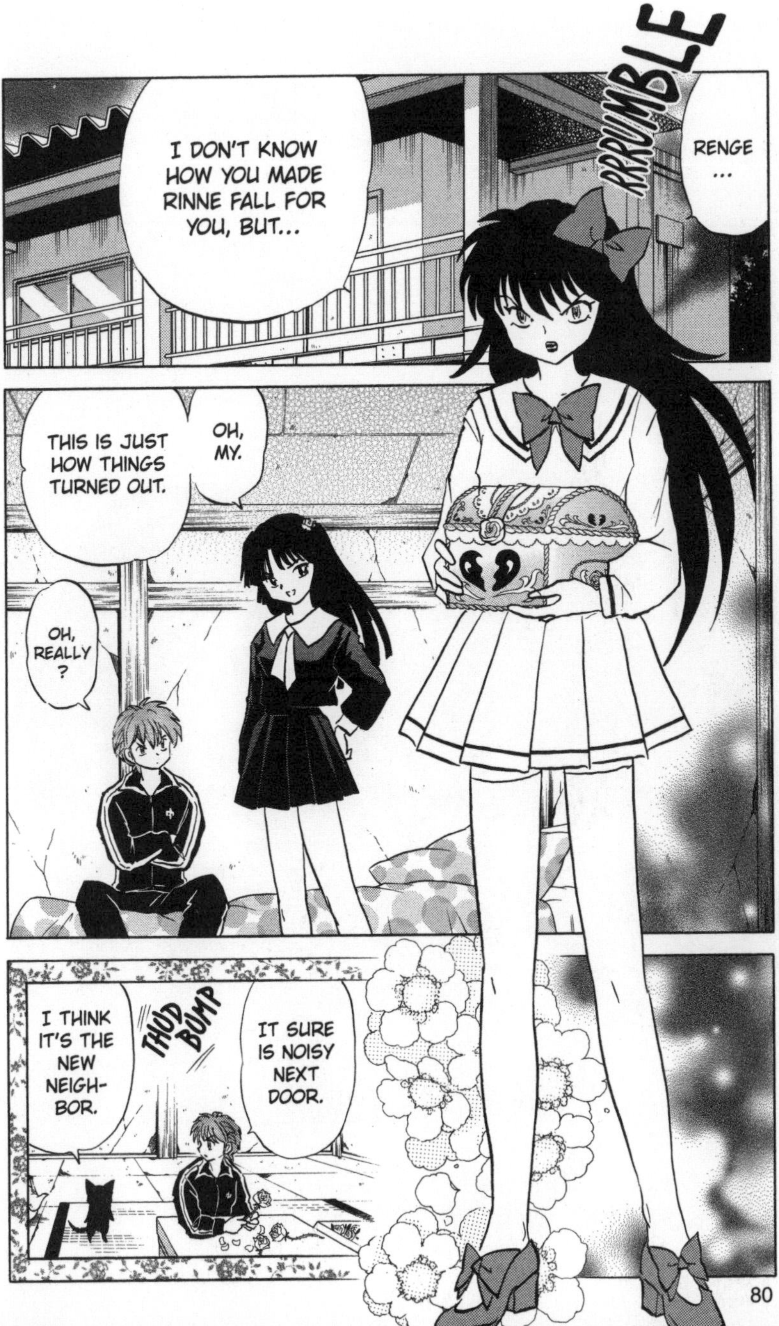
RRRUMBLE
RENGE ...
I DON'T KNOW HOW YOU MADE RINNE FALL FOR YOU, BUT...
OH, MY.
THIS IS JUST HOW THINGS TURNED OUT.
OH, REALLY ?
IT SURE IS NOISY NEXT DOOR.
THUD BUMP
I THINK IT'S THE NEW NEIGH-BOR.

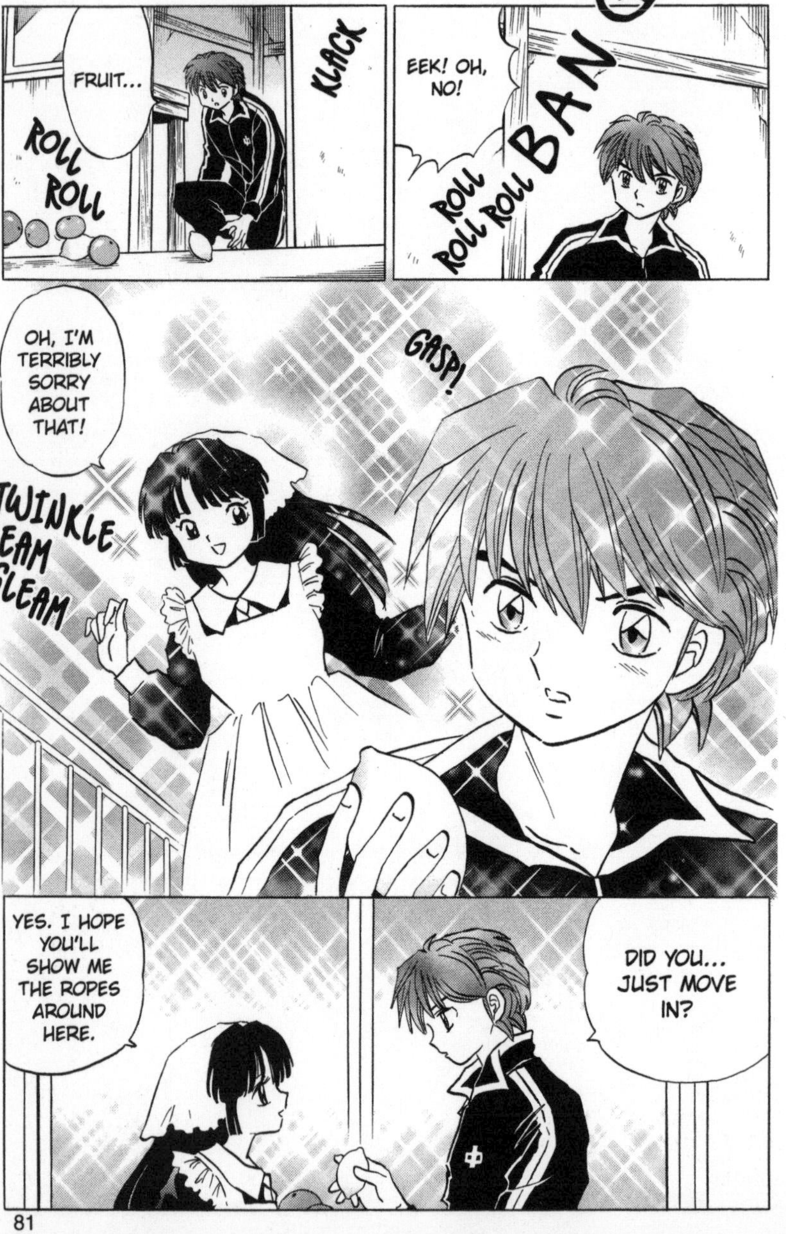
BANG
EEK! OH, NO!
ROLL ROLL ROLL ROLL
KLACK
FRUIT...
ROLL ROLL
GASP!
OH, I'M TERRIBLY SORRY ABOUT THAT!
TWINKLE GLEAM GLEAM
DID YOU... JUST MOVE IN?
YES. I HOPE YOU'LL SHOW ME THE ROPES AROUND HERE.

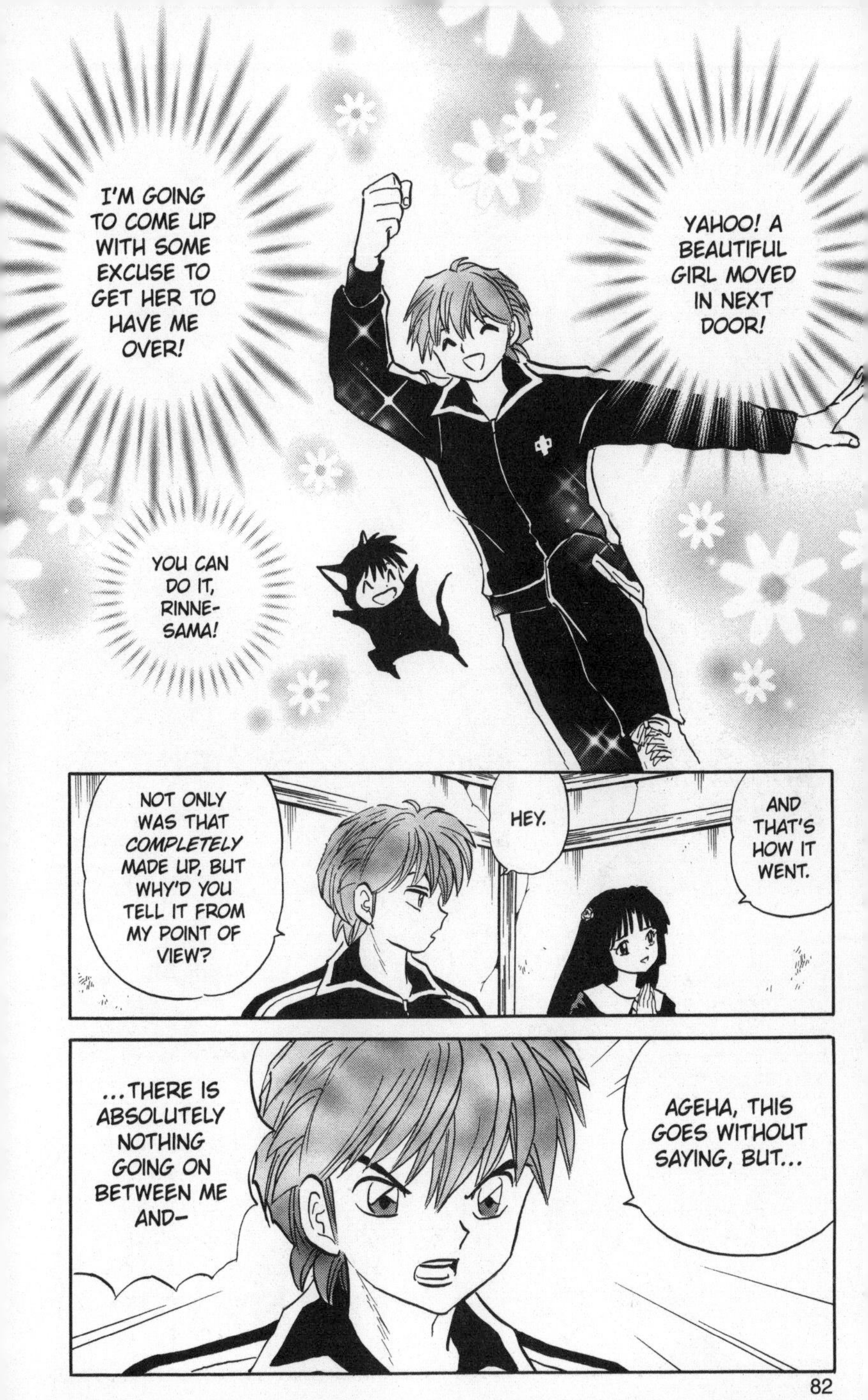
YAHOO! A BEAUTIFUL GIRL MOVED IN NEXT DOOR!
I'M GOING TO COME UP WITH SOME EXCUSE TO GET HER TO HAVE ME OVER!
YOU CAN DO IT, RINNE-SAMA!
AND THAT'S HOW IT WENT.
HEY.
NOT ONLY WAS THAT *COMPLETELY* MADE UP, BUT WHY'D YOU TELL IT FROM MY POINT OF VIEW?
AGEHA, THIS GOES WITHOUT SAYING, BUT...
...THERE IS ABSOLUTELY NOTHING GOING ON BETWEEN ME AND–

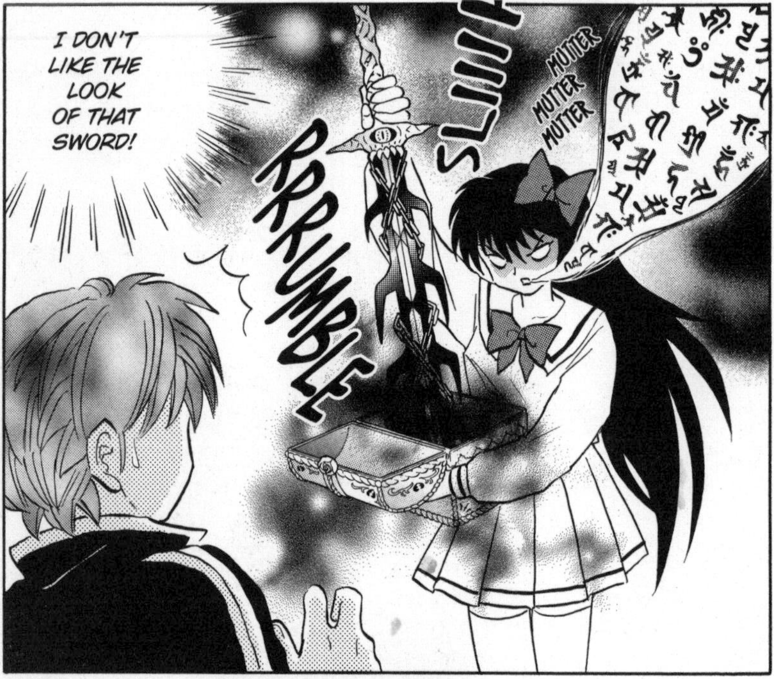
MUTTER MUTTER MUTTER
SLIIIP
RRRUMBLE
I DON'T LIKE THE LOOK OF THAT SWORD!

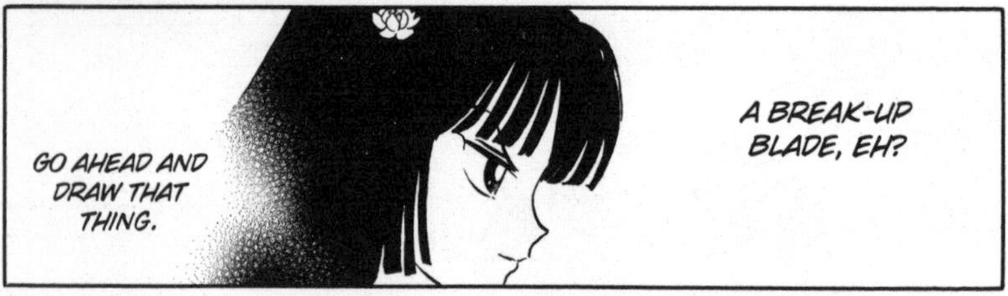
A BREAK-UP BLADE, EH?
GO AHEAD AND DRAW THAT THING.

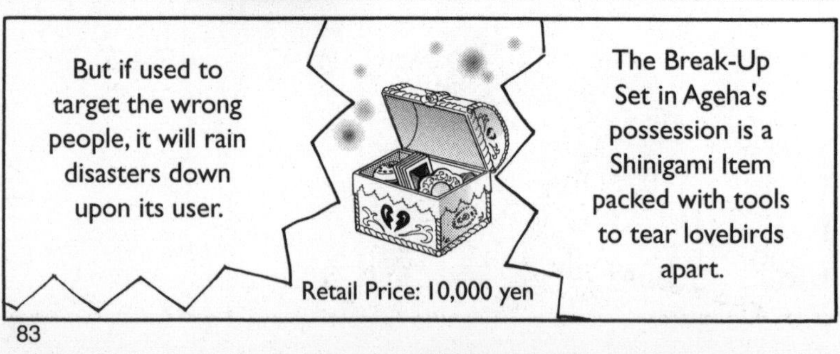
The Break-Up Set in Ageha's possession is a Shinigami Item packed with tools to tear lovebirds apart.
But if used to target the wrong people, it will rain disasters down upon its user.
Retail Price: 10,000 yen

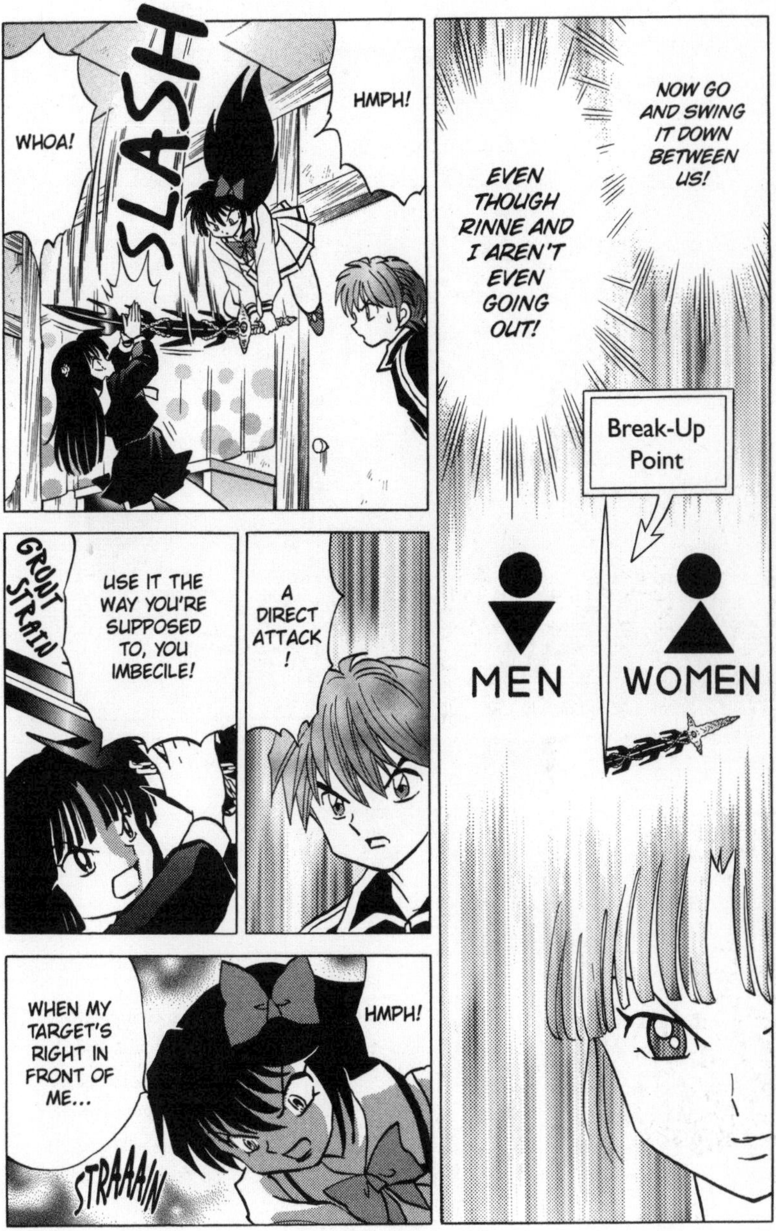
NOW GO AND SWING IT DOWN BETWEEN US!
EVEN THOUGH RINNE AND I AREN'T EVEN GOING OUT!
Break-Up Point
MEN
WOMEN
HMPH!
SLASH
WHOA!
A DIRECT ATTACK!
USE IT THE WAY YOU'RE SUPPOSED TO, YOU IMBECILE!
GRUNT STRAIN
HMPH!
WHEN MY TARGET'S RIGHT IN FRONT OF ME...
STRAAAIN

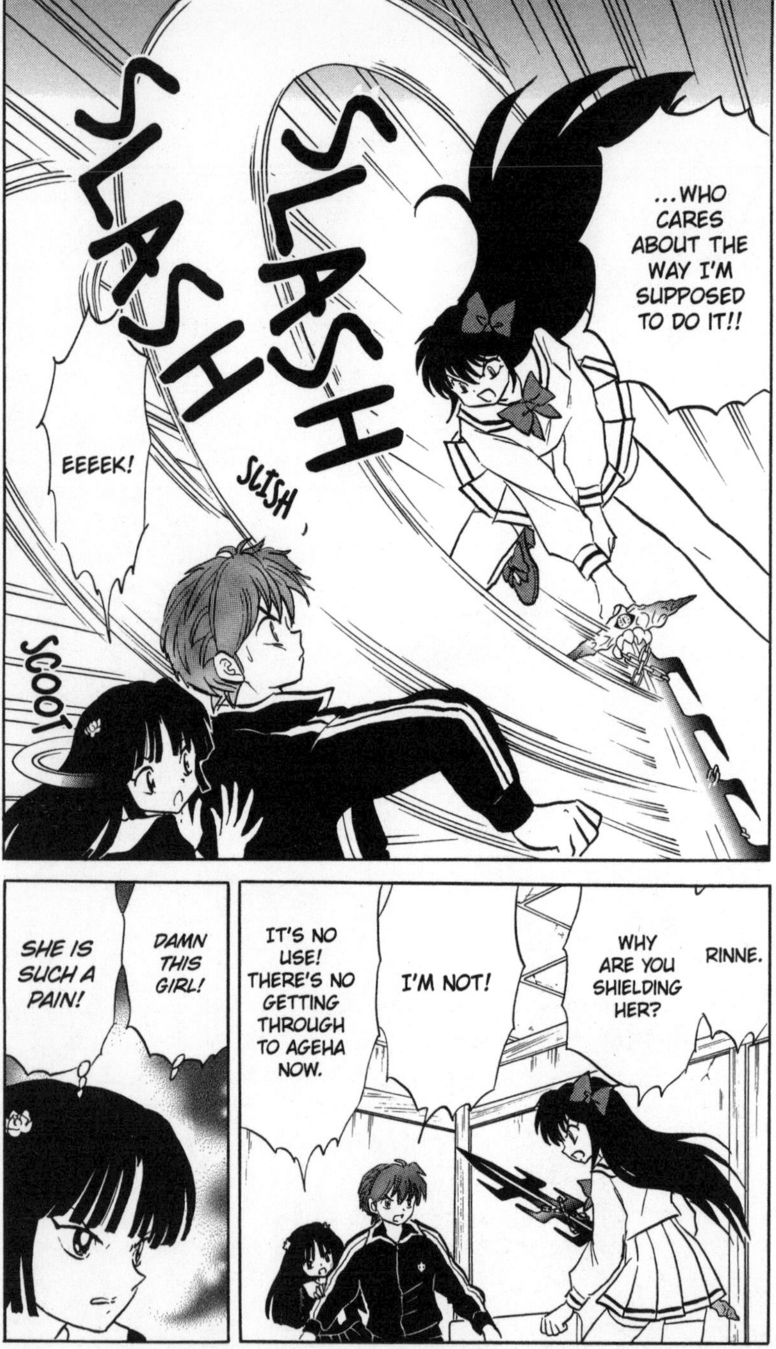
...WHO CARES ABOUT THE WAY I'M SUPPOSED TO DO IT!!
SLASH
SLASH
SLISH
EEEEK!
SCOOT
RINNE.
WHY ARE YOU SHIELDING HER?
I'M NOT!
IT'S NO USE! THERE'S NO GETTING THROUGH TO AGEHA NOW.
DAMN THIS GIRL!
SHE IS SUCH A PAIN!

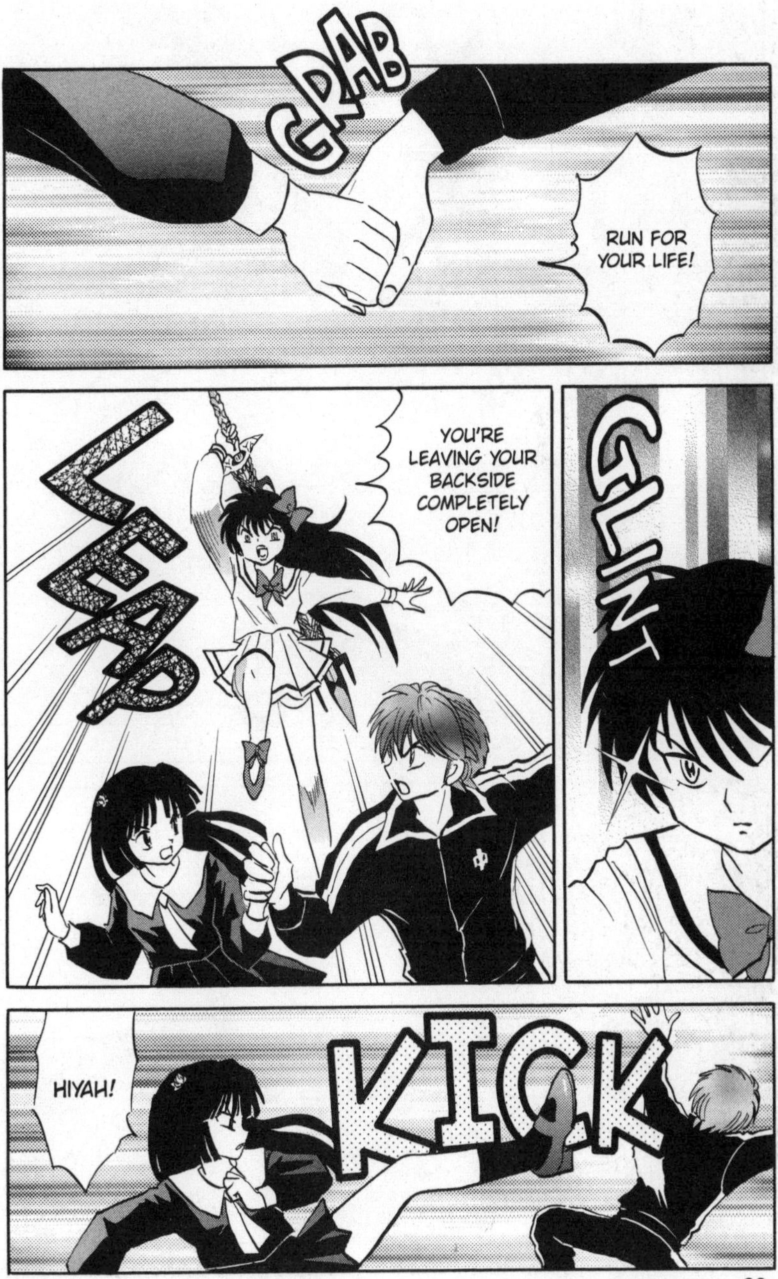
GRAB
RUN FOR YOUR LIFE!
GLINT
YOU'RE LEAVING YOUR BACKSIDE COMPLETELY OPEN!
LEAP
KICK
HIYAH!

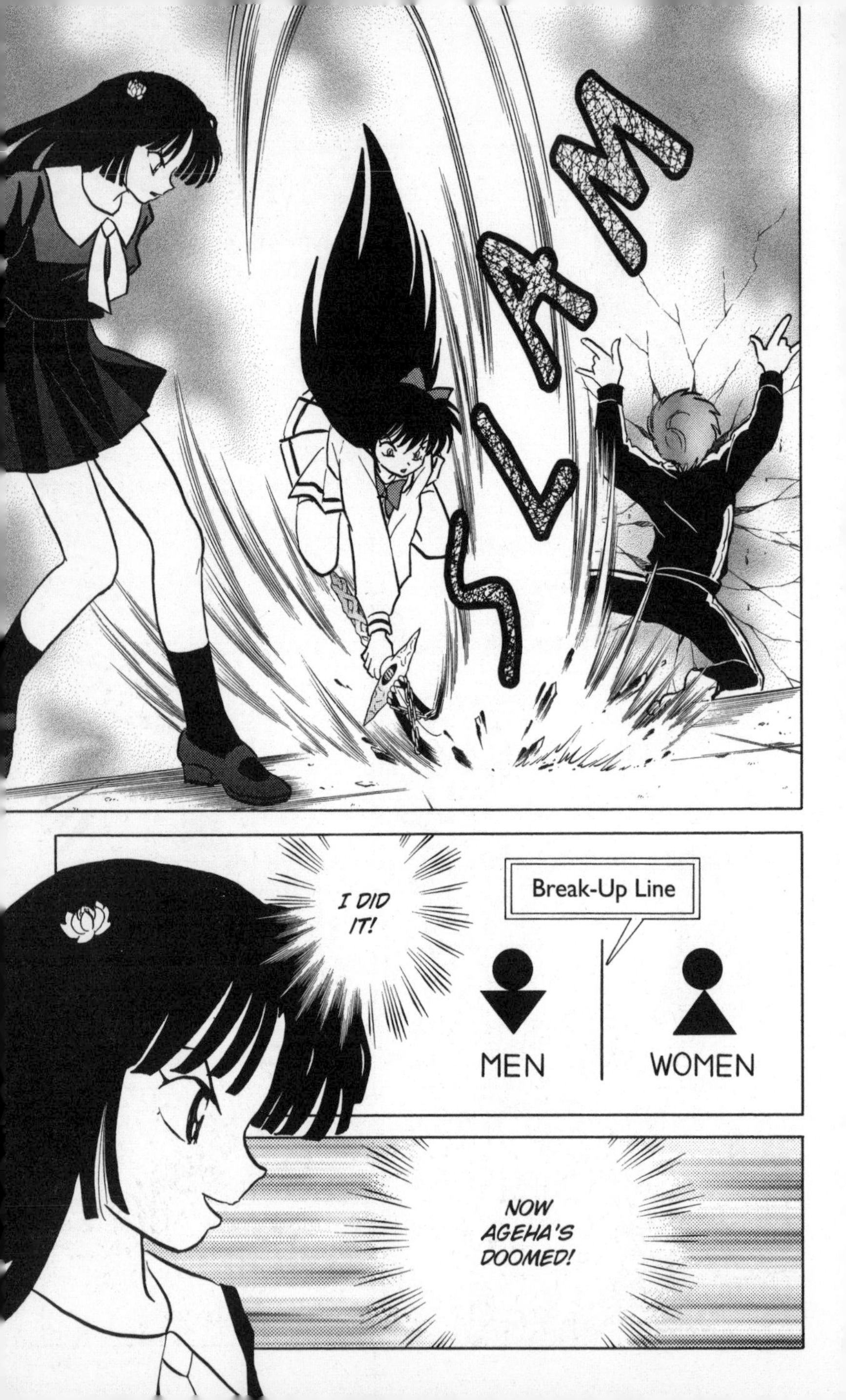
SLAM
Break-Up Line
MEN
WOMEN
I DID IT!
NOW AGEHA'S DOOMED!

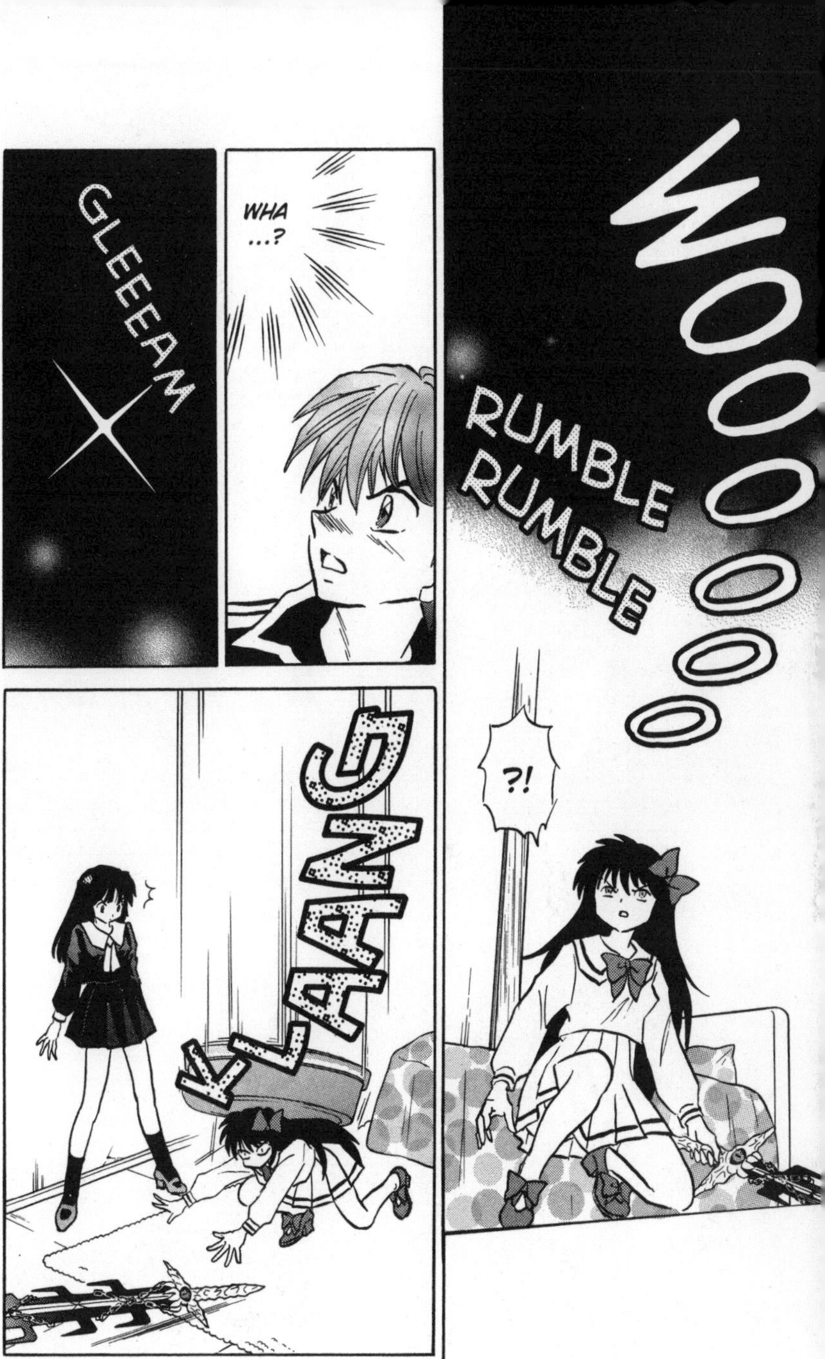
WOOOOOOO
RUMBLE RUMBLE
?!
WHA ...?
GLEEEAM
KLANG

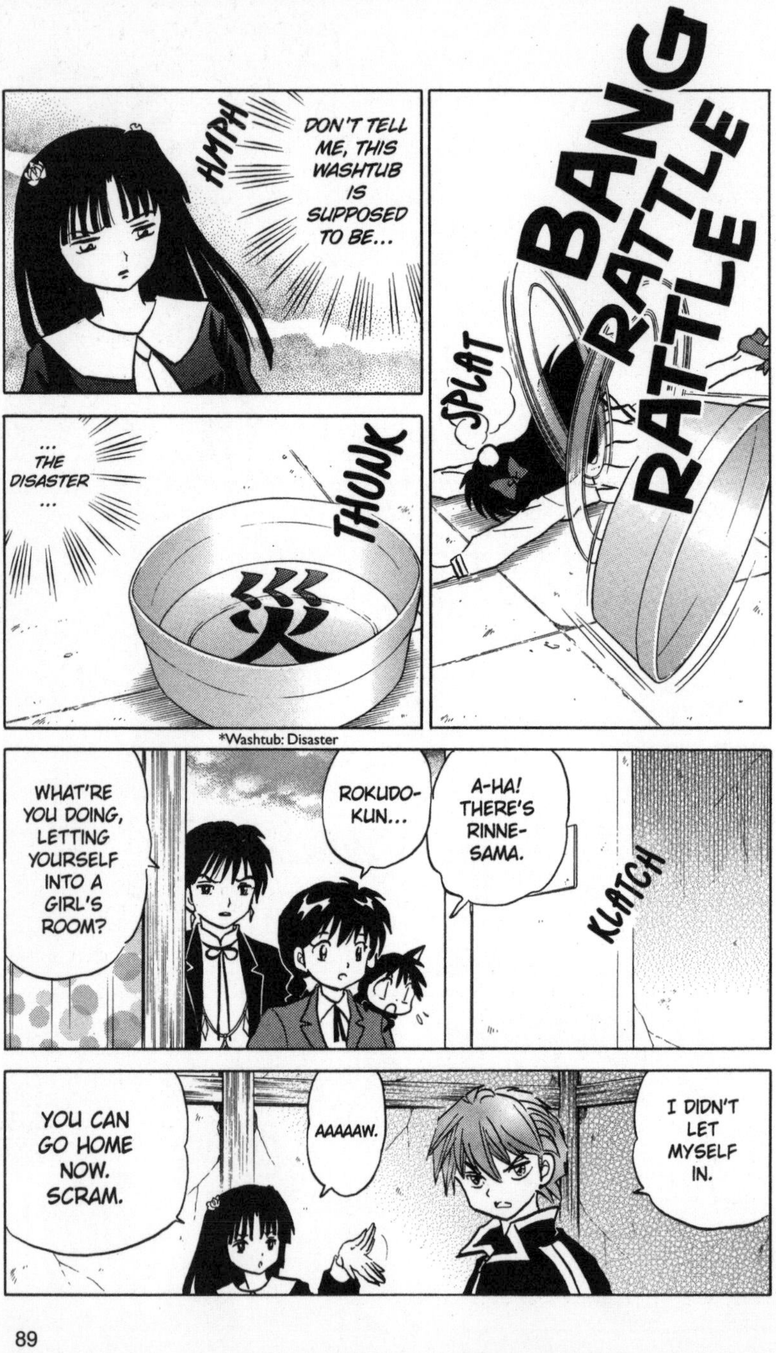
BANG
RATTLE RATTLE
SPLAT
HMPH
DON'T TELL ME, THIS WASHTUB IS SUPPOSED TO BE...
... THE DISASTER ...
THUNK
KLATCH
A-HA! THERE'S RINNE-SAMA.
ROKUDO-KUN...
WHAT'RE YOU DOING, LETTING YOURSELF INTO A GIRL'S ROOM?
I DIDN'T LET MYSELF IN.
AAAAAW.
YOU CAN GO HOME NOW. SCRAM.

*Washtub: Disaster

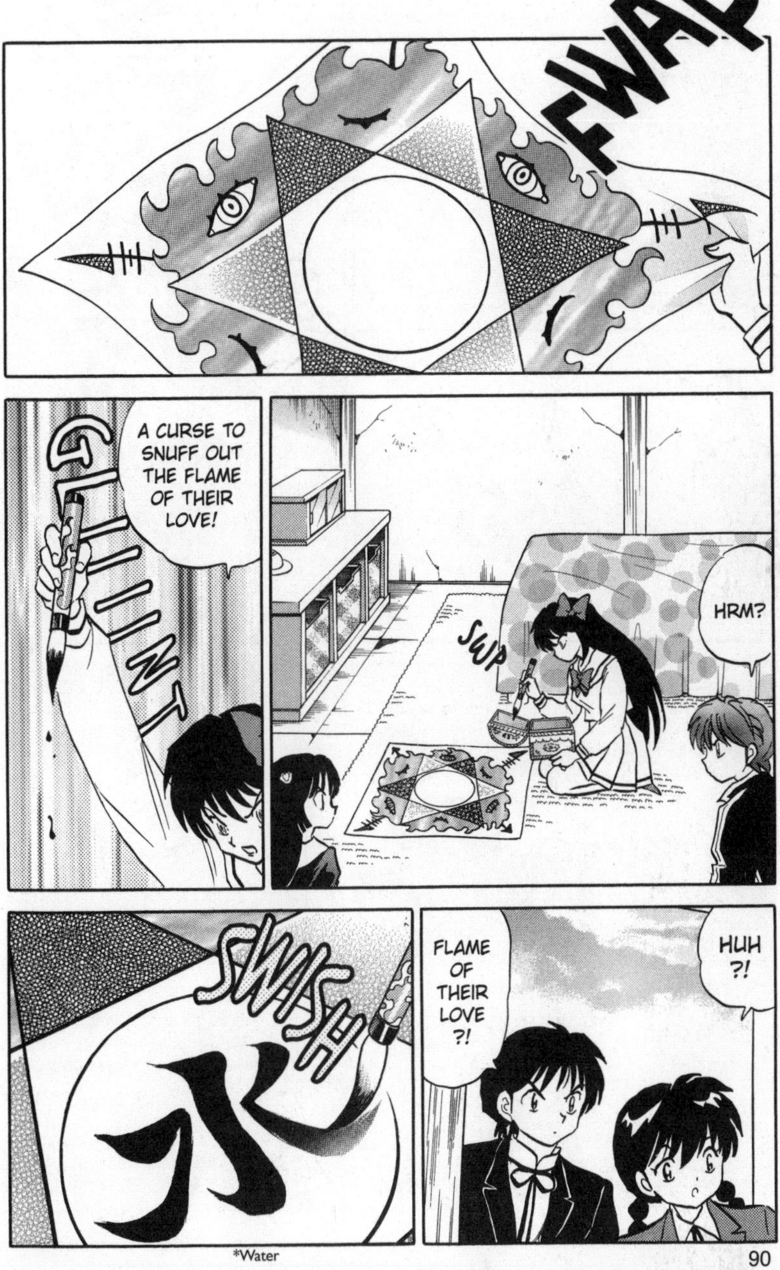
FWAP
HRM?
SWP
A CURSE TO SNUFF OUT THE FLAME OF THEIR LOVE!
GLINT
HUH ?!
FLAME OF THEIR LOVE ?!
SWISH
水

*Water

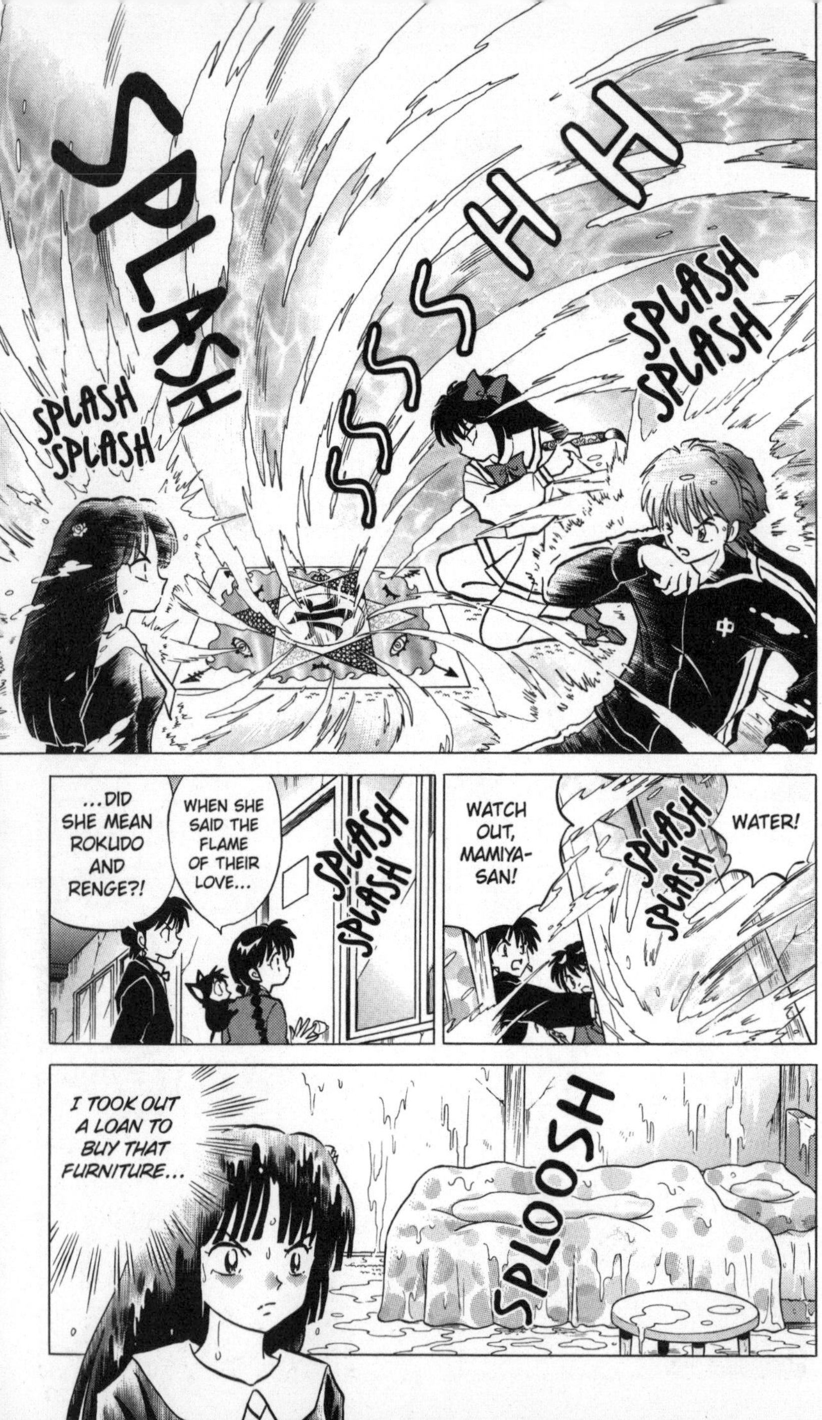
SPLASH SPLASH
SSSSHH
SPLASH
SPLASH SPLASH
WATER!
WATCH OUT, MAMIYA-SAN!
SPLASH SPLASH
WHEN SHE SAID THE FLAME OF THEIR LOVE...
...DID SHE MEAN ROKUDO AND RENGE?!
SPLASH SPLASH
SPLOOSH
I TOOK OUT A LOAN TO BUY THAT FURNITURE...

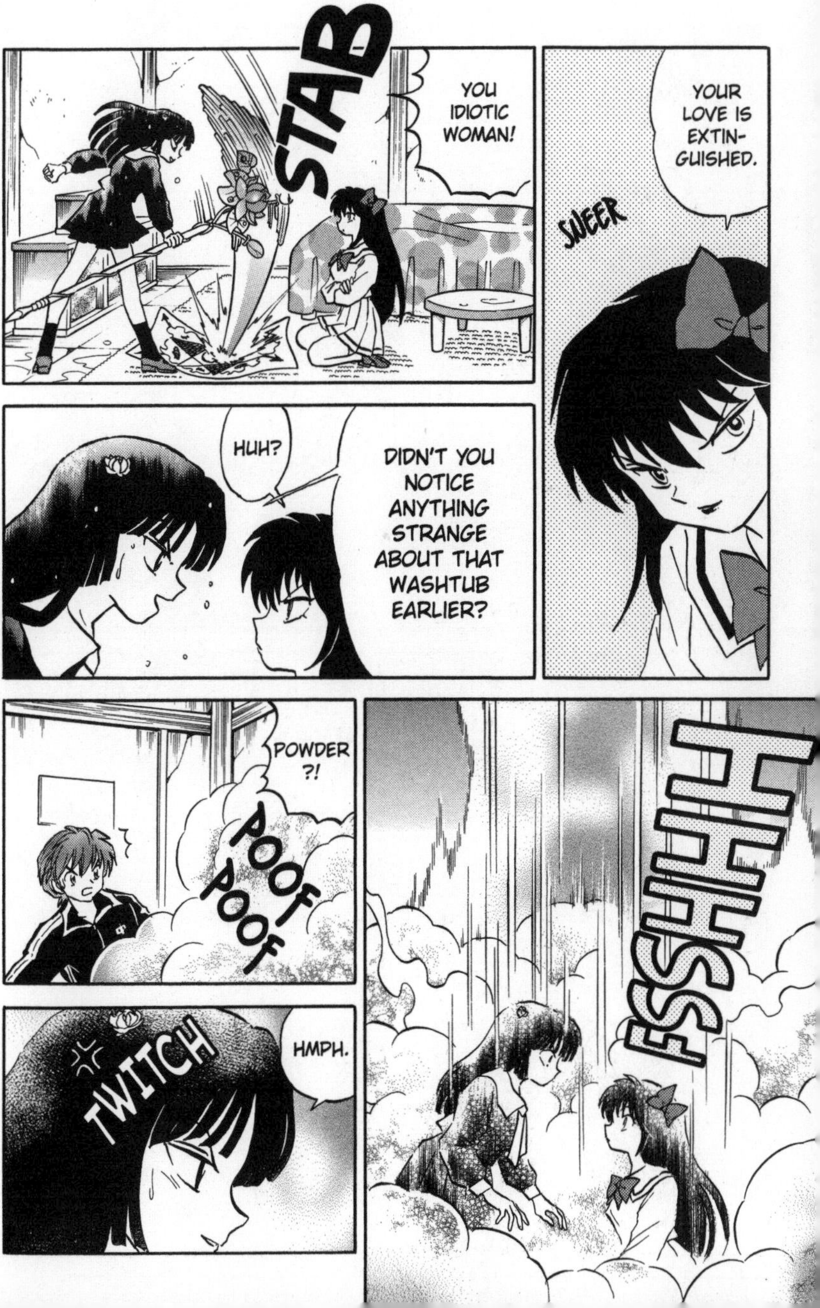
YOUR LOVE IS EXTIN-GUISHED.
SNEER
STAB
YOU IDIOTIC WOMAN!
DIDN'T YOU NOTICE ANYTHING STRANGE ABOUT THAT WASHTUB EARLIER?
HUH?
FSSHHHH
POWDER ?!
POOF POOF
HMPH.
TWITCH

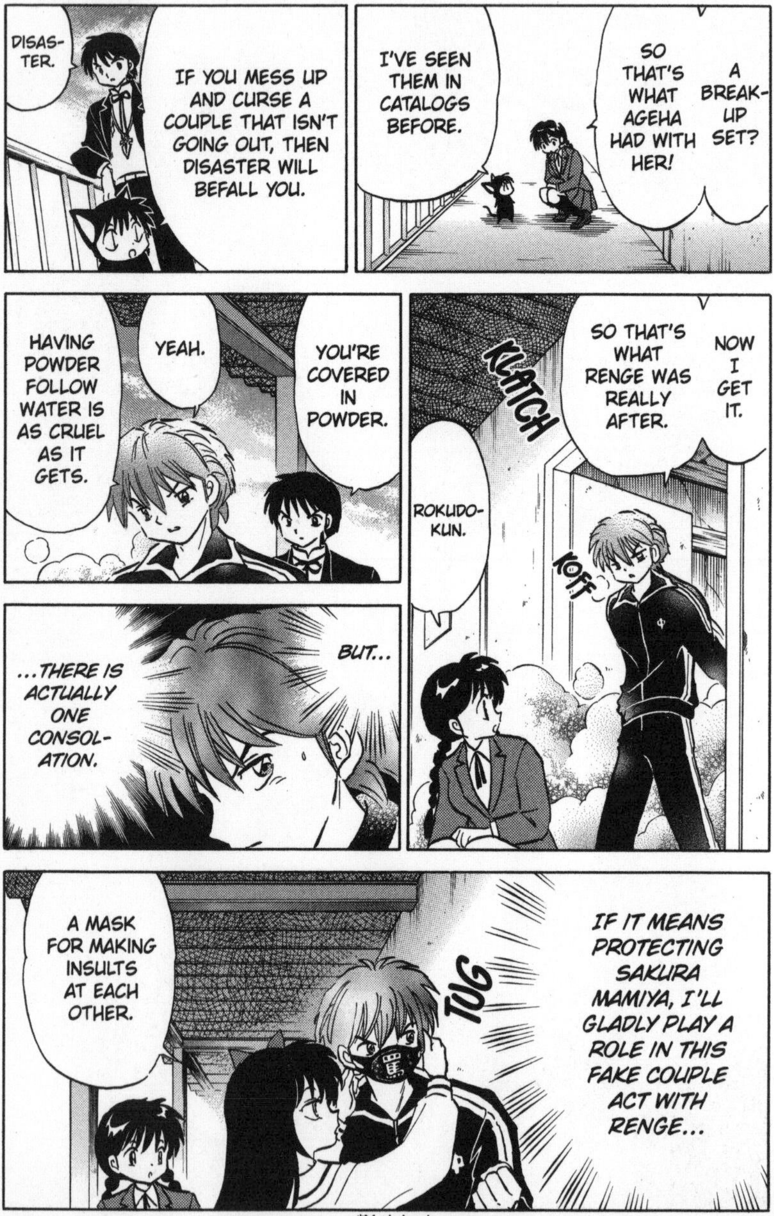
A BREAK-UP SET?
SO THAT'S WHAT AGEHA HAD WITH HER!
I'VE SEEN THEM IN CATALOGS BEFORE.
IF YOU MESS UP AND CURSE A COUPLE THAT ISN'T GOING OUT, THEN DISASTER WILL BEFALL YOU.
DISASTER.
NOW I GET IT.
SO THAT'S WHAT RENGE WAS REALLY AFTER.
KLATCH
ROKUDO-KUN.
KOFF
YOU'RE COVERED IN POWDER.
YEAH.
HAVING POWDER FOLLOW WATER IS AS CRUEL AS IT GETS.
BUT...
...THERE IS ACTUALLY ONE CONSOLATION.
IF IT MEANS PROTECTING SAKURA MAMIYA, I'LL GLADLY PLAY A ROLE IN THIS FAKE COUPLE ACT WITH RENGE...
TUG
A MASK FOR MAKING INSULTS AT EACH OTHER.

*Mask: Insult

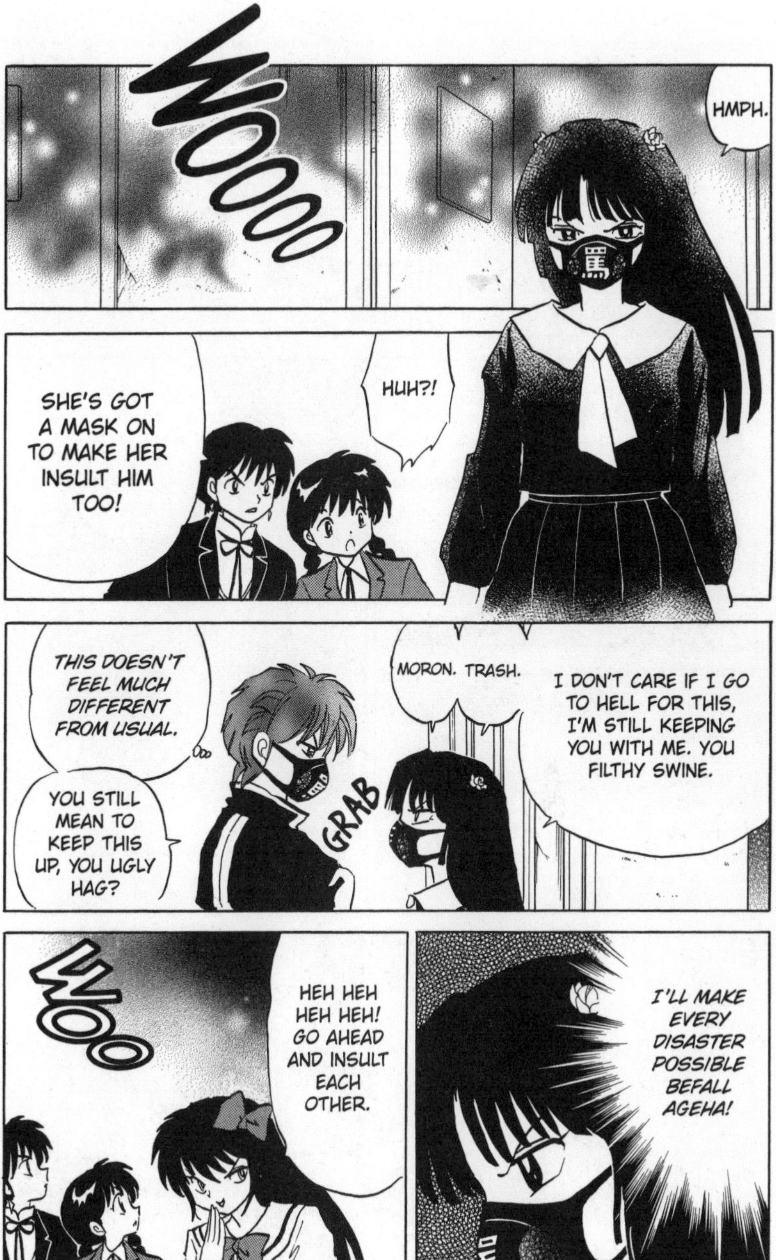
HMPH.
WOOOOO
HUH?!
SHE'S GOT A MASK ON TO MAKE HER INSULT HIM TOO!
I DON'T CARE IF I GO TO HELL FOR THIS, I'M STILL KEEPING YOU WITH ME. YOU FILTHY SWINE.
MORON. TRASH.
GRAB
THIS DOESN'T FEEL MUCH DIFFERENT FROM USUAL.
YOU STILL MEAN TO KEEP THIS UP, YOU UGLY HAG?
I'LL MAKE EVERY DISASTER POSSIBLE BEFALL AGEHA!
HEH HEH HEH HEH! GO AHEAD AND INSULT EACH OTHER.
WOO

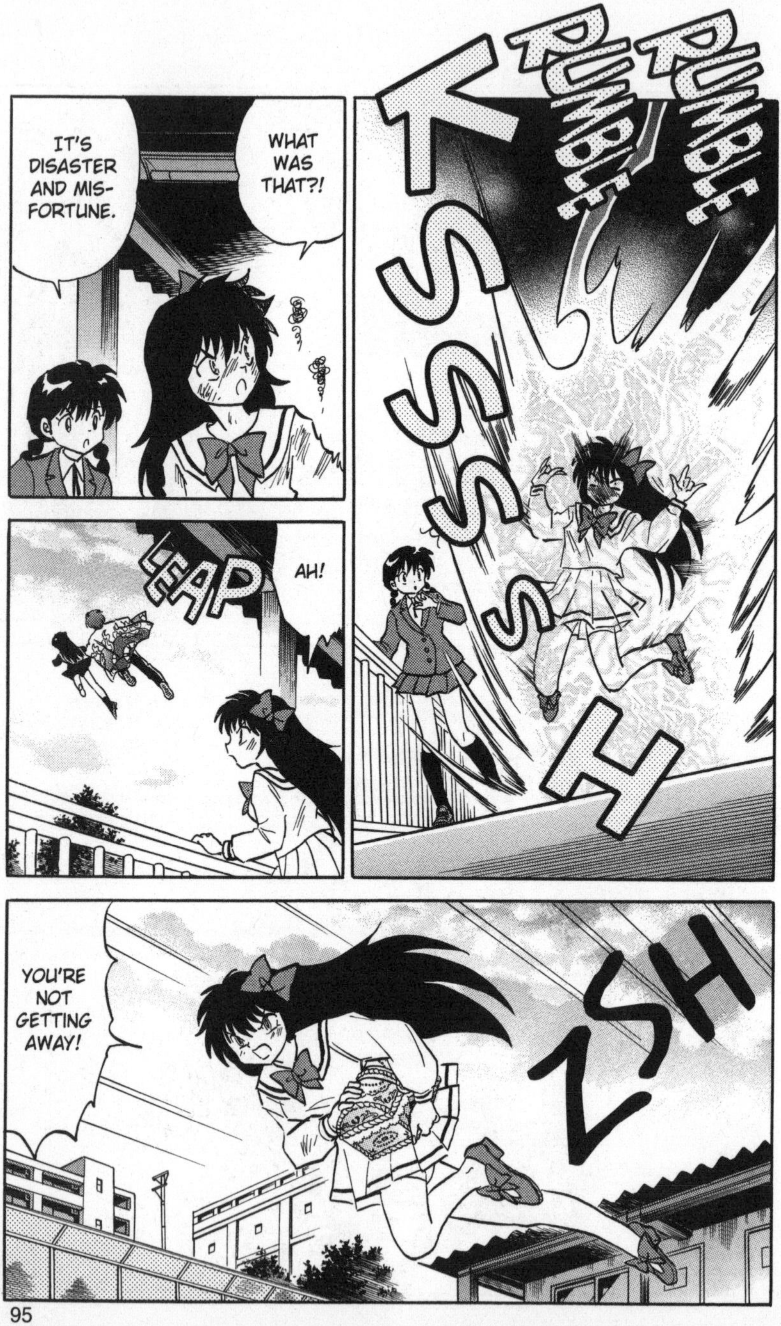

RUMBLE
RUMBLE
KSSSSH
WHAT WAS THAT?!
IT'S DISASTER AND MIS-FORTUNE.
AH!
LEAP
ZSH
YOU'RE NOT GETTING AWAY!

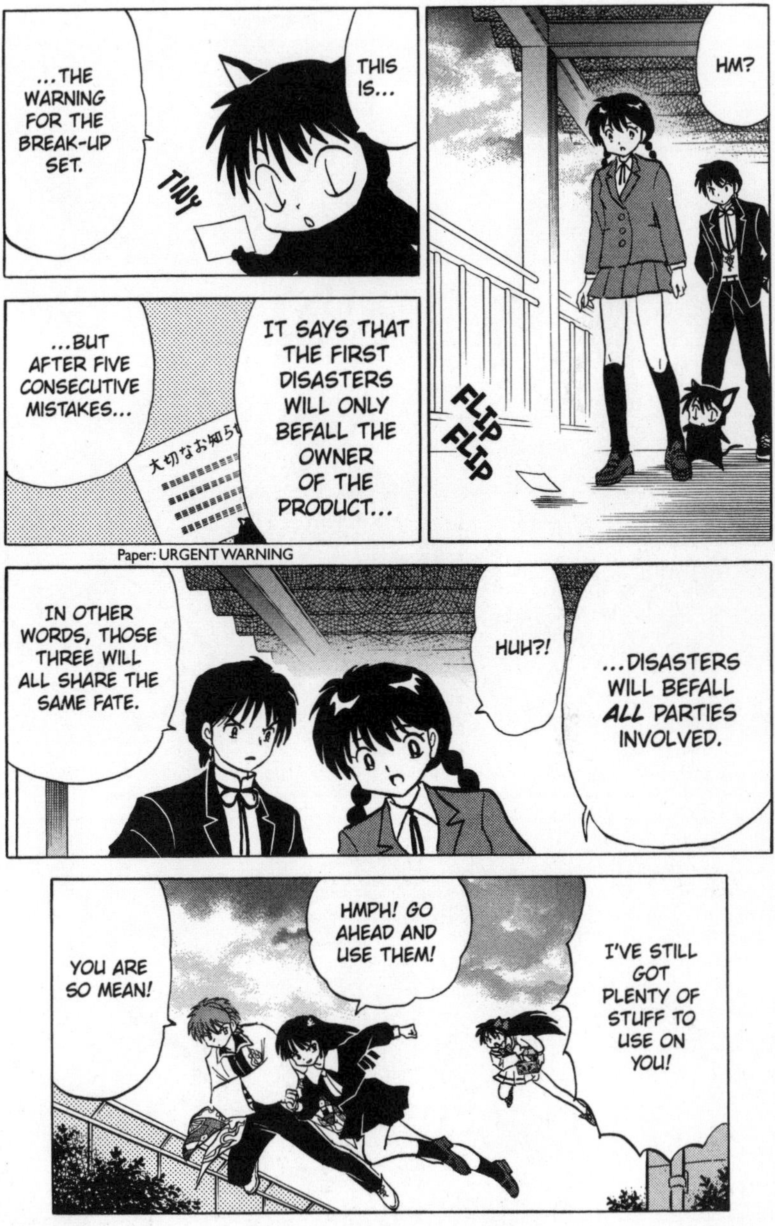
HM?
FLIP
FLIP
THIS IS...
TINY
...THE WARNING FOR THE BREAK-UP SET.
IT SAYS THAT THE FIRST DISASTERS WILL ONLY BEFALL THE OWNER OF THE PRODUCT...
...BUT AFTER FIVE CONSECUTIVE MISTAKES...
Paper: URGENT WARNING
...DISASTERS WILL BEFALL ALL PARTIES INVOLVED.
HUH?!
IN OTHER WORDS, THOSE THREE WILL ALL SHARE THE SAME FATE.
I'VE STILL GOT PLENTY OF STUFF TO USE ON YOU!
HMPH! GO AHEAD AND USE THEM!
YOU ARE SO MEAN!

CHAPTER 144: THE BREAK-UP GOD

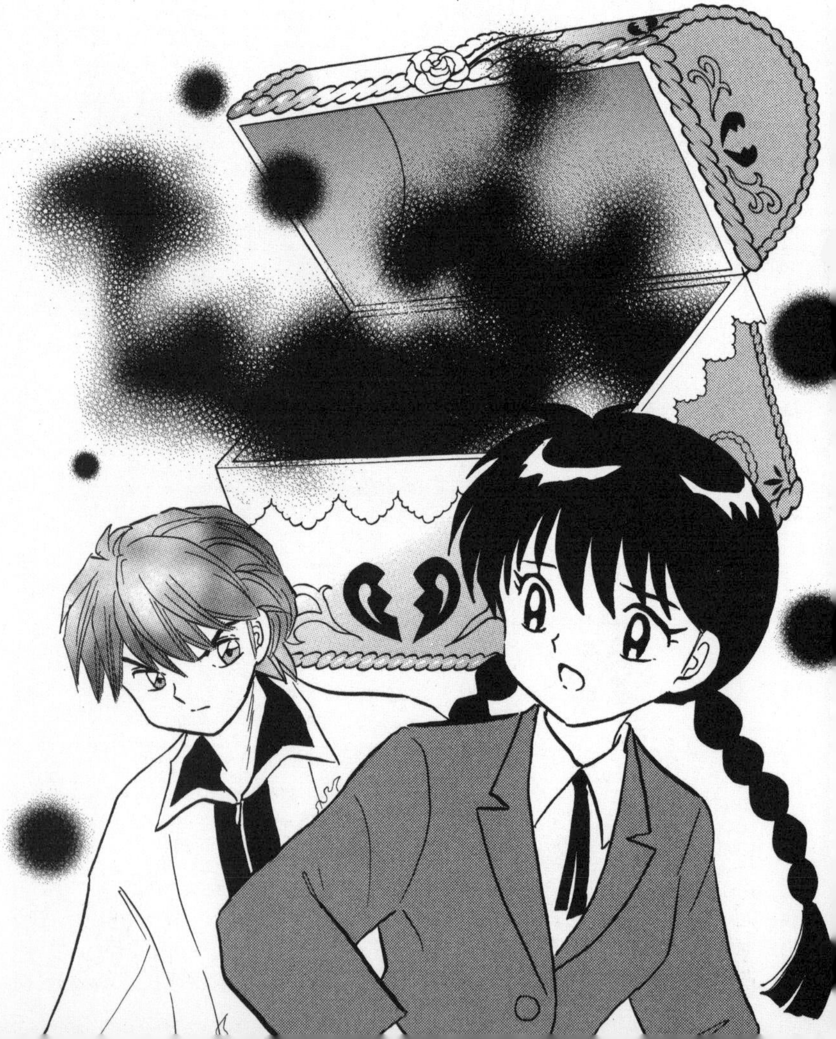

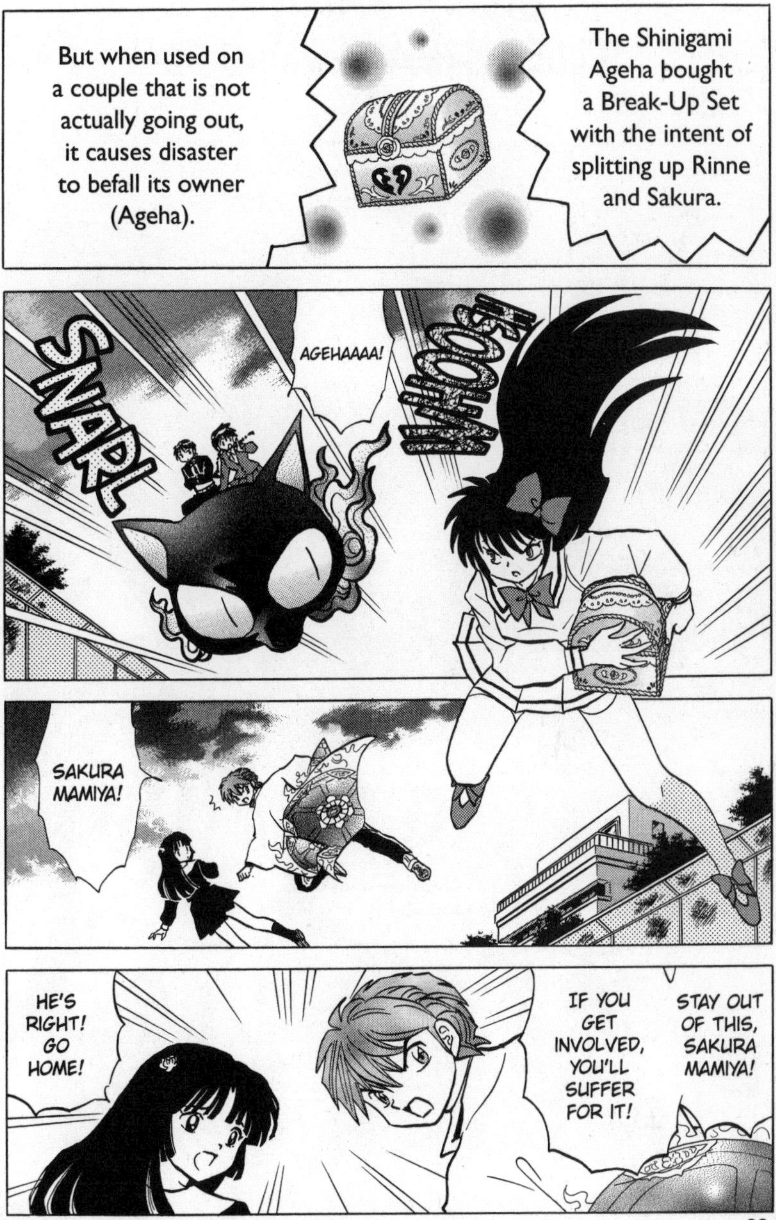
The Shinigami Ageha bought a Break-Up Set with the intent of splitting up Rinne and Sakura.
But when used on a couple that is not actually going out, it causes disaster to befall its owner (Ageha).
WHOOSH
AGEHAAAA!
SNARL
SAKURA MAMIYA!
STAY OUT OF THIS, SAKURA MAMIYA!
IF YOU GET INVOLVED, YOU'LL SUFFER FOR IT!
HE'S RIGHT! GO HOME!

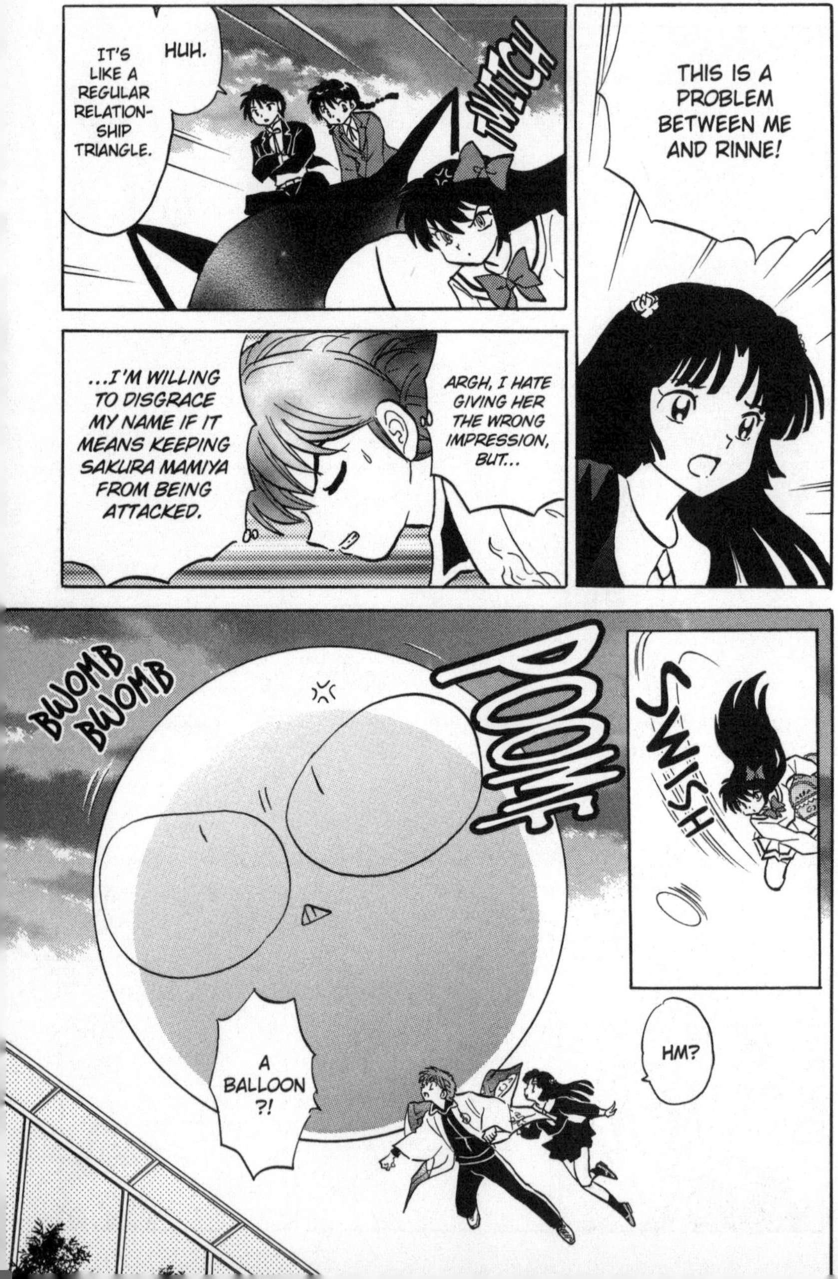
THIS IS A PROBLEM BETWEEN ME AND RINNE!
HUH.
IT'S LIKE A REGULAR RELATION-SHIP TRIANGLE.
TWITCH
ARGH, I HATE GIVING HER THE WRONG IMPRESSION, BUT...
...I'M WILLING TO DISGRACE MY NAME IF IT MEANS KEEPING SAKURA MAMIYA FROM BEING ATTACKED.
SWISH
POOMF
BWOMB BWOMB
HM?
A BALLOON ?!

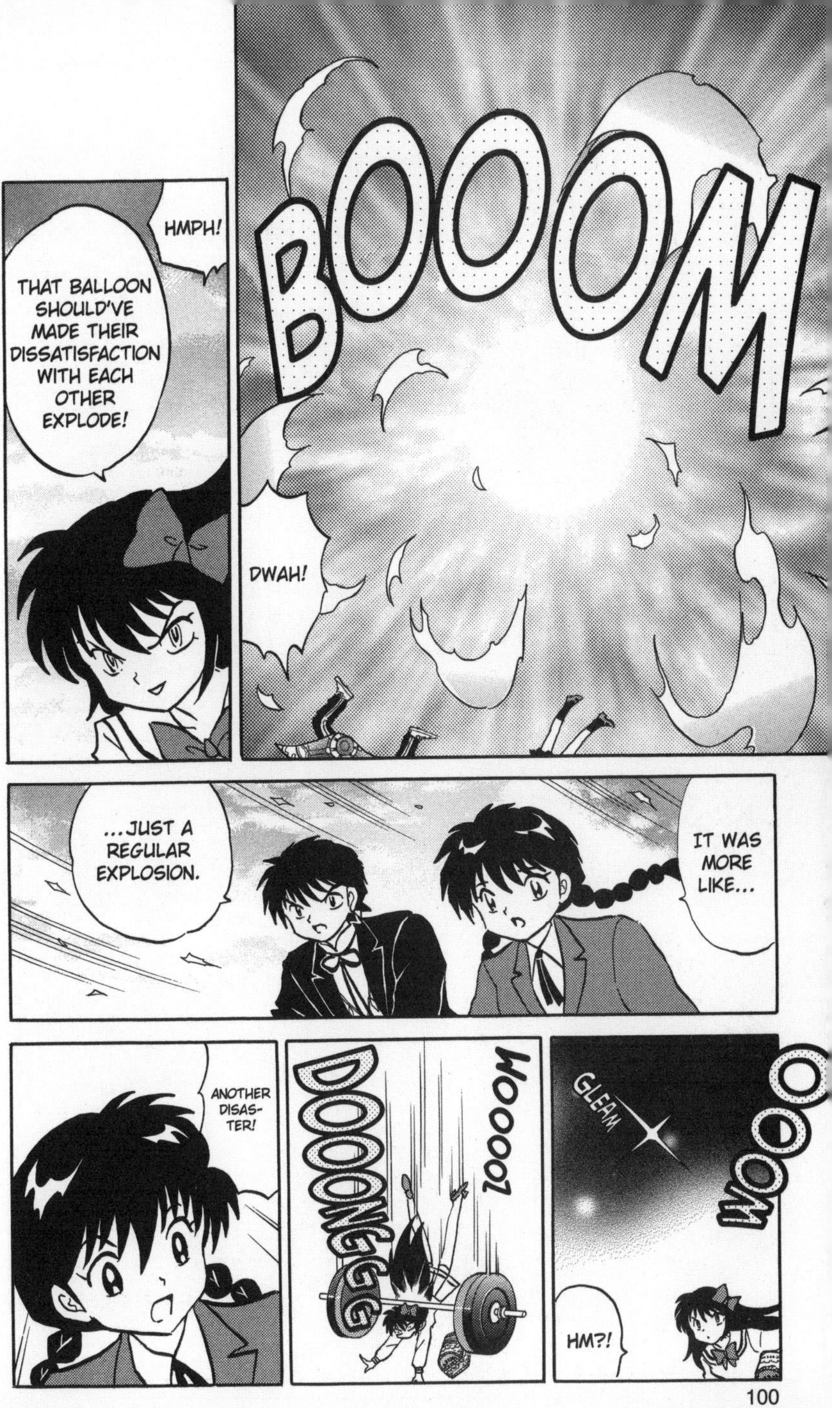
BOOOM
DWAH!
HMPH!
THAT BALLOON SHOULD'VE MADE THEIR DISSATISFACTION WITH EACH OTHER EXPLODE!
IT WAS MORE LIKE...
...JUST A REGULAR EXPLOSION.
WOOOO
GLEAM
HM?!
DOOONGG
ANOTHER DISAS-TER!

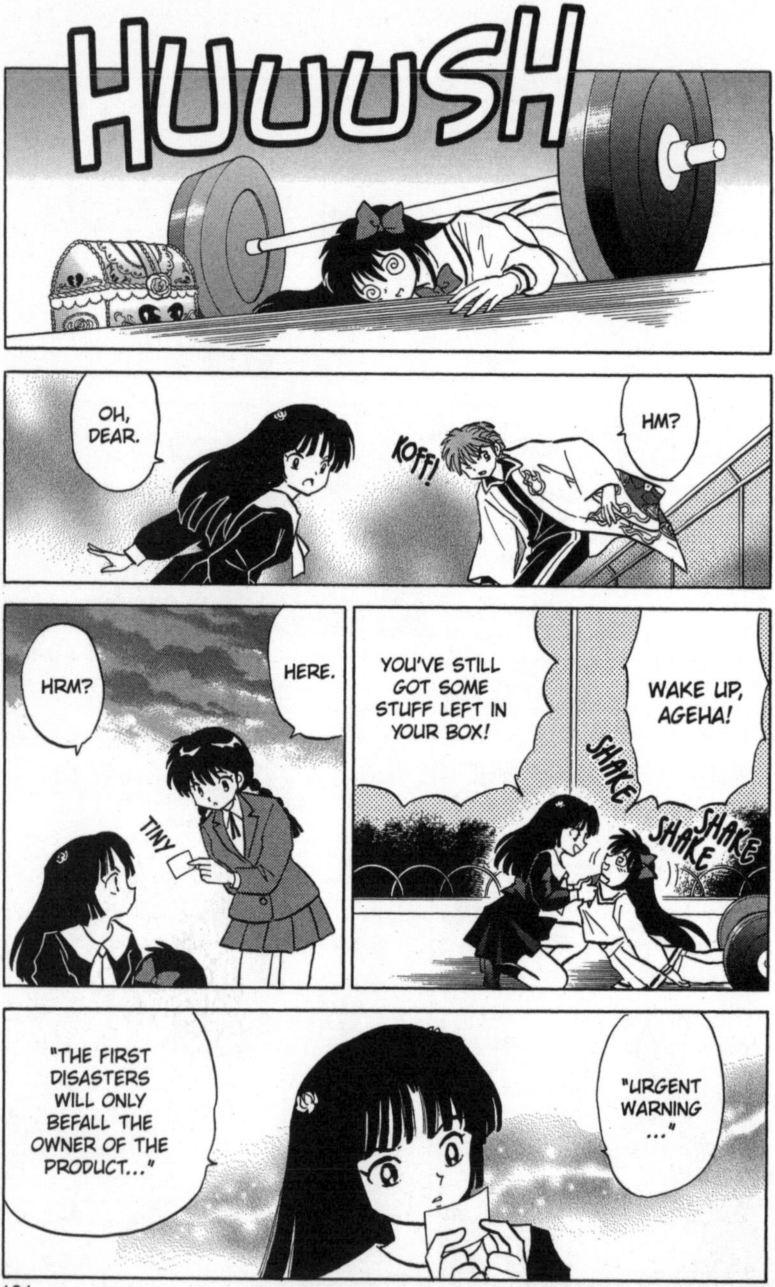
HUUUSH
HM?
KOFF!
OH, DEAR.
WAKE UP, AGEHA!
YOU'VE STILL GOT SOME STUFF LEFT IN YOUR BOX!
SHAKE
SHAKE SHAKE
HERE.
HRM?
TINY
"URGENT WARNING ..."
"THE FIRST DISASTERS WILL ONLY BEFALL THE OWNER OF THE PRODUCT..."

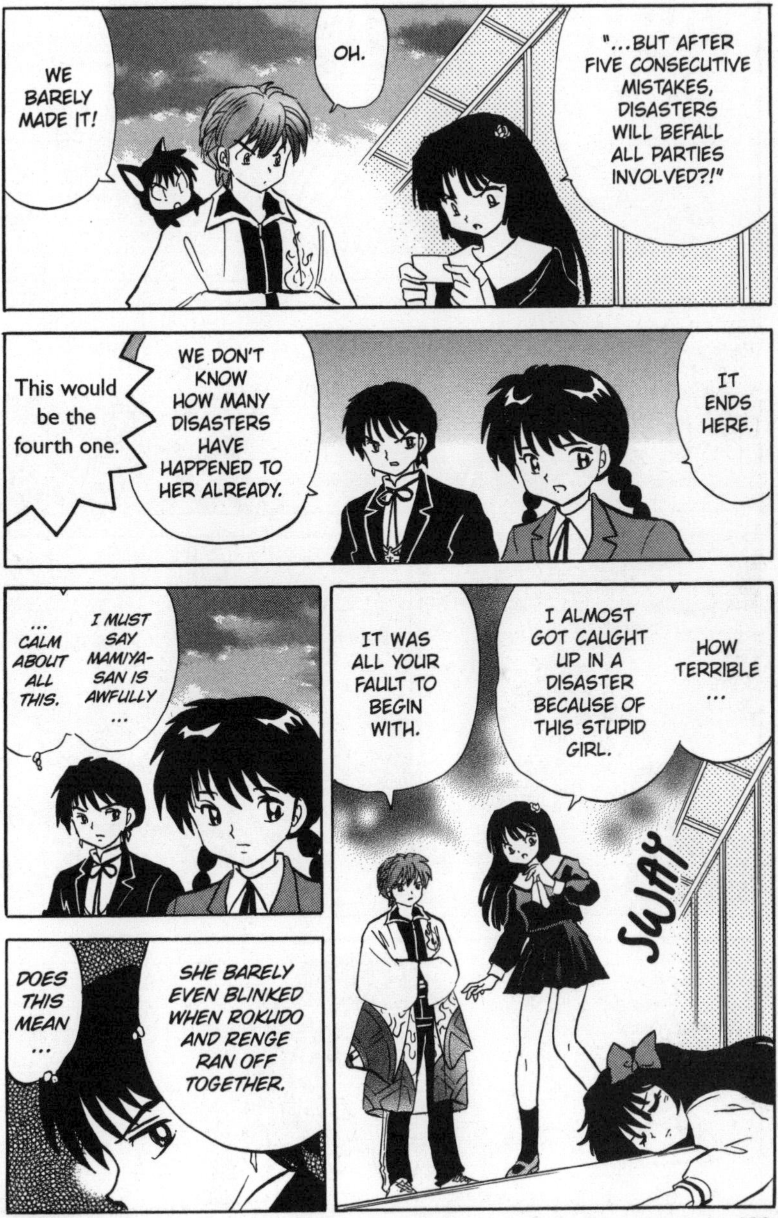
"...BUT AFTER FIVE CONSECUTIVE MISTAKES, DISASTERS WILL BEFALL ALL PARTIES INVOLVED?!"
OH.
WE BARELY MADE IT!
IT ENDS HERE.
WE DON'T KNOW HOW MANY DISASTERS HAVE HAPPENED TO HER ALREADY.
This would be the fourth one.
HOW TERRIBLE...
I ALMOST GOT CAUGHT UP IN A DISASTER BECAUSE OF THIS STUPID GIRL.
IT WAS ALL YOUR FAULT TO BEGIN WITH.
SWAY
I MUST SAY MAMIYA-SAN IS AWFULLY...
...CALM ABOUT ALL THIS.
SHE BARELY EVEN BLINKED WHEN ROKUDO AND RENGE RAN OFF TOGETHER.
DOES THIS MEAN...

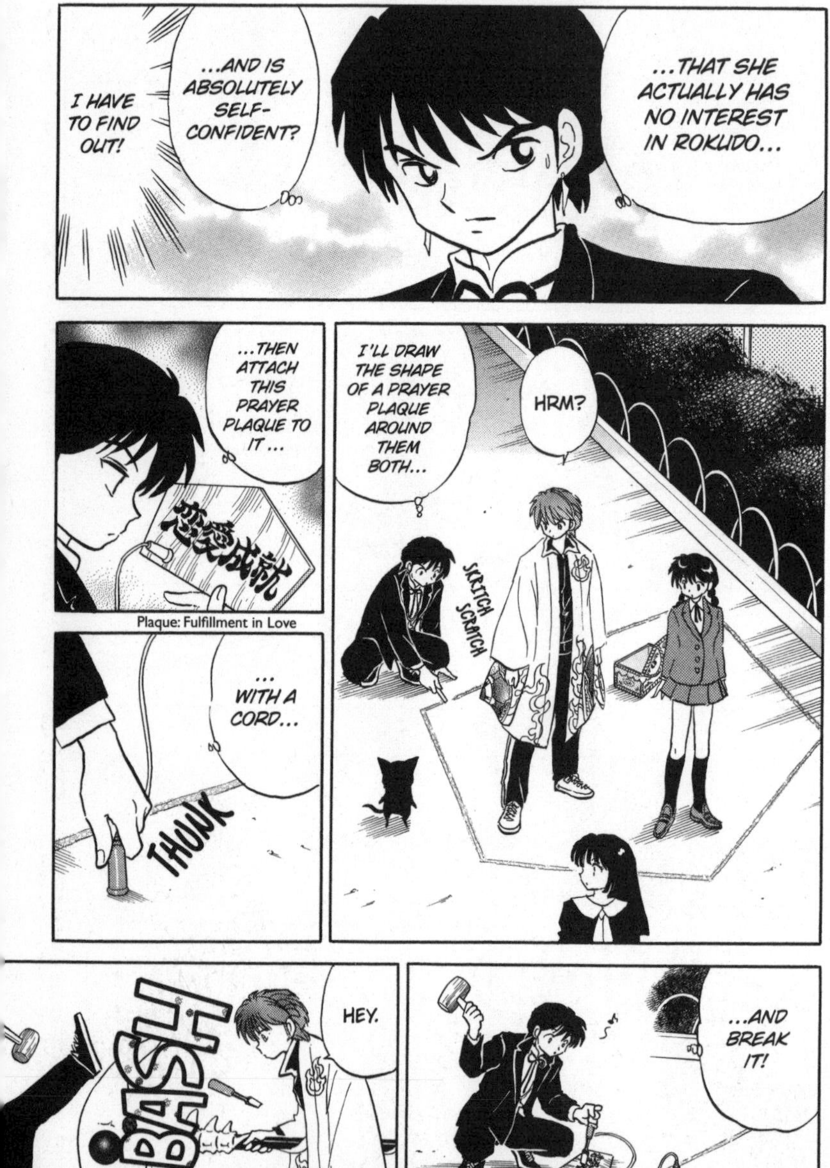
...THAT SHE ACTUALLY HAS NO INTEREST IN ROKUDO...
...AND IS ABSOLUTELY SELF-CONFIDENT?
I HAVE TO FIND OUT!
HRM?
I'LL DRAW THE SHAPE OF A PRAYER PLAQUE AROUND THEM BOTH...
SKRITCH SCRATCH
...THEN ATTACH THIS PRAYER PLAQUE TO IT...
恋愛成就
Plaque: Fulfillment in Love
... WITH A CORD...
THUNK
...AND BREAK IT!
HEY.
BASH

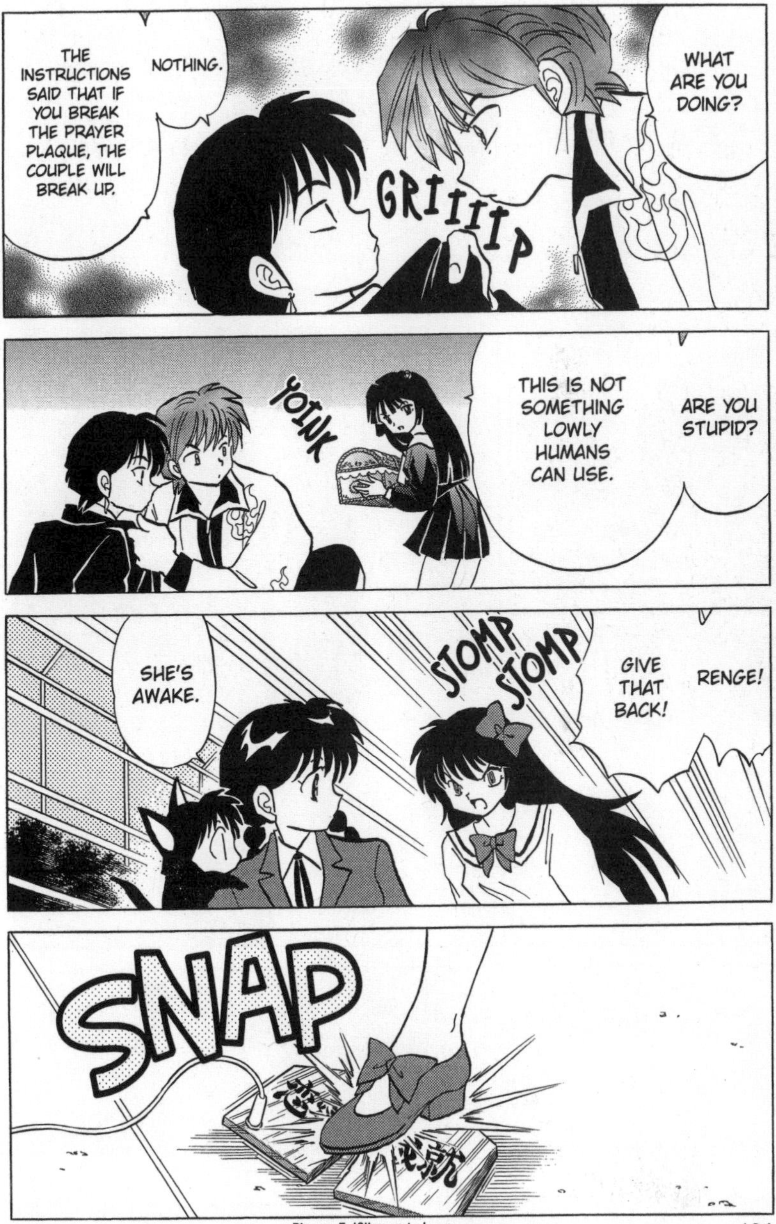
WHAT ARE YOU DOING?
GRIIIIP
NOTHING.
THE INSTRUCTIONS SAID THAT IF YOU BREAK THE PRAYER PLAQUE, THE COUPLE WILL BREAK UP.
ARE YOU STUPID?
THIS IS NOT SOMETHING LOWLY HUMANS CAN USE.
YOINK
RENGE!
GIVE THAT BACK!
STOMP STOMP
SHE'S AWAKE.
SNAP
Plaque: Fulfillment in Love

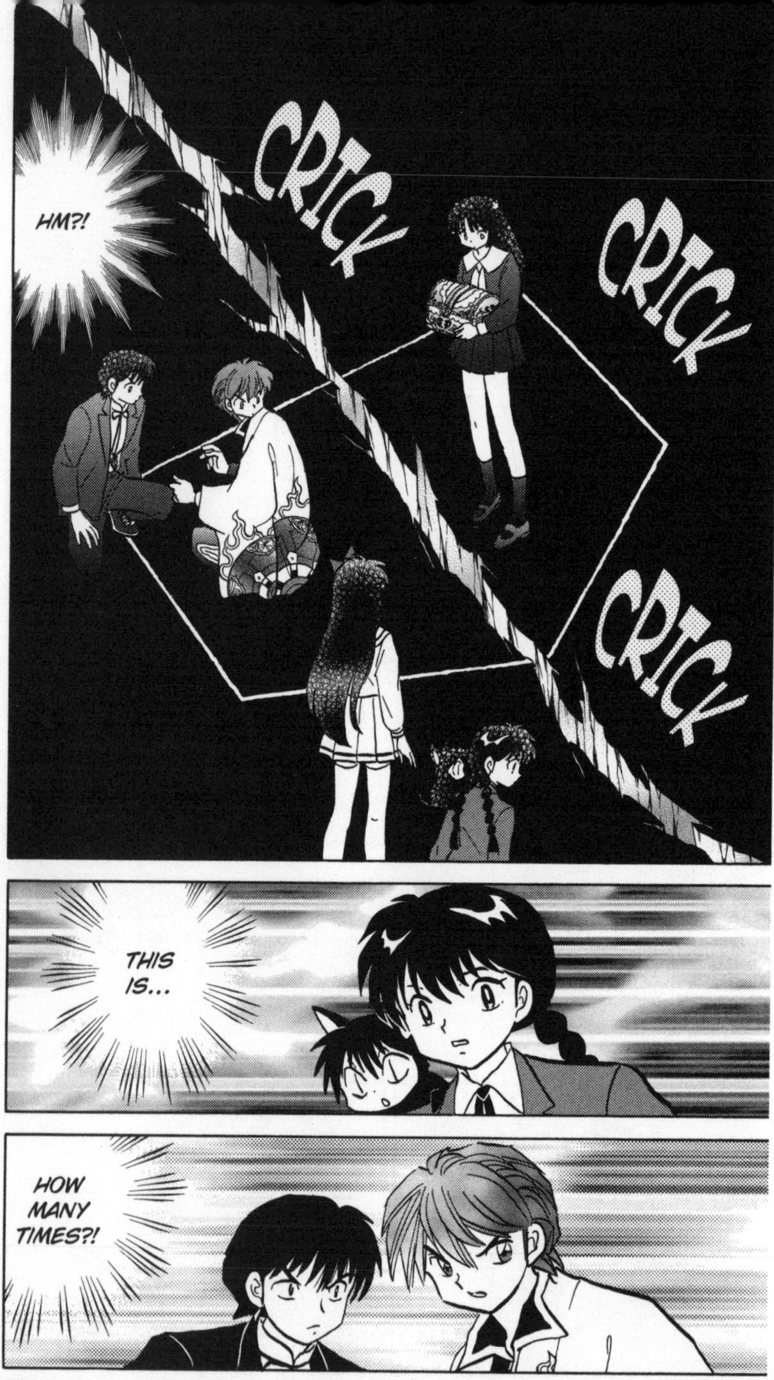
CRICK
CRICK
CRICK
HM?!
THIS IS...
HOW MANY TIMES?!

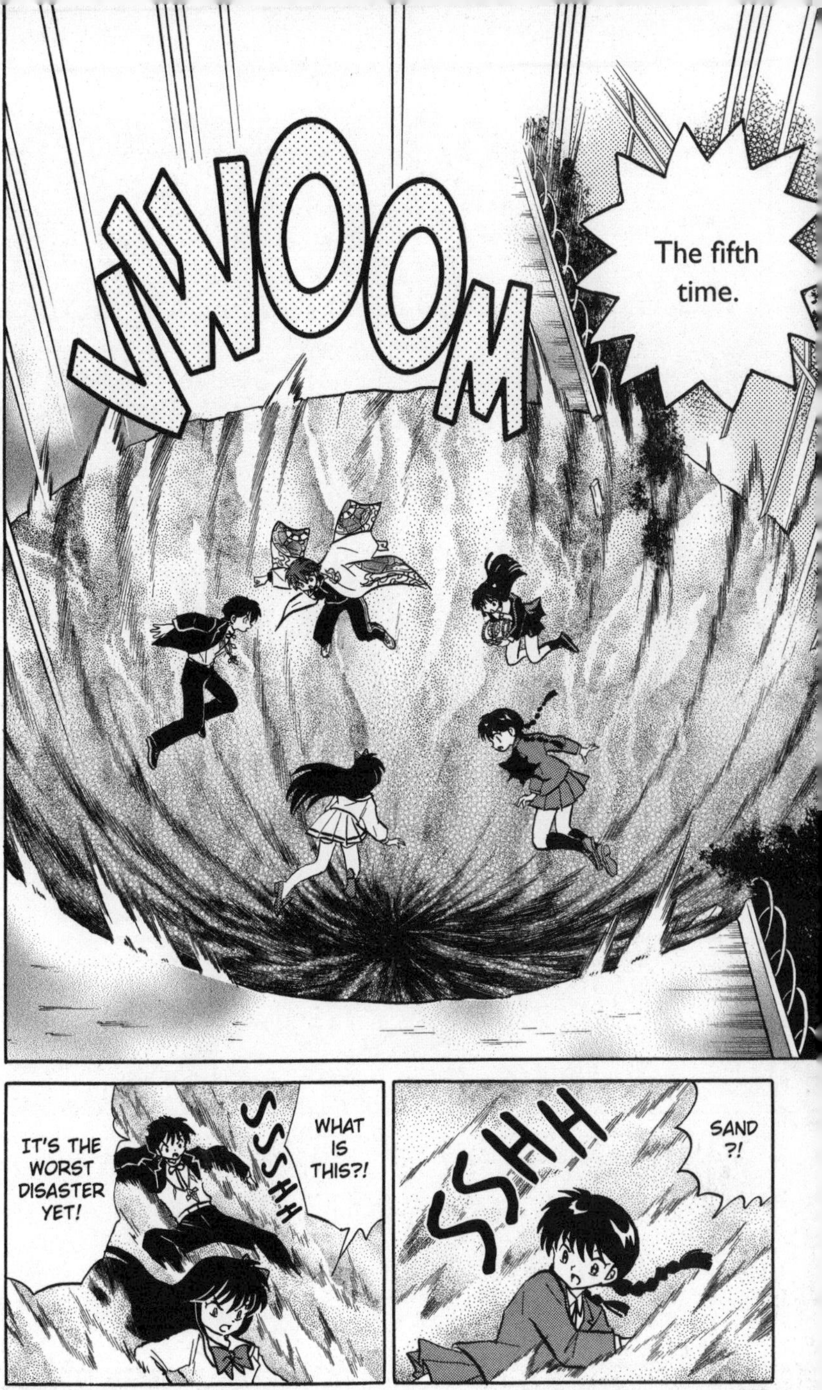
The fifth time.
VWOOM
SAND ?!
SHH
WHAT IS THIS?!
SSSHH
IT'S THE WORST DISASTER YET!

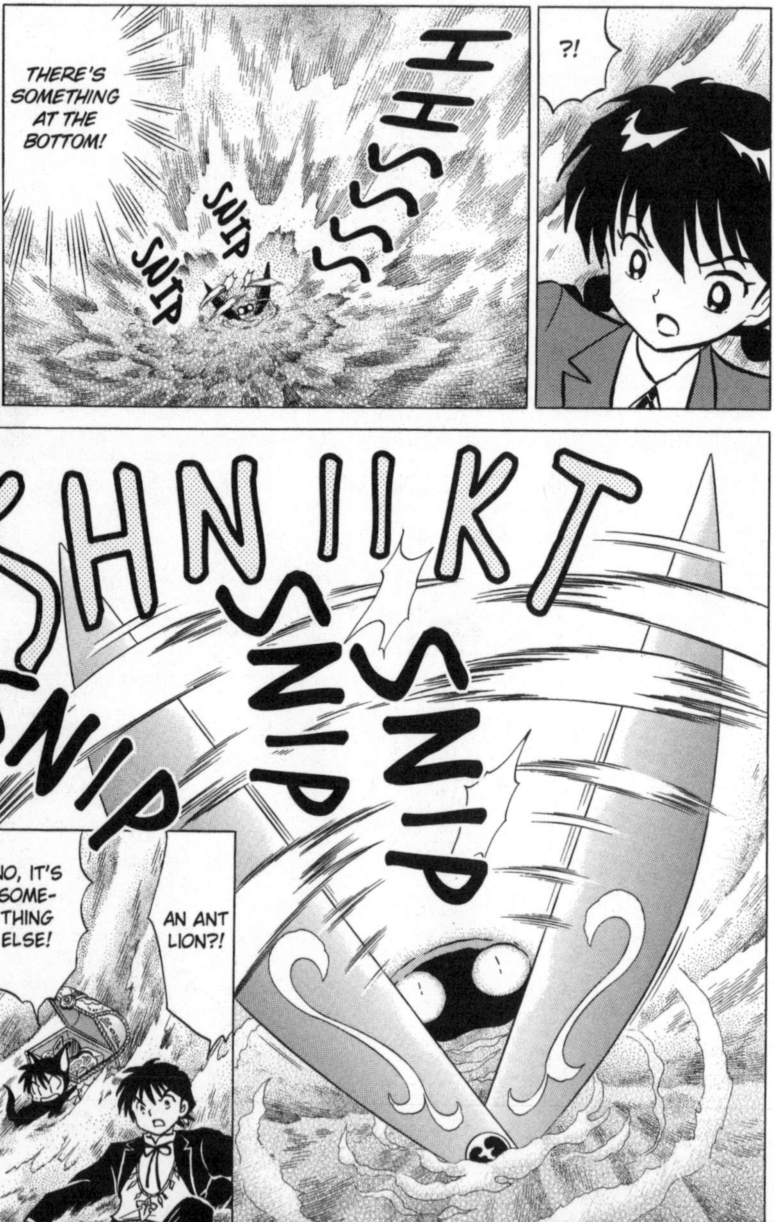
?!
THERE'S SOMETHING AT THE BOTTOM!
SNIP
SNIP
SHNIIKT
SNIP
SNIP
SNIP
AN ANT LION?!
NO, IT'S SOME-THING ELSE!

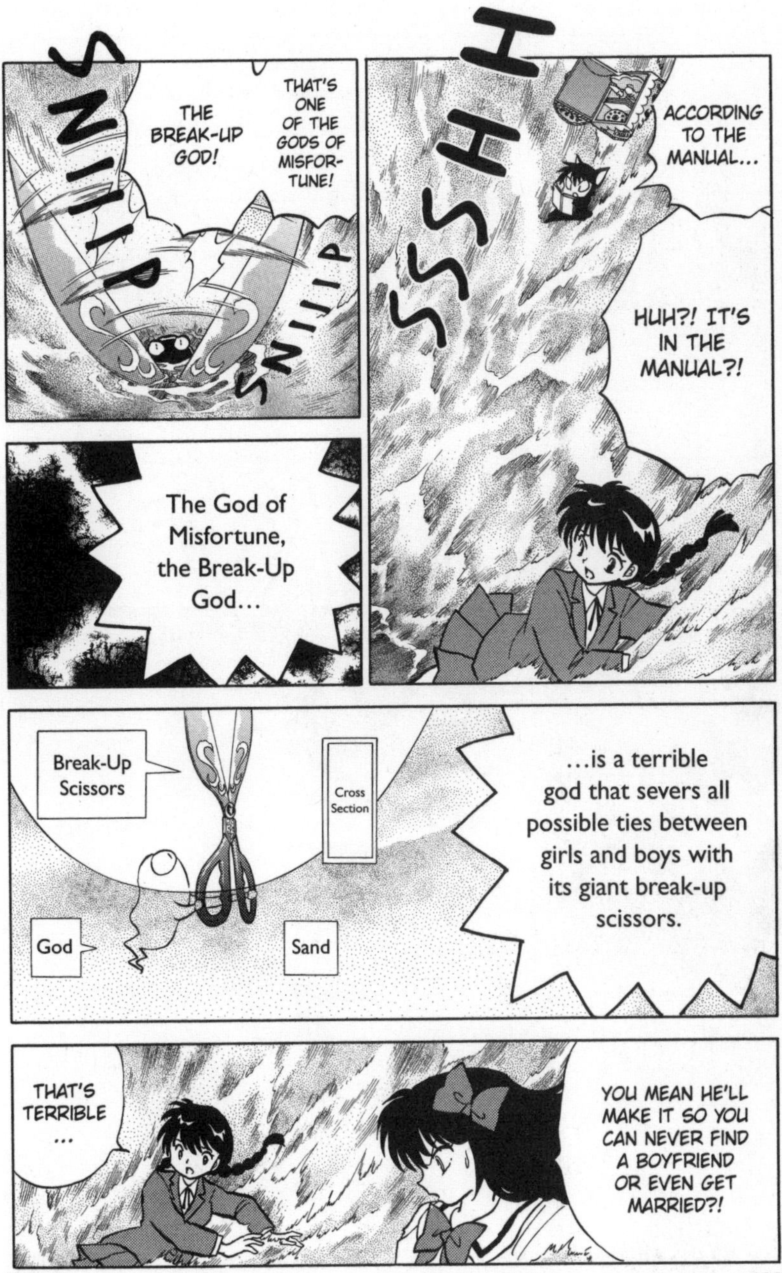
SSSHH
ACCORDING TO THE MANUAL...
HUH?! IT'S IN THE MANUAL?!
SNIIIP
THAT'S ONE OF THE GODS OF MISFORTUNE!
THE BREAK-UP GOD!
SNIIIP
The God of Misfortune, the Break-Up God...
...is a terrible god that severs all possible ties between girls and boys with its giant break-up scissors.
Cross Section
Break-Up Scissors
Sand
God
YOU MEAN HE'LL MAKE IT SO YOU CAN NEVER FIND A BOYFRIEND OR EVEN GET MARRIED?!
THAT'S TERRIBLE ...

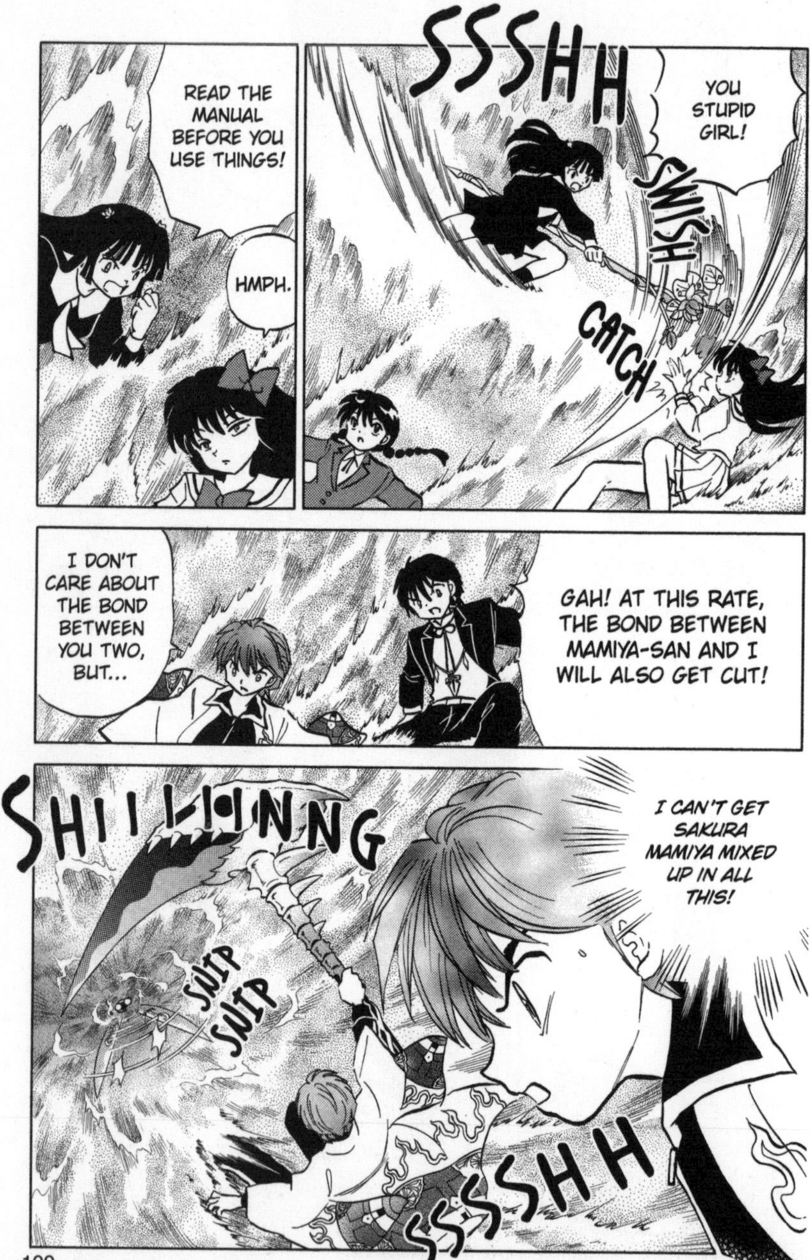
SSSHH
YOU STUPID GIRL!
SWISH
CATCH
READ THE MANUAL BEFORE YOU USE THINGS!
HMPH.
GAH! AT THIS RATE, THE BOND BETWEEN MAMIYA-SAN AND I WILL ALSO GET CUT!
I DON'T CARE ABOUT THE BOND BETWEEN YOU TWO, BUT...
I CAN'T GET SAKURA MAMIYA MIXED UP IN ALL THIS!
SHIIIINNG
SNIP SNIP
SSSSHH

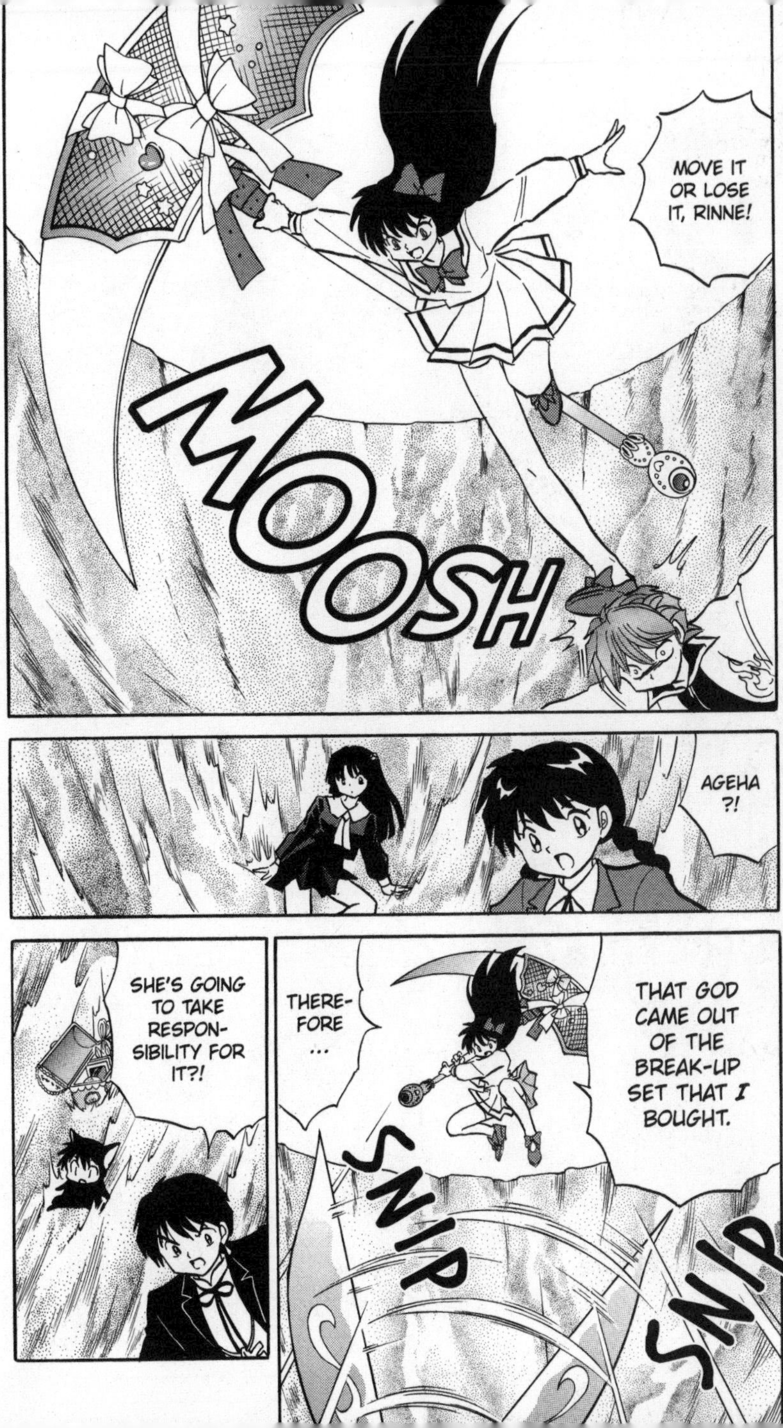
MOVE IT OR LOSE IT, RINNE!
MOOSH
AGEHA ?!
THAT GOD CAME OUT OF THE BREAK-UP SET THAT *I* BOUGHT.
THERE-FORE ...
SNIP
SNIP
SHE'S GOING TO TAKE RESPON-SIBILITY FOR IT?!

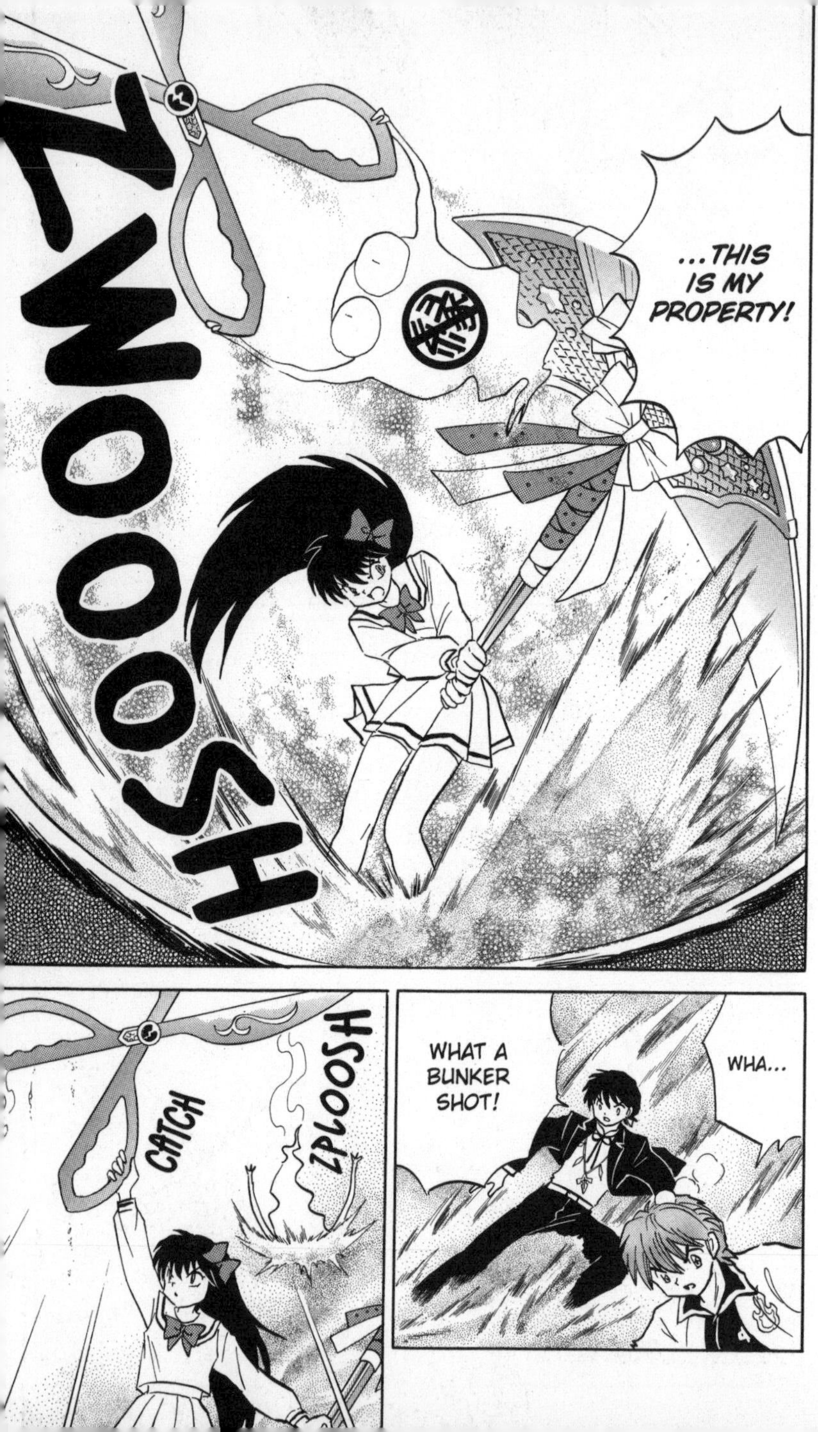
...THIS IS MY PROPERTY!
ZWOOSH
WHA...
WHAT A BUNKER SHOT!
ZPLOOSH
CATCH

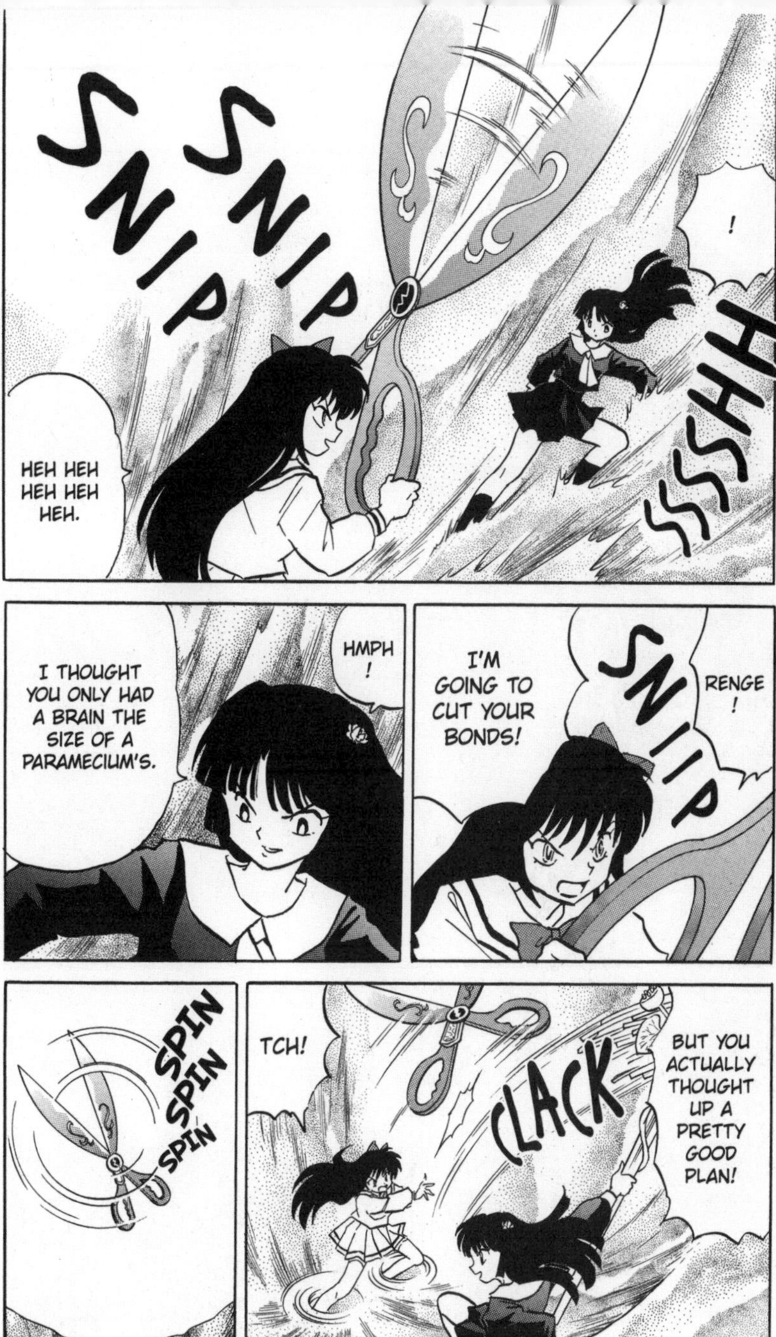
!
SSSHH
SNIP SNIP
HEH HEH HEH HEH HEH.
RENGE!
SNIIP
I'M GOING TO CUT YOUR BONDS!
HMPH!
I THOUGHT YOU ONLY HAD A BRAIN THE SIZE OF A PARAMECIUM'S.
BUT YOU ACTUALLY THOUGHT UP A PRETTY GOOD PLAN!
CLACK
TCH!
SPIN SPIN SPIN

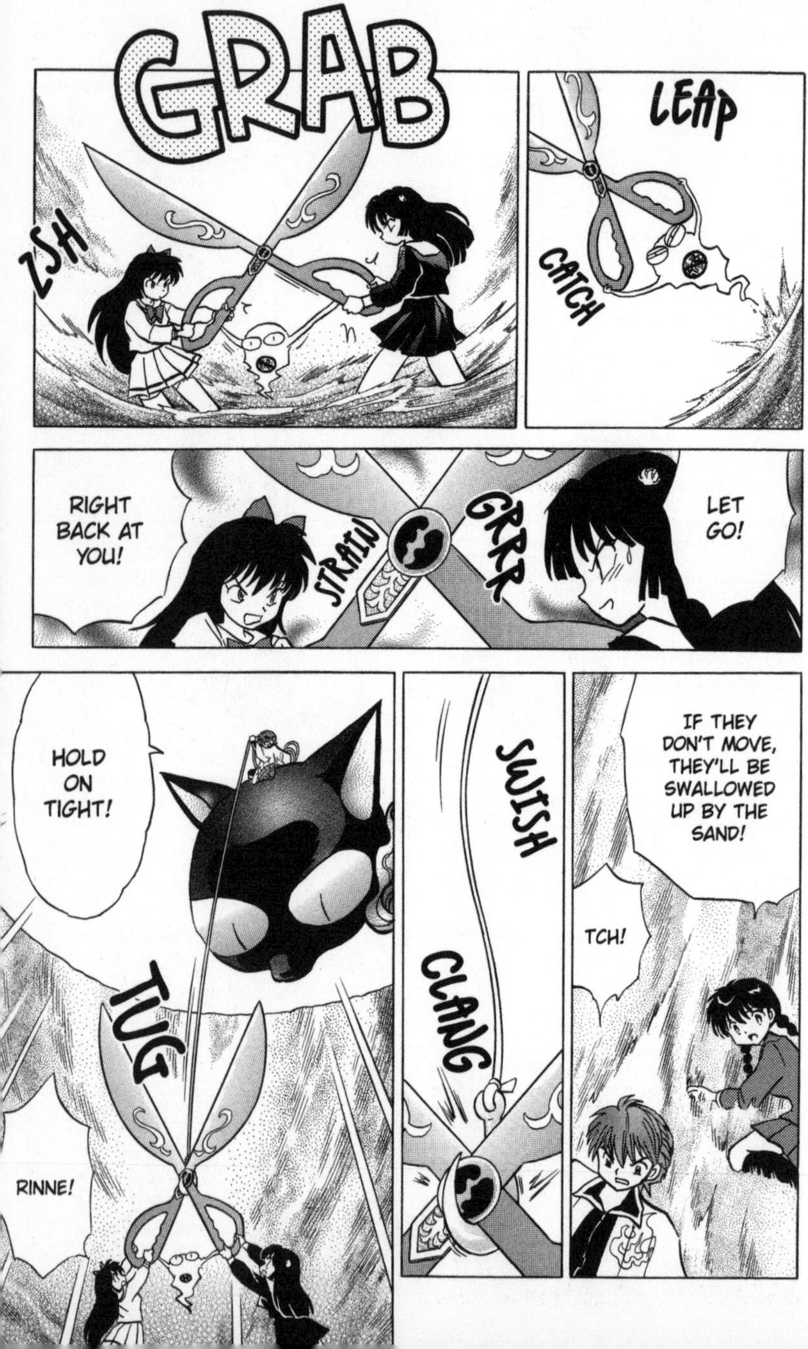
LEAP
CATCH
GRAB
ZSH
LET GO!
GRRR
STRAIN
RIGHT BACK AT YOU!
IF THEY DON'T MOVE, THEY'LL BE SWALLOWED UP BY THE SAND!
TCH!
SWISH
CLANG
HOLD ON TIGHT!
TUG
RINNE!

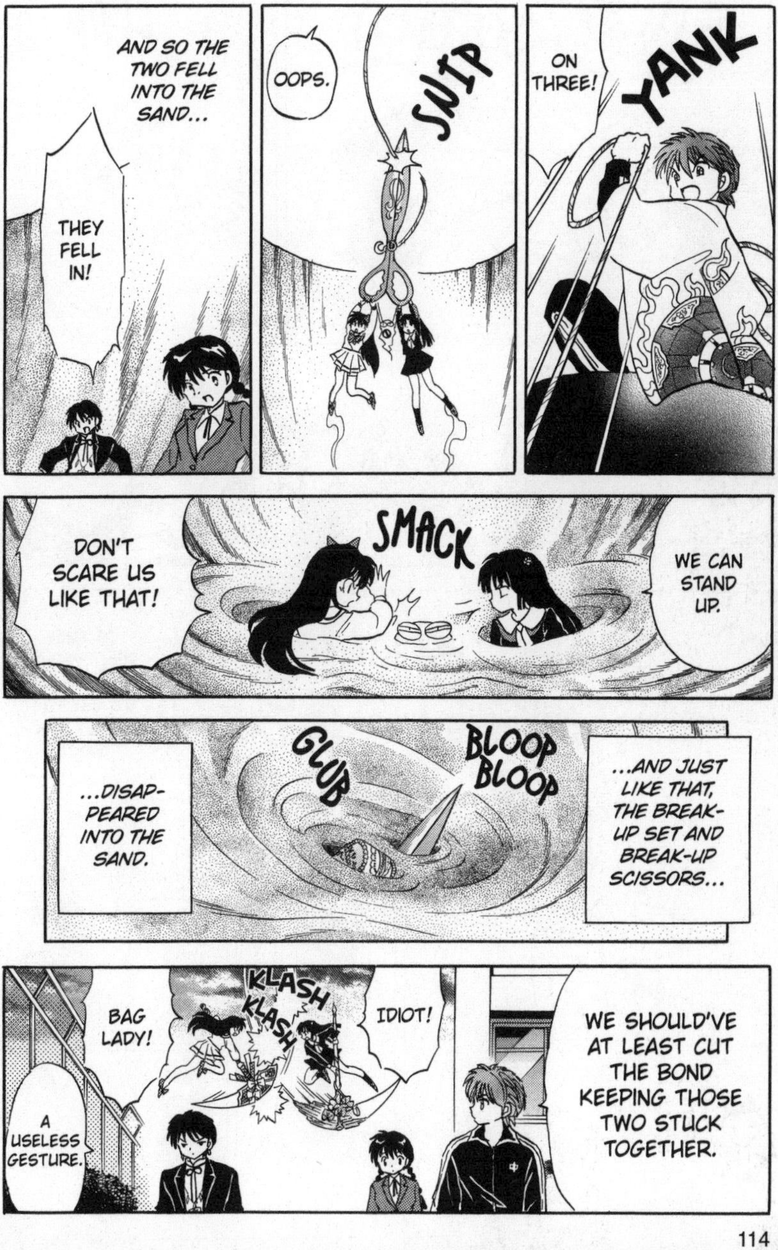
ON THREE!
YANK
OOPS.
SNIP
AND SO THE TWO FELL INTO THE SAND...
THEY FELL IN!
WE CAN STAND UP.
SMACK
DON'T SCARE US LIKE THAT!
...AND JUST LIKE THAT, THE BREAK-UP SET AND BREAK-UP SCISSORS...
BLOOP BLOOP
GLUB
...DISAP-PEARED INTO THE SAND.
WE SHOULD'VE AT LEAST CUT THE BOND KEEPING THOSE TWO STUCK TOGETHER.
IDIOT!
KLASH KLASH
BAG LADY!
A USELESS GESTURE.

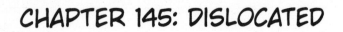

CHAPTER 145: DISLOCATED

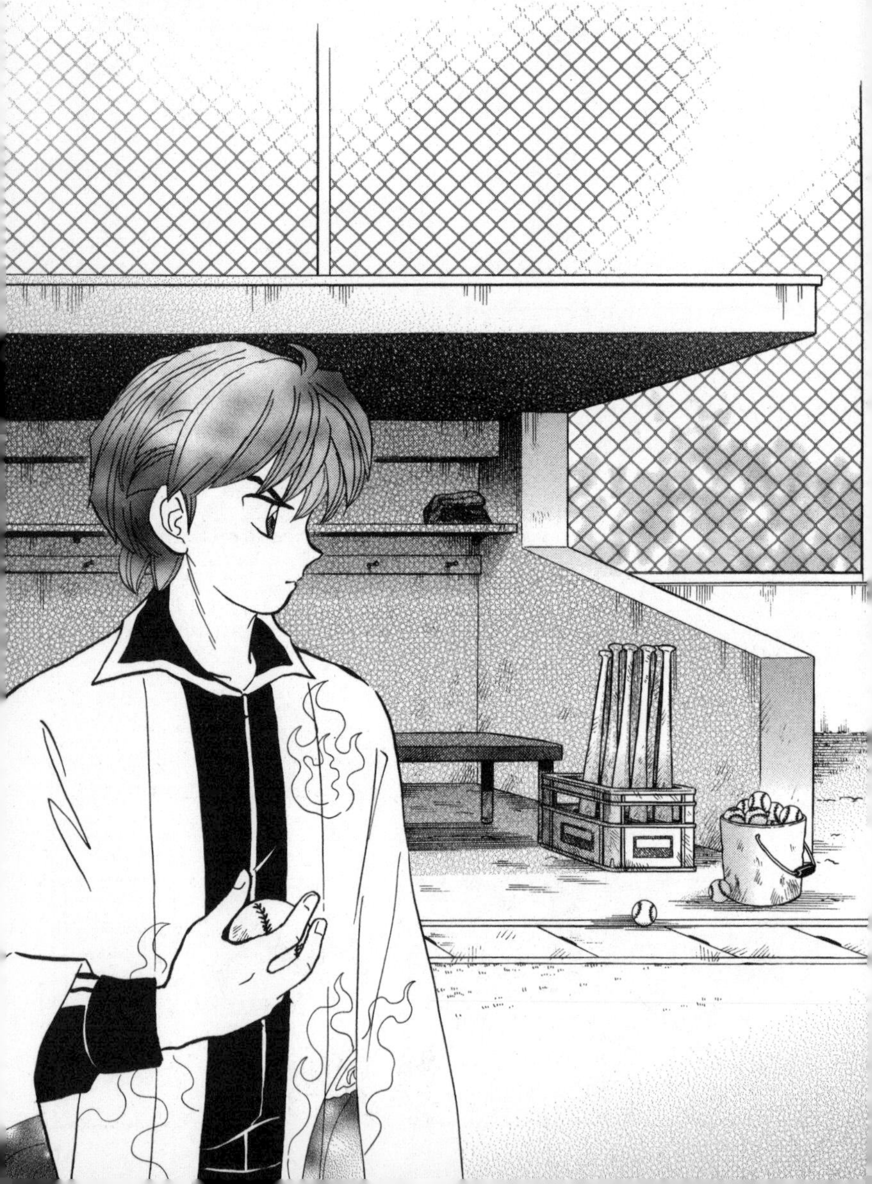

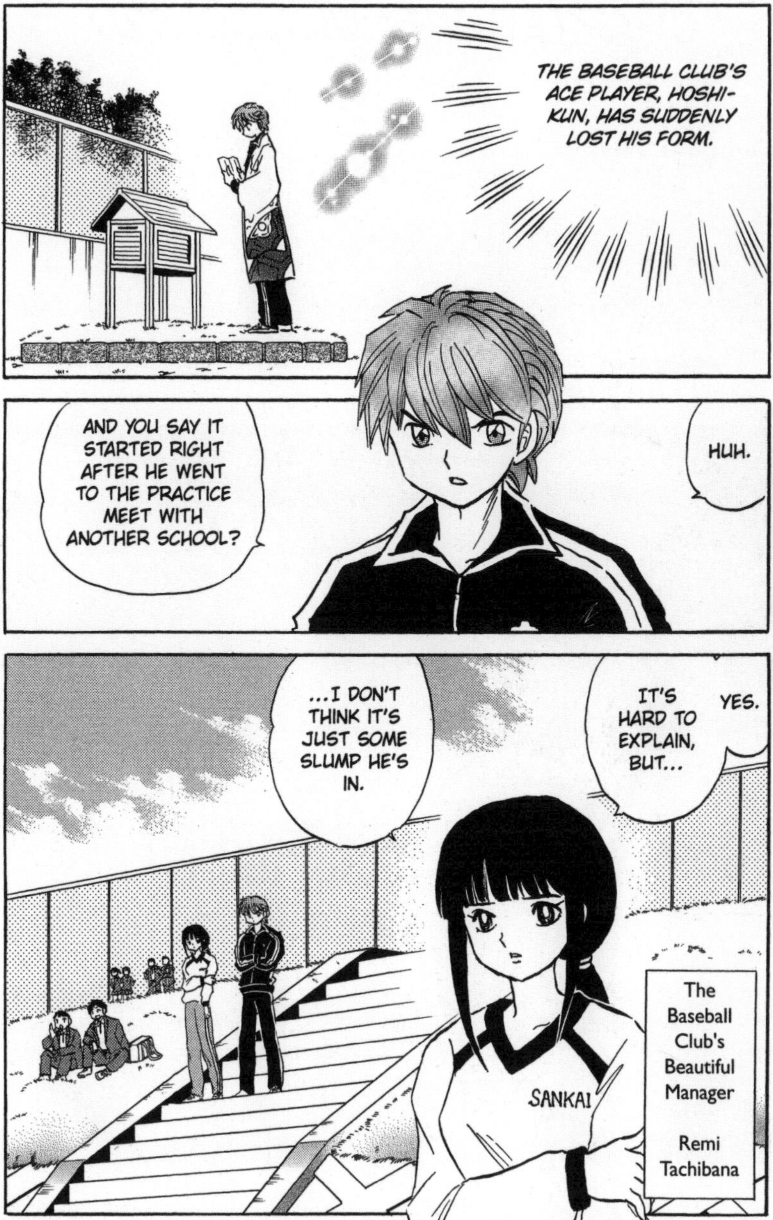
THE BASEBALL CLUB'S ACE PLAYER, HOSHI-KUN, HAS SUDDENLY LOST HIS FORM.
HUH.
AND YOU SAY IT STARTED RIGHT AFTER HE WENT TO THE PRACTICE MEET WITH ANOTHER SCHOOL?
YES.
IT'S HARD TO EXPLAIN, BUT...
...I DON'T THINK IT'S JUST SOME SLUMP HE'S IN.
SANKAI
The Baseball Club's Beautiful Manager
Remi Tachibana

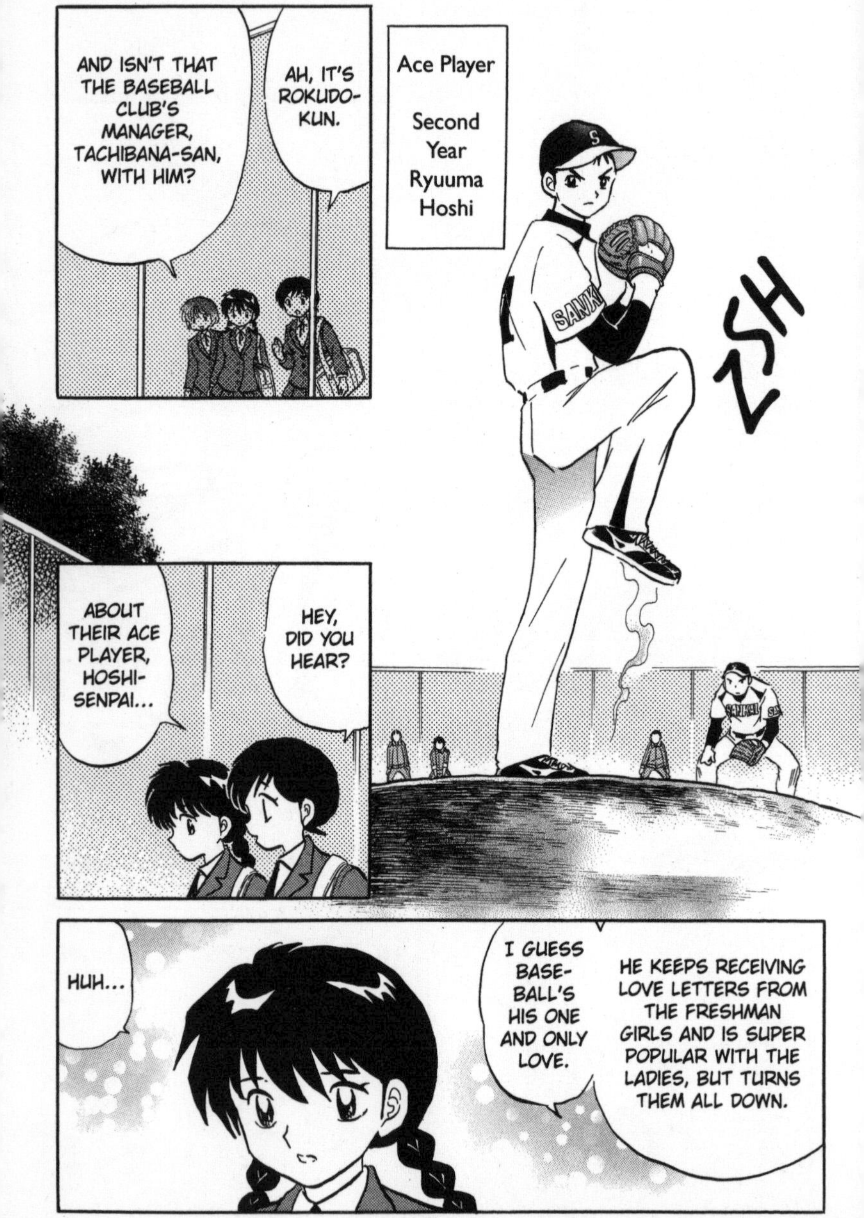
Ace Player
Second Year Ryuuma Hoshi
ZSH
AH, IT'S ROKUDO-KUN.
AND ISN'T THAT THE BASEBALL CLUB'S MANAGER, TACHIBANA-SAN, WITH HIM?
HEY, DID YOU HEAR?
ABOUT THEIR ACE PLAYER, HOSHI-SENPAI...
HE KEEPS RECEIVING LOVE LETTERS FROM THE FRESHMAN GIRLS AND IS SUPER POPULAR WITH THE LADIES, BUT TURNS THEM ALL DOWN.
I GUESS BASE-BALL'S HIS ONE AND ONLY LOVE.
HUH...

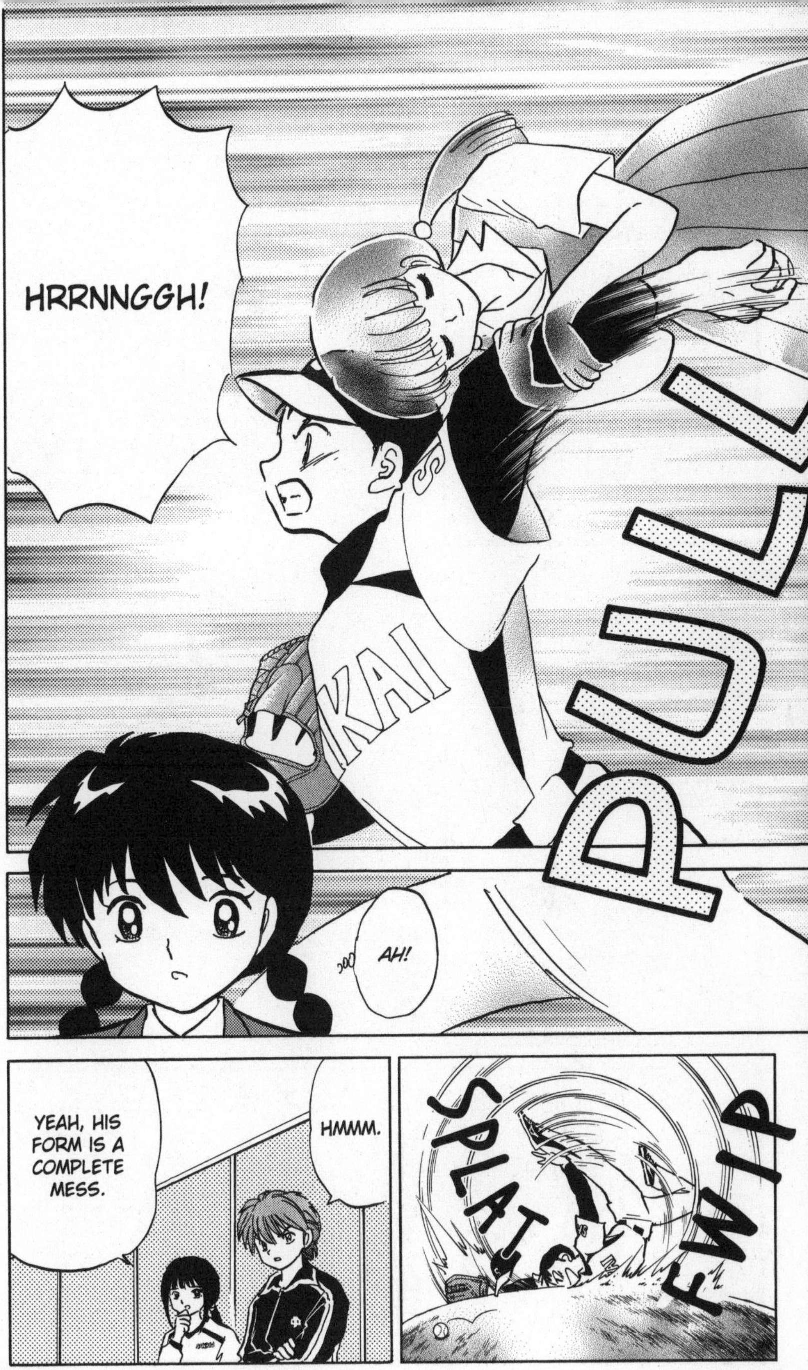
HRRNNGGH!
PULL
AH!
SPLAT
FWIP
HMMM.
YEAH, HIS FORM IS A COMPLETE MESS.

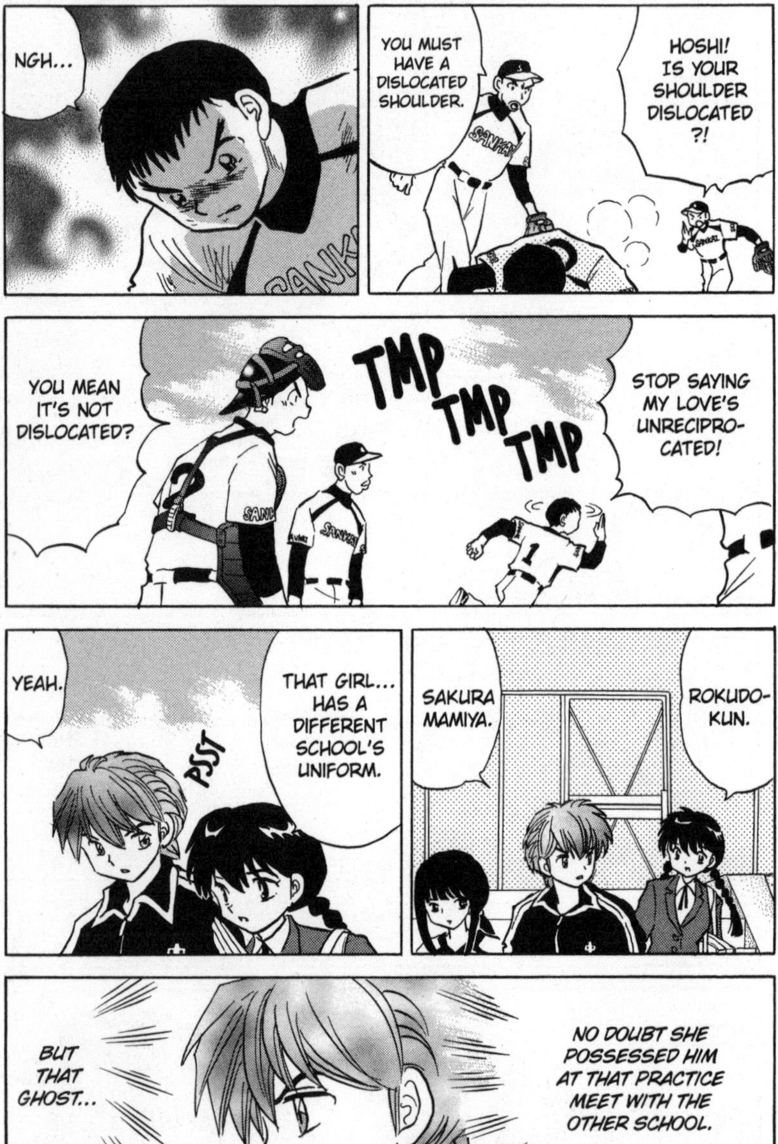
HOSHI! IS YOUR SHOULDER DISLOCATED ?!
YOU MUST HAVE A DISLOCATED SHOULDER.
NGH...
STOP SAYING MY LOVE'S UNRECIPRO-CATED!
TMP TMP TMP
YOU MEAN IT'S NOT DISLOCATED?
ROKUDO-KUN.
SAKURA MAMIYA.
THAT GIRL... HAS A DIFFERENT SCHOOL'S UNIFORM.
PSST
YEAH.
NO DOUBT SHE POSSESSED HIM AT THAT PRACTICE MEET WITH THE OTHER SCHOOL.
BUT THAT GHOST...

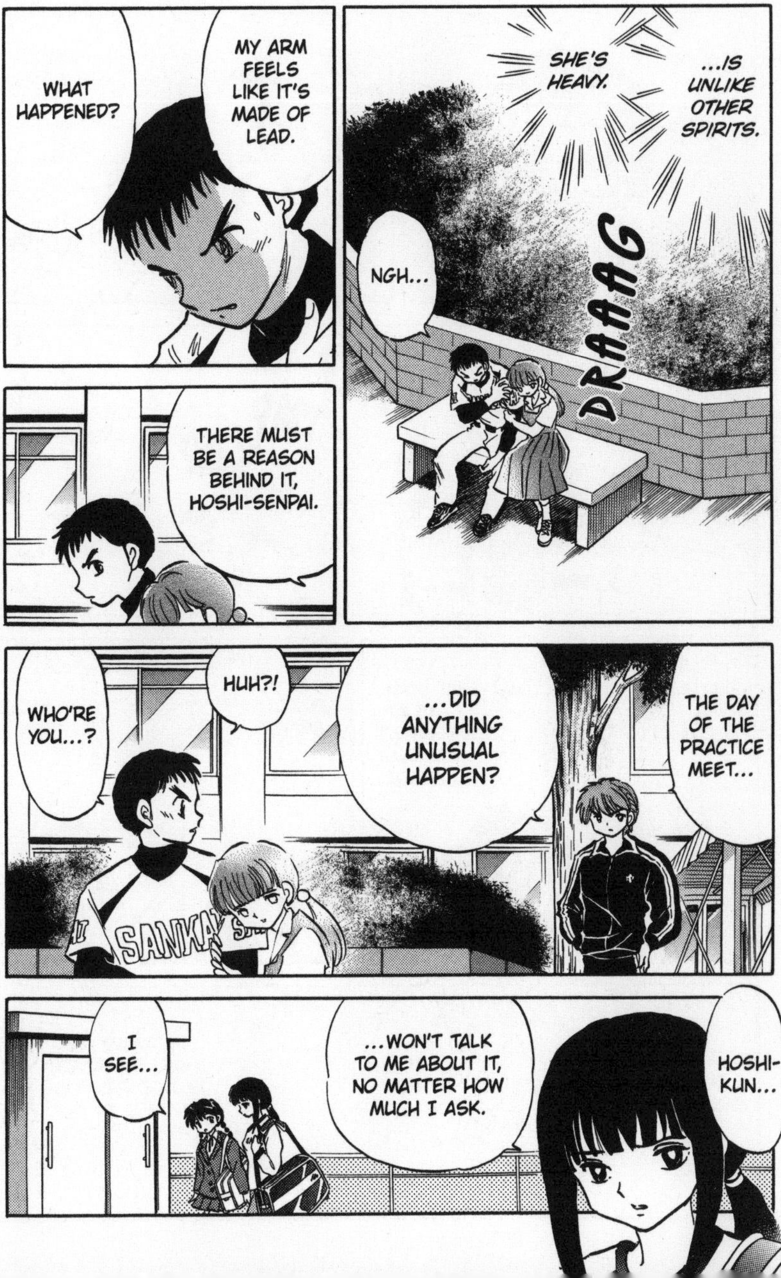
...IS UNLIKE OTHER SPIRITS.
SHE'S HEAVY.
DRAAAG
NGH...
MY ARM FEELS LIKE IT'S MADE OF LEAD.
WHAT HAPPENED?
THERE MUST BE A REASON BEHIND IT, HOSHI-SENPAI.
THE DAY OF THE PRACTICE MEET...
...DID ANYTHING UNUSUAL HAPPEN?
HUH?!
WHO'RE YOU...?
SANKAI
HOSHI-KUN...
...WON'T TALK TO ME ABOUT IT, NO MATTER HOW MUCH I ASK.
I SEE...

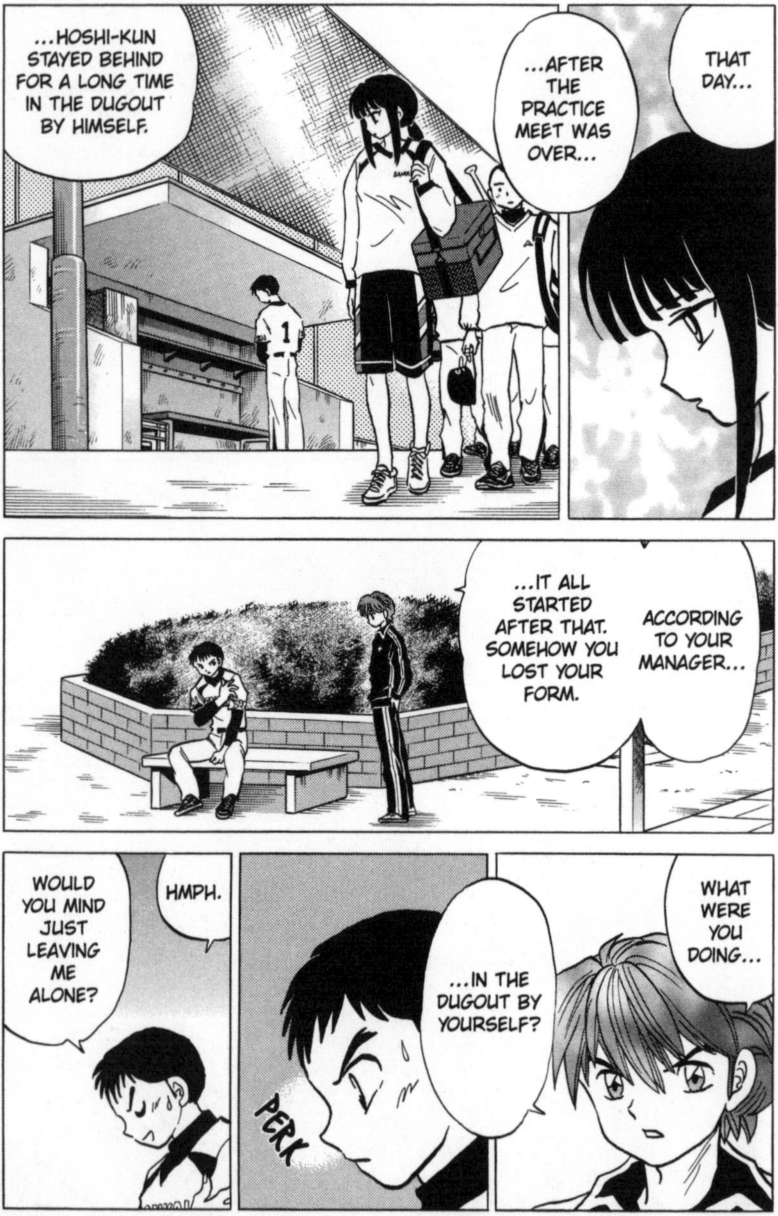
THAT DAY...
...AFTER THE PRACTICE MEET WAS OVER...
...HOSHI-KUN STAYED BEHIND FOR A LONG TIME IN THE DUGOUT BY HIMSELF.
ACCORDING TO YOUR MANAGER...
...IT ALL STARTED AFTER THAT. SOMEHOW YOU LOST YOUR FORM.
WHAT WERE YOU DOING...
...IN THE DUGOUT BY YOURSELF?
PERK
HMPH.
WOULD YOU MIND JUST LEAVING ME ALONE?

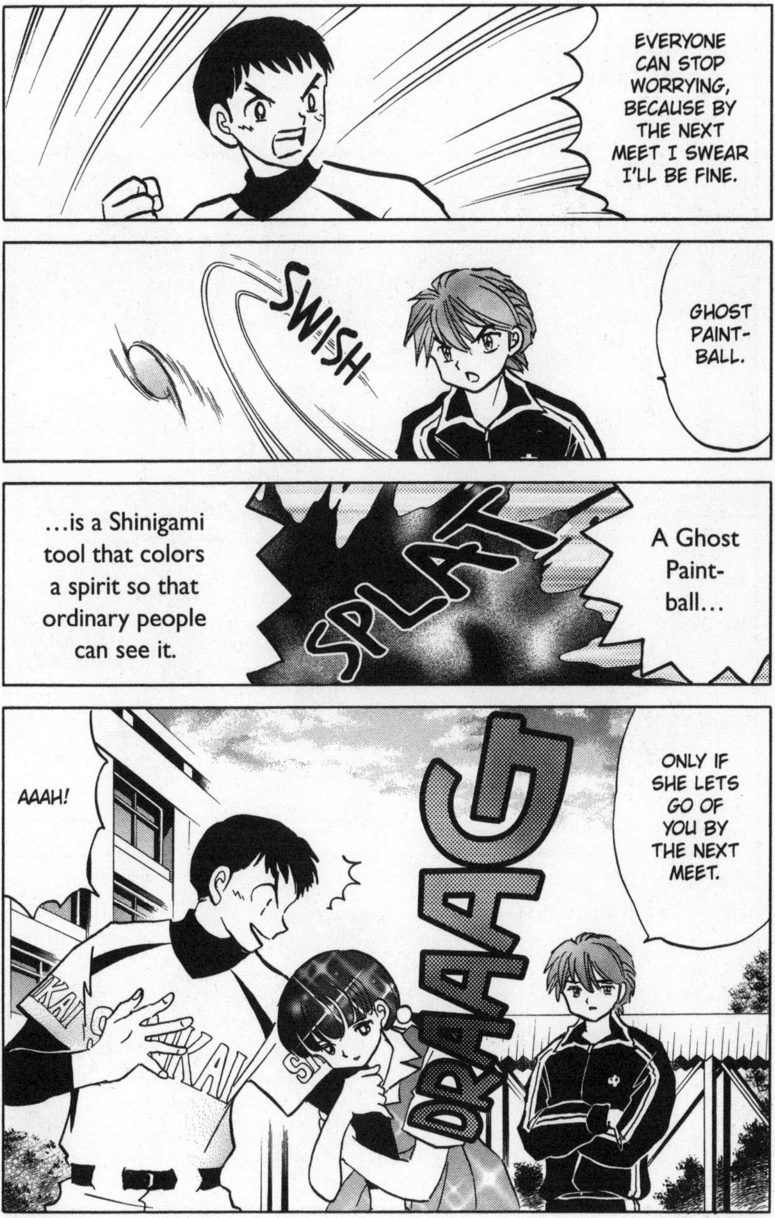
EVERYONE CAN STOP WORRYING, BECAUSE BY THE NEXT MEET I SWEAR I'LL BE FINE.
GHOST PAINT-BALL.
SWISH
A Ghost Paint-ball…
SPLAT
…is a Shinigami tool that colors a spirit so that ordinary people can see it.
ONLY IF SHE LETS GO OF YOU BY THE NEXT MEET.
DRAAAG
AAAH!

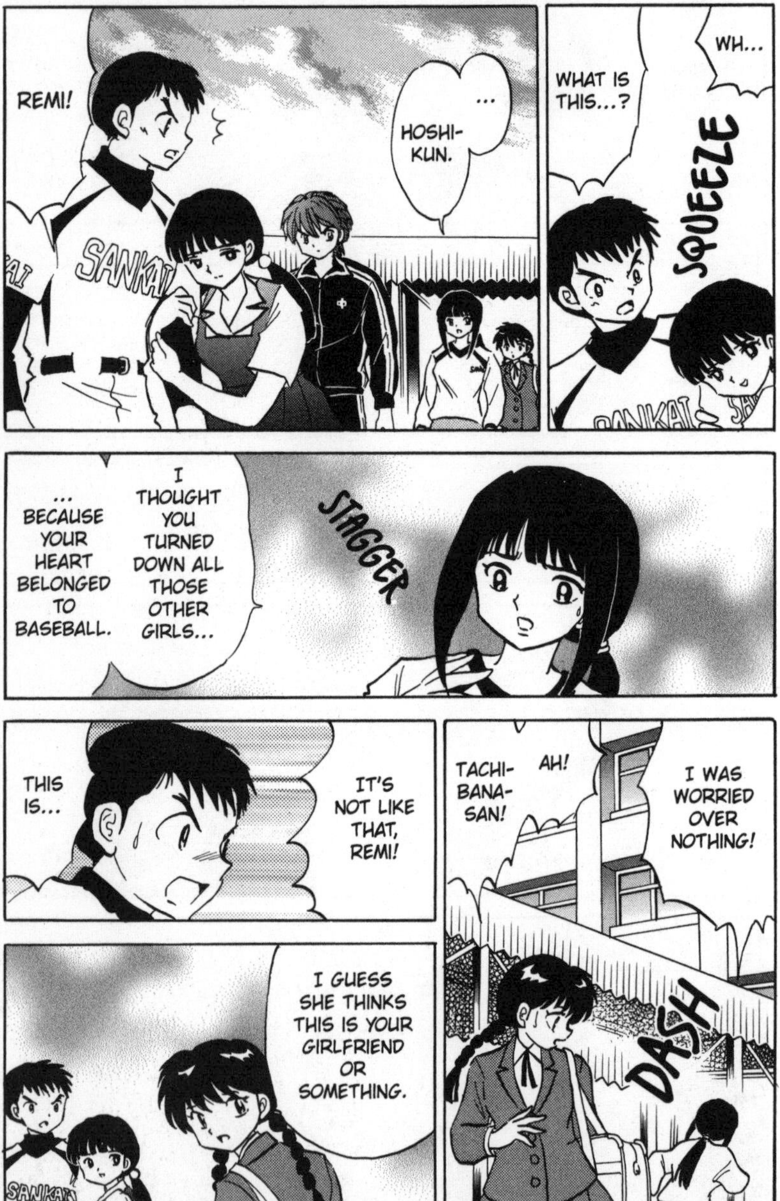
WH...
WHAT IS THIS...?
SQUEEZE
... HOSHI-KUN.
REMI!
STAGGER
I THOUGHT YOU TURNED DOWN ALL THOSE OTHER GIRLS...
... BECAUSE YOUR HEART BELONGED TO BASEBALL.
I WAS WORRIED OVER NOTHING!
AH!
TACHI-BANA-SAN!
DASH
IT'S NOT LIKE THAT, REMI!
THIS IS...
I GUESS SHE THINKS THIS IS YOUR GIRLFRIEND OR SOMETHING.

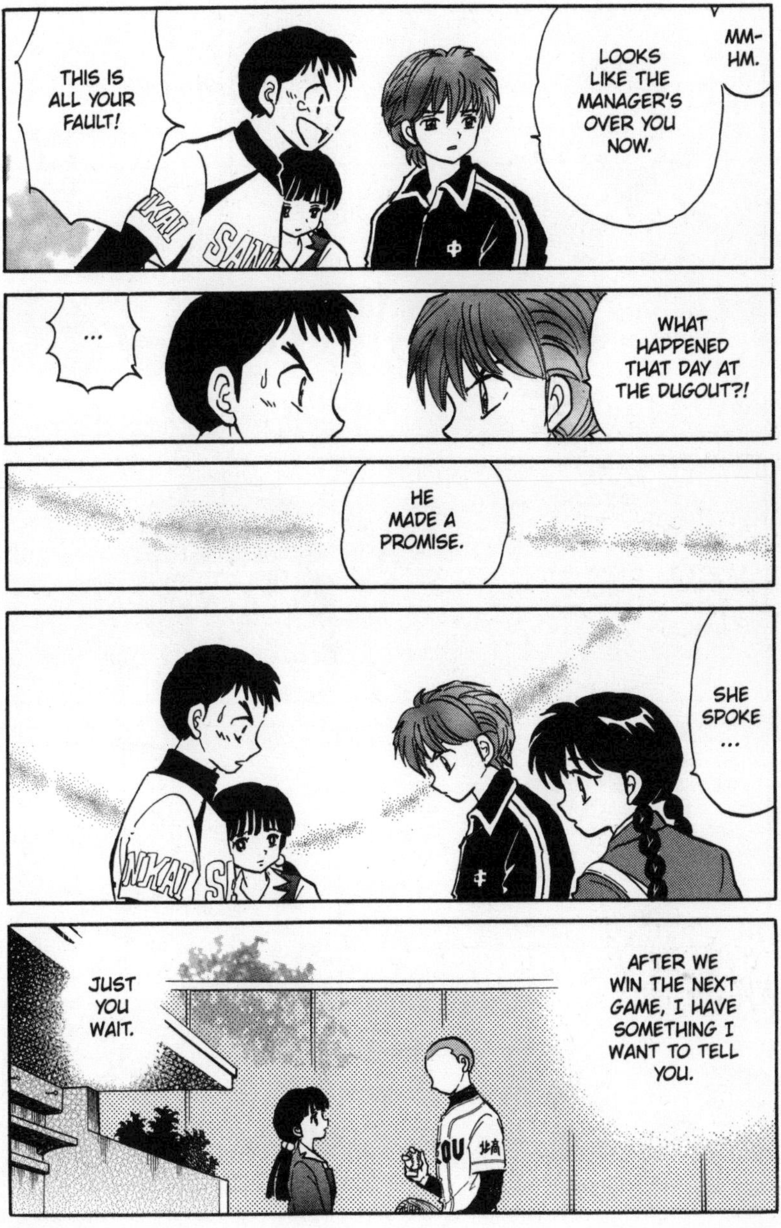
MM-HM.
LOOKS LIKE THE MANAGER'S OVER YOU NOW.
THIS IS ALL YOUR FAULT!
WHAT HAPPENED THAT DAY AT THE DUGOUT?!
...
HE MADE A PROMISE.
SHE SPOKE ...
AFTER WE WIN THE NEXT GAME, I HAVE SOMETHING I WANT TO TELL YOU.
JUST YOU WAIT.

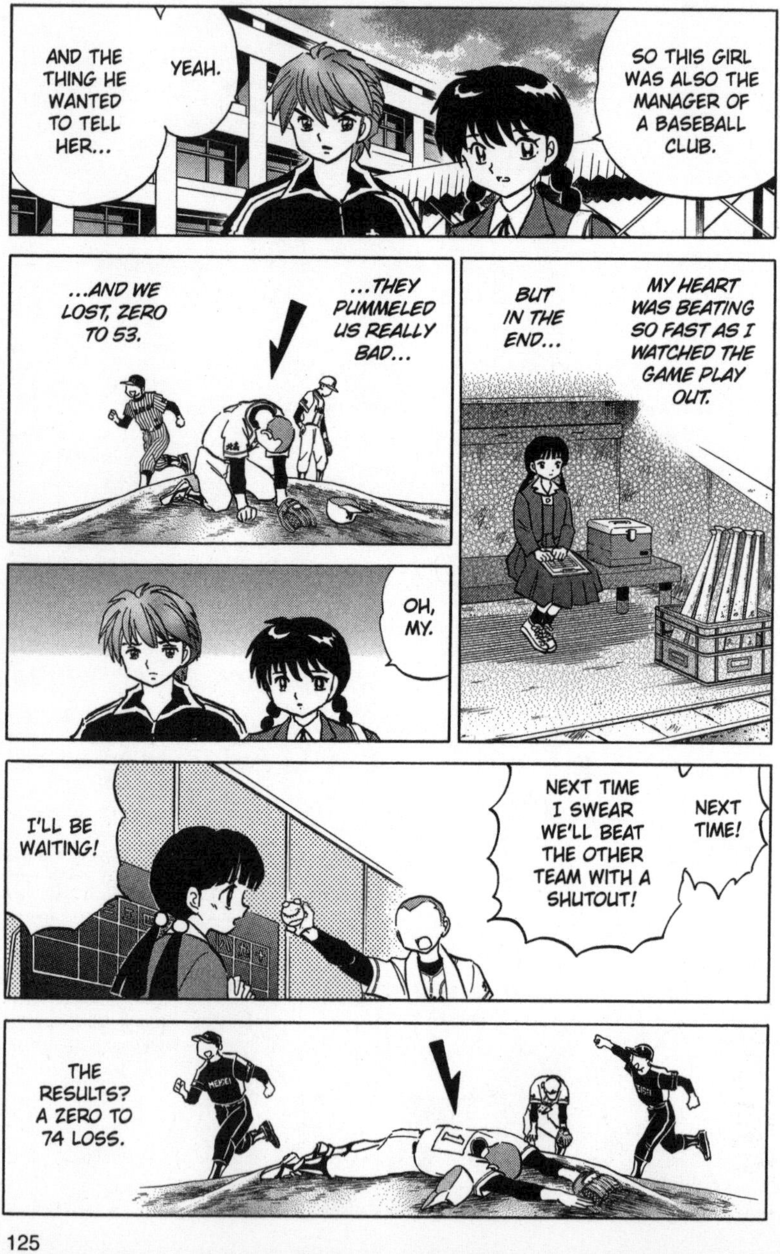
SO THIS GIRL WAS ALSO THE MANAGER OF A BASEBALL CLUB.
YEAH.
AND THE THING HE WANTED TO TELL HER...
MY HEART WAS BEATING SO FAST AS I WATCHED THE GAME PLAY OUT.
BUT IN THE END...
...THEY PUMMELED US REALLY BAD...
...AND WE LOST, ZERO TO 53.
OH, MY.
NEXT TIME!
NEXT TIME I SWEAR WE'LL BEAT THE OTHER TEAM WITH A SHUTOUT!
I'LL BE WAITING!
THE RESULTS? A ZERO TO 74 LOSS.

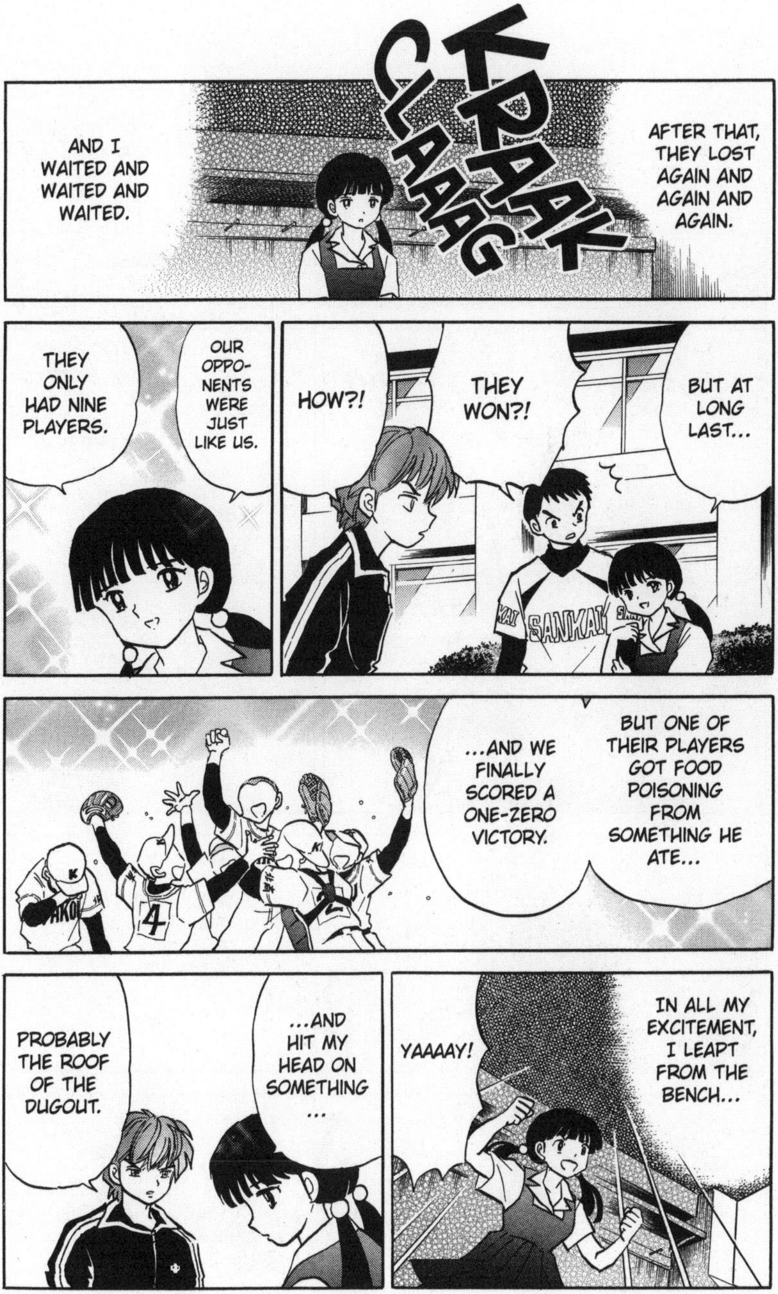
AFTER THAT, THEY LOST AGAIN AND AGAIN AND AGAIN.
KRAAK
CLAAAG
AND I WAITED AND WAITED AND WAITED.
BUT AT LONG LAST...
THEY WON?!
HOW?!
OUR OPPONENTS WERE JUST LIKE US.
THEY ONLY HAD NINE PLAYERS.
BUT ONE OF THEIR PLAYERS GOT FOOD POISONING FROM SOMETHING HE ATE...
...AND WE FINALLY SCORED A ONE-ZERO VICTORY.
IN ALL MY EXCITEMENT, I LEAPT FROM THE BENCH...
YAAAAY!
...AND HIT MY HEAD ON SOMETHING...
PROBABLY THE ROOF OF THE DUGOUT.

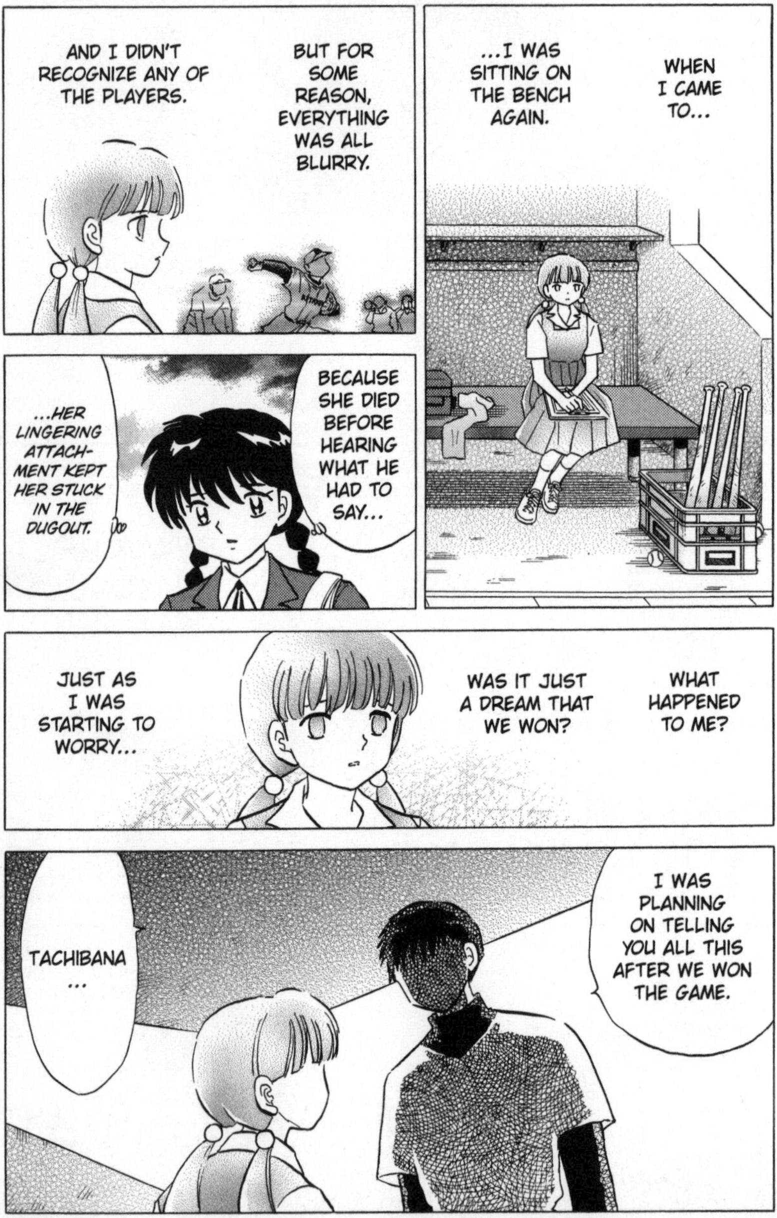
WHEN I CAME TO...
...I WAS SITTING ON THE BENCH AGAIN.
BUT FOR SOME REASON, EVERYTHING WAS ALL BLURRY.
AND I DIDN'T RECOGNIZE ANY OF THE PLAYERS.
BECAUSE SHE DIED BEFORE HEARING WHAT HE HAD TO SAY...
...HER LINGERING ATTACHMENT KEPT HER STUCK IN THE DUGOUT.
WHAT HAPPENED TO ME?
WAS IT JUST A DREAM THAT WE WON?
JUST AS I WAS STARTING TO WORRY...
I WAS PLANNING ON TELLING YOU ALL THIS AFTER WE WON THE GAME.
TACHIBANA ...

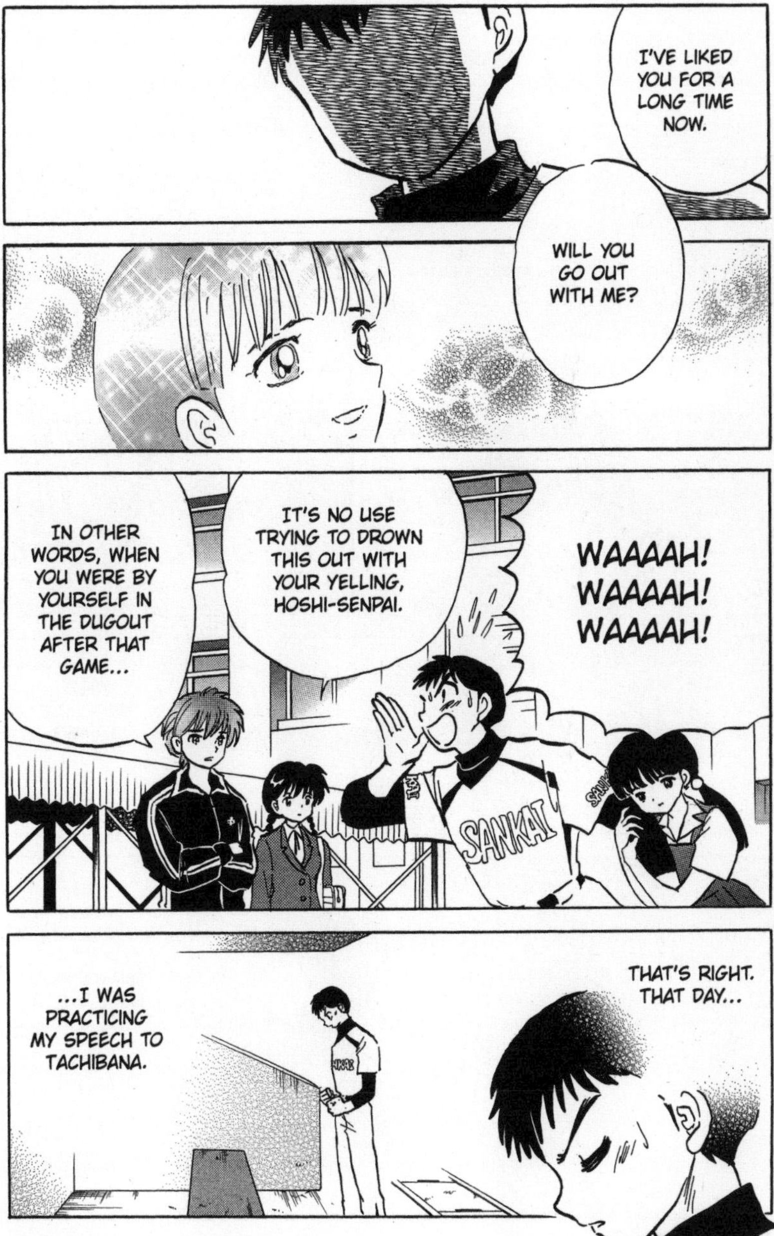
I'VE LIKED YOU FOR A LONG TIME NOW.
WILL YOU GO OUT WITH ME?
WAAAAH! WAAAAH! WAAAAH!
IT'S NO USE TRYING TO DROWN THIS OUT WITH YOUR YELLING, HOSHI-SENPAI.
IN OTHER WORDS, WHEN YOU WERE BY YOURSELF IN THE DUGOUT AFTER THAT GAME...
THAT'S RIGHT. THAT DAY...
...I WAS PRACTICING MY SPEECH TO TACHIBANA.

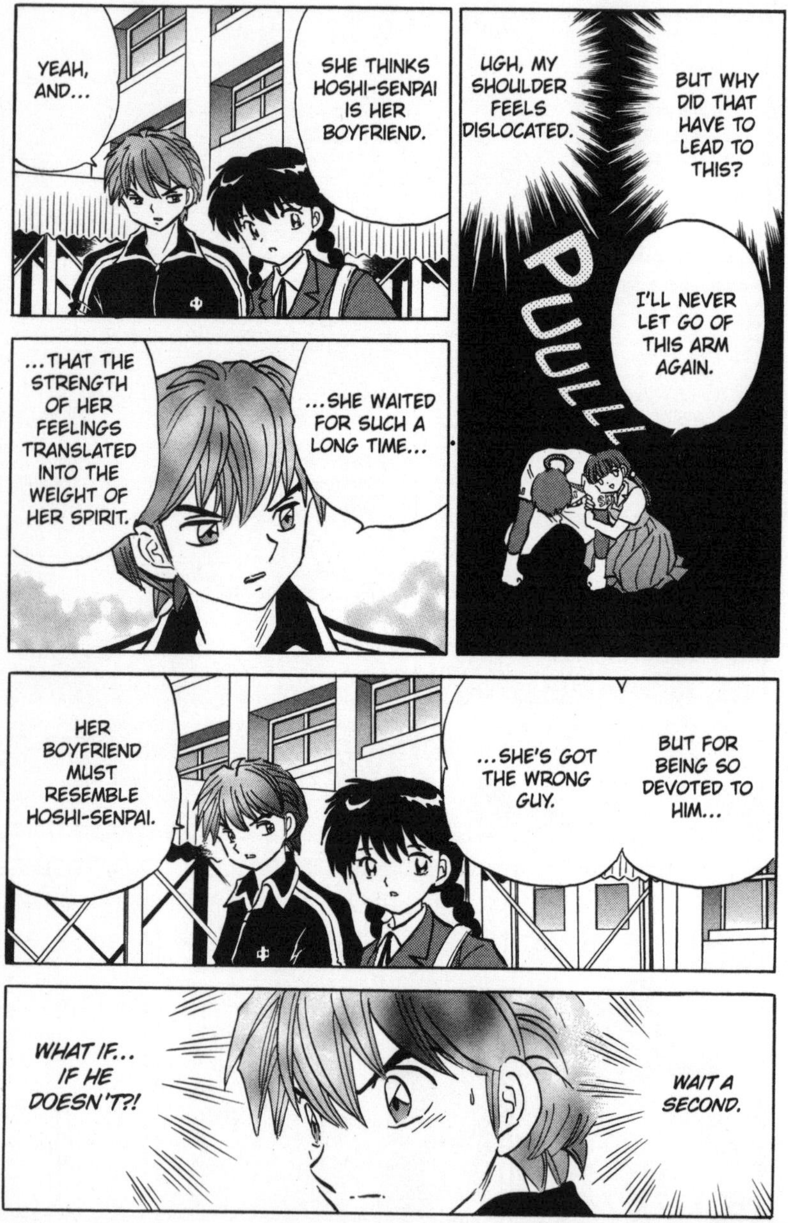
BUT WHY DID THAT HAVE TO LEAD TO THIS?
UGH, MY SHOULDER FEELS DISLOCATED.
PULL
I'LL NEVER LET GO OF THIS ARM AGAIN.
SHE THINKS HOSHI-SENPAI IS HER BOYFRIEND.
YEAH, AND...
...SHE WAITED FOR SUCH A LONG TIME...
...THAT THE STRENGTH OF HER FEELINGS TRANSLATED INTO THE WEIGHT OF HER SPIRIT.
BUT FOR BEING SO DEVOTED TO HIM...
...SHE'S GOT THE WRONG GUY.
HER BOYFRIEND MUST RESEMBLE HOSHI-SENPAI.
WAIT A SECOND.
WHAT IF... IF HE DOESN'T?!

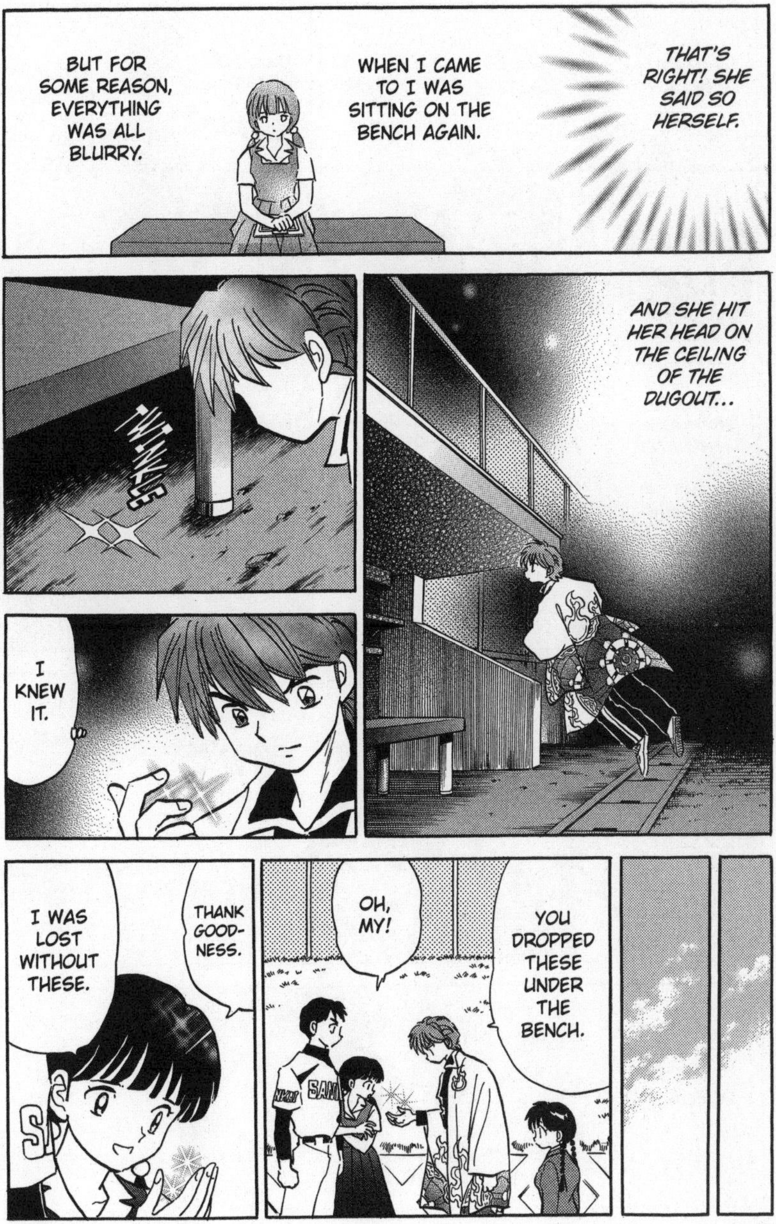
THAT'S RIGHT! SHE SAID SO HERSELF.
WHEN I CAME TO I WAS SITTING ON THE BENCH AGAIN.
BUT FOR SOME REASON, EVERYTHING WAS ALL BLURRY.
AND SHE HIT HER HEAD ON THE CEILING OF THE DUGOUT...
TWINKLE
I KNEW IT.
YOU DROPPED THESE UNDER THE BENCH.
OH, MY!
THANK GOODNESS.
I WAS LOST WITHOUT THESE.

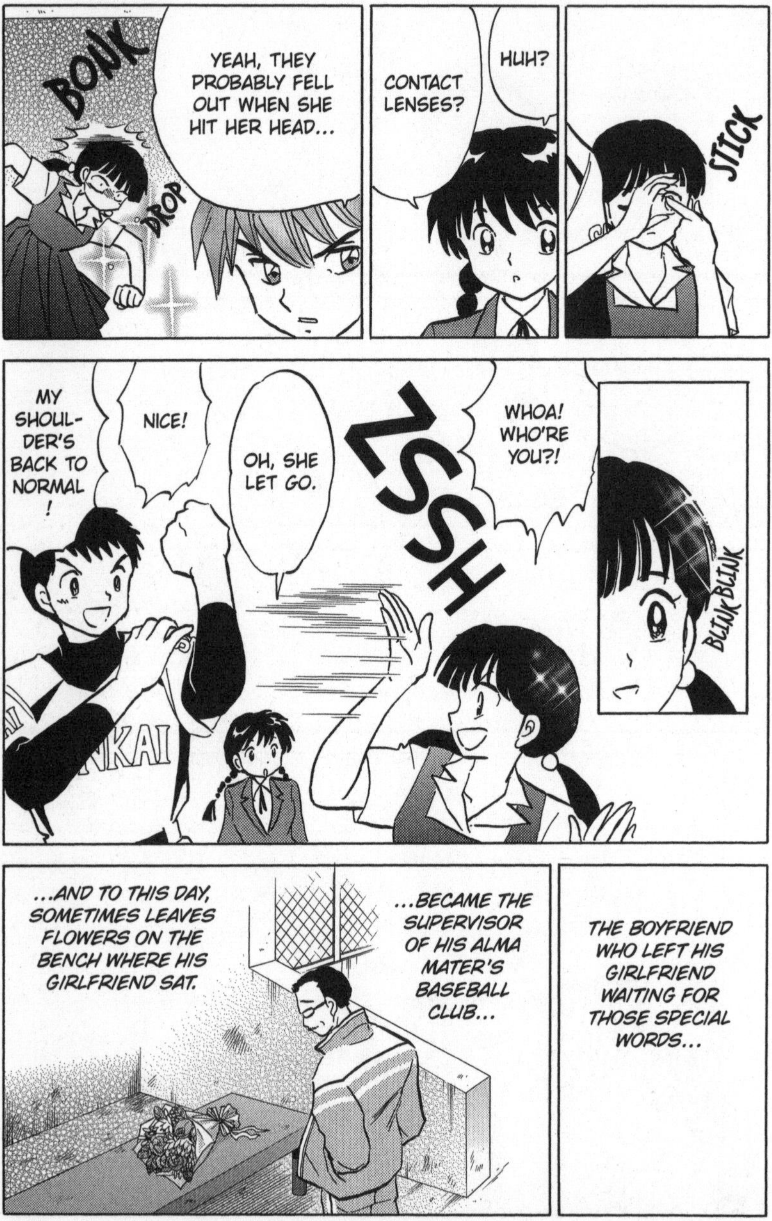
STICK
HUH?
CONTACT LENSES?
YEAH, THEY PROBABLY FELL OUT WHEN SHE HIT HER HEAD...
BONK
DROP
WHOA! WHO'RE YOU?!
BLINK BLINK
ZSSH
OH, SHE LET GO.
NICE!
MY SHOULDER'S BACK TO NORMAL!
THE BOYFRIEND WHO LEFT HIS GIRLFRIEND WAITING FOR THOSE SPECIAL WORDS...
...BECAME THE SUPERVISOR OF HIS ALMA MATER'S BASEBALL CLUB...
...AND TO THIS DAY, SOMETIMES LEAVES FLOWERS ON THE BENCH WHERE HIS GIRLFRIEND SAT.

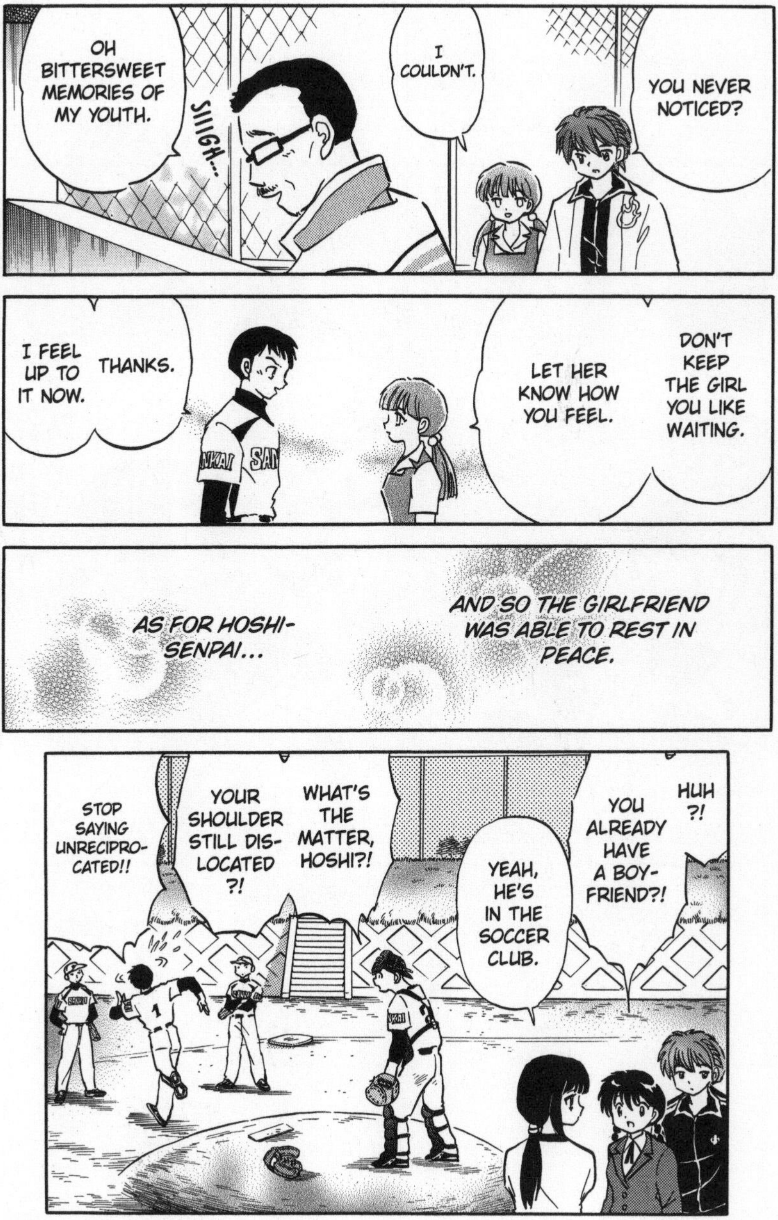
YOU NEVER NOTICED?
I COULDN'T.
SIIIGH...
OH BITTERSWEET MEMORIES OF MY YOUTH.
DON'T KEEP THE GIRL YOU LIKE WAITING.
LET HER KNOW HOW YOU FEEL.
THANKS.
I FEEL UP TO IT NOW.
AND SO THE GIRLFRIEND WAS ABLE TO REST IN PEACE.
AS FOR HOSHI-SENPAI...
HUH?!
YOU ALREADY HAVE A BOY-FRIEND?!
YEAH, HE'S IN THE SOCCER CLUB.
WHAT'S THE MATTER, HOSHI?!
YOUR SHOULDER STILL DIS-LOCATED?!
STOP SAYING UNRECIPRO-CATED!!

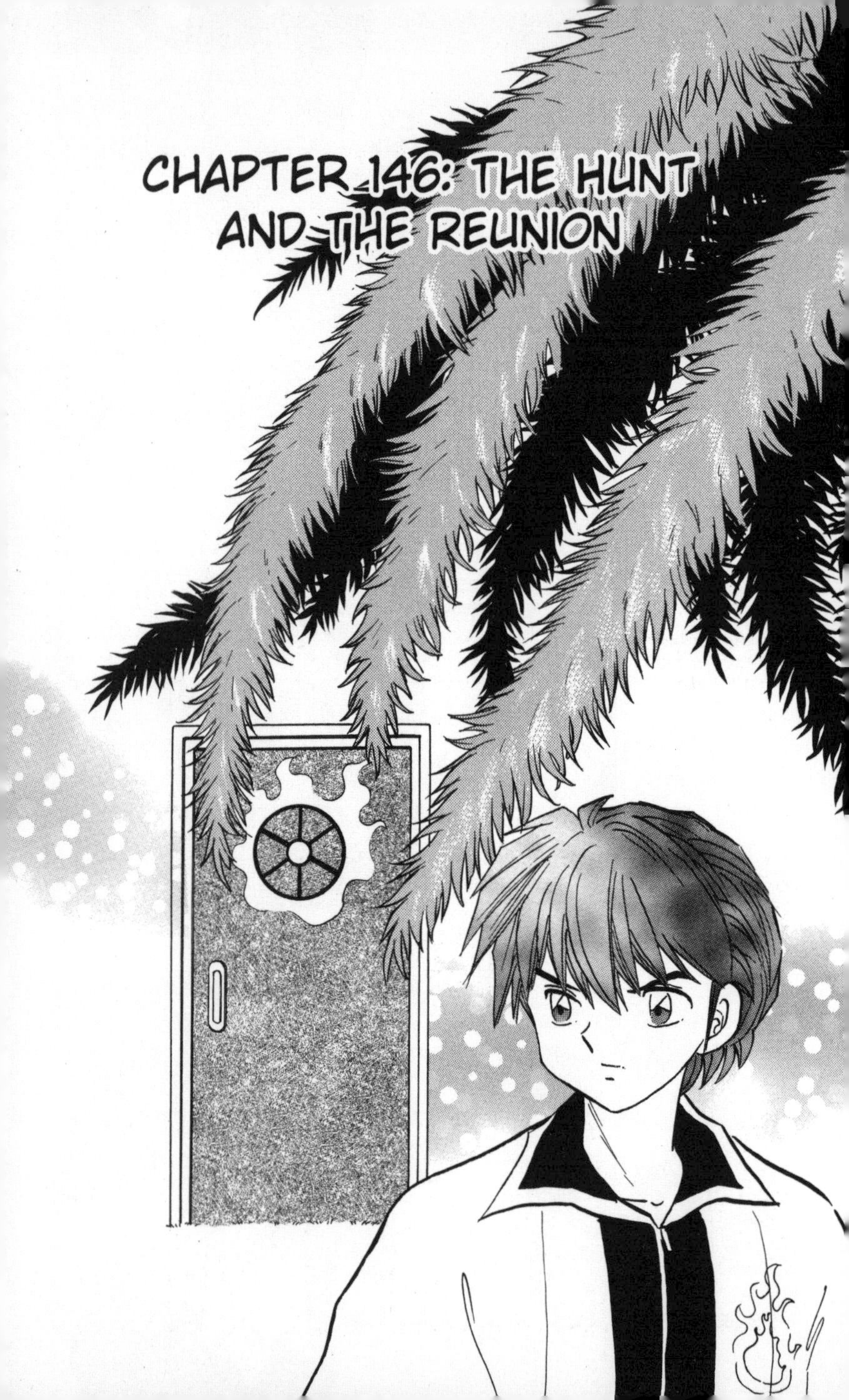
CHAPTER 146: THE HUNT AND THE REUNION

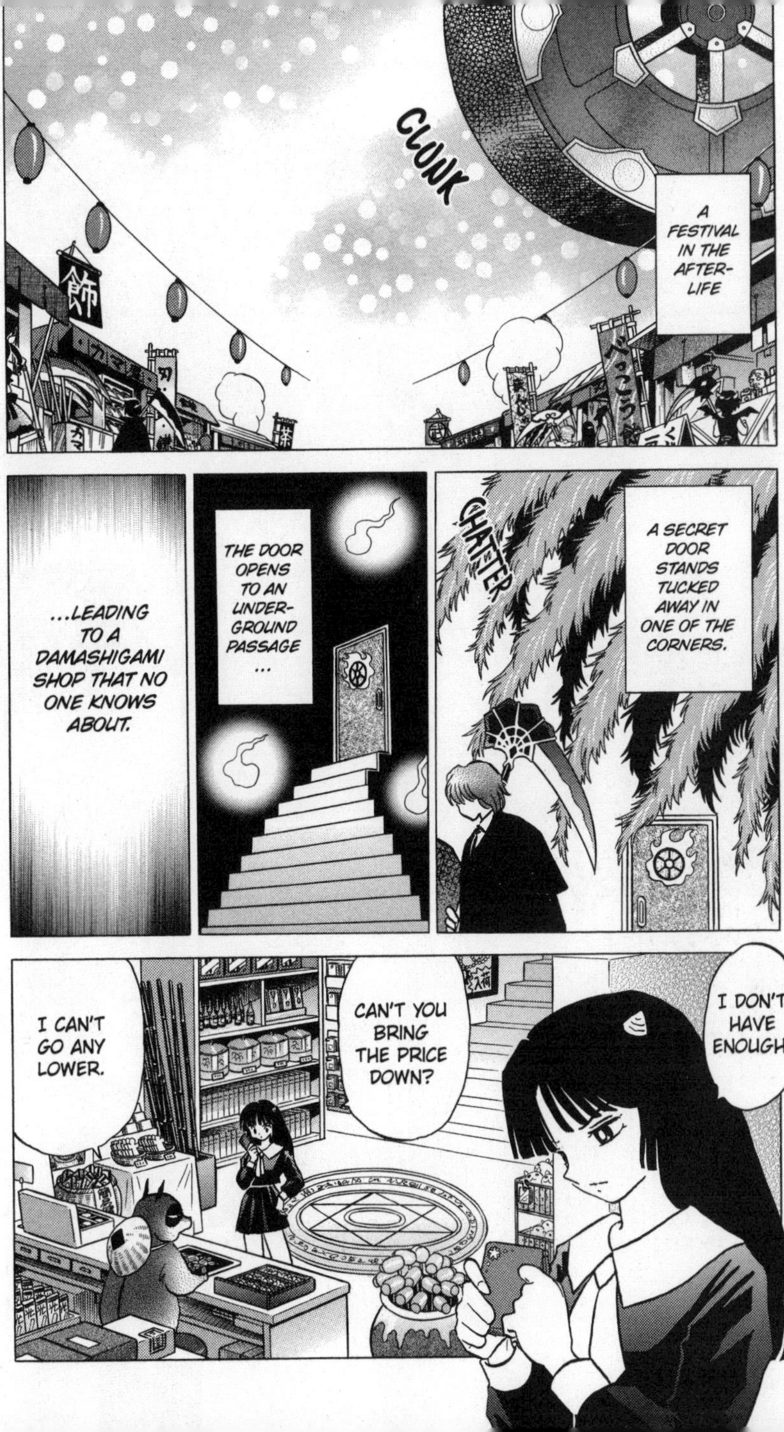
A FESTIVAL IN THE AFTER-LIFE
CLUNK
A SECRET DOOR STANDS TUCKED AWAY IN ONE OF THE CORNERS.
CHATTER
THE DOOR OPENS TO AN UNDER-GROUND PASSAGE ...
...LEADING TO A DAMASHIGAMI SHOP THAT NO ONE KNOWS ABOUT.
I DON'T HAVE ENOUGH.
CAN'T YOU BRING THE PRICE DOWN?
I CAN'T GO ANY LOWER.

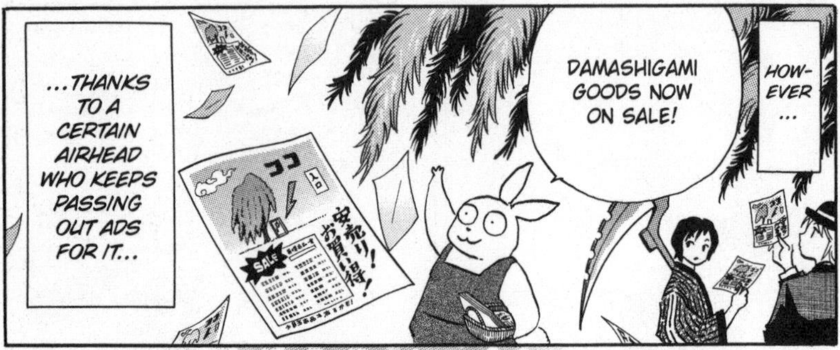
HOW-EVER...
DAMASHIGAMI GOODS NOW ON SALE!
...THANKS TO A CERTAIN AIRHEAD WHO KEEPS PASSING OUT ADS FOR IT...
Paper: Here Cheap! Bargains!

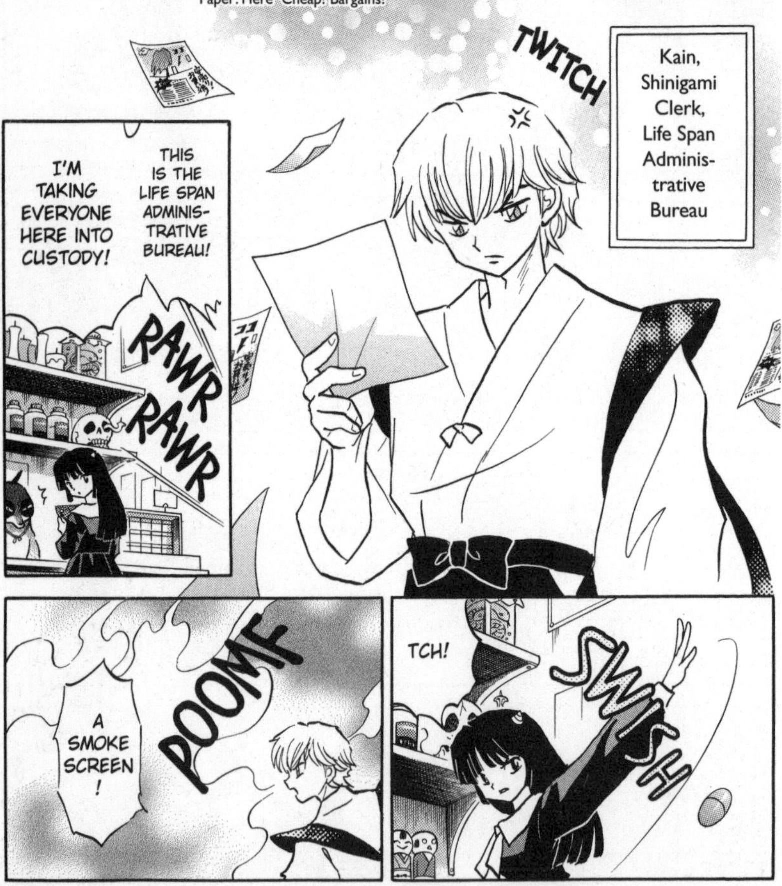
TWITCH
Kain, Shinigami Clerk, Life Span Administrative Bureau
THIS IS THE LIFE SPAN ADMINISTRATIVE BUREAU!
I'M TAKING EVERYONE HERE INTO CUSTODY!
RAWR RAWR
TCH!
SWISH
POOMF
A SMOKE SCREEN!

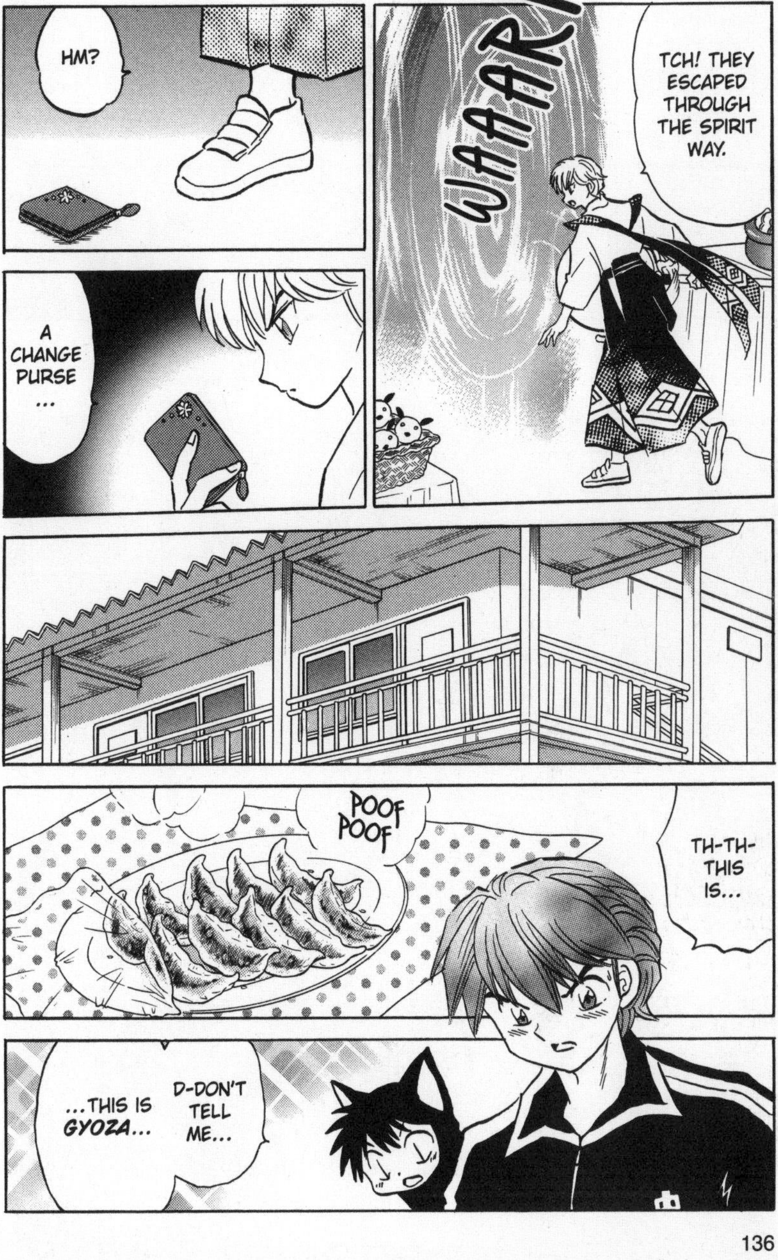
TCH! THEY ESCAPED THROUGH THE SPIRIT WAY.
WAAARP
HM?
A CHANGE PURSE ...
TH-TH-THIS IS...
POOF POOF
D-DON'T TELL ME...
...THIS IS *GYOZA*...

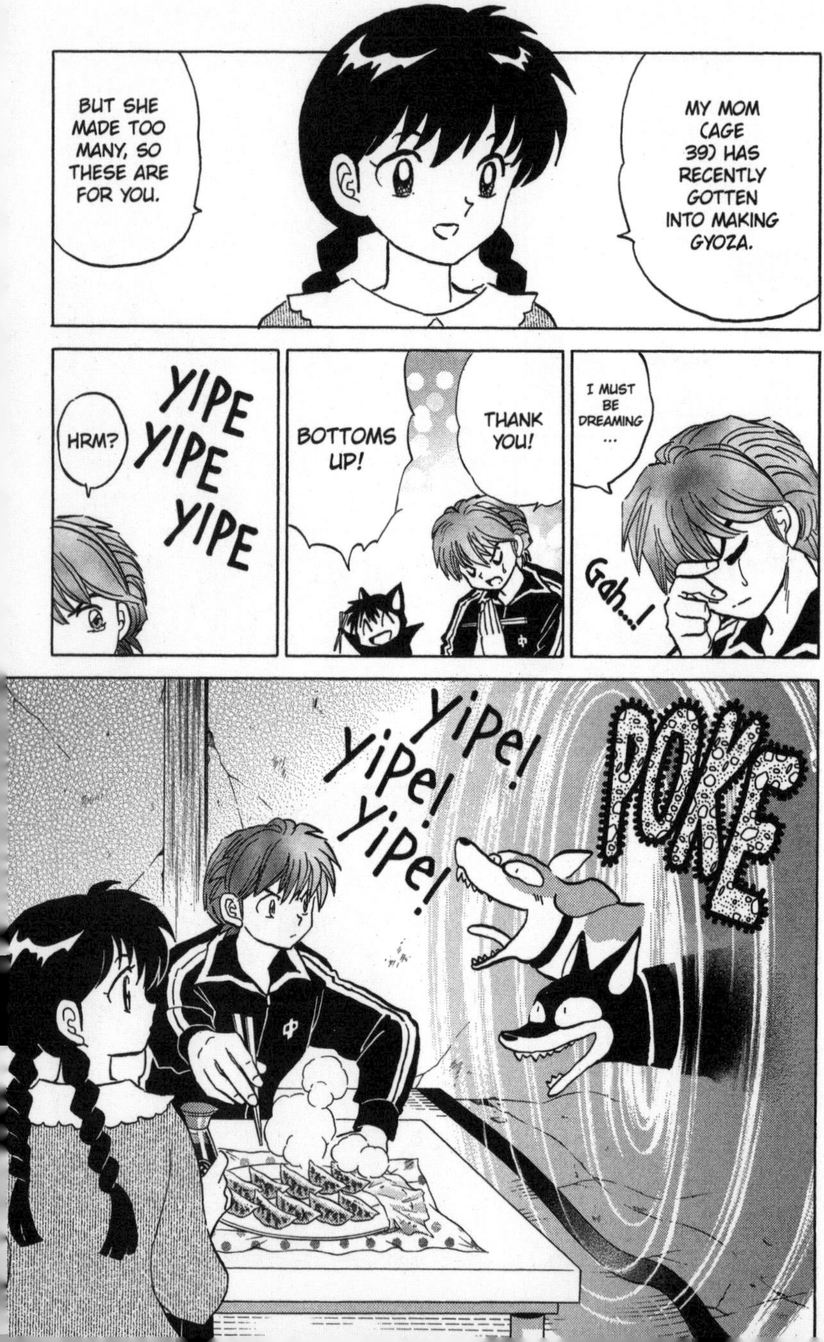
MY MOM (AGE 39) HAS RECENTLY GOTTEN INTO MAKING GYOZA.
BUT SHE MADE TOO MANY, SO THESE ARE FOR YOU.
I MUST BE DREAMING...
Gah...!
THANK YOU!
BOTTOMS UP!
YIPE YIPE YIPE
HRM?
POKE
Yipe! Yipe! Yipe!

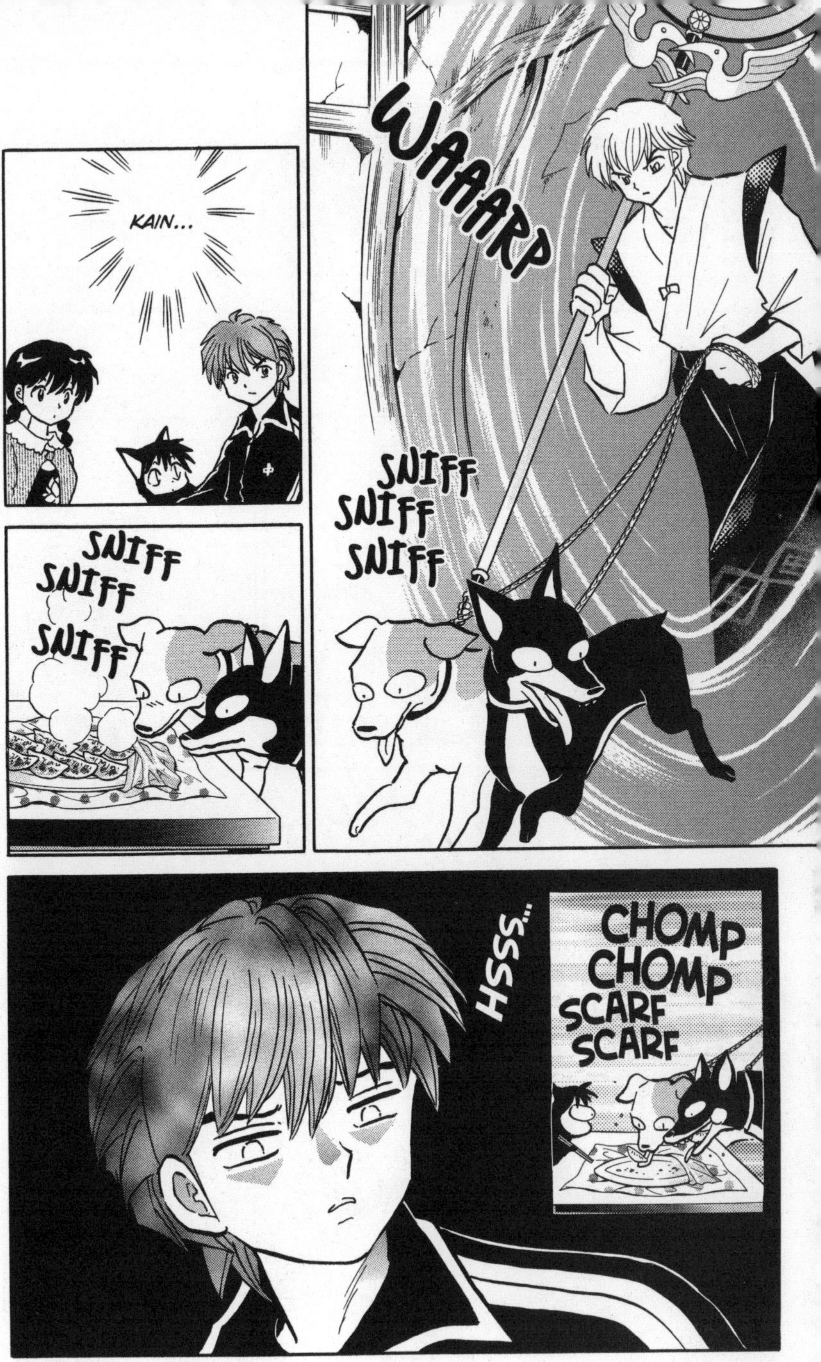
WAAARP
SNIFF SNIFF SNIFF
KAIN...
SNIFF SNIFF SNIFF
CHOMP CHOMP SCARF SCARF
HSSS...

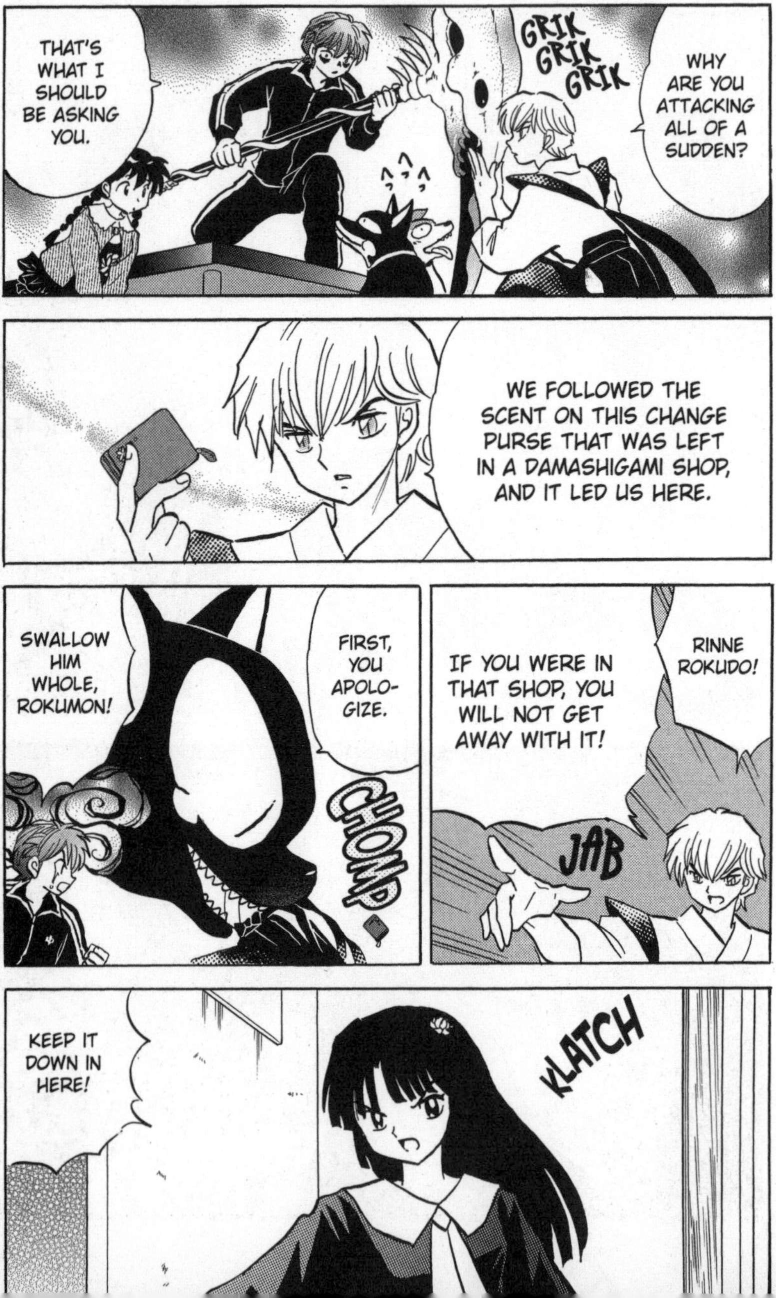
WHY ARE YOU ATTACKING ALL OF A SUDDEN?
GRIK GRIK GRIK
THAT'S WHAT I SHOULD BE ASKING YOU.
WE FOLLOWED THE SCENT ON THIS CHANGE PURSE THAT WAS LEFT IN A DAMASHIGAMI SHOP, AND IT LED US HERE.
RINNE ROKUDO!
IF YOU WERE IN THAT SHOP, YOU WILL NOT GET AWAY WITH IT!
JAB
FIRST, YOU APOLOGIZE.
SWALLOW HIM WHOLE, ROKUMON!
CHOMP
KLATCH
KEEP IT DOWN IN HERE!

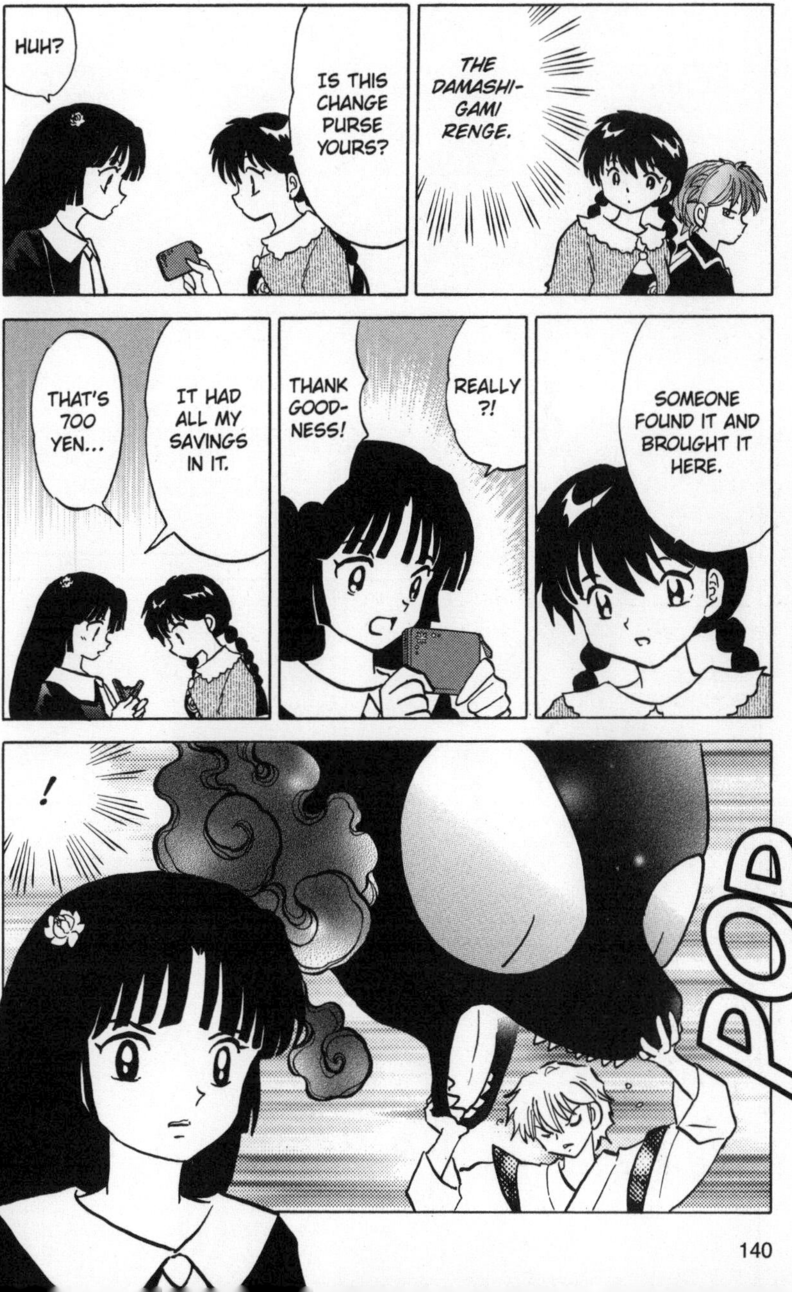
THE DAMASHI-GAMI RENGE.
IS THIS CHANGE PURSE YOURS?
HUH?
SOMEONE FOUND IT AND BROUGHT IT HERE.
REALLY?!
THANK GOODNESS!
IT HAD ALL MY SAVINGS IN IT.
THAT'S 700 YEN...
POP
!

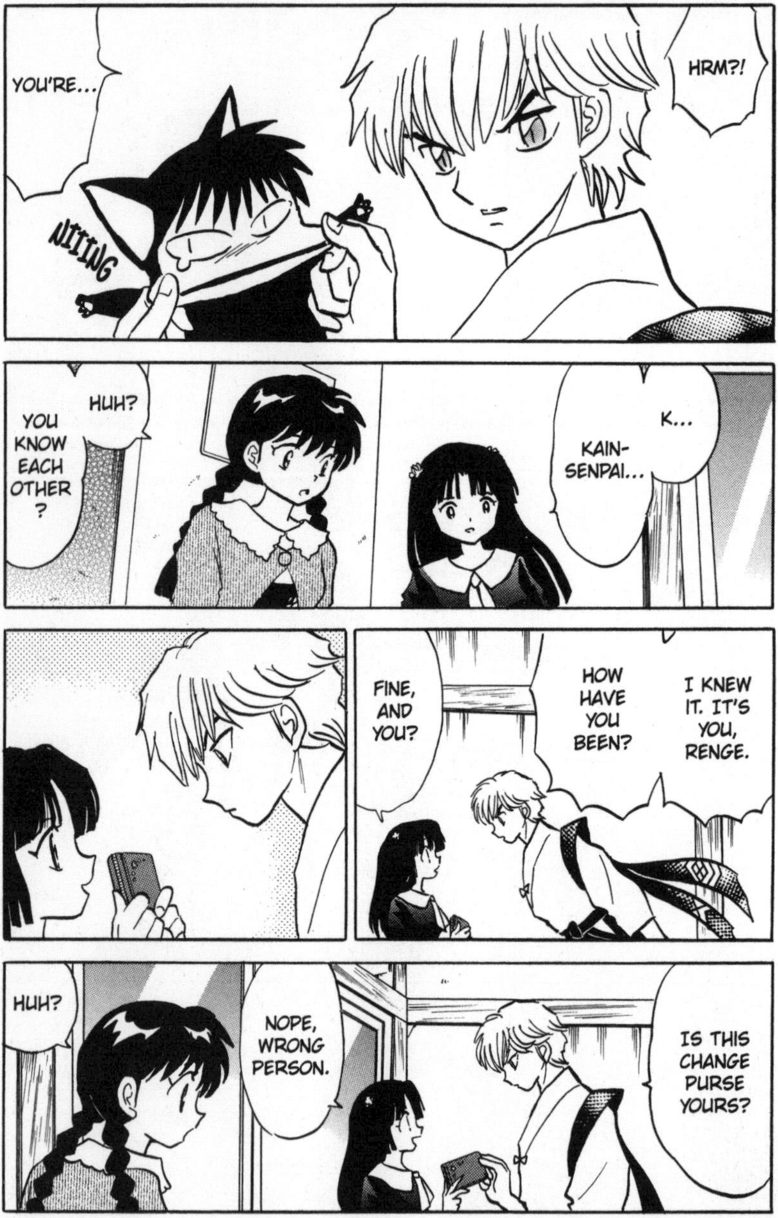
HRM?!
YOU'RE...
NIIING
K... KAIN-SENPAI...
HUH?
YOU KNOW EACH OTHER?
I KNEW IT. IT'S YOU, RENGE.
HOW HAVE YOU BEEN?
FINE, AND YOU?
IS THIS CHANGE PURSE YOURS?
NOPE, WRONG PERSON.
HUH?

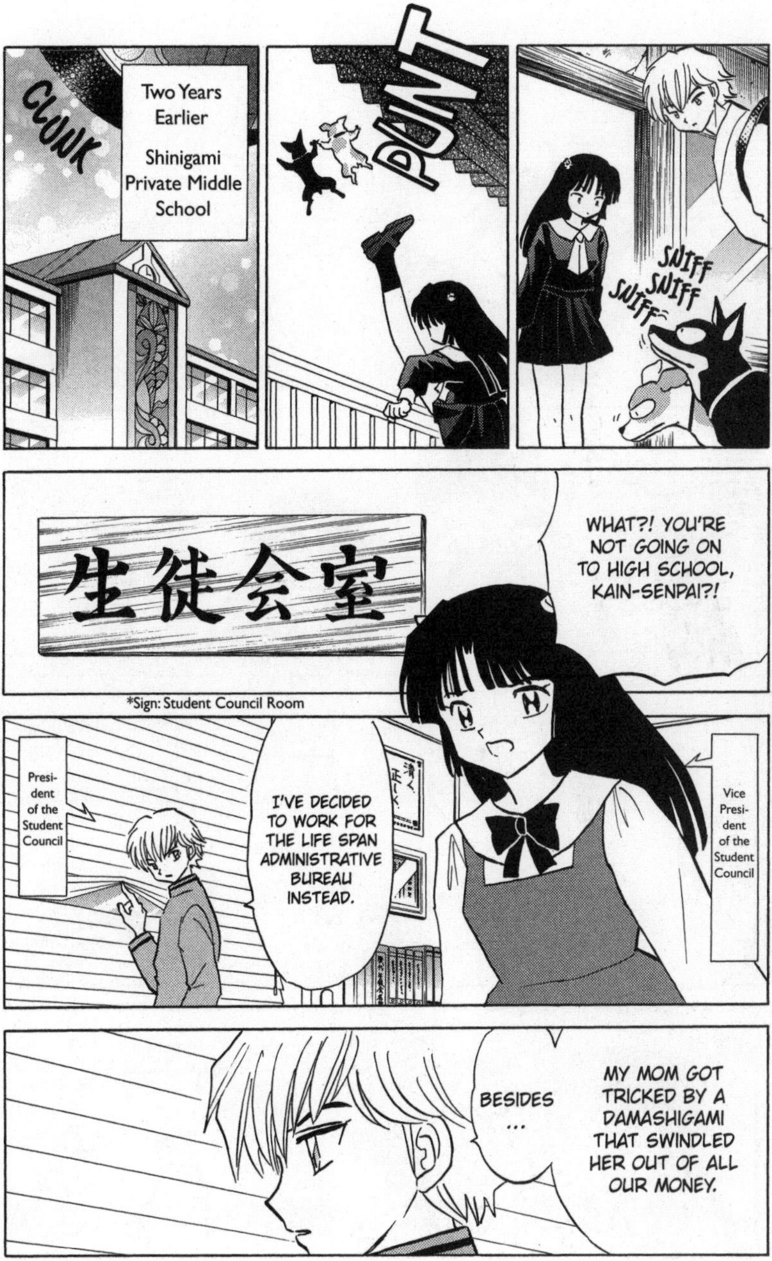
SNIFF SNIFF SNIFF
PUNT
Two Years Earlier
Shinigami Private Middle School
CLUNK
WHAT?! YOU'RE NOT GOING ON TO HIGH SCHOOL, KAIN-SENPAI?!
生徒会室
*Sign: Student Council Room
Vice President of the Student Council
I'VE DECIDED TO WORK FOR THE LIFE SPAN ADMINISTRATIVE BUREAU INSTEAD.
President of the Student Council
MY MOM GOT TRICKED BY A DAMASHIGAMI THAT SWINDLED HER OUT OF ALL OUR MONEY.
BESIDES ...

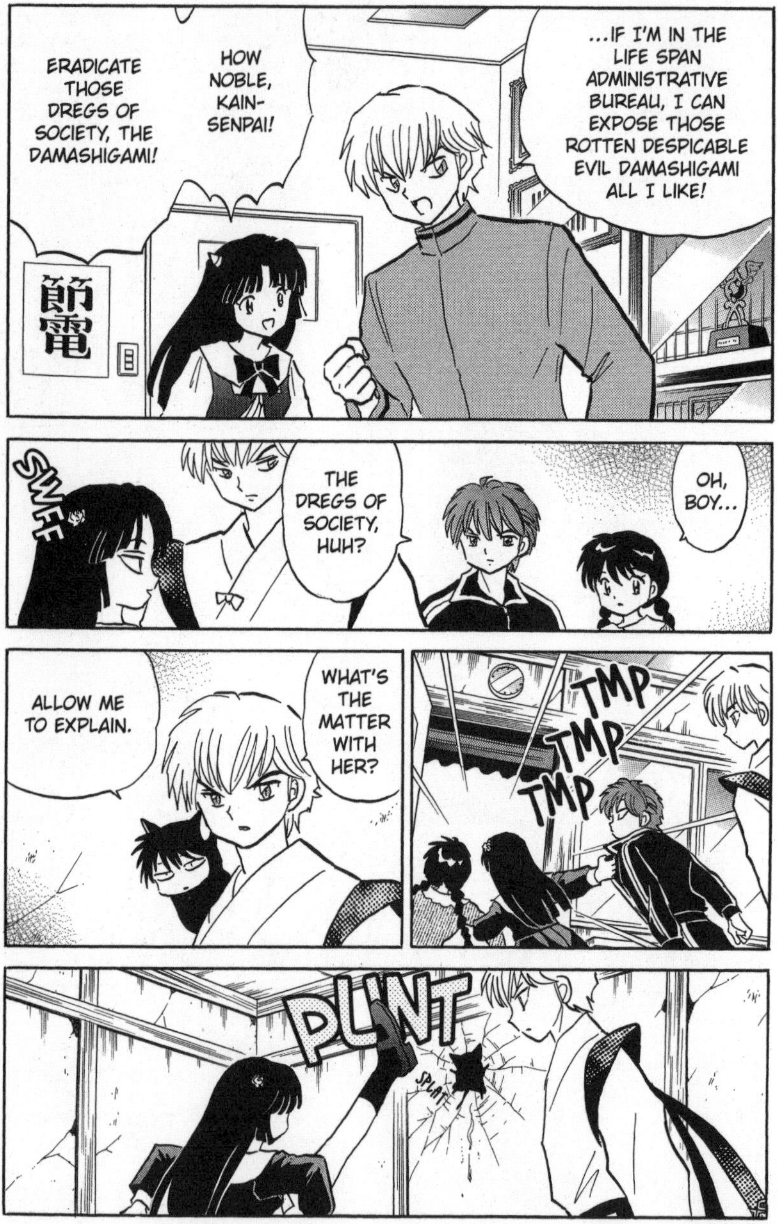
...IF I'M IN THE LIFE SPAN ADMINISTRATIVE BUREAU, I CAN EXPOSE THOSE ROTTEN DESPICABLE EVIL DAMASHIGAMI ALL I LIKE!
HOW NOBLE, KAIN-SENPAI!
ERADICATE THOSE DREGS OF SOCIETY, THE DAMASHIGAMI!
節電
OH, BOY...
THE DREGS OF SOCIETY, HUH?
SWFF
TMP
TMP
TMP
WHAT'S THE MATTER WITH HER?
ALLOW ME TO EXPLAIN.
PUNT
SPLAT

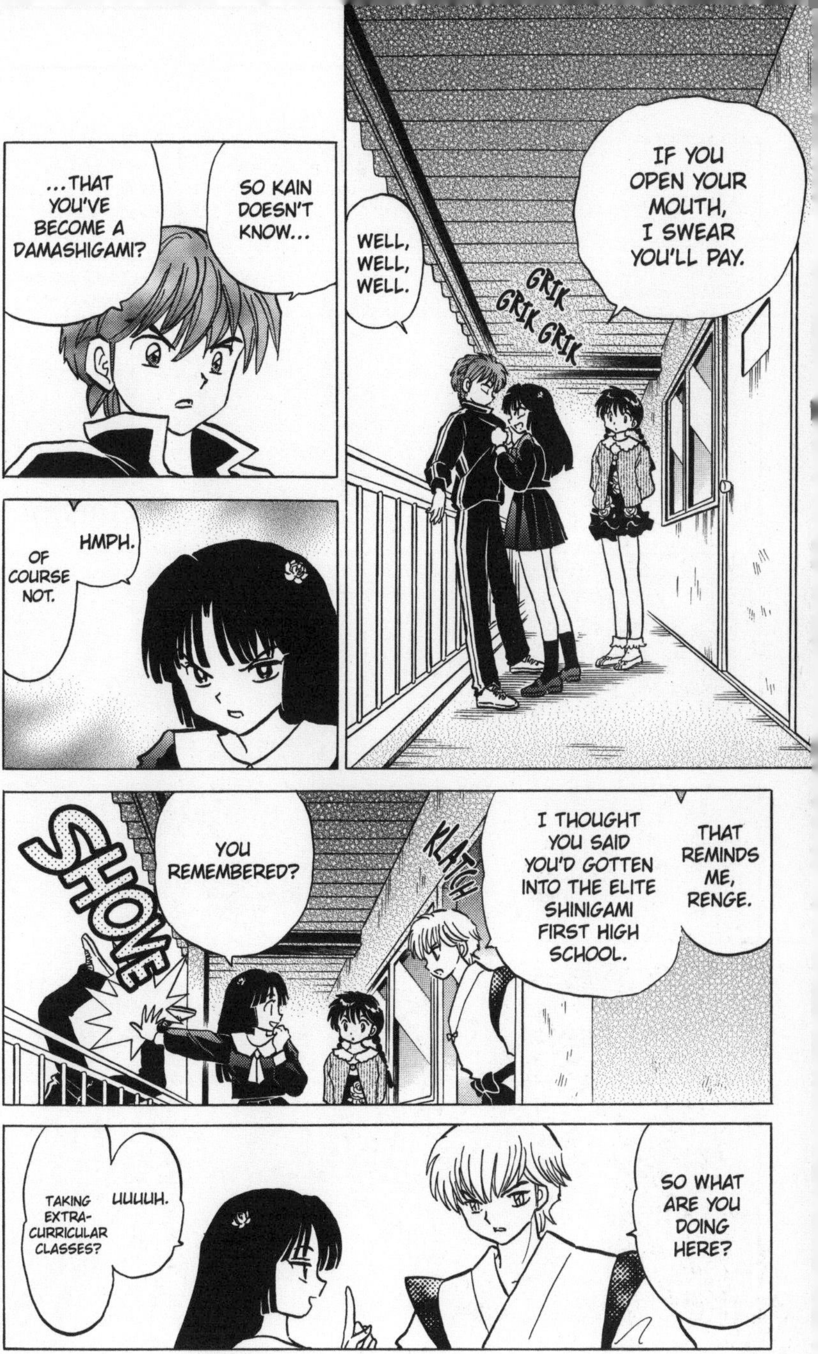
IF YOU OPEN YOUR MOUTH, I SWEAR YOU'LL PAY.
GRIK GRIK GRIK
WELL, WELL, WELL.
SO KAIN DOESN'T KNOW...
...THAT YOU'VE BECOME A DAMASHIGAMI?
HMPH.
OF COURSE NOT.
THAT REMINDS ME, RENGE.
I THOUGHT YOU SAID YOU'D GOTTEN INTO THE ELITE SHINIGAMI FIRST HIGH SCHOOL.
KLATCH
YOU REMEMBERED?
SHOVE
SO WHAT ARE YOU DOING HERE?
UUUUH.
TAKING EXTRA-CURRICULAR CLASSES?

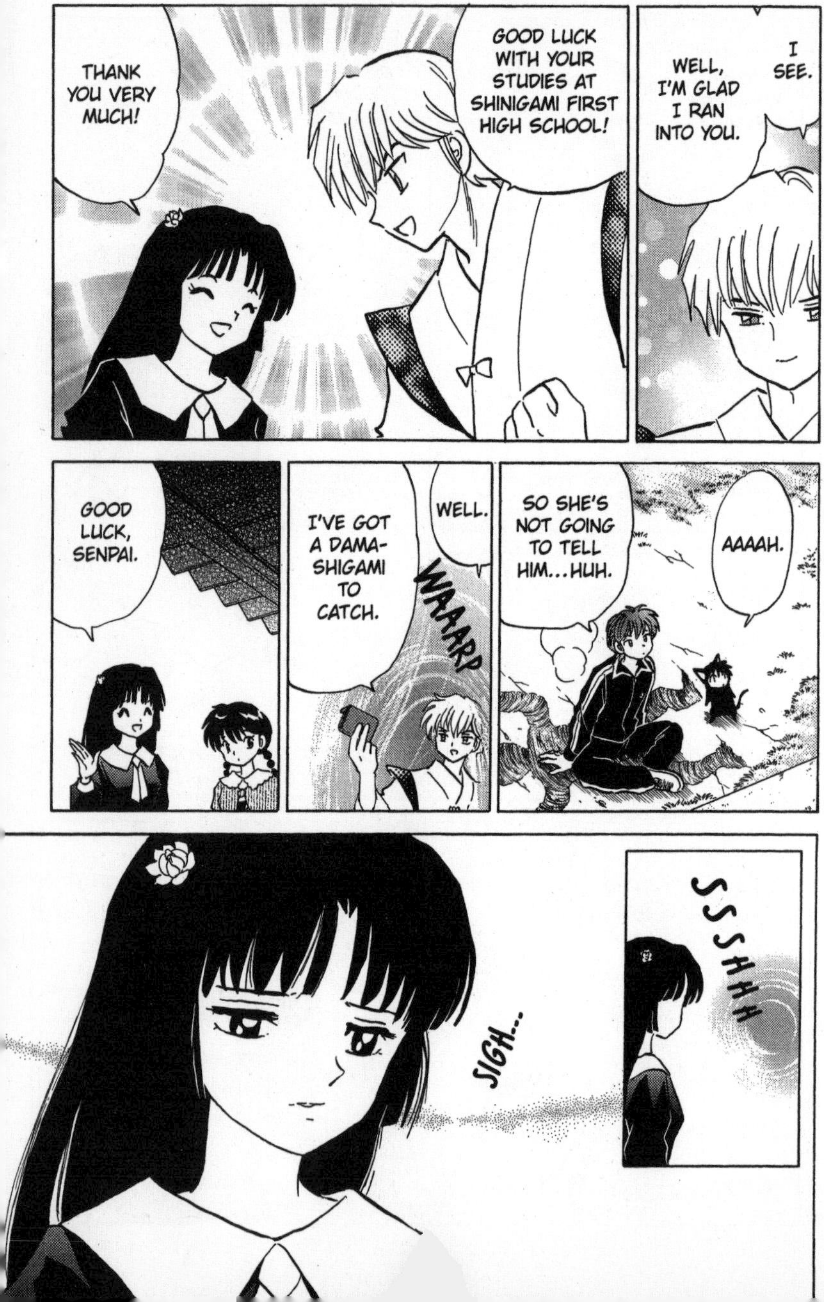
I SEE.
WELL, I'M GLAD I RAN INTO YOU.
GOOD LUCK WITH YOUR STUDIES AT SHINIGAMI FIRST HIGH SCHOOL!
THANK YOU VERY MUCH!
AAAAH.
SO SHE'S NOT GOING TO TELL HIM...HUH.
WELL.
I'VE GOT A DAMA-SHIGAMI TO CATCH.
WAAARP
GOOD LUCK, SENPAI.
SSSHHH
SIGH...

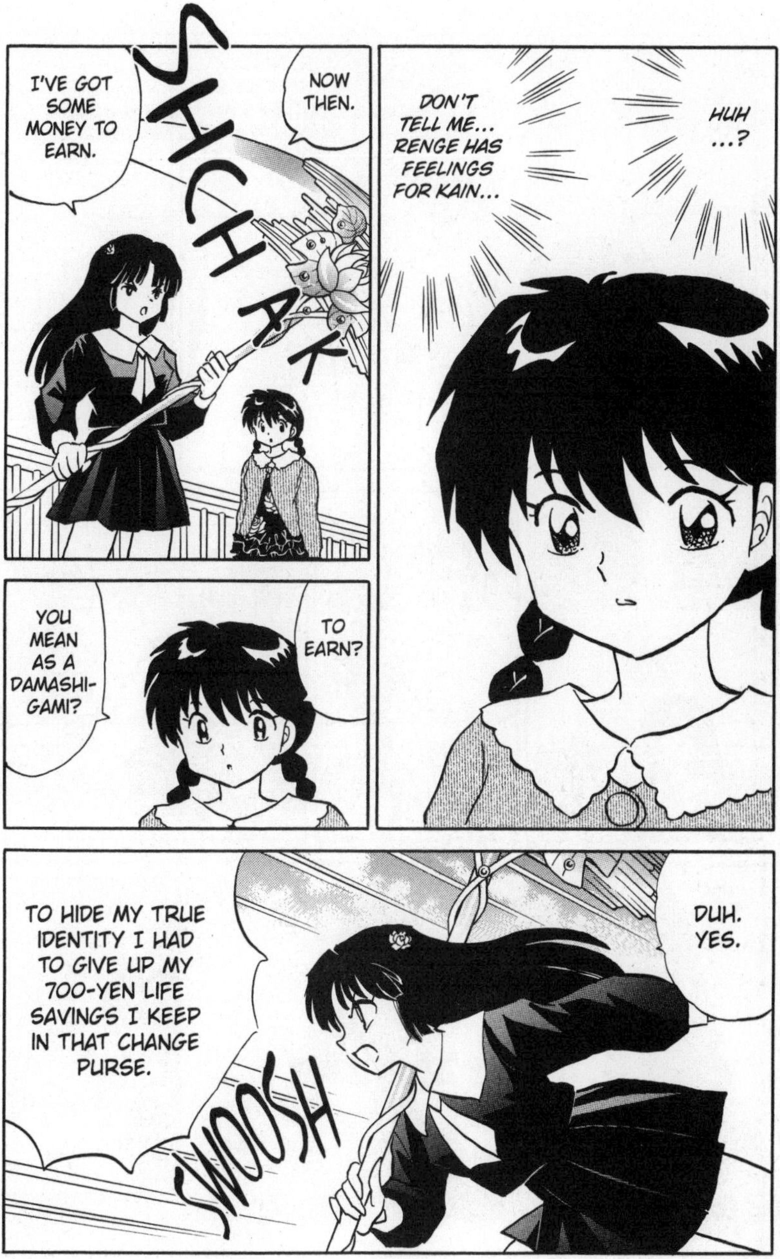
HUH ...?
DON'T TELL ME... RENGE HAS FEELINGS FOR KAIN...
NOW THEN.
I'VE GOT SOME MONEY TO EARN.
SHICHAK
TO EARN?
YOU MEAN AS A DAMASHI-GAMI?
DUH. YES.
TO HIDE MY TRUE IDENTITY I HAD TO GIVE UP MY 700-YEN LIFE SAVINGS I KEEP IN THAT CHANGE PURSE.
SWOOSH

SHE WAS WILLING TO SACRIFICE THE EXORBITANT AMOUNT OF 700 YEN TO PRESERVE HER ALIAS.
ROKUDO-KUN.
CLANG
SHE MUST REALLY...
...FEEL THAT STRONGLY ABOUT KAIN.
HUSH
AREN'T YOU GOING TO FOLLOW HER?
OH, THAT'S RIGHT.
SHE SEEMED PRETTY DETERMINED TO DO SOME KILLING TO MAKE A KILLING.
TCH!
WHOOSH

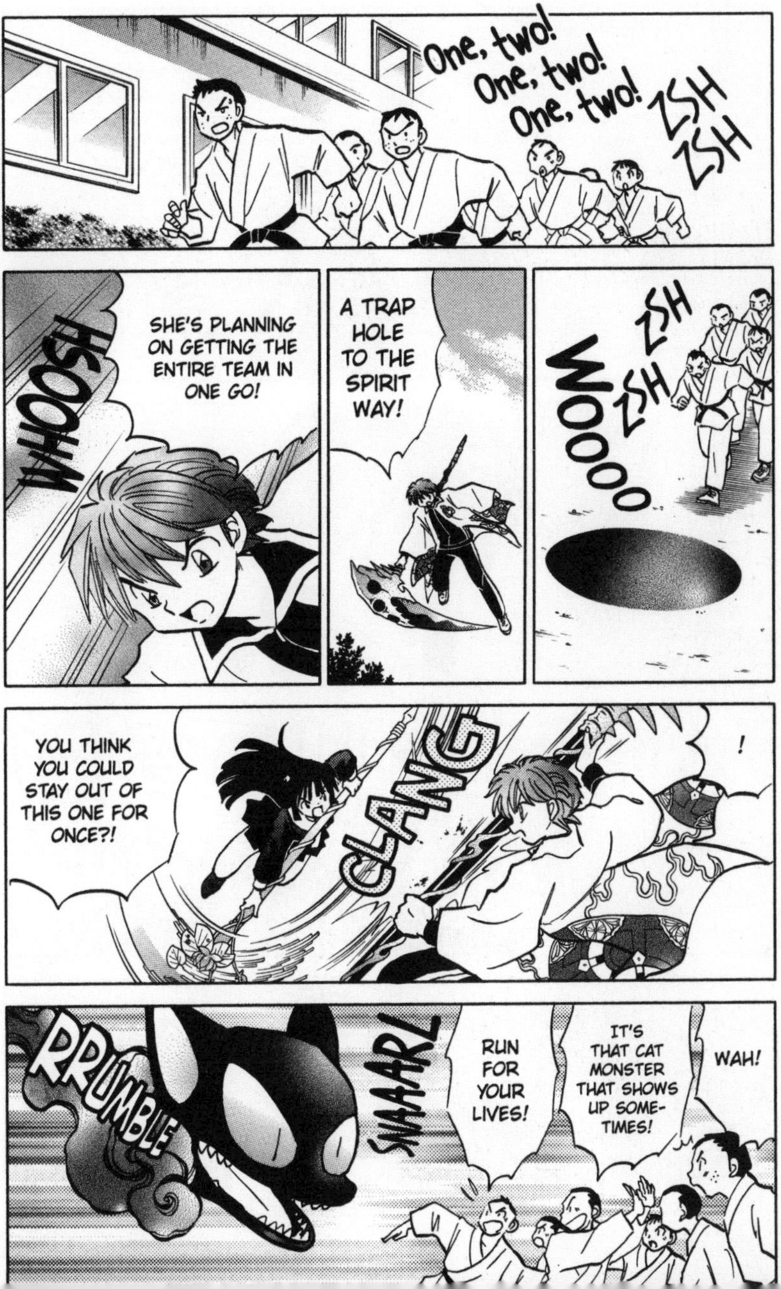
One, two!
One, two!
One, two!
ZSH
ZSH
ZSH
ZSH
WOOOOO
A TRAP HOLE TO THE SPIRIT WAY!
SHE'S PLANNING ON GETTING THE ENTIRE TEAM IN ONE GO!
WHOOSH
!
CLANG
YOU THINK YOU COULD STAY OUT OF THIS ONE FOR ONCE?!
WAH!
IT'S THAT CAT MONSTER THAT SHOWS UP SOME-TIMES!
RUN FOR YOUR LIVES!
SNAAARL
RRUMBLE

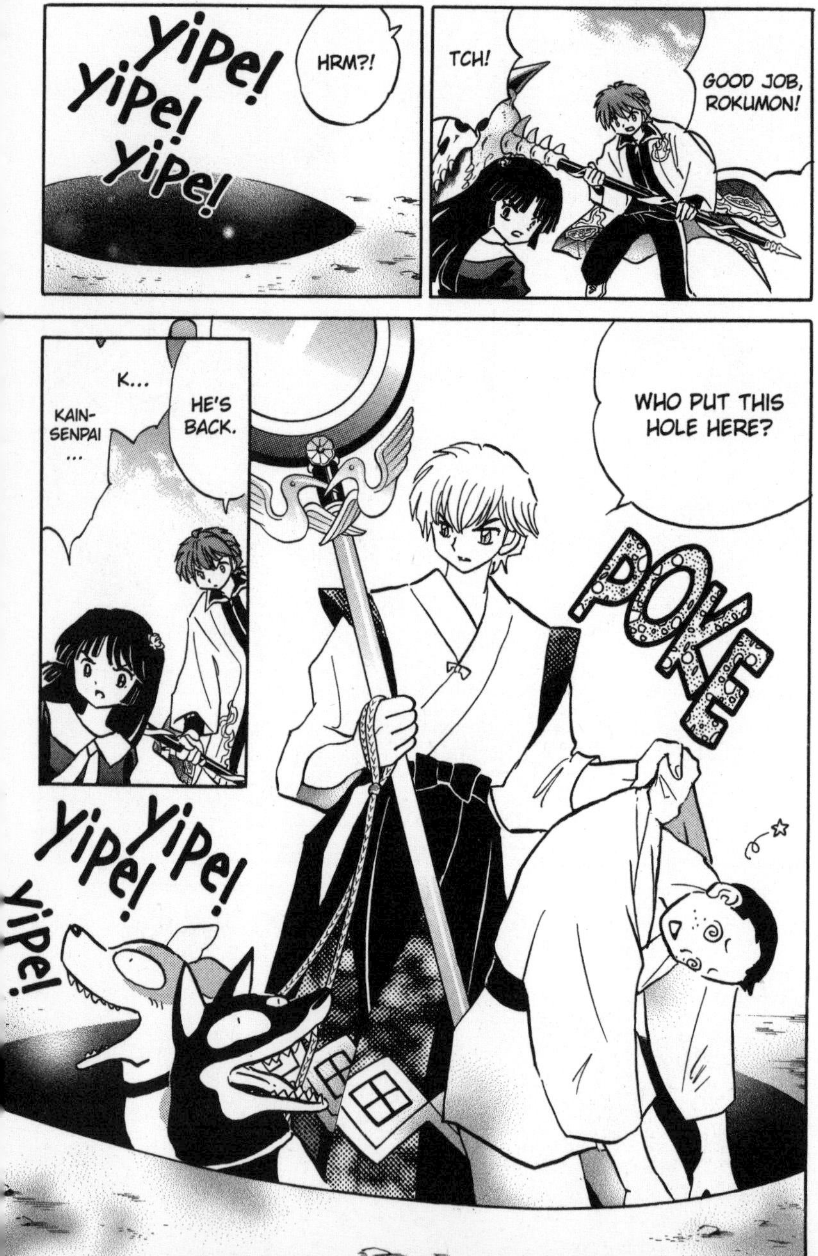
GOOD JOB, ROKUMON!
TCH!
HRM?!
Yipe! Yipe! Yipe!
WHO PUT THIS HOLE HERE?
POKE
HE'S BACK.
K...
KAIN-SENPAI ...
Yipe! Yipe! yipe!

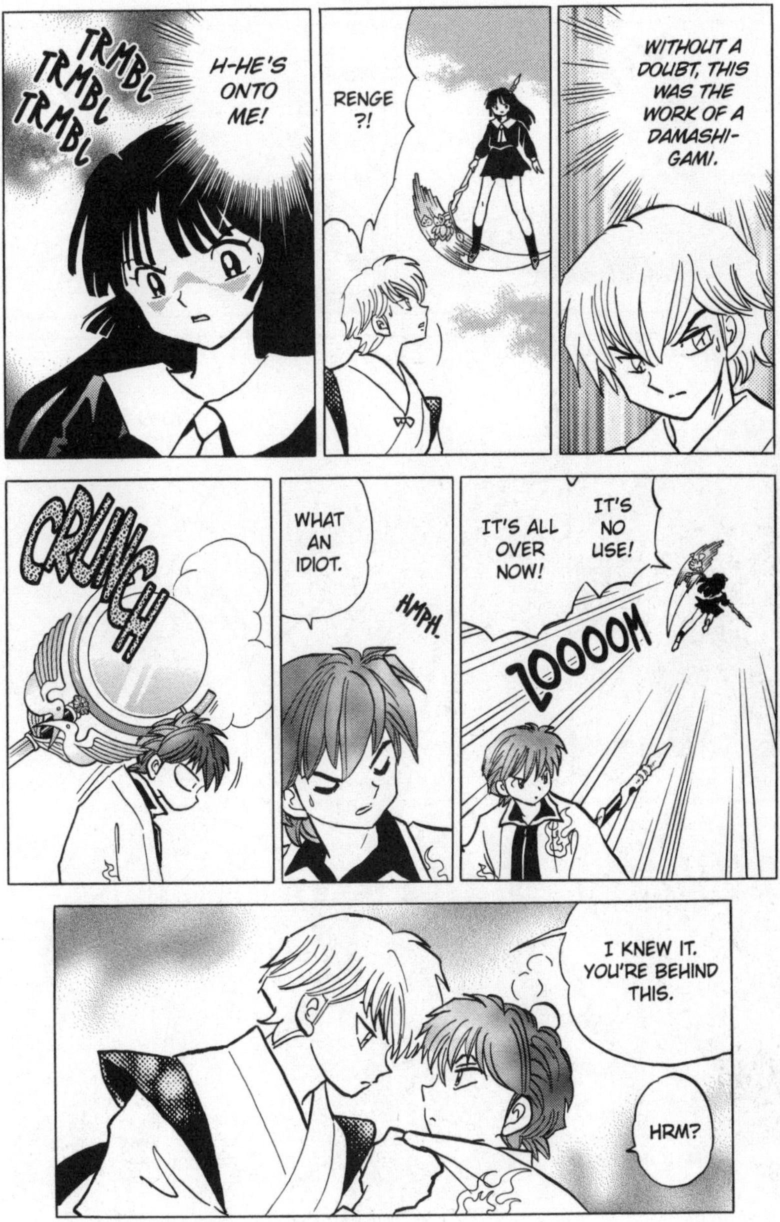
WITHOUT A DOUBT, THIS WAS THE WORK OF A DAMASHI-GAMI.
RENGE ?!
H-HE'S ONTO ME!
TRMBL TRMBL TRMBL
IT'S NO USE!
IT'S ALL OVER NOW!
ZOOOOM
WHAT AN IDIOT.
HMPH.
CRUNCH
I KNEW IT. YOU'RE BEHIND THIS.
HRM?

CHAPTER 147: SUSPICION

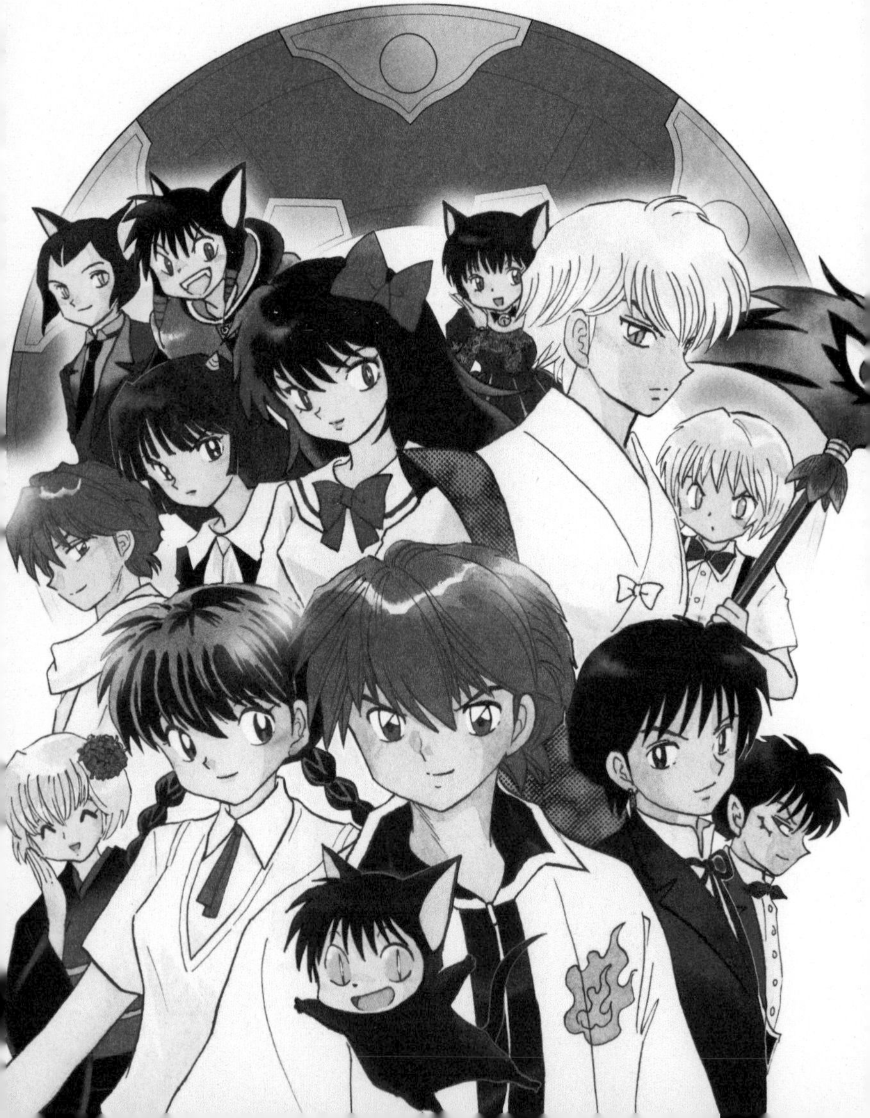

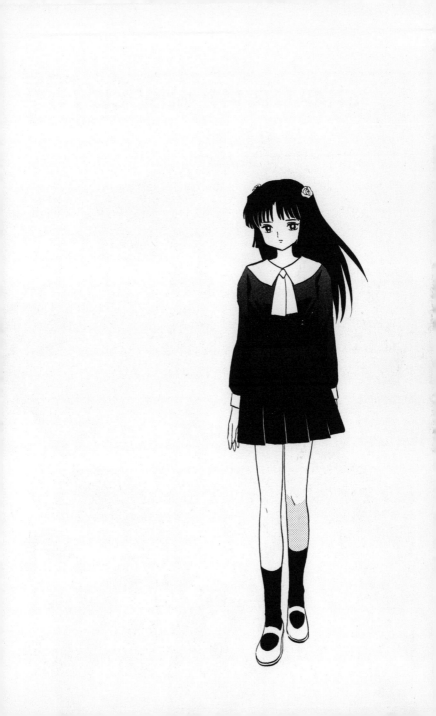

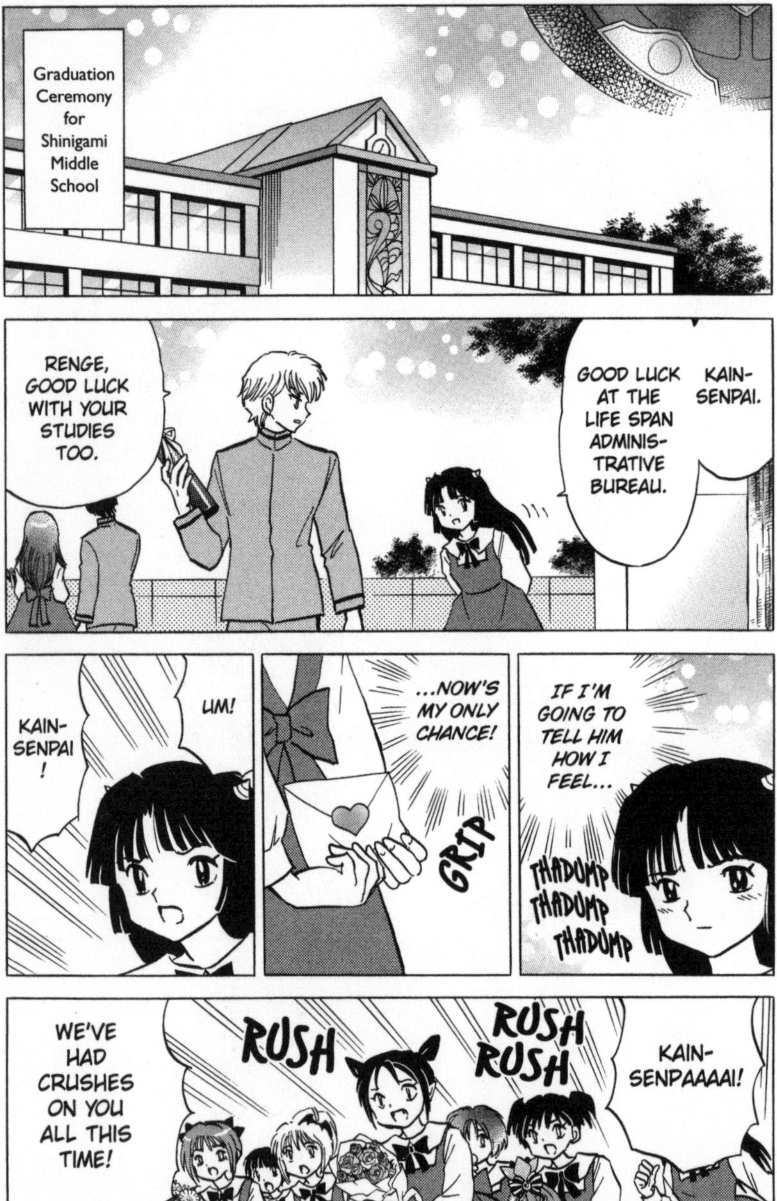

Graduation Ceremony for Shinigami Middle School
KAIN-SENPAI.
GOOD LUCK AT THE LIFE SPAN ADMINISTRATIVE BUREAU.
RENGE, GOOD LUCK WITH YOUR STUDIES TOO.
IF I'M GOING TO TELL HIM HOW I FEEL...
THADUMP THADUMP THADUMP
...NOW'S MY ONLY CHANCE!
GRIP
UM!
KAIN-SENPAI!
KAIN-SENPAAAAI!
RUSH RUSH
RUSH
WE'VE HAD CRUSHES ON YOU ALL THIS TIME!

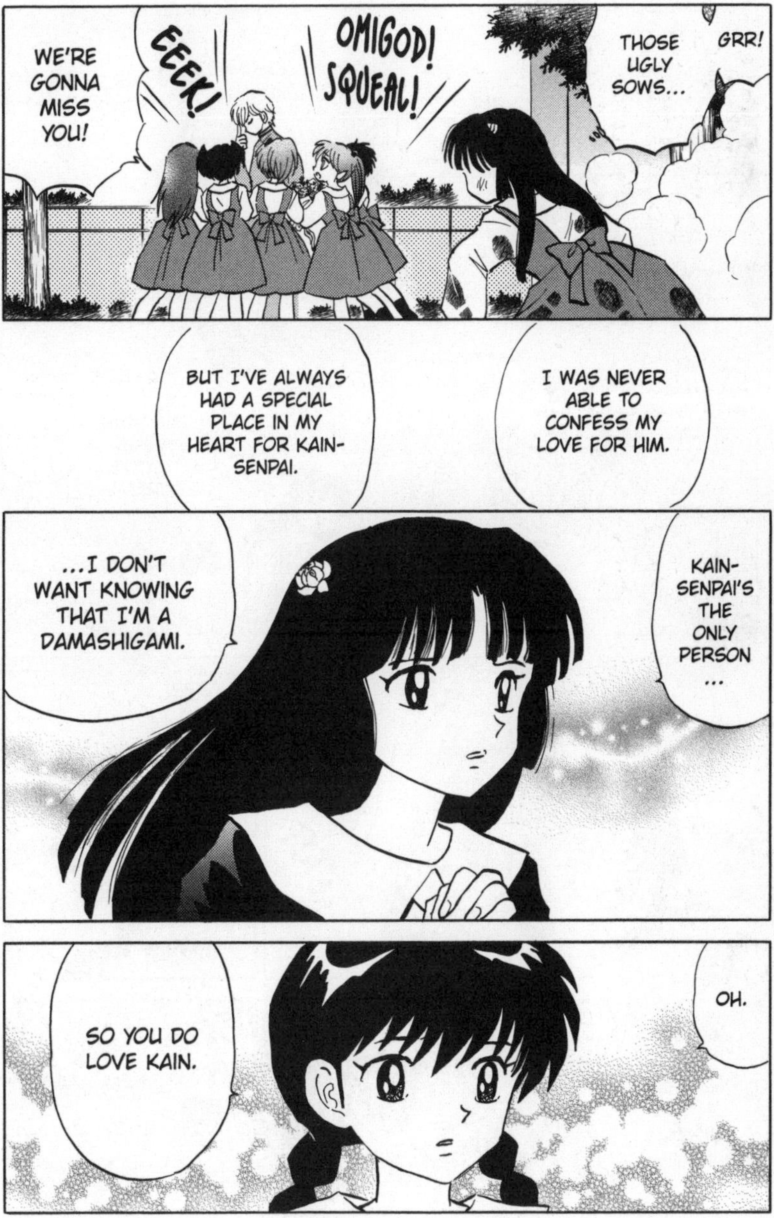
GRR!
THOSE UGLY SOWS...
OMIGOD! SQUEAL!
EEEK!
WE'RE GONNA MISS YOU!
I WAS NEVER ABLE TO CONFESS MY LOVE FOR HIM.
BUT I'VE ALWAYS HAD A SPECIAL PLACE IN MY HEART FOR KAIN-SENPAI.
KAIN-SENPAI'S THE ONLY PERSON ...
...I DON'T WANT KNOWING THAT I'M A DAMASHIGAMI.
OH.
SO YOU DO LOVE KAIN.

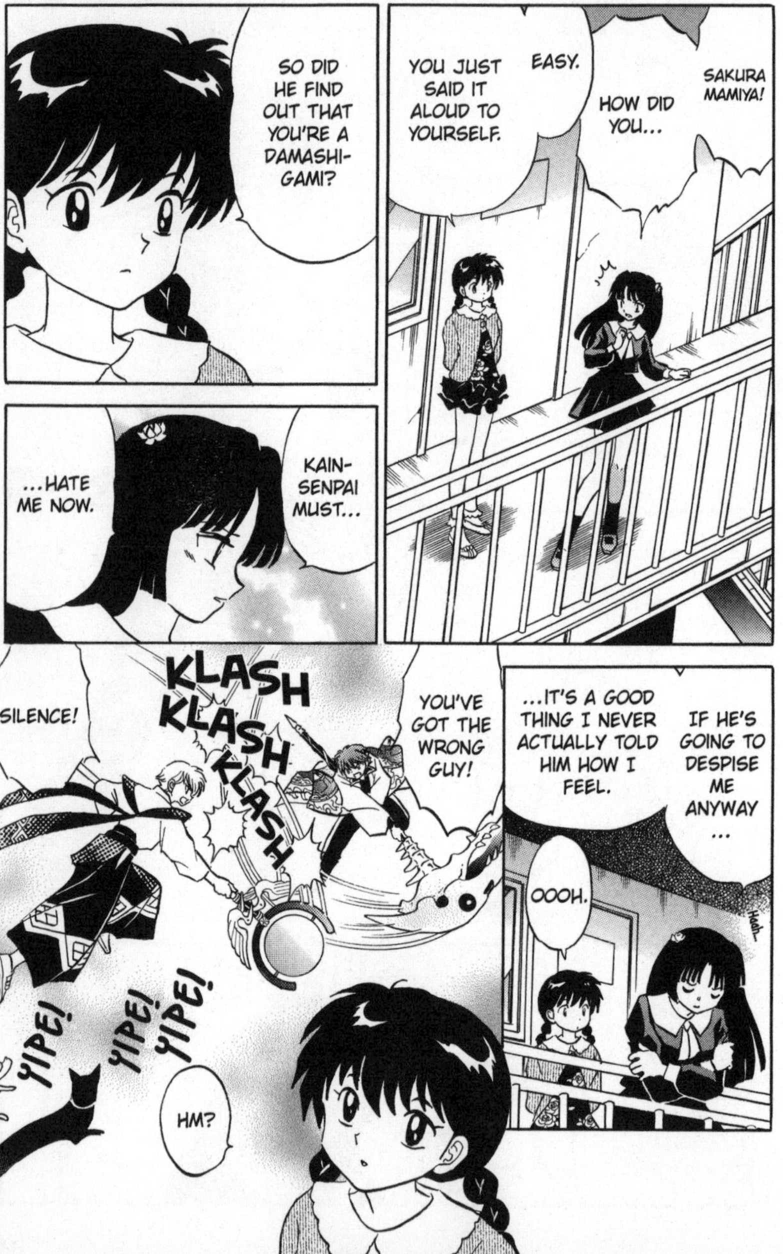
SAKURA MAMIYA!
HOW DID YOU...
EASY.
YOU JUST SAID IT ALOUD TO YOURSELF.
SO DID HE FIND OUT THAT YOU'RE A DAMASHI-GAMI?
KAIN-SENPAI MUST...
...HATE ME NOW.
IF HE'S GOING TO DESPISE ME ANYWAY...
...IT'S A GOOD THING I NEVER ACTUALLY TOLD HIM HOW I FEEL.
OOOH.
YOU'VE GOT THE WRONG GUY!
KLASH
KLASH
KLASH
KLASH
SILENCE!
YIPE!
YIPE!
YIPE!
HM?

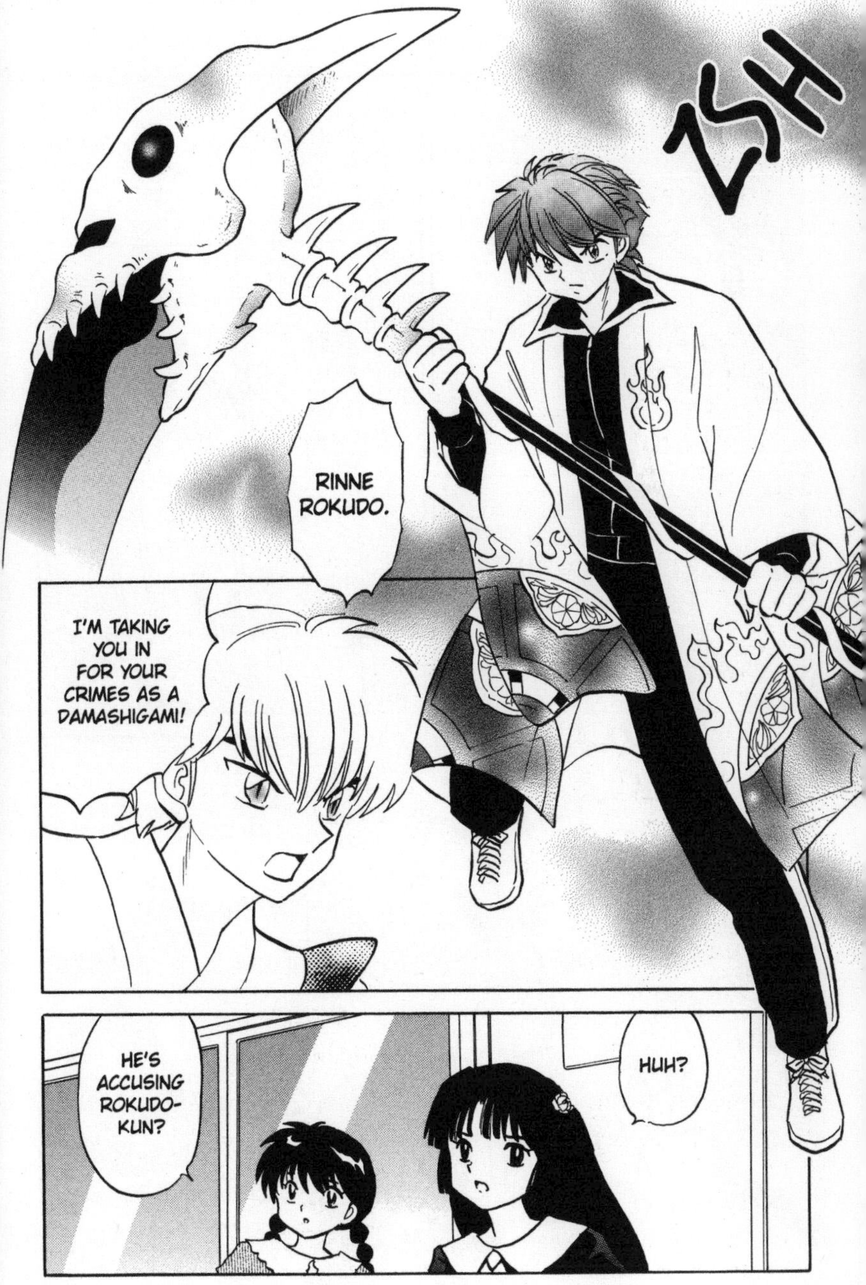
ZSH
RINNE ROKUDO.
I'M TAKING YOU IN FOR YOUR CRIMES AS A DAMASHIGAMI!
HUH?
HE'S ACCUSING ROKUDO-KUN?

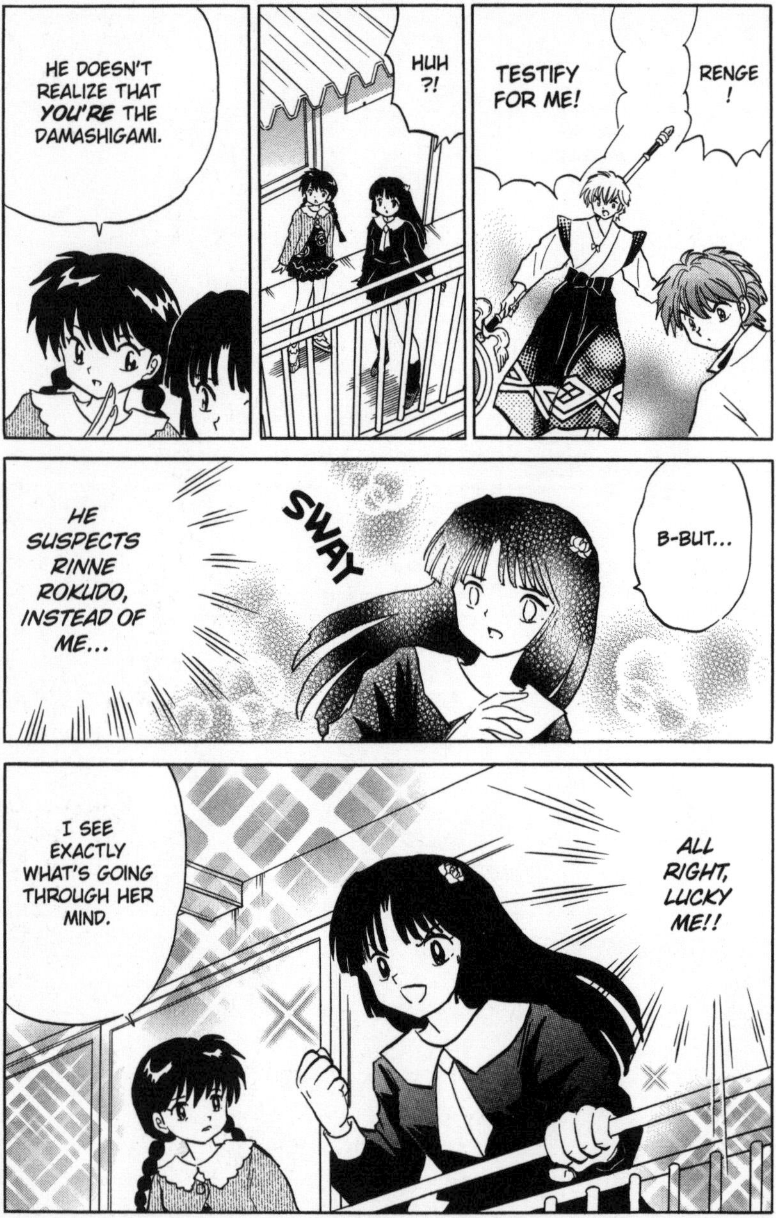
RENGE!
TESTIFY FOR ME!
HUH?!
HE DOESN'T REALIZE THAT *YOU'RE* THE DAMASHIGAMI.
B-BUT...
SWAY
HE SUSPECTS RINNE ROKUDO, INSTEAD OF ME...
ALL RIGHT, LUCKY ME!!
I SEE EXACTLY WHAT'S GOING THROUGH HER MIND.

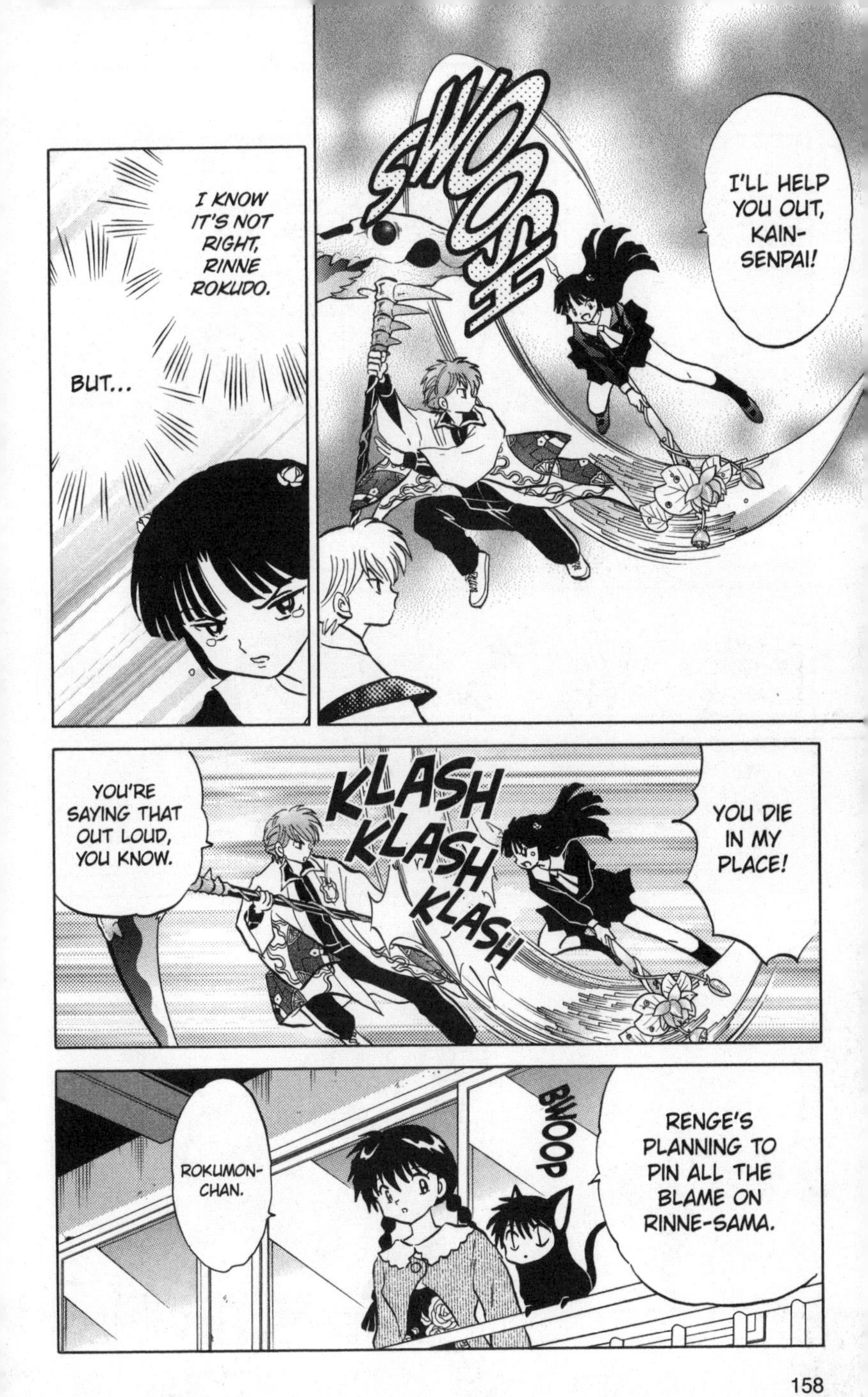
I'LL HELP YOU OUT, KAIN-SENPAI!
SWOOSH
I KNOW IT'S NOT RIGHT, RINNE ROKUDO.
BUT...
YOU DIE IN MY PLACE!
KLASH KLASH KLASH
YOU'RE SAYING THAT OUT LOUD, YOU KNOW.
RENGE'S PLANNING TO PIN ALL THE BLAME ON RINNE-SAMA.
BWOOP
ROKUMON-CHAN.

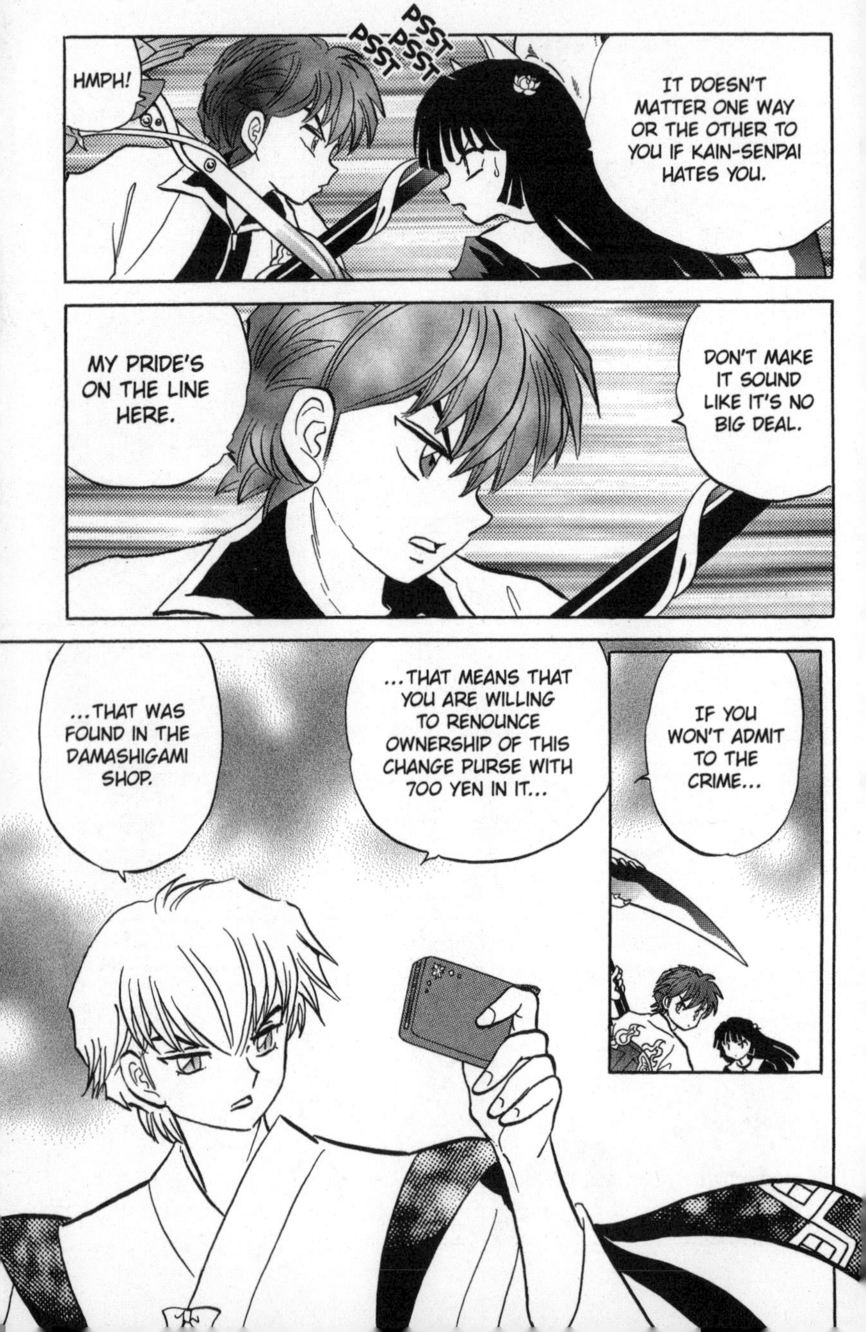
IT DOESN'T MATTER ONE WAY OR THE OTHER TO YOU IF KAIN-SENPAI HATES YOU.
PSST PSST PSST
HMPH!
DON'T MAKE IT SOUND LIKE IT'S NO BIG DEAL.
MY PRIDE'S ON THE LINE HERE.
IF YOU WON'T ADMIT TO THE CRIME...
...THAT MEANS THAT YOU ARE WILLING TO RENOUNCE OWNERSHIP OF THIS CHANGE PURSE WITH 700 YEN IN IT...
...THAT WAS FOUND IN THE DAMASHIGAMI SHOP.

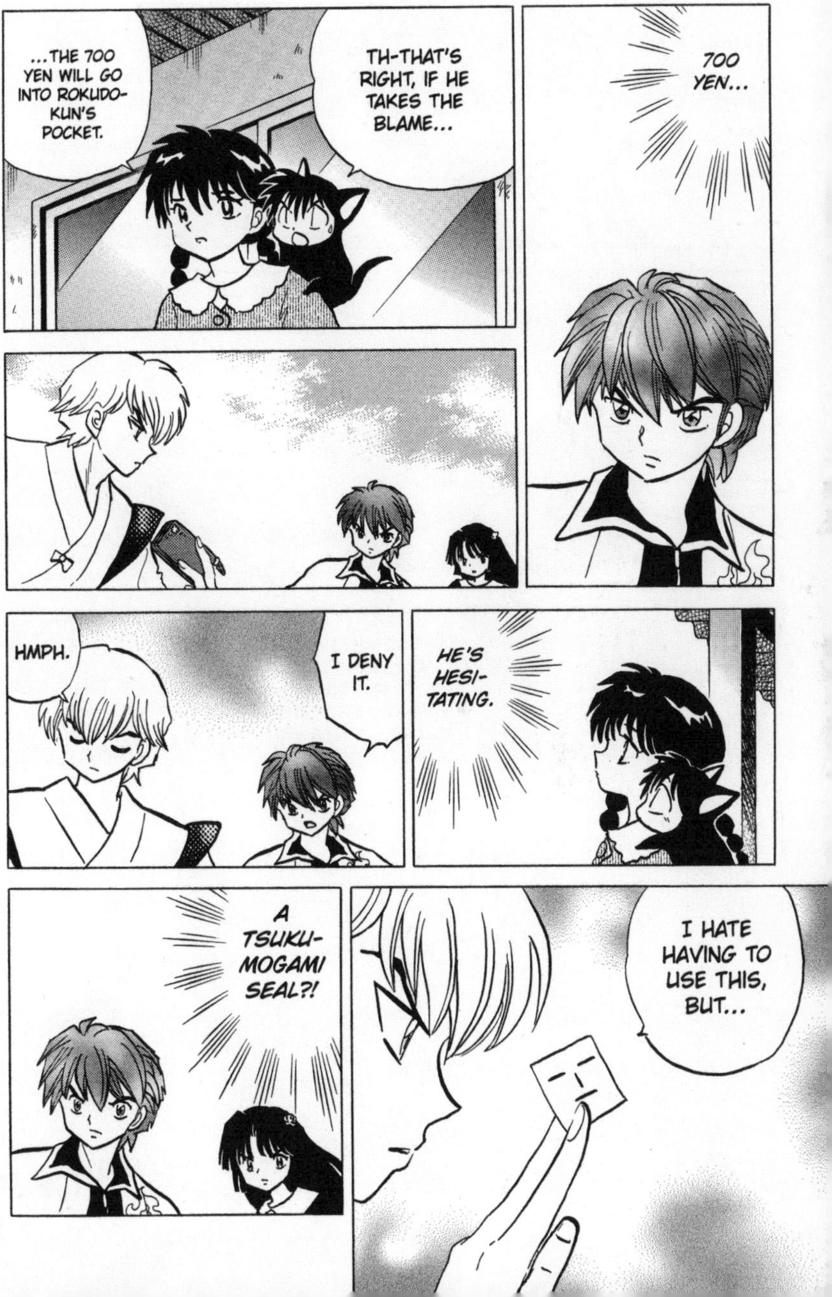
700 YEN...
TH-THAT'S RIGHT, IF HE TAKES THE BLAME...
...THE 700 YEN WILL GO INTO ROKUDO-KUN'S POCKET.
HE'S HESI-TATING.
I DENY IT.
HMPH.
I HATE HAVING TO USE THIS, BUT...
A TSUKU-MOGAMI SEAL?!

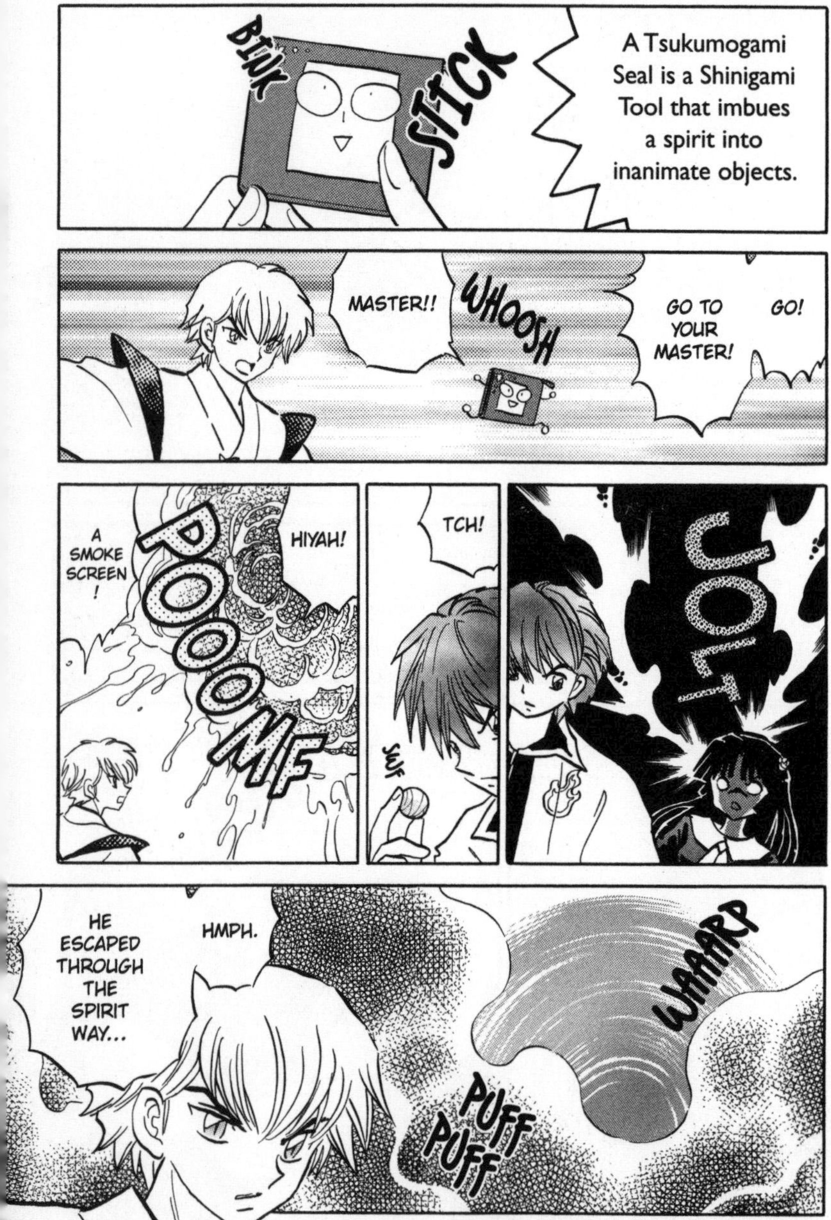
A Tsukumogami Seal is a Shinigami Tool that imbues a spirit into inanimate objects.
STICK
BLINK
GO!
GO TO YOUR MASTER!
WHOOSH
MASTER!!
JOLT
TCH!
SWF
HIYAH!
A SMOKE SCREEN!
POOOOMF
WHAARP
PUFF PUFF
HMPH.
HE ESCAPED THROUGH THE SPIRIT WAY...

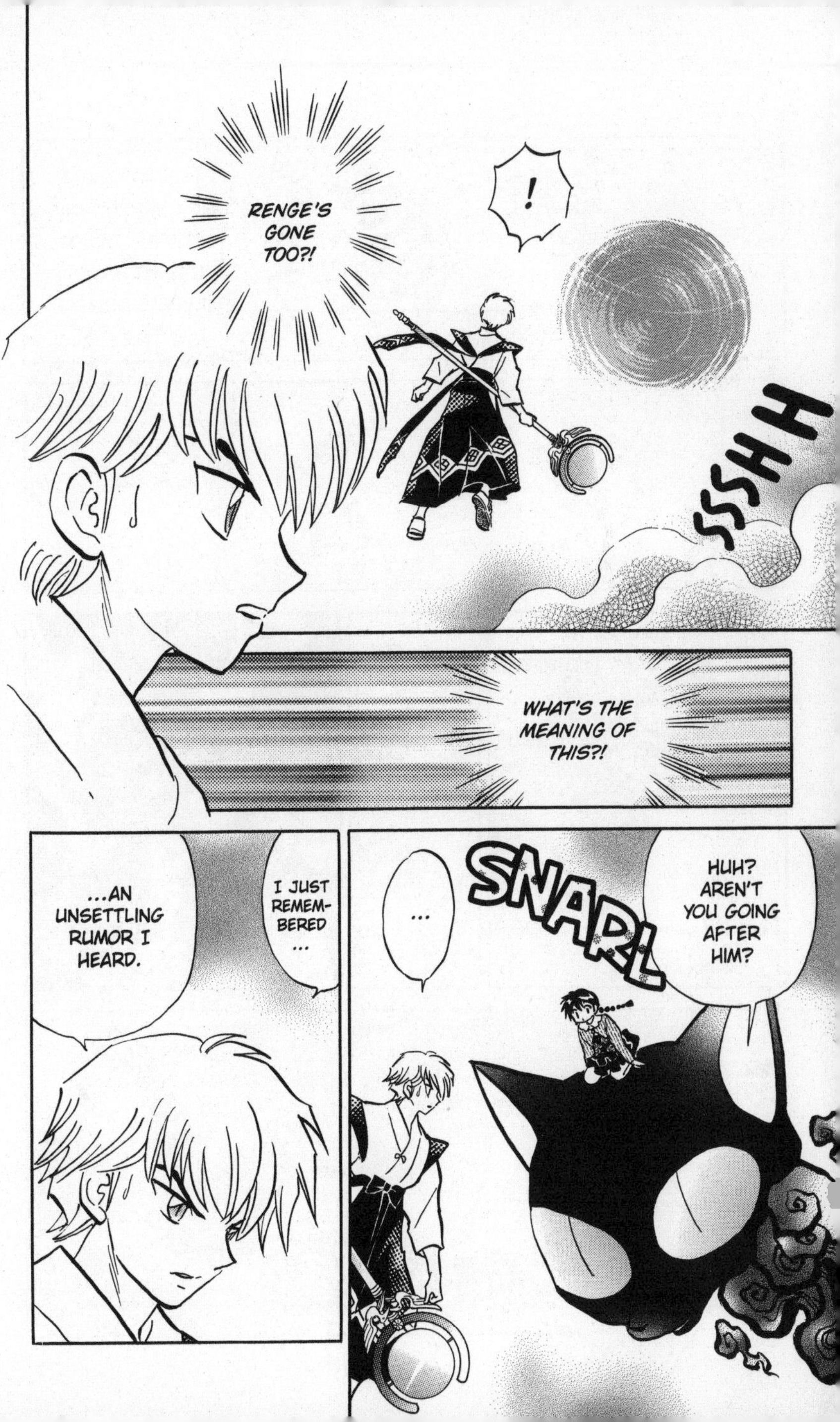
!
SSSHH
RENGE'S GONE TOO?!
WHAT'S THE MEANING OF THIS?!
HUH? AREN'T YOU GOING AFTER HIM?
SNARL
...
I JUST REMEMBERED...
...AN UNSETTLING RUMOR I HEARD.

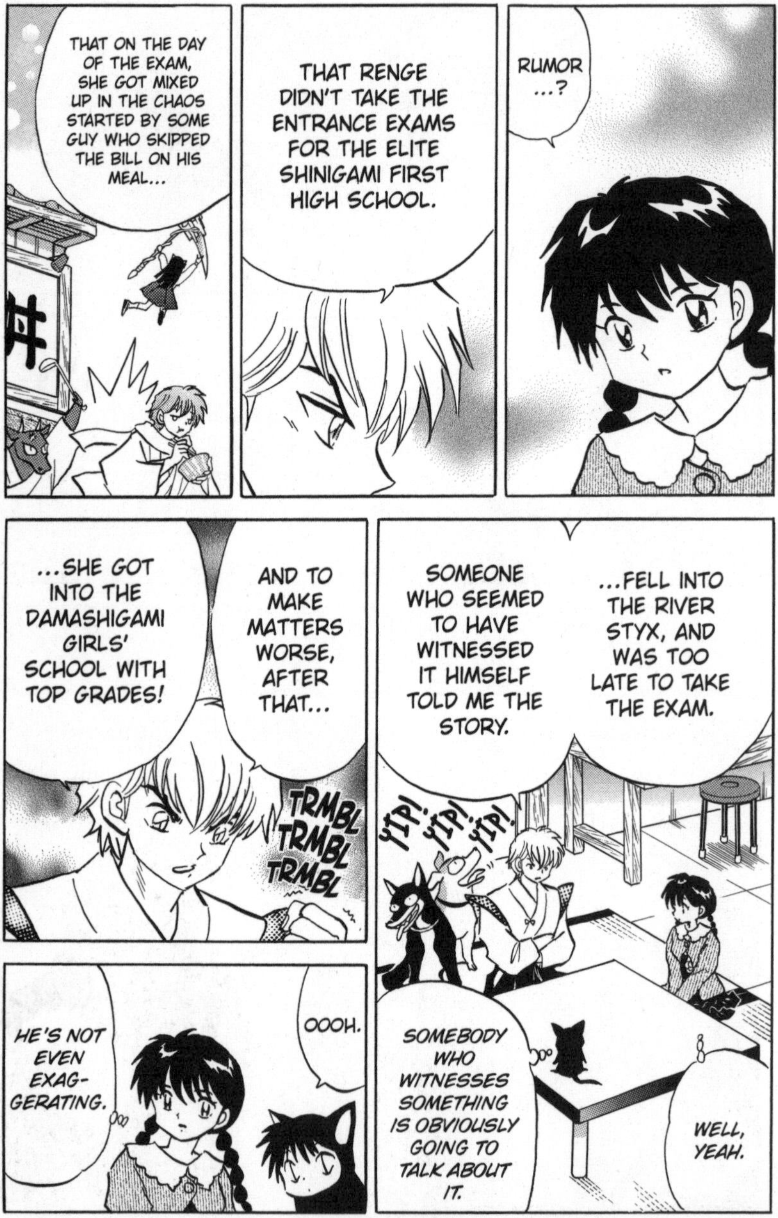
RUMOR ...?
THAT RENGE DIDN'T TAKE THE ENTRANCE EXAMS FOR THE ELITE SHINIGAMI FIRST HIGH SCHOOL.
THAT ON THE DAY OF THE EXAM, SHE GOT MIXED UP IN THE CHAOS STARTED BY SOME GUY WHO SKIPPED THE BILL ON HIS MEAL...
...FELL INTO THE RIVER STYX, AND WAS TOO LATE TO TAKE THE EXAM.
SOMEONE WHO SEEMED TO HAVE WITNESSED IT HIMSELF TOLD ME THE STORY.
YIP! YIP! YIP!
WELL, YEAH.
SOMEBODY WHO WITNESSES SOMETHING IS OBVIOUSLY GOING TO TALK ABOUT IT.
AND TO MAKE MATTERS WORSE, AFTER THAT...
...SHE GOT INTO THE DAMASHIGAMI GIRLS' SCHOOL WITH TOP GRADES!
TRMBL TRMBL TRMBL
OOOH.
HE'S NOT EVEN EXAG-GERATING.

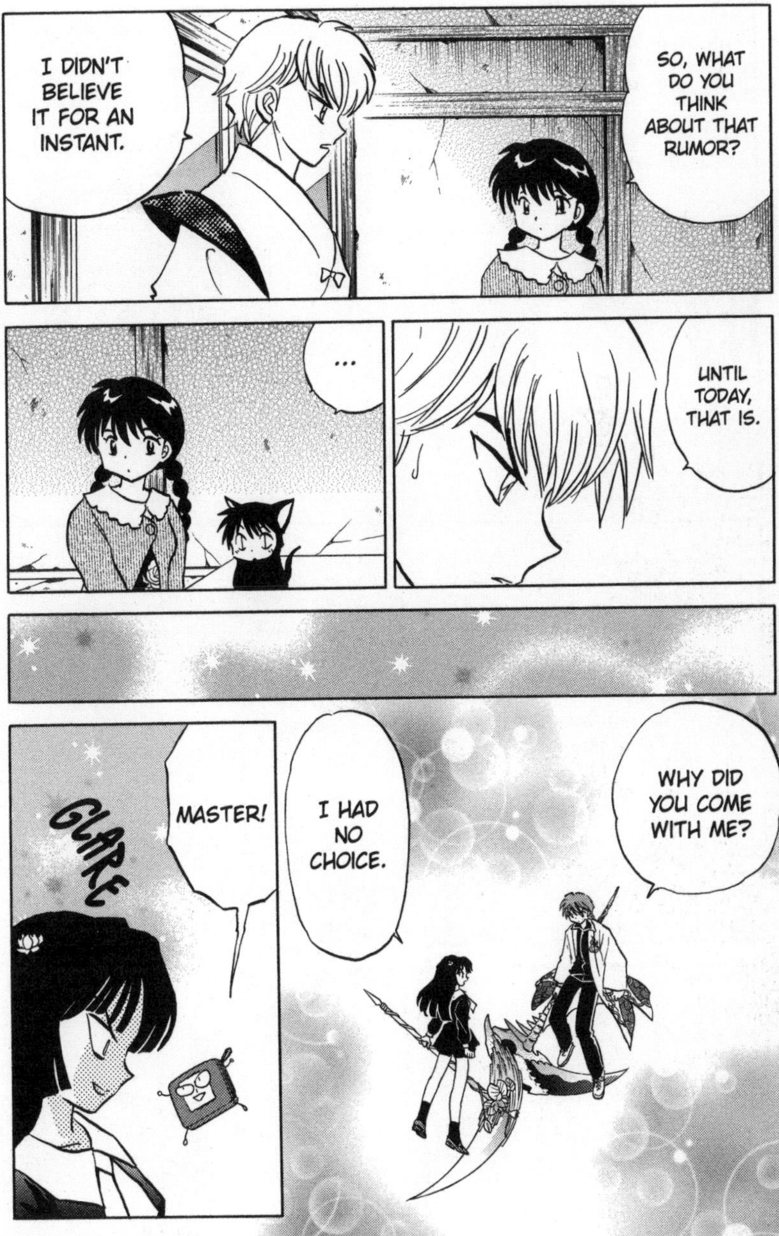

SO, WHAT DO YOU THINK ABOUT THAT RUMOR?
I DIDN'T BELIEVE IT FOR AN INSTANT.
UNTIL TODAY, THAT IS.
...
WHY DID YOU COME WITH ME?
I HAD NO CHOICE.
MASTER!
GLARE

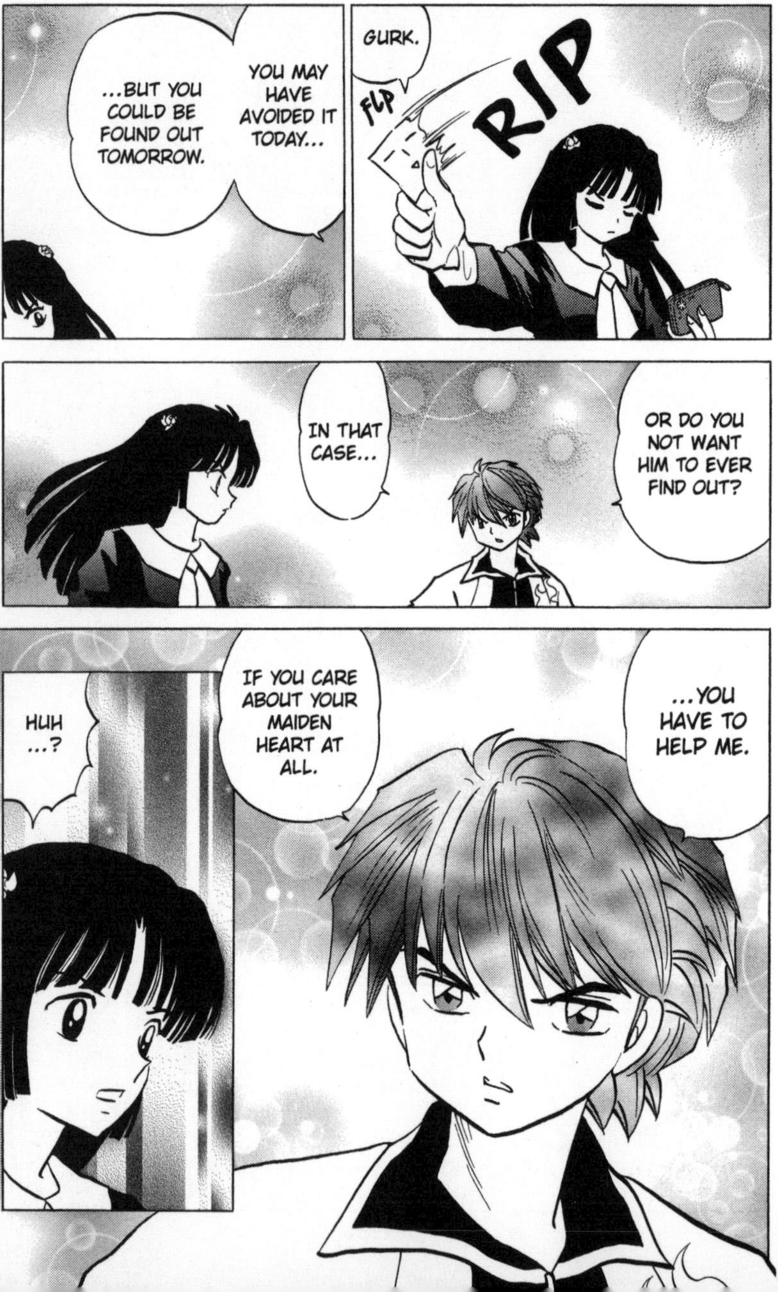
GURK.
FLP
RIP
YOU MAY HAVE AVOIDED IT TODAY...
...BUT YOU COULD BE FOUND OUT TOMORROW.
OR DO YOU NOT WANT HIM TO EVER FIND OUT?
IN THAT CASE...
...YOU HAVE TO HELP ME.
IF YOU CARE ABOUT YOUR MAIDEN HEART AT ALL.
HUH ...?

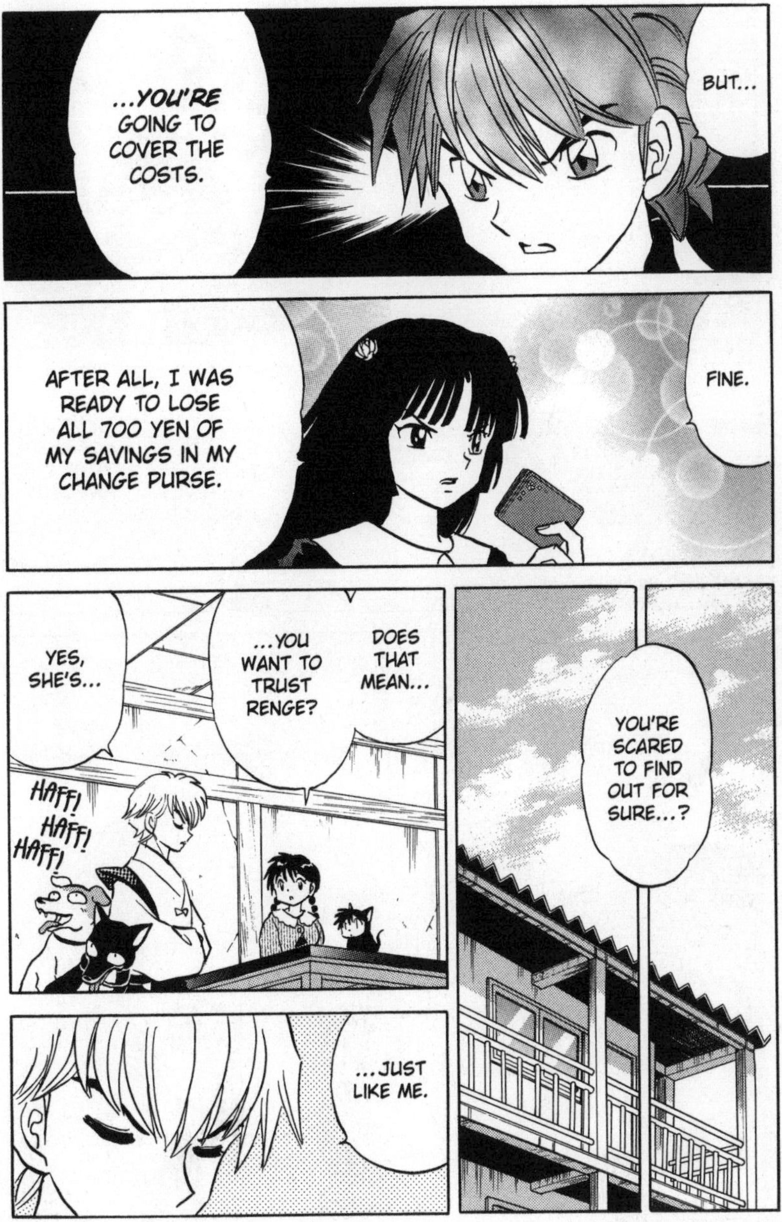
BUT...
...YOU'RE GOING TO COVER THE COSTS.
FINE.
AFTER ALL, I WAS READY TO LOSE ALL 700 YEN OF MY SAVINGS IN MY CHANGE PURSE.
YOU'RE SCARED TO FIND OUT FOR SURE...?
DOES THAT MEAN...
...YOU WANT TO TRUST RENGE?
YES, SHE'S...
HAFF! HAFF! HAFF!
...JUST LIKE ME.

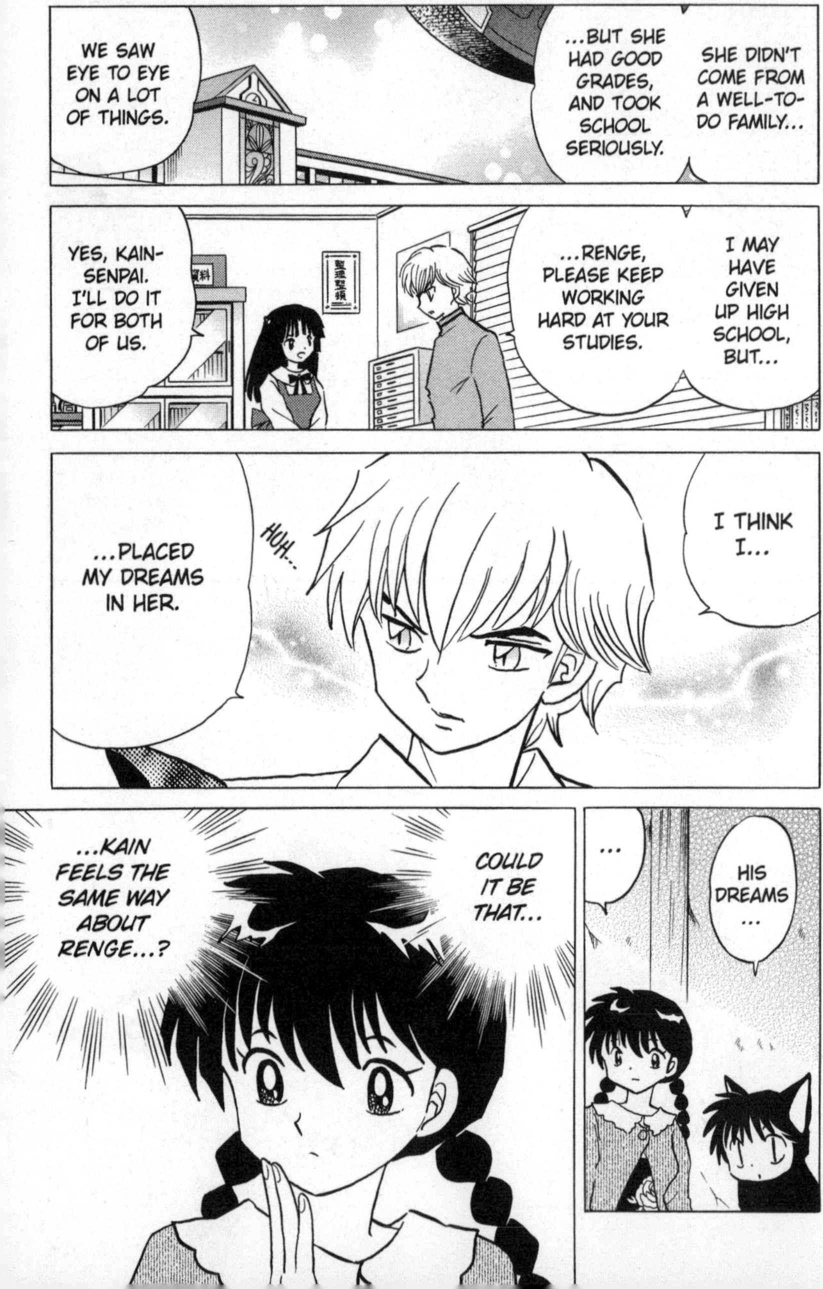
SHE DIDN'T COME FROM A WELL-TO-DO FAMILY...
...BUT SHE HAD GOOD GRADES, AND TOOK SCHOOL SERIOUSLY.
WE SAW EYE TO EYE ON A LOT OF THINGS.
I MAY HAVE GIVEN UP HIGH SCHOOL, BUT...
...RENGE, PLEASE KEEP WORKING HARD AT YOUR STUDIES.
YES, KAIN-SENPAI. I'LL DO IT FOR BOTH OF US.
I THINK I...
HUH...
...PLACED MY DREAMS IN HER.
HIS DREAMS ...
...
COULD IT BE THAT...
...KAIN FEELS THE SAME WAY ABOUT RENGE...?

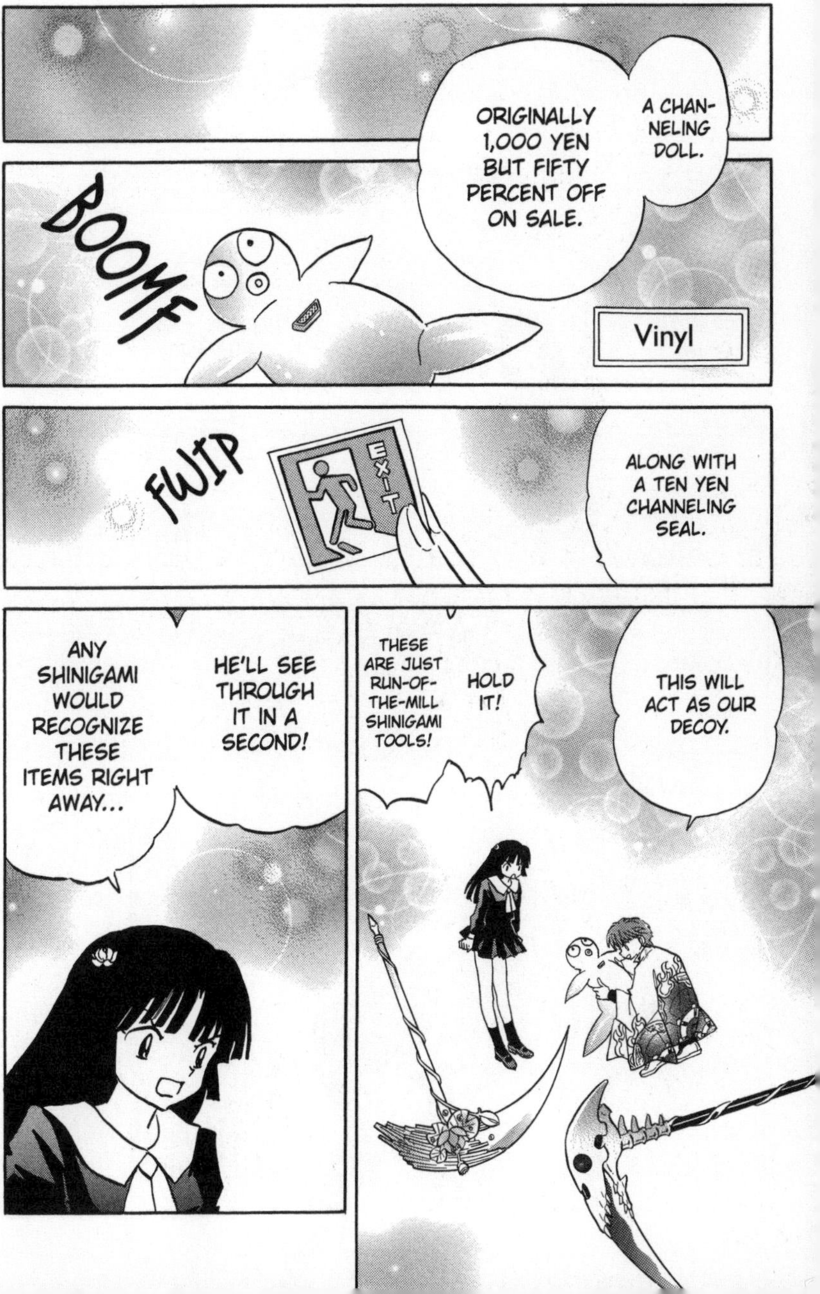
A CHAN-NELING DOLL.
ORIGINALLY 1,000 YEN BUT FIFTY PERCENT OFF ON SALE.
Vinyl
BOOMF
ALONG WITH A TEN YEN CHANNELING SEAL.
EXIT
FWIP
THIS WILL ACT AS OUR DECOY.
HOLD IT!
THESE ARE JUST RUN-OF-THE-MILL SHINIGAMI TOOLS!
HE'LL SEE THROUGH IT IN A SECOND!
ANY SHINIGAMI WOULD RECOGNIZE THESE ITEMS RIGHT AWAY...

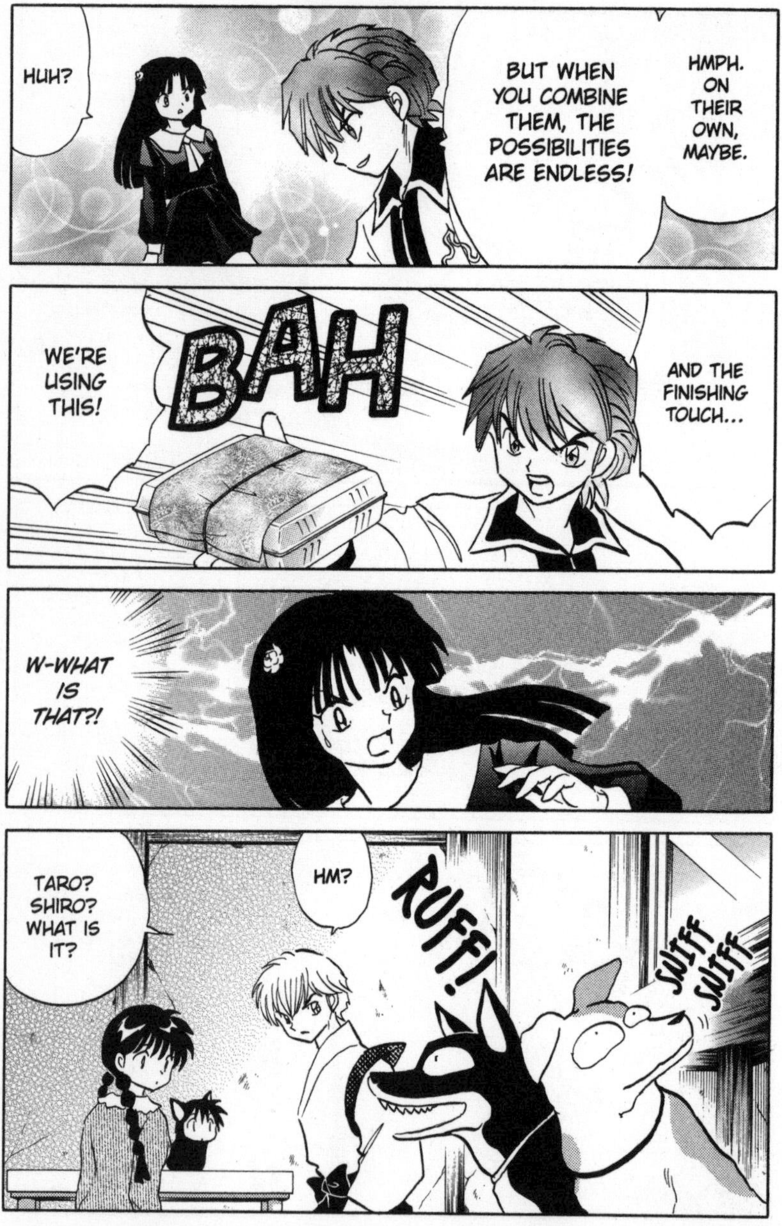
HMPH. ON THEIR OWN, MAYBE.
BUT WHEN YOU COMBINE THEM, THE POSSIBILITIES ARE ENDLESS!
HUH?
AND THE FINISHING TOUCH...
BAH
WE'RE USING THIS!
W-WHAT IS THAT?!
SNIFF SNIFF
RUFF!
HM?
TARO? SHIRO? WHAT IS IT?

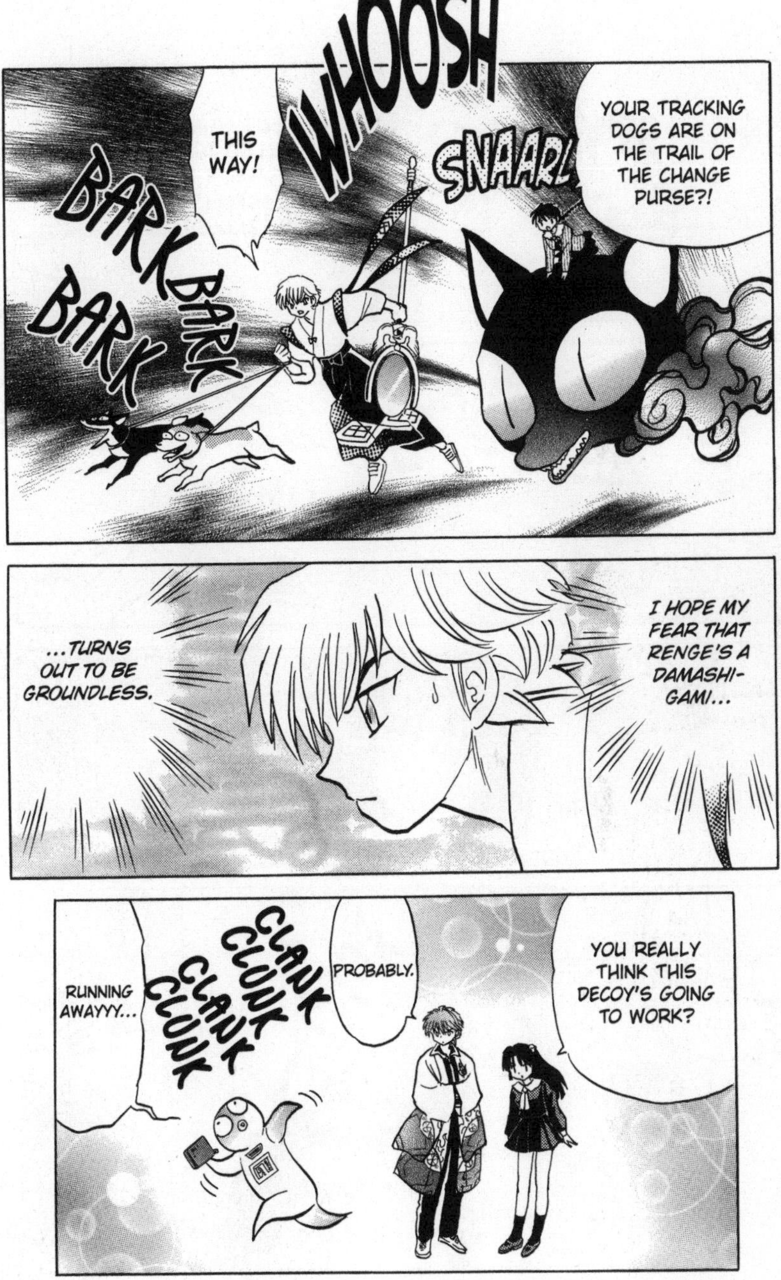
YOUR TRACKING DOGS ARE ON THE TRAIL OF THE CHANGE PURSE?!
SNAARL
WHOOSH
THIS WAY!
BARK BARK BARK
I HOPE MY FEAR THAT RENGE'S A DAMASHI-GAMI...
...TURNS OUT TO BE GROUNDLESS.
YOU REALLY THINK THIS DECOY'S GOING TO WORK?
PROBABLY.
CLANK CLUNK CLANK CLUNK
RUNNING AWAYYY...

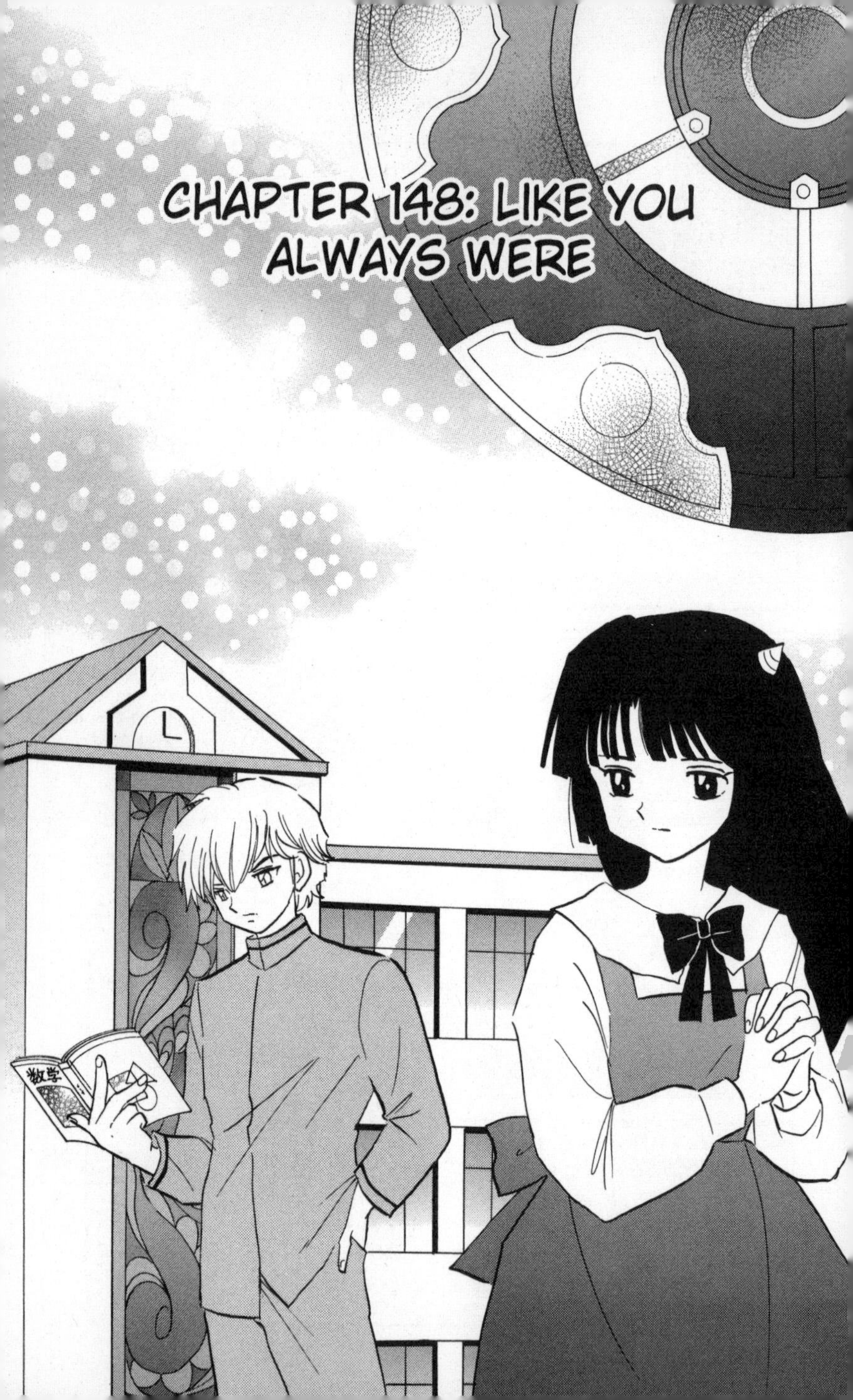
CHAPTER 148: LIKE YOU ALWAYS WERE
数学

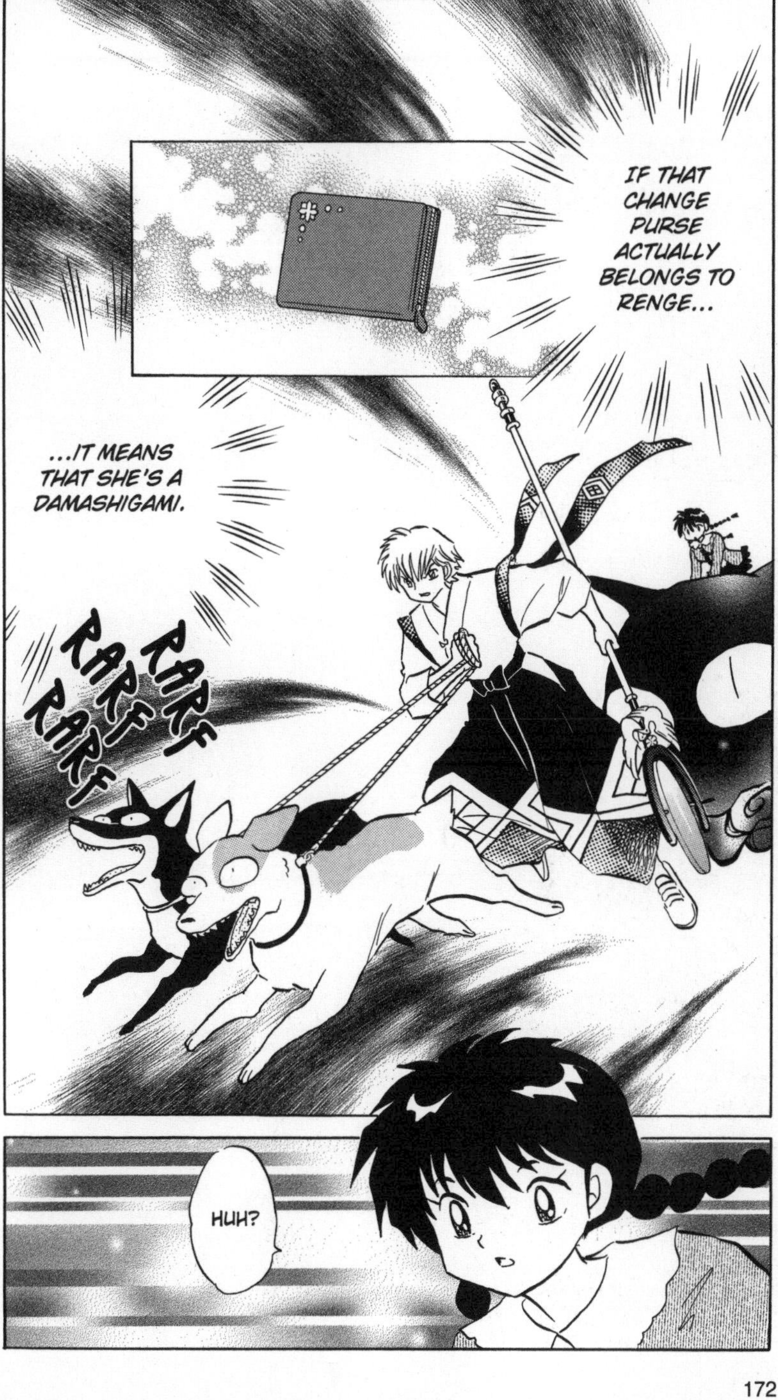
IF THAT CHANGE PURSE ACTUALLY BELONGS TO RENGE...
...IT MEANS THAT SHE'S A DAMASHIGAMI.
RARF RARF RARF
HUH?

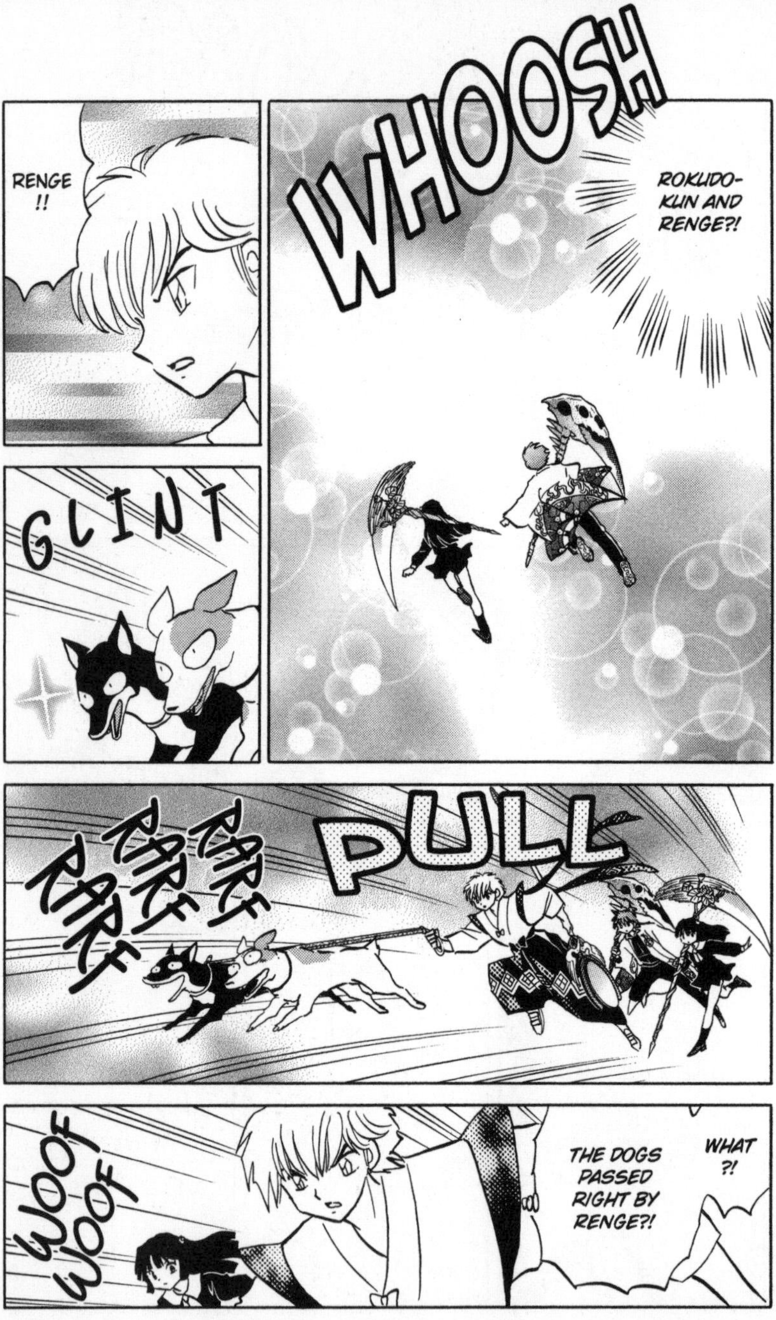
WHOOSH
ROKUDO-KUN AND RENGE?!
RENGE !!
GLINT
PULL
RARF RARF RARF
WHAT ?!
THE DOGS PASSED RIGHT BY RENGE?!
WOOF WOOF

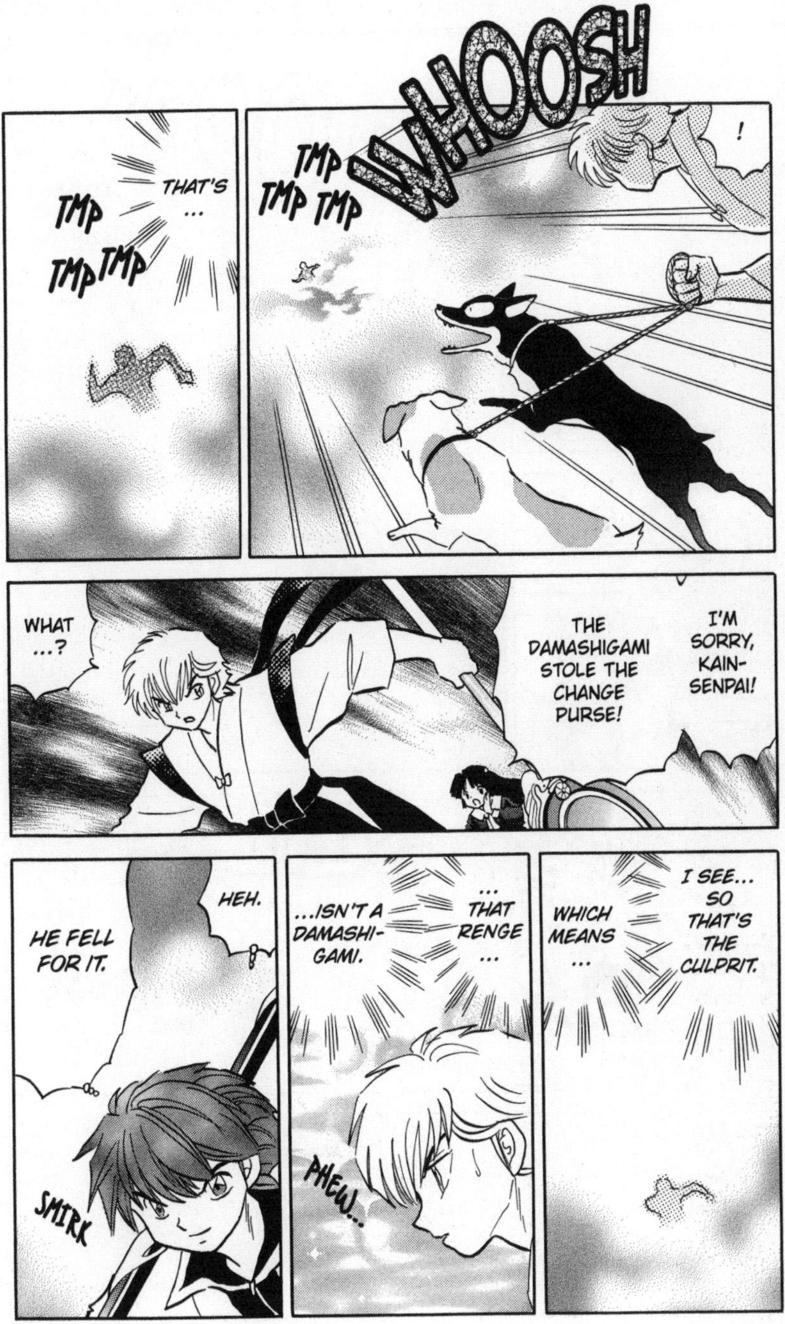
!
WHOOSH
TMP
TMP TMP
TMP
TMP TMP
THAT'S ...
I'M SORRY, KAIN-SENPAI!
THE DAMASHIGAMI STOLE THE CHANGE PURSE!
WHAT ...?
I SEE... SO THAT'S THE CULPRIT.
WHICH MEANS ...
... THAT RENGE ...
...ISN'T A DAMASHI-GAMI.
PHEW...
HEH.
HE FELL FOR IT.
SMIRK

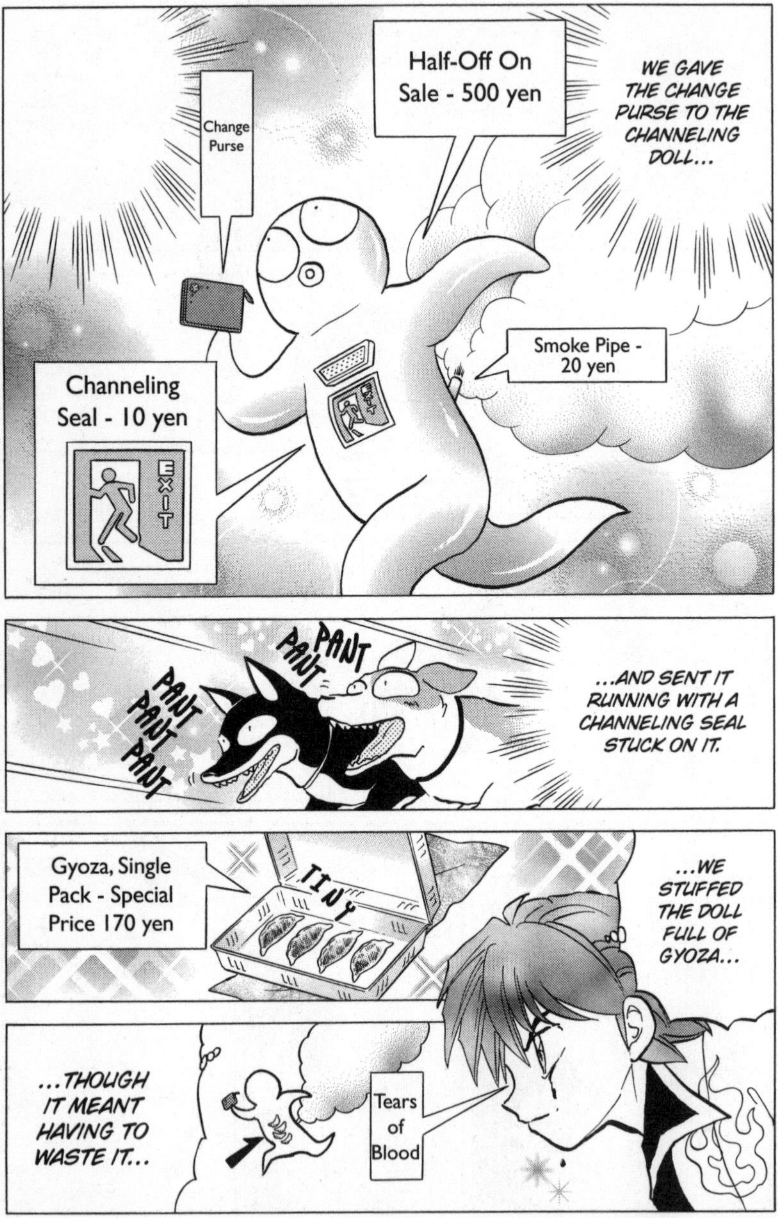
WE GAVE THE CHANGE PURSE TO THE CHANNELING DOLL...
Half-Off On Sale - 500 yen
Change Purse
Smoke Pipe - 20 yen
Channeling Seal - 10 yen
EXIT
...AND SENT IT RUNNING WITH A CHANNELING SEAL STUCK ON IT.
PANT PANT
PANT PANT PANT
...WE STUFFED THE DOLL FULL OF GYOZA...
TINY
Gyoza, Single Pack - Special Price 170 yen
Tears of Blood
...THOUGH IT MEANT HAVING TO WASTE IT...

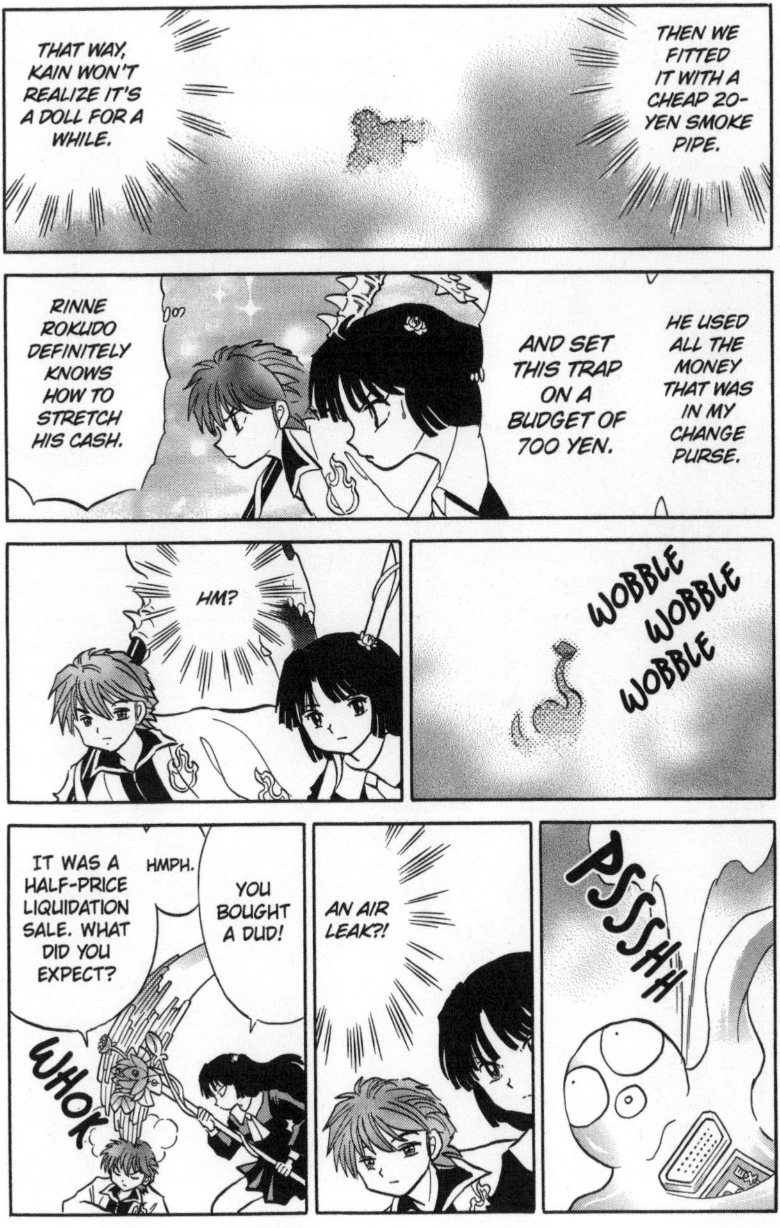
THEN WE FITTED IT WITH A CHEAP 20-YEN SMOKE PIPE.
THAT WAY, KAIN WON'T REALIZE IT'S A DOLL FOR A WHILE.
HE USED ALL THE MONEY THAT WAS IN MY CHANGE PURSE.
AND SET THIS TRAP ON A BUDGET OF 700 YEN.
RINNE ROKUDO DEFINITELY KNOWS HOW TO STRETCH HIS CASH.
WOBBLE WOBBLE WOBBLE
HM?
PSSSHH
AN AIR LEAK?!
YOU BOUGHT A DUD!
HMPH.
IT WAS A HALF-PRICE LIQUIDATION SALE. WHAT DID YOU EXPECT?
WHOK

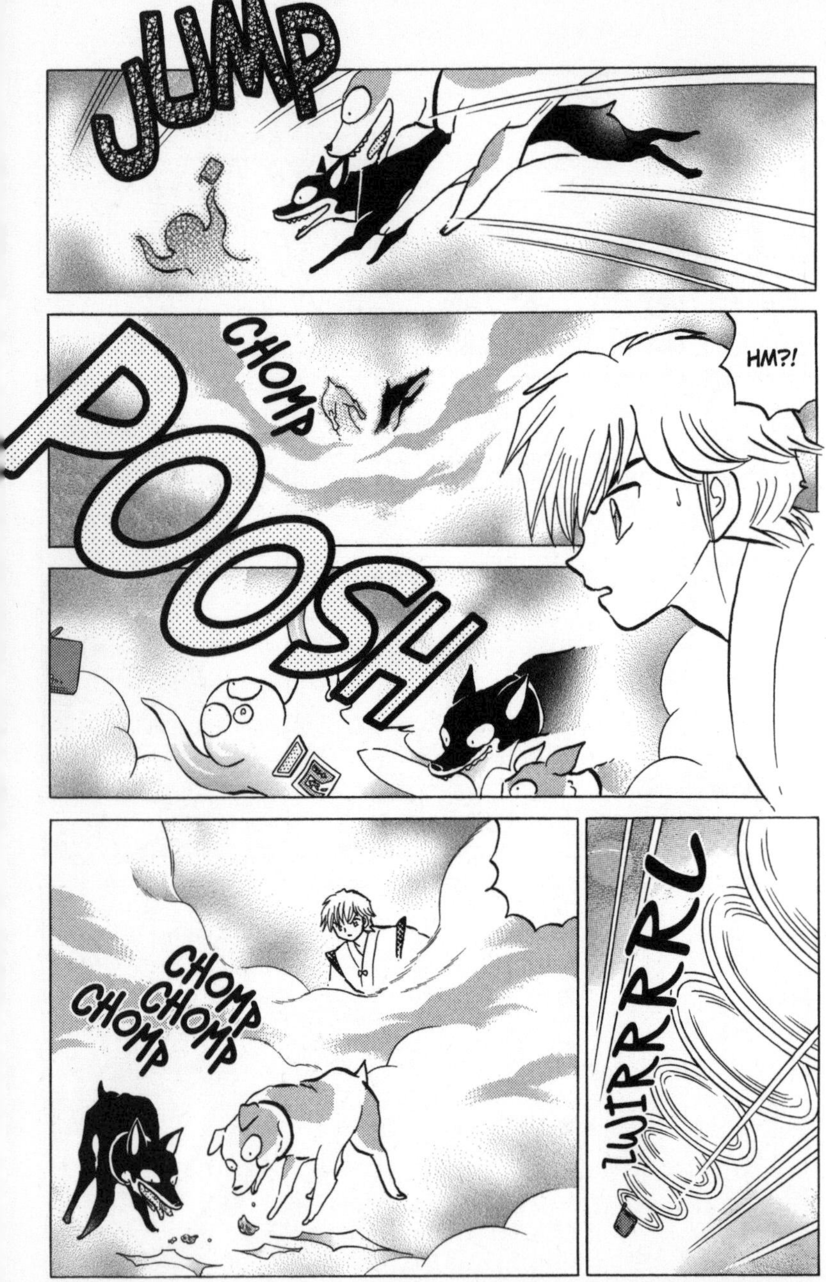
JUMP
HM?!
CHOMP
POOSH
WHIRRRRL
CHOMP
CHOMP
CHOMP

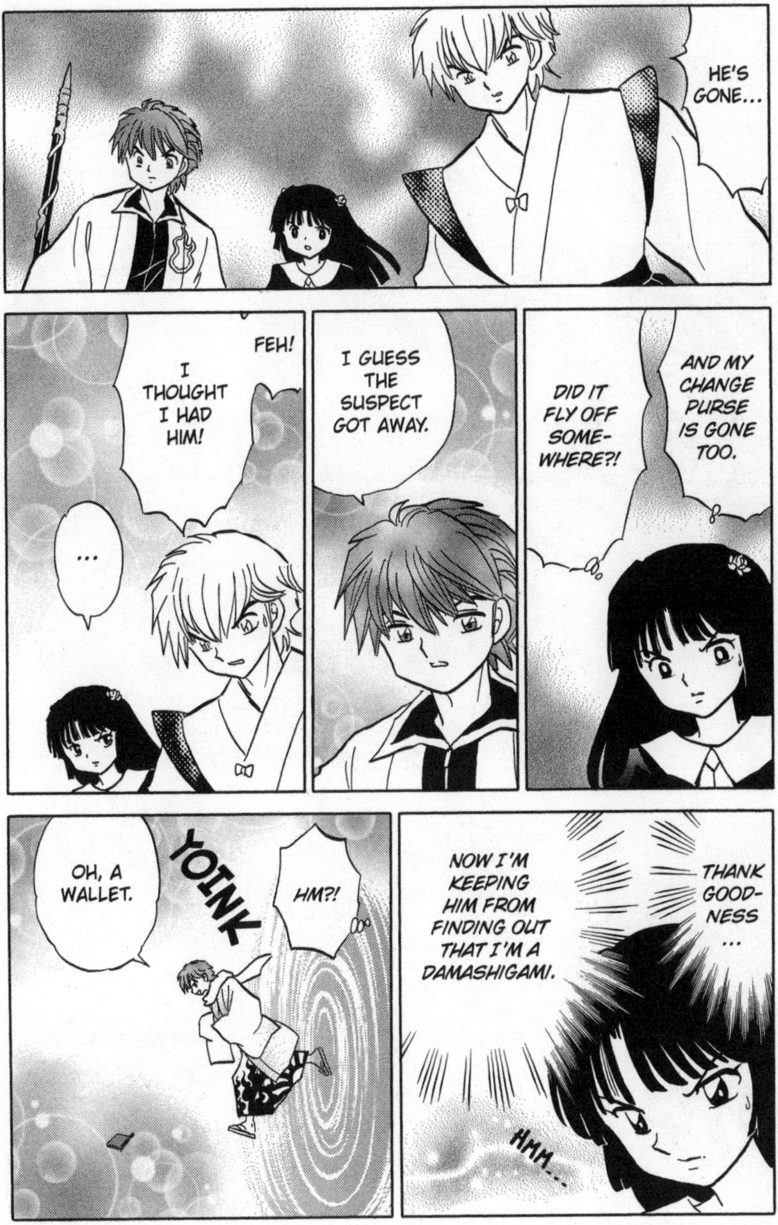
HE'S GONE...
AND MY CHANGE PURSE IS GONE TOO.
DID IT FLY OFF SOME-WHERE?!
I GUESS THE SUSPECT GOT AWAY.
FEH!
I THOUGHT I HAD HIM!
...
THANK GOOD-NESS...
NOW I'M KEEPING HIM FROM FINDING OUT THAT I'M A DAMASHIGAMI.
HMM...
HM?!
YOINK
OH, A WALLET.

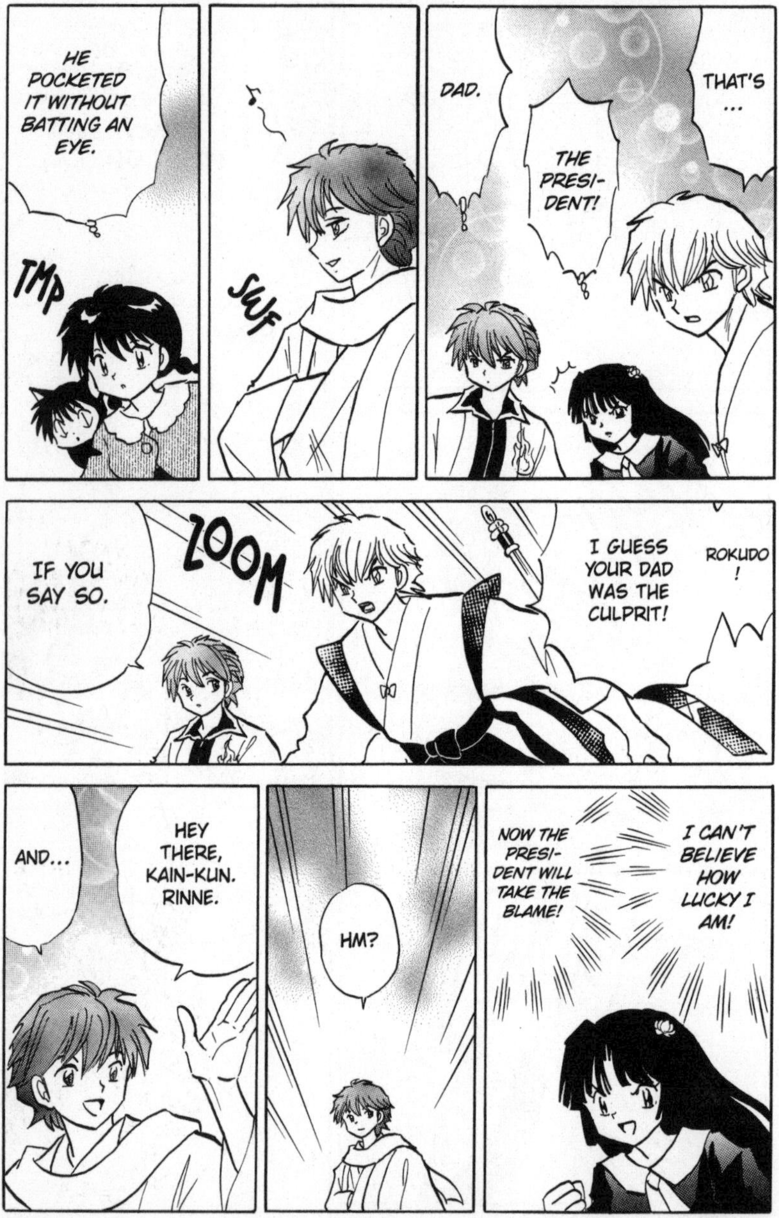
THAT'S ...
DAD.
THE PRESIDENT!
SWF
HE POCKETED IT WITHOUT BATTING AN EYE.
TMP
ROKUDO!
I GUESS YOUR DAD WAS THE CULPRIT!
ZOOM
IF YOU SAY SO.
I CAN'T BELIEVE HOW LUCKY I AM!
NOW THE PRESIDENT WILL TAKE THE BLAME!
HM?
HEY THERE, KAIN-KUN. RINNE.
AND...

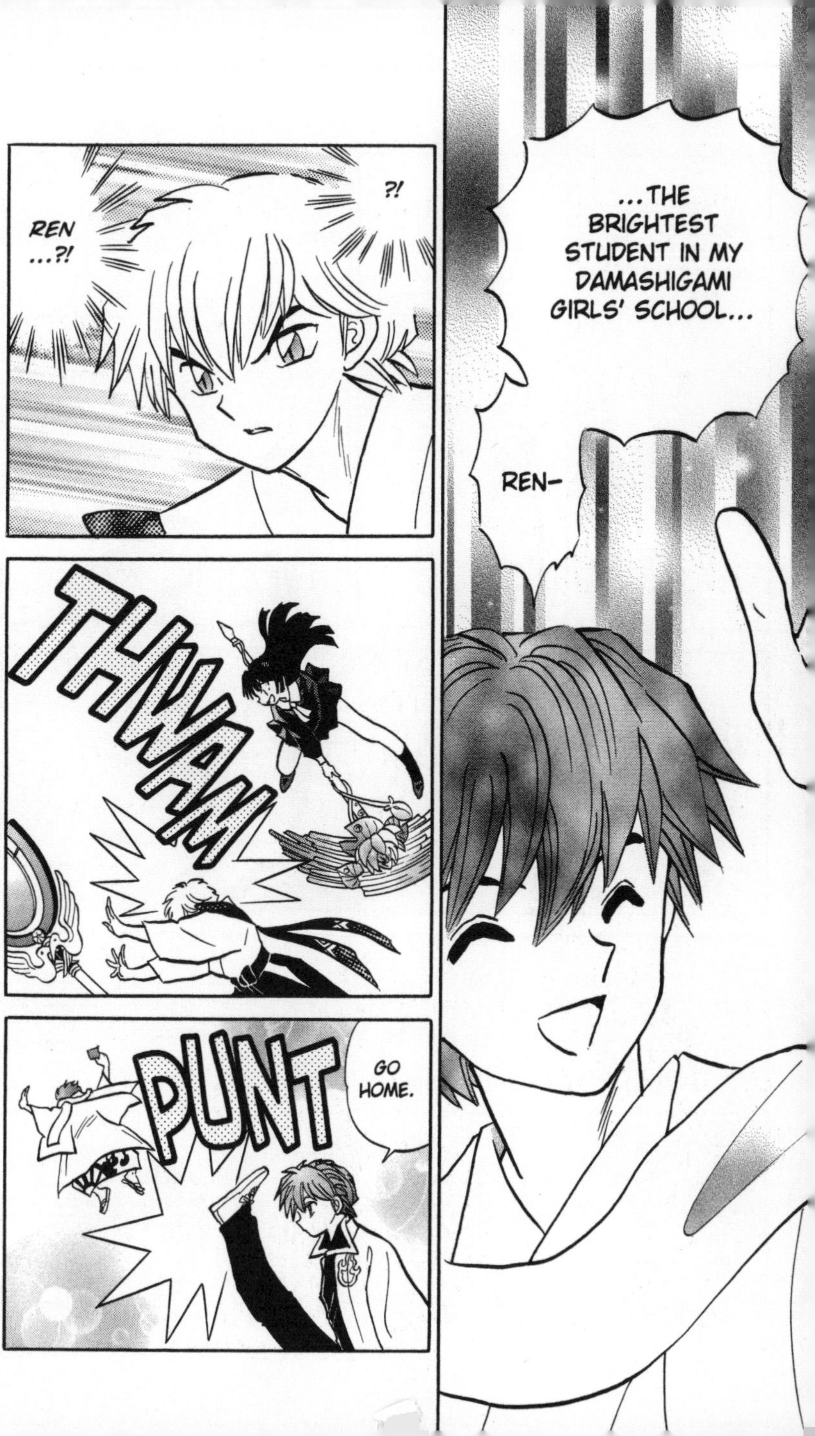
...THE BRIGHTEST STUDENT IN MY DAMASHIGAMI GIRLS' SCHOOL...
REN-
?!
REN ...?!
THWAM
GO HOME.
PUNT

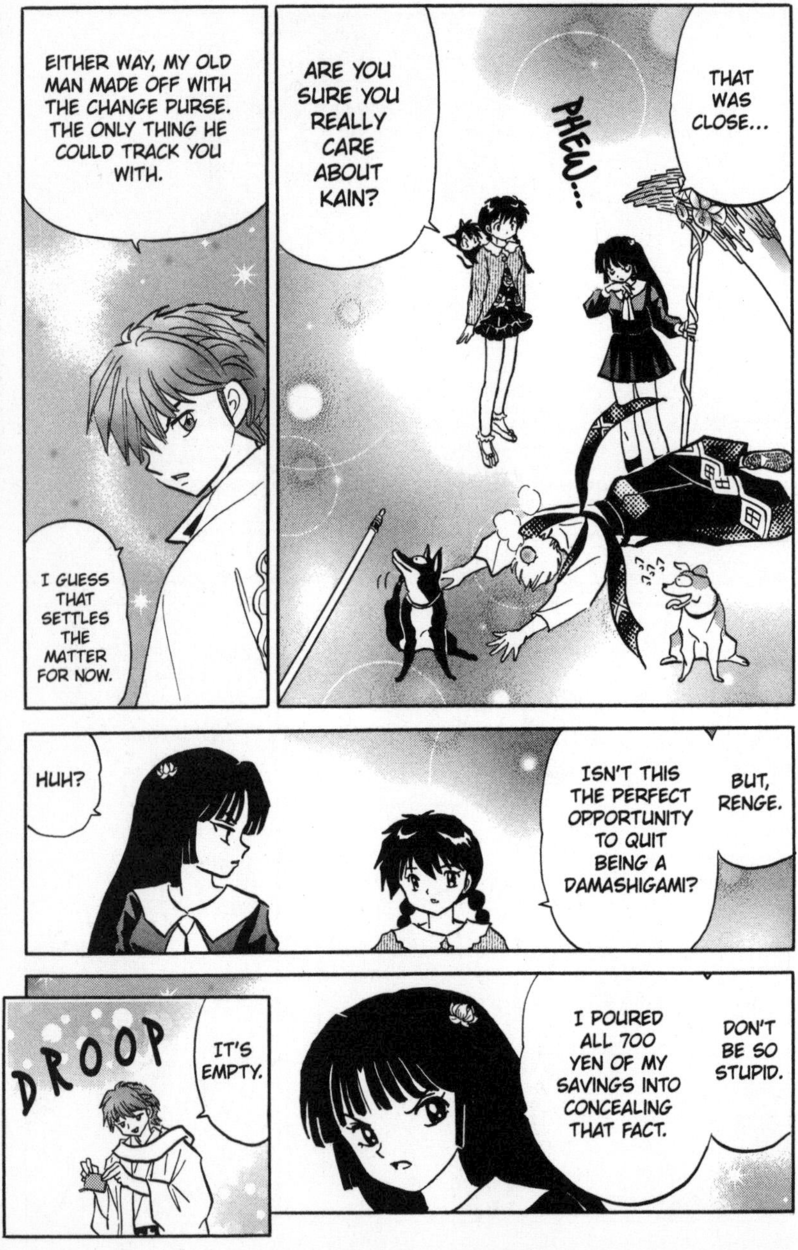
THAT WAS CLOSE...
PHEW...
ARE YOU SURE YOU REALLY CARE ABOUT KAIN?
EITHER WAY, MY OLD MAN MADE OFF WITH THE CHANGE PURSE. THE ONLY THING HE COULD TRACK YOU WITH.
I GUESS THAT SETTLES THE MATTER FOR NOW.
BUT, RENGE.
ISN'T THIS THE PERFECT OPPORTUNITY TO QUIT BEING A DAMASHIGAMI?
HUH?
DON'T BE SO STUPID.
I POURED ALL 700 YEN OF MY SAVINGS INTO CONCEALING THAT FACT.
IT'S EMPTY.
DROOP

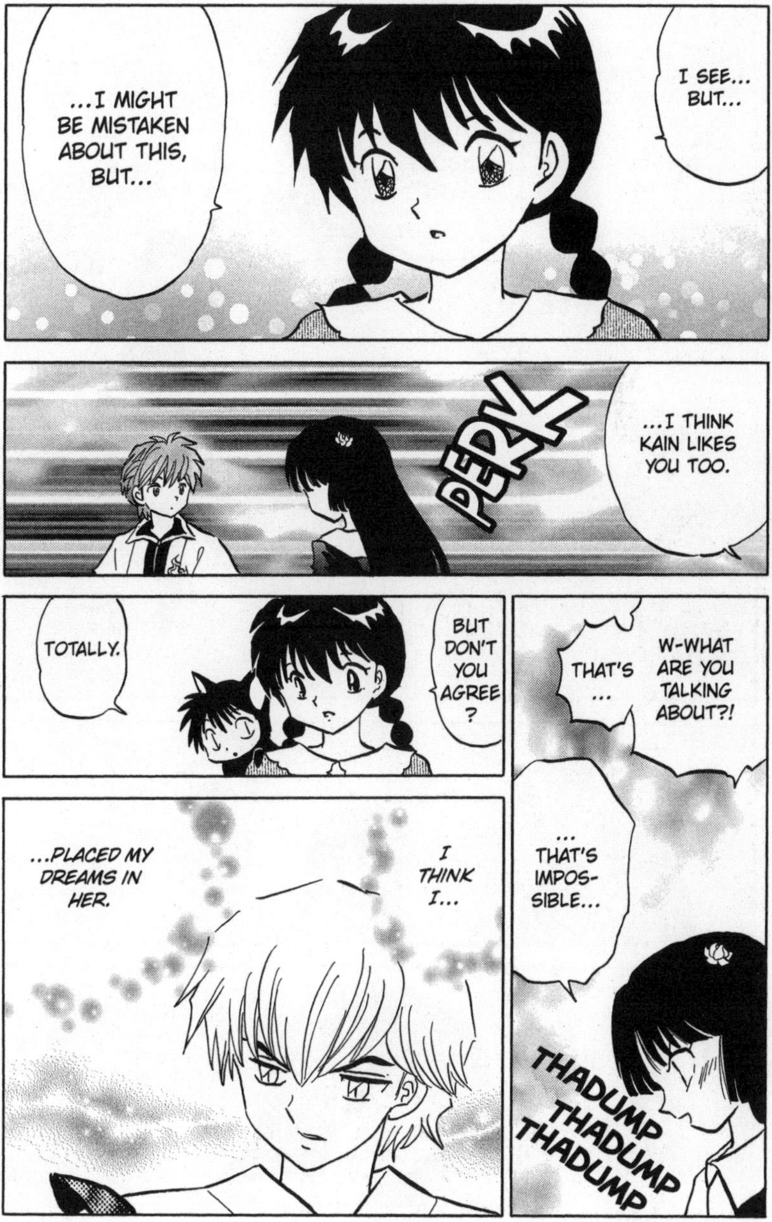
I SEE... BUT...
...I MIGHT BE MISTAKEN ABOUT THIS, BUT...
...I THINK KAIN LIKES YOU TOO.
PERK
W-WHAT ARE YOU TALKING ABOUT?!
THAT'S...
...THAT'S IMPOS-SIBLE...
THADUMP THADUMP THADUMP
BUT DON'T YOU AGREE?
TOTALLY.
I THINK I...
...PLACED MY DREAMS IN HER.

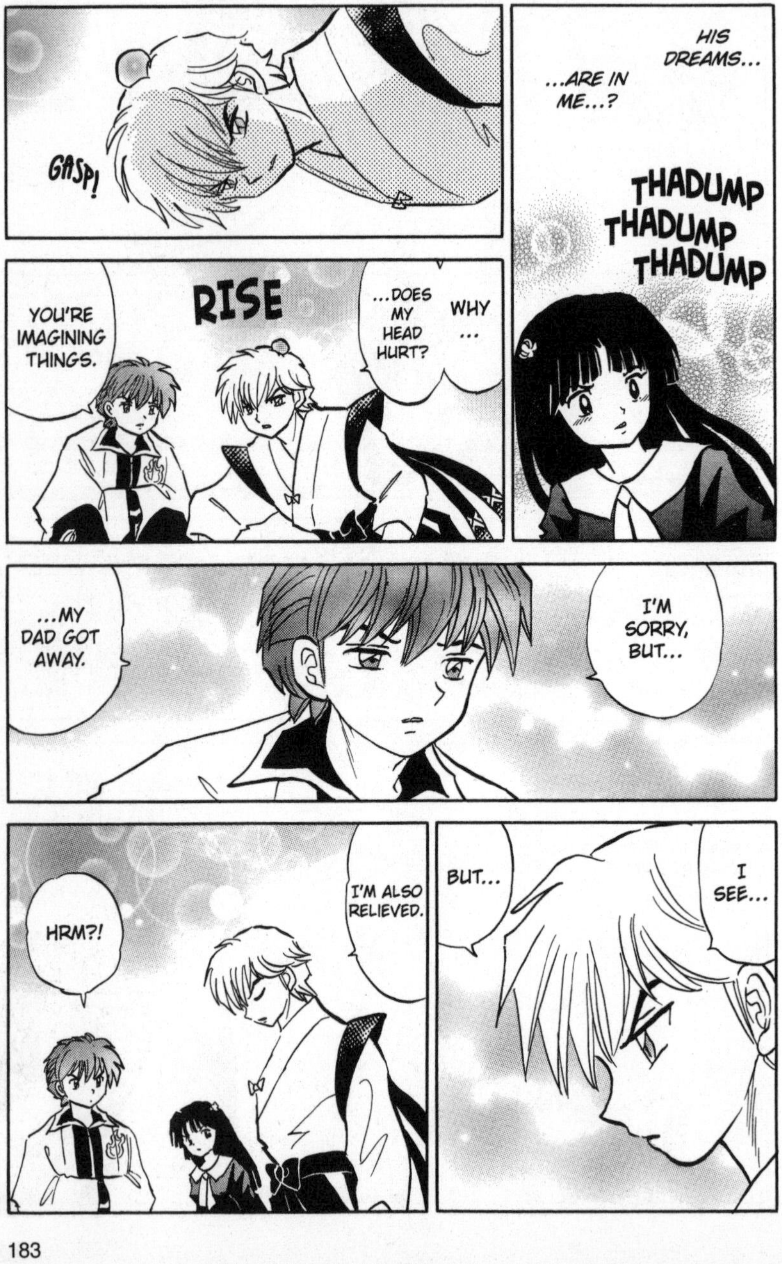
HIS DREAMS...
...ARE IN ME...?
THADUMP THADUMP THADUMP
GASP!
WHY...
...DOES MY HEAD HURT?
RISE
YOU'RE IMAGINING THINGS.
I'M SORRY, BUT...
...MY DAD GOT AWAY.
I SEE...
BUT...
I'M ALSO RELIEVED.
HRM?!

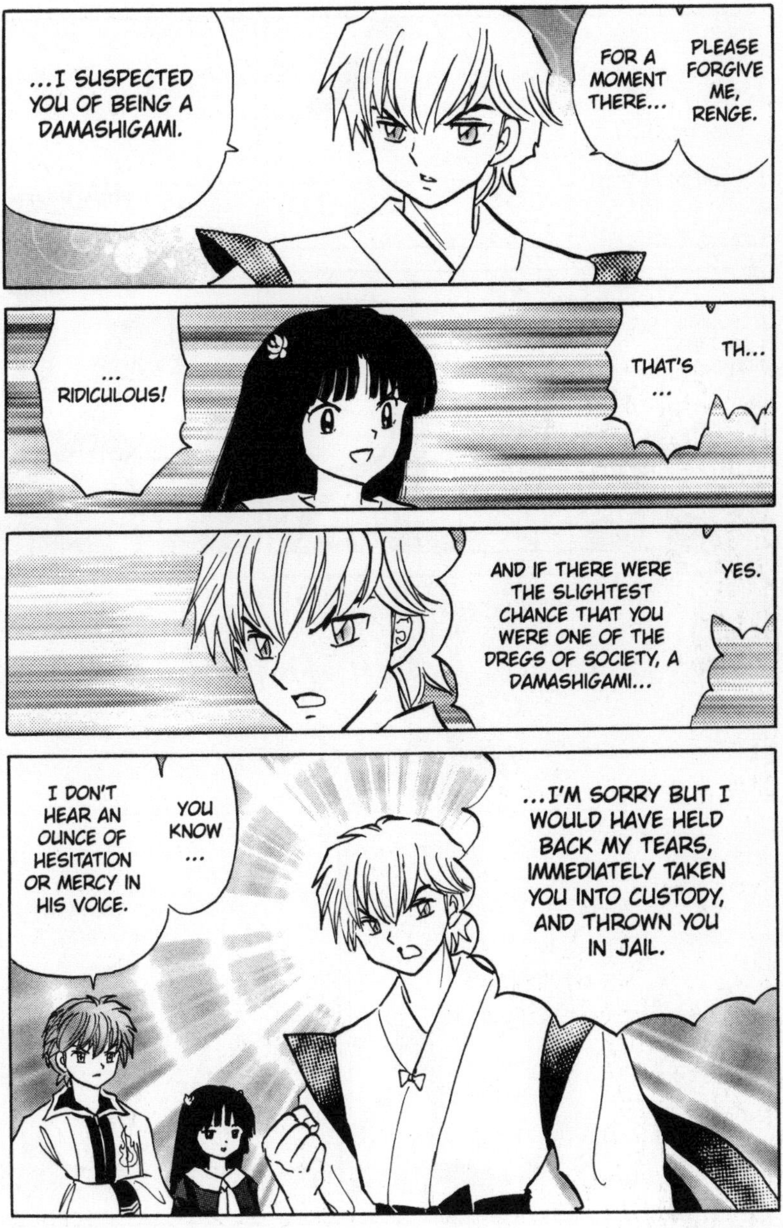
PLEASE FORGIVE ME, RENGE.
FOR A MOMENT THERE...
...I SUSPECTED YOU OF BEING A DAMASHIGAMI.
TH...
THAT'S ...
... RIDICULOUS!
YES.
AND IF THERE WERE THE SLIGHTEST CHANCE THAT YOU WERE ONE OF THE DREGS OF SOCIETY, A DAMASHIGAMI...
...I'M SORRY BUT I WOULD HAVE HELD BACK MY TEARS, IMMEDIATELY TAKEN YOU INTO CUSTODY, AND THROWN YOU IN JAIL.
YOU KNOW ...
I DON'T HEAR AN OUNCE OF HESITATION OR MERCY IN HIS VOICE.

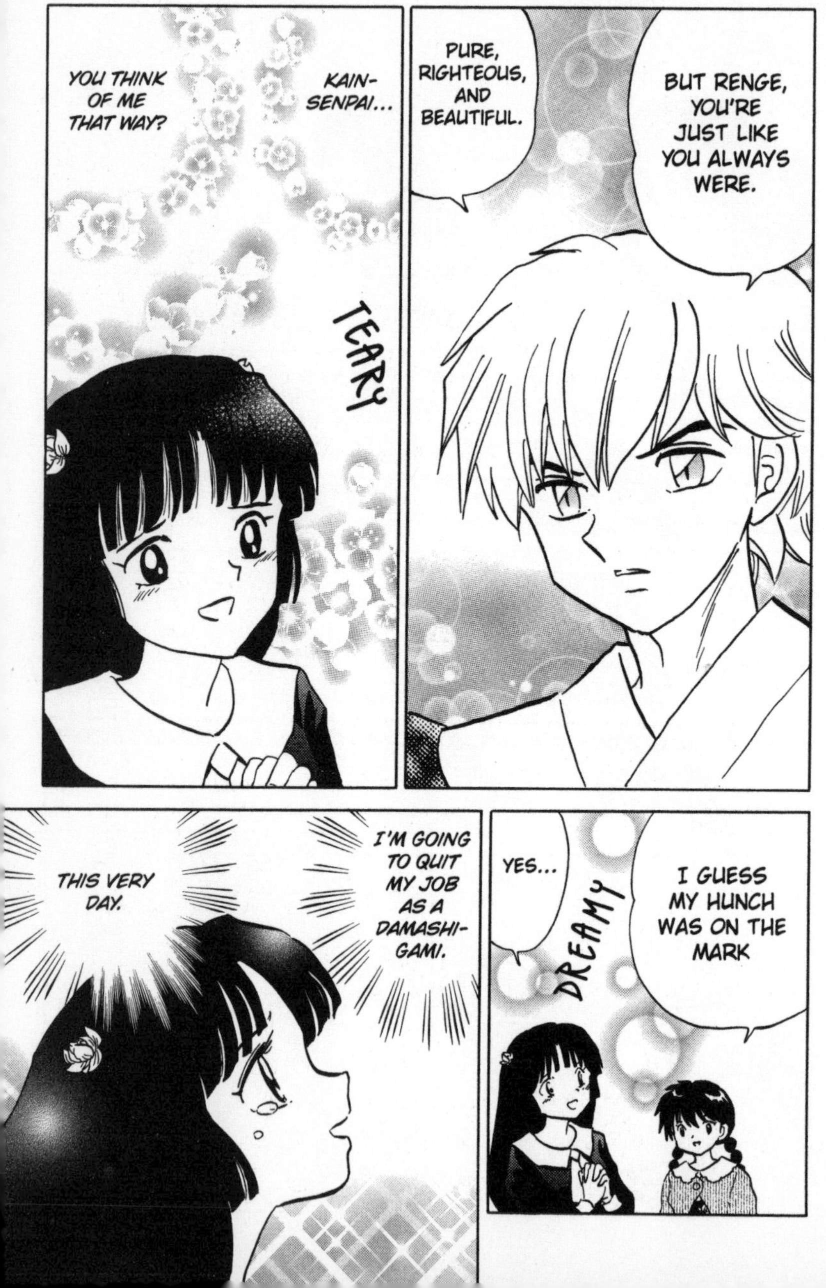
BUT RENGE, YOU'RE JUST LIKE YOU ALWAYS WERE.
PURE, RIGHTEOUS, AND BEAUTIFUL.
KAIN-SENPAI...
YOU THINK OF ME THAT WAY?
TEARY
I GUESS MY HUNCH WAS ON THE MARK
YES...
DREAMY
I'M GOING TO QUIT MY JOB AS A DAMASHI-GAMI.
THIS VERY DAY.

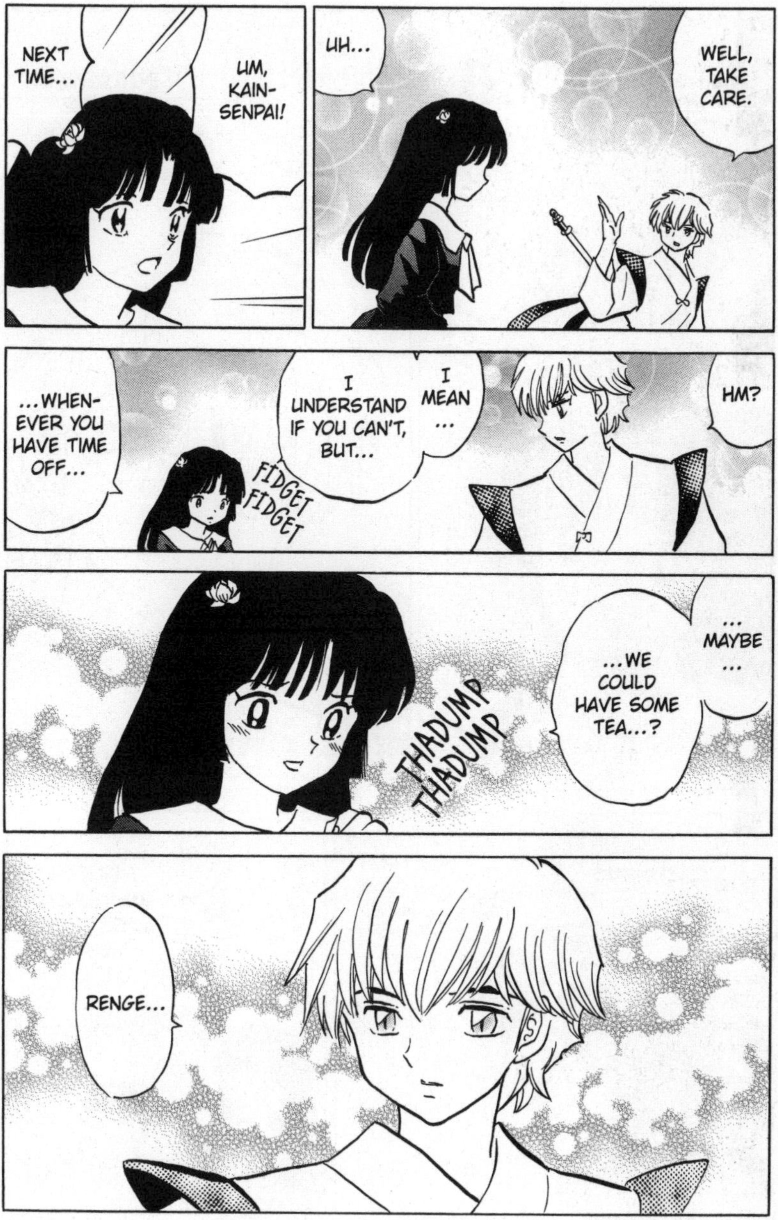
WELL, TAKE CARE.
UH...
UM, KAIN-SENPAI!
NEXT TIME...
HM?
I MEAN...
I UNDERSTAND IF YOU CAN'T, BUT...
FIDGET FIDGET
...WHEN-EVER YOU HAVE TIME OFF...
...MAYBE...
...WE COULD HAVE SOME TEA...?
THADUMP THADUMP
RENGE...

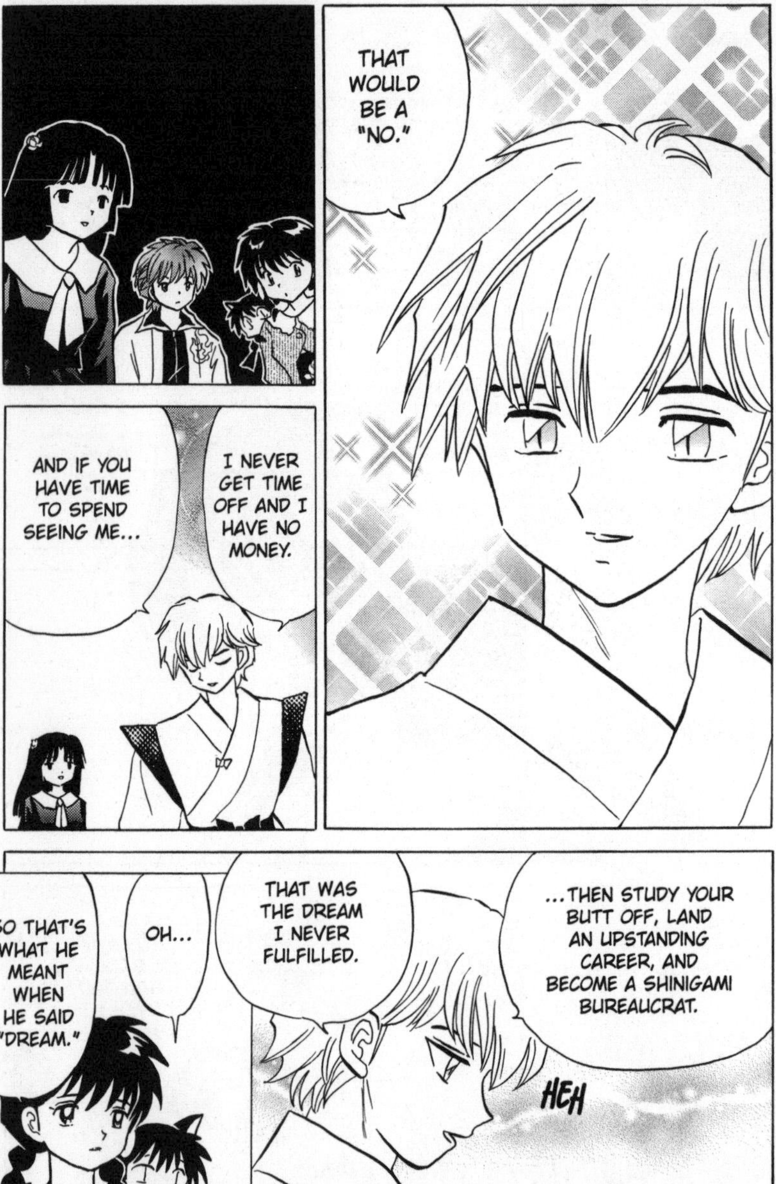
THAT WOULD BE A "NO."
I NEVER GET TIME OFF AND I HAVE NO MONEY.
AND IF YOU HAVE TIME TO SPEND SEEING ME...
...THEN STUDY YOUR BUTT OFF, LAND AN UPSTANDING CAREER, AND BECOME A SHINIGAMI BUREAUCRAT.
HEH
THAT WAS THE DREAM I NEVER FULFILLED.
OH...
SO THAT'S WHAT HE MEANT WHEN HE SAID "DREAM."

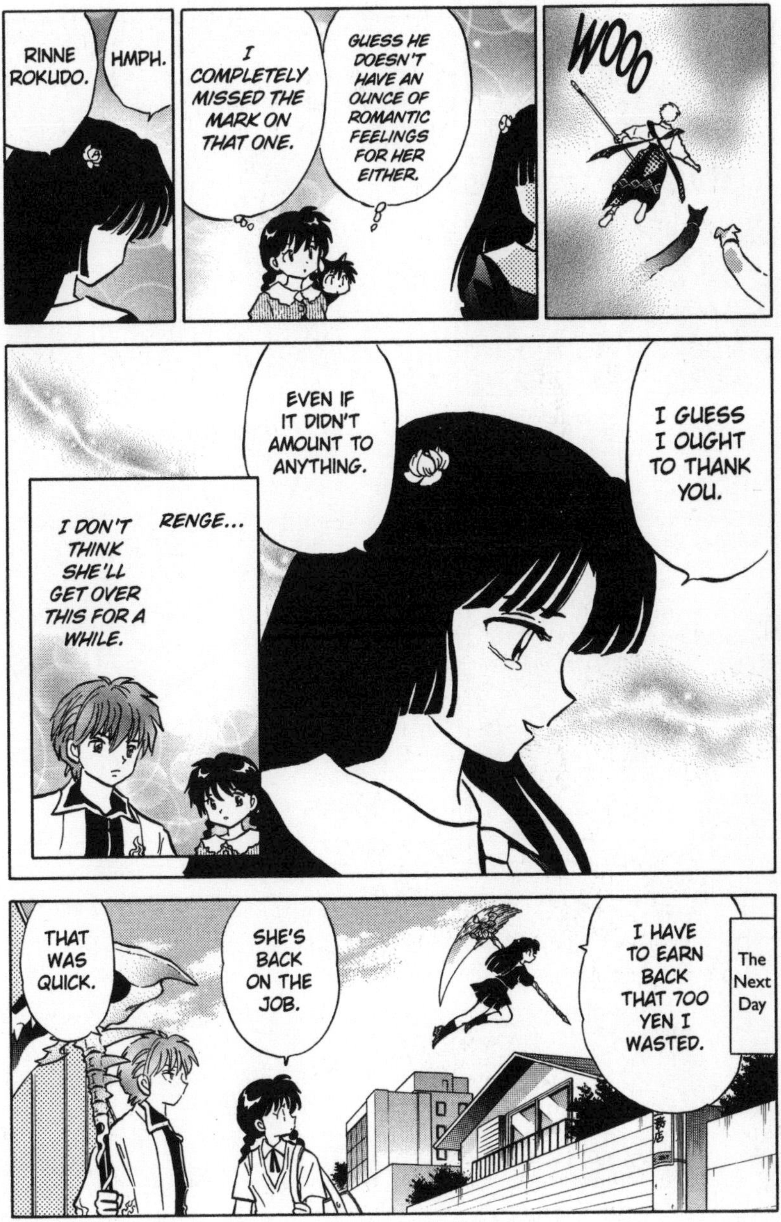
WOOO
GUESS HE DOESN'T HAVE AN OUNCE OF ROMANTIC FEELINGS FOR HER EITHER.
I COMPLETELY MISSED THE MARK ON THAT ONE.
HMPH.
RINNE ROKUDO.
I GUESS I OUGHT TO THANK YOU.
EVEN IF IT DIDN'T AMOUNT TO ANYTHING.
RENGE...
I DON'T THINK SHE'LL GET OVER THIS FOR A WHILE.
The Next Day
I HAVE TO EARN BACK THAT 700 YEN I WASTED.
SHE'S BACK ON THE JOB.
THAT WAS QUICK.

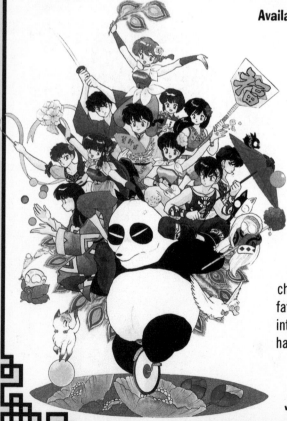

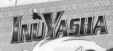

VIZMANGA
Read manga anytime, anywhere!

From our newest hit series to the classics you know and love, the best manga in the world is now available digitally. Buy a volume* of digital manga for your:

- iOS device (**iPad®**, **iPhone®**, **iPod®** touch) through the **VIZ Manga** app

- Android-powered device (**phone or tablet**) with a browser by visiting **VIZManga.com**

- **Mac or PC computer** by visiting **VIZManga.com**

VIZ Digital has loads to offer:

- 500+ ready-to-read volumes
- New volumes each week
- FREE previews
- Access on multiple devices! Create a log-in through the app so you buy a book once, and read it on your device of choice!*

To learn more, visit www.viz.com/apps

* Some series may not be available for multiple devices. Check the app on your device to find out what's available.

Hey! You're R̶e̶a̶d̶i̶n̶g̶ the Wrong Direction!

This is the end of this graphic novel!

To properly enjoy this VIZ graphic novel, please turn it around and begin reading from right to left. Unlike English, Japanese is read right to left, so Japanese comics are read in reverse order from the way English comics are typically read.

This book has been printed in the original Japanese format in order to preserve the orientation of the original artwork. Have fun with it!

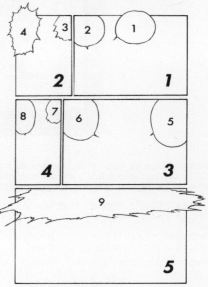

Follow the action this way